Desktop Video Markets

Table of Contents

Chapter 3: Forecasts of the Total U.S. Desktop Video Products Market

Chapter 4: Forecasts of the Total U.S. Desktop Video Preproduction Products Market

Chapter 5: Forecasts of the Total U.S. Desktop Video Production Products Market

Chapter 6: Forecasts of the Total U.S. Desktop Video Postproduction Products Market

Chapter 7: Strategies For Success

Chapter 8: Profiles of Selected Companies

List of Figures

Chapter 1
Executive Summary

The Growing Importance of Desktop Video

Pepsi had it wrong: ours is the video generation. We grew up getting our entertainment, news, product advertising, and a great deal of our education from a dynamic, visual media, television. Previous generations relied on printed media such as newspapers and magazines, or the audio-only media of radio. Future generations may depend on other forms of communication, but for today and the foreseeable future, video presentations are the most effective way of communicating persuasive, entertaining, or informative messages to an audience.

Demand for Video

The demand for video programming is substantial and continues to grow each year. Almost every home in the United States has at least one television set; many have two or more. Each television has access to at least one channel of programming; many have access to CATV systems offering between 15 and 35 channels, 24 hours a day, and some have access to satellite systems offering 200 or more channels of video programming. Over 77% of American households also own a VCR, accounting for over 100 million units sold. The VCR allows the user to select exactly the programming he or she desires from the available inputs and to view it at convenient times.

Not even the available broadcast programming is enough to meet the user demand augmented by the VCR. Videotape rentals of feature films now provide more viewers of that programming than theaters. Even so, the feature film entertainment videotape market has flattened out in recent years, following nearly a decade of rapid growth. The largest growing segment of the commercial videotape market (over 300 percent CAGR) is special interest programming, such as exercise tapes, instructional tapes, travel tapes, "how-to" tapes, etc.

Special interest programming is generally produced for smaller markets than traditional entertainment programming, hence cost is a major factor in determining whether or not a particular program can be produced and brought to market. Up until recently, these financial barriers have prevented many special interest programs from making their way from the content providers to the consumers.

Businesses have also begun to catch the video programming wave. For many applications, such as employee training, customer demonstrations, or corporate publicity, videotape programs make cost-effective and eye-catching supplements or replacements for existing media and methods, including manuals, brochures, or direct sales calls. The same cost factors mentioned above have limited the number of companies using video for these purposes.

Supply of Video Development Tools

Until very recently, video development has required access to suites of very specialized and expensive equipment, as well as the personnel necessary to operate that equipment. For those desiring to obtain this equipment, equipment budgets of $500,000 to $2,000,000 are commonplace, and overhead/personnel budgets of $200,000 to $500,000 annually are within reason. Obviously, most video producers cannot opt for ownership of such a conventional video suite. Even renting the equipment or contracting for development of programming using such equipment and personnel is costly, ranging up to $2000 per hour of use.

Recent technological innovations have offered a substitute solution for many video development applications. Innovations in personal computer-based video equipment, collectively denoted as "desktop video", have begun to revolutionize the development of videotape programming. It is now possible to own a high-quality video production studio for under $100,000, or to rent such studios for under $100 per hour.

Economics of Desktop Video

Desktop video is defined as the technology which facilitates the production of video presentations destined for final or intermediate output via videotape through the use of personal computers and other microprocessor-based desktop equipment. The advent of desktop video as a viable video programming development technology has several immediate effects. First, and perhaps most importantly, it increases the supply of video programming to the market, since more subjects can now be covered cost effectively and since more businesses can afford to use video to supplant or supplement existing tools. Second, it opens video development to a whole new range of creative talent, who could not afford to buy into the conventional video technologies, but who can very well afford desktop video equipment. This expands the talent pool from the 300,000 people currently working in professional video development to the multiple millions.

Desktop video is forcing radical changes on the existing professional video industry, including the major broadcast networks, cable television stations, production studios, and postproduction houses. Computers are intruding where none existed before, the economies of the business are changing, job skill requirements are changing, and equipment and personnel are becoming obsolete.

Market Size

The technology for desktop video has emerged largely in the last three years. 1993 is anticipated as the year in which desktop video comes into its own. Revenues from sales of desktop video products are anticipated to reach nearly $2 billion in 1993, reflecting sales of dedicated desktop video products as well as those destined for other existing markets such as multimedia or conventional video postproduction, but actually being used in desktop video applications. As the 90's wear on, the desktop video market is forecasted to grow dramatically, reaching $4.8 billion in 1995 and $20.4 billion in 1999.

Desktop video as a market is a new concept. Prior studies of the multimedia and conventional video markets have failed to define desktop video as a discrete segment. Hence, the magnitude of the market revenue numbers quoted above reflect some overlap with some forecasts of the multimedia and conventional video markets.

Major Market Trends

Computerization

Video development has been dominated by complicated, expensive, special-purpose equipment and the personnel with the narrow skill sets necessary to operate it. The professional video industry has been insulated and remains largely computer-illiterate. The emergence of desktop video is a major shock to this stable, isolated market and community.

Because of the economies allowed by desktop video, existing video professionals will not be able to ignore it. They must adapt, either by adopting the technology, or by seeking different markets. Adopting the technology will mean replacing or augmenting their special-purpose equipment with general-purpose desktop video systems, acquiring computer-literate personnel, or training existing personnel. Those organizations who resist the onslaught of desktop video must specialize in those markets for which desktop video is inappropriate (at least in the near future), e.g., broadcast-quality, large live productions, etc.

Influx of New Participants

Desktop video allows a vast new supply of creative talent to begin producing video presentations. The lowering of the cost barrier alone allows hundreds of thousands of producers to obtain production systems. The ease of use of personal-computer based systems, versus conventional video, allows these and other new entrants the ability to actually perform video development with the now-affordable equipment.

Although the ability to obtain and use desktop video equipment is now within reach of a much larger market, it does not mean that the skills necessary to create professional quality video presentations are available as well. Just because one can afford a hammer, a level, and an electric saw, and one can operate them as intended, does not mean one is a carpenter and can build a house. Video production has historically been a team sport, requiring players with individual, arcane skill sets such as video editing, graphics development, animation, camera work, lighting, audio engineering, etc. It has been this lack of skills among the general populace that has been a limiting factor in the growth of desktop video in its early years. This, however, is changing rapidly as users acquire these skills, either through trial and error, or through instruction from special interest books and videos.

New markets also bring new participants in terms of products and services providers. Familiar video names such as Grass Valley Group, FOR.A, and Ampex, are being joined by the likes of Avid Technology, Adobe, and Digidesign. Desktop video production and postproduction houses are springing up almost overnight, providing serious competition to existing market participants, at least for special interest and corporate programming.

Distribution

There is currently very little established distribution means appropriate for desktop video. Desktop video overlaps and contains elements from the professional video, professional audio, multimedia, and personal computer markets, each of which have differing structures and capabilities, but none of which are suitable for moving desktop video products from the manufacturers to the consumers.

Personal computer distributors and dealers, while offering a great deal of computer expertise, know little about video production techniques, markets, and ancillary equipment. Professional audio dealers are typically both computer- and video-illiterate, although they may be well versed in digital audio, a prime component of desktop video. Professional video dealers are unaccustomed in selling to the general market, having historically focused on video production and postproduction houses, who in turn sell services to end users in the video market.

This disorganized distribution mechanism has hindered the growth of the desktop video market to date, although things are beginning to get sorted out. A new class of reseller, the desktop video VAR, is beginning to emerge. These resellers combine computer, video, and audio skills and offer both products and services to the end users of desktop video systems.

Major Technology Trends

Digitization

A key trend brought on by desktop video is the transition of the previously all-analog environments of video production and postproduction to ones incorporating predominantly digital elements. The technological trend has multiple effects on the existing conventional video market as well as the emerging desktop video market.

First, digitization brings the holy grail of nonlinear, disk-based video editing to fruition. The time, effort, and cost of editing videotape programming are much reduced if the random access nature of digital storage and the functionality of digital processing can be utilized. As of 1993, moderate (industrial) quality digital video processing is available from products like the Avid Media Suite Pro. More will come in 1993 adding increasing functionality and performance and spelling the eventual obsolescence of the much of the analog environment.

Second, the beginning of the migration to all-digital environments has allowed a rethinking of what quality levels are required for video acquisition. Previously, video had to be acquired at the highest resolution possible, because subsequent processing, duplication, and editing progressively reduced the resolution of the final output. Digital processing techniques are allowing video acquisition at lower quality levels (translation: lower equipment cost), since digital processes (except compression) do not affect picture quality. As compression techniques improve, or become less needed, and as the signal path from camera input to videotape output become more digital in nature, the quality level delta between the acquisition media and the output media (television/VHS videotape) will decrease significantly, thus lowering the cost of the overall video production system.

Improving Compression Algorithms

Key to the market acceptance and the technological feasibility of digital desktop video processing will be the continued improvement of the compression algorithms. Compression is the technique that allows the massive amounts of data necessary to describe full-motion, full-size, full-bandwidth video and audio to be processed by desktop computer systems and stored on reasonably sized storage media. The benefits of compression are obvious: 25 - 100:1 decreases in file sizes, allowing storage of reasonable-length programming on affordable devices.

The downside of compression is the fact that most compression and decompression algorithms introduce imperfections, called "artifacts", into the digital representation of the video image. These artifacts can range from barely noticeable to very objectionable.

Compression algorithms are improving constantly, thanks to the tireless work of a number of developers. Most are implementing their algorithms in VLSI hardware. Eventually, it will be both common and affordable to achieve lossless, 25:1 or greater compression, improving the acceptance of desktop video output.

Growing Quality of Digital Video

Allied somewhat with the compression issue is the overall issue of acquiring, storing, retrieving, and playing back digital representations of video images in real-time. To date, there have been many claims in this area, but much less in terms of actual performance. Many digital video products developed for the multimedia market allow only reduced picture sizes or reduced frame capture and playback rates. These products are clearly not sufficient for central desktop video applications, although they are suitable for concept development purposes during the video preproduction phase.

These products are improving steadily in functionality. As of this writing, it is common to find products that can support 320x240 video resolutions at 15 to 20 frames per second, along with support for 8 or 10-bit stereo audio. Only a very few have improved beyond this point, although the day is coming soon when one can acquire a 30 frame per second, 640x480 resolution video digitization and playback system that supports two channels of 16-bit, CD-quality audio.

Integration

One of the major drawbacks of conventional video systems is the specialization of each piece of the required equipment. This is a distinct factor in favor of desktop video systems, in which many functions are provided by a single, multipurpose system. This allows the sharing of data among the various video development functions, saving time and effort, and reducing the overall expense of the labor side of video production.

It is conceivable that someday a single desktop video system can be used for script and storyboard development, teleprompting and camera direction, video and audio acquisition, processing, editing, and storage, budgeting and scheduling, graphics, animation, and titling creation, as well as integration of the finished output product and control of videotape duplication equipment.

Major Competitive Factors

Functionality

A key competitive attribute for any desktop video product is the functionality it provides. Substitute products already exist, both for the eventual output videotape, as well as for the products used to create it. Competitive products must provide significant functionality improvements over these substitutes at equivalent or lower pricing in order to encourage existing video developers to make the switch to desktop video.

Price

Desktop video is all about price, or rather cost, from the perspective of the videotape developer. Desktop video products must provide an acceptable level of overall functionality, in terms of ease of use, output quality, and integrated functions at a price affordable to the mass market, in order to achieve the rapid growth forecasted in this report. To a great extent, desktop video product pricing will be driven by the computer technologies it incorporates, rather than the less volatile conventional video technologies.

Support / Ease of Use

At the present time, desktop video products are not well integrated and are not particularly easy to use. For desktop video competitors to succeed in capturing market share, they will have to focus on improving the user interfaces to their products, integrating their products with others in the industry according to developing standards, and provide the technical support, documentation, training, and services, either directly or via their sales channels, to the emerging consumers of their products.

Because of the complexities of desktop video systems in their current incarnations, as well as the video-illiteracy, computer-illiteracy, and audio-illiteracy prevalent in the mass market, the distribution channel elements for desktop video also will differentiate themselves by the level of support provided to the end users of desktop video products.

Availability

Desktop video is currently a "tweener" product category. It sits somewhere between the technologies of professional video products, professional audio products, multimedia products, personal computer products, and consumer audio and video products. Each of these markets has defined distribution channels. Desktop video currently does not. Accordingly, desktop video products, as such, are difficult for potential purchasers to find. This condition will not exist for long as desktop video VARs emerge, and some computer and video dealers transition to handle this emerging market.

Conclusions

Desktop Video: The Next PC Revolution

There are a number of personal computer industry leaders who compare the desktop video market with the desktop publishing market of the late 80's. Both technologies represent significant productivity improvements over previously existing techniques and allow the development of output by the mass market, versus a highly-skilled, highly-capitalized, and highly-focused few.

The best analogy of the coming desktop video revolution is the personal computer revolution of the 80's, supplanting minicomputers and mainframes in many environments. The PC brought computational power to the masses, it was far less costly than the previous technology, and it was dismissed as "a toy" by the established data processing incumbents. Today, there are over 125 million personal computers in the world, they are even less costly than they were originally, they perform at many times the level of the original units, and millions of businesses and individuals rely on them for their daily work and recreation. Meanwhile, the data processing establishment has had to adapt to personal computers, specialize on niche markets, or go out of business. The suppliers who persisted in supplying "big iron", e.g., IBM, Data General, DEC, NCR, Prime, Unisys, etc. have all had their problems adapting to the market evolution.

Desktop video represents the same paradigm shift for the video development industry. There are the incumbents who will resist its integration in their work flows, and dismiss the technology as another "toy", and perhaps even fear a loss of control from computerization. Other users will happily seize the potential of the new technology and run with it. Some suppliers will resist developing compatible or competitive products and continue pushing their conventional video product lines. Many will go out of business. Innovative suppliers will recognize the market potentials and develop new product lines in order to exploit opportunities there.

We forecast that the 90's will be the era of desktop video and that 1993 will be the breakthrough year. By the end of the decade, desktop video will have revolutionized the video industry. In a few years, we'll see who made the right decisions.

"Those who cannot remember the past are condemned to repeat it."

George Santayana 1863-1952

Chapter 2
Introduction to the Industry

Desktop video is an exciting new industry combining the technologies of video production with personal computers. In this chapter we will explore the differences between desktop video and existing technologies as well as between desktop video and other new technologies, such as multimedia. We will also explore qualitatively the history, structure, and key technologies of the industry.

Industry Definitions

What is desktop video? The answer depends upon whom you ask. Broadly defined, desktop video is the process of capturing, editing, and playing video images utilizing desktop computer equipment. Under this definition, desktop video includes such elements as video teleconferencing, presentation products such as still stores and projection panels, digital TV and HDTV, and even the majority of the elements normally considered to fall under the broad umbrella of "multimedia".

There has been much discussion about multimedia (or interactive media or integrated media), digital video, and desktop video over the past few years. There seems to be a number of definitions of what each constitutes and these definitions often overlap or contradict each other. The trade press and the manufacturers of products in these categories themselves often disagree on exact definitions and whether or not a given product falls into a given category or another. We have chosen to describe each field as separate and definable, although with some overlap, in order to segregate the technologies and markets associated with desktop video for this report.

Desktop Video Defined

We choose a narrow definition of desktop video, as follows:

Desktop video is the technology which facilitates the production of video presentations destined for final or intermediate output via videotape using personal computers and other microprocessor-based desktop equipment.

Per our definition, the production platform (e.g. a personal computer upon which a video presentation is developed or edited) is not necessarily the same as the delivery platform (e.g. a VCR and television used to display the output) in a desktop video system.

Contrast with Multimedia

The term multimedia generally connotes technology which incorporates elements of video, audio, computer graphics, animations, and still frame captures into a cohesive presentation, destined for output on a computer monitor and audio system. Some people in and out of the industry use the terms "interactive media" or "integrated media" as synonyms for the more broadly used term, multimedia.

Multimedia output can be incorporated into desktop video presentations, e.g. a multimedia presentation can be edited onto a videotape. Multimedia animations can also be an input into desktop video productions. Desktop video output can be incorporated into a multimedia presentation, e.g. a video clip can be merged with graphics and text information in a computerized, perhaps even interactive, multimedia kiosk package.

In a multimedia or integrated media system, the development and delivery platforms are typically computer devices. Multimedia tends to be event-based, whereas desktop video is time-based. Multimedia tends to be dominated by graphics and animation, with video and audio as an adjuncts, whereas desktop video tends to focus on live video and audio, and utilizes graphics and animations as supplementary materials.

Fig 2-1:	Desktop Video vs. Multimedia

```
Graphics/CG/Animation->              -> Video/audio in window ->
Video/audio live/tape ->                  <- Multimedia animation -<
                        DTV                                 Multimedia
Direct Transmission <--                              -> Computer display
        Videotape <--
```

Contrast with Digital Video

We consider digital video to be a component of both desktop video and multimedia; the term describes the conversion of analog video signals to and from digital storage. Products which digitize analog input signals for storage in computer systems and provide the reverse conversion for output to analog monitors and VTR decks are digital video devices. Software which controls the acquisition, storage, editing, retrieval, and display of these digital representations of analog video also fall into this category.

Contrast with Conventional Video

Desktop video can be differentiated from conventional video systems by the required presence of a desktop computer and software. Also, a desktop video system is multifunctional and is controlled by a multipurpose computer, and all functions can typically be performed by a single operator.

Conventional videotape programs are typically created on systems comprised of single-function elements by a number of trained professionals. Some of these systems are computerized, as in character generation systems, but the platform is proprietary and the system is single-function. Desktop video implies the use of a standardized desktop platform and multiple functions.

Industry Development

Although the desktop video industry is very new, it is a logical development of trends in computer and video technologies, as well as a consequence of the increasing demand for video programming.

Opportunities for Video

It is commonly said that "a picture is worth a thousand words". If so, then video, a series of pictures which when sequenced simulates real life action, must be worth many thousands of words for every running minute. The fact is, video can educate, inform, persuade, motivate, and entertain us more than any other medium because of its ability to convey vast information content in a way which incorporates the elements of color, movement, and sound. We're powerfully drawn to such a medium; Few trends are more powerful today than our growing dependence on video-based information.

One reason for this is the impact television has had to the U.S. population. Over 80% of the U.S. population alive in 1992 was born in the television era. This population has learned to acquire its news, entertainment, education, and other information via video presentations, rather than more traditional media, such as newspaper or magazines. MTV has supplanted Top 40 radio as a prime delivery mechanism for popular music. CNN and network news have replaced the daily newspaper as the means by which most Americans learn of current events. Televised interviews and debates have revised our political processes. Television advertisements have supplanted billboards and print ads in terms of effectiveness. Nova and other public broadcasting features have brought education into our homes far more effectively than magazines or encyclopedias.

Until the 1980's, television networks and the fledgling CATV organizations developed and distributed the vast majority of video presentations in the United States. During the 80's, the advent of the VCR changed the market for video presentations dramatically. According to recent studies, there are now over 100 million VCRs in the U.S. alone and over 300 million worldwide.

Over 77% of American households have at least one VCR. With the VCR, consumers could now access programming according to their individual schedules and requirements by renting or purchasing videotapes with the desired content. Most of the growth of this market was based on the conversion of feature films previously aired in cinemas into videotape format. Consumers were freed from the time and programming constraints imposed by the networks and cable organizations.

Although the entertainment videotape market grew dramatically in the 80's and remains quite large ($____B in 1992), it has flattened recently as video rental outlets have completed the acquisition of their basic stock inventories and as private consumers have collected their favorite programs. Special interest programming, e.g. exercise tapes, how-to tapes, etc., is now the fastest growing segment of the videotape market, expanding at a compound annual rate of over 400% in the last seven years, to $______B in 1992, according to a recent market study.

Consumers have recognized that video is the most effective means of acquiring specialized information and have turned to it for self-help, training, education, and coaching, in addition to entertainment. Special interest videotapes, with a VCR and television, offer the advantages of time utility (vis a vis the consumer) as well as the ability to repeat programming as desired. Special interest programming has to date been focused on large potential audiences because of the costs involved in producing high-quality videotape presentations. This has limited special interest programming to niches like exercise tapes, a niche likely to provide sales similar to that of feature films converted to videotape.

There are a myriad of specialized market segments for video presentations besides the mass market. At-home consumers have learned that video is an excellent media from which to acquire more specialized programming, such as musical instruction, gardening tips, business skills, formal education, sports skills, and other topics for which the market is limited. Government agencies have also turned to video as a means of documenting meetings, police operations, court proceedings, and the like. Colleges have offered video extensions allowing students to take classes without ever appearing on campus. Also, businesses have learned that video is as effective in point-to-point education and persuasion as it is in broadcast applications. Many businesses have turned to video as a means of educating its personnel or agents, demonstrating its products, and even providing sales persuasion.

The primary limiting factor in the growth of this limited-distribution videotape market segment has been purely economic: historically, videotape programming has cost more that it returned. The costs of developing video presentations has forced the producers to go after the larger, safer market niches and avoid the segments which would produce less than hundreds of thousands of videotape sales. Whereas there are a few niches, e.g. exercise tapes, which might produce sales of this volume, there are multitudes more that would produce sales ranging from a few hundred to tens of thousands.   The same holds for business and government use of video: the costs of producing the programming have to date been excessive as compared to alternative media such as brochures, manuals, demonstration software, etc. These businesses and government entities, along with other special interest video creators, await only the technology necessary to make small- to medium-scale productions economically feasible. This is the opportunity served by desktop video.

Video Technology Developments

Video technology has been with us since the turn of the century in the form of motion pictures (film), and videotape technology has been around since the late 1940's. The process of creating a video presentation has historically been very labor intensive and has required the use of very expensive and specialized equipment.

A typical video production consists of 4 primary phases: preproduction, production, postproduction, and distribution. All four phases require a great deal of specialized expertise in the form of trained professionals, which complicates a video project and adds personnel costs. Where tools and other gear are required and available, as in the phases of production and postproduction, it is very specialized and costly. In some cases, tools which would make the job much easier have not been developed.

The equipment necessary for production and postproduction has historically been analog and single-function in nature. An analog camera would capture live action and send it to an analog VTR for recording. An analog edit controller would control a bank of VTRs during the editing process, sending the output signals to an analog video switcher, which would interface with an analog special effects generator (for scene transitions) and a character generator (for titling). A typical video postproduction suite could cost upwards of $1M. A typical video production camera and recorder could cost in excess of $25,000. Many video production suites charged in excess of $500 per hour for studio time in both production and post-production modes. It is clear that video production was an expensive process.

The electronics explosion of the 60's, 70's, and 80's has led to ever-improving technologies in the video production process. The development of the microprocessor and the subsequent personal computer technologies, largely in the 80's, is just beginning to revolutionize the video industry. The personal computer has begun to insinuate itself into the video production and post-production process and has brought about entirely new economies in the market.

The Motivation for Desktop Video

The increasing importance of desktop video is based on two simple principles:

1) people want video delivery of their entertainment, education, and persuasion programming, and

2) Desktop video is the most economic means of delivering that programming.

Why video delivery? As an entertainment medium, video combines the elements of motion, sound, and color, attracting and holding the attention of the viewer. As an educational medium, video is able to present information in context, making it more relevant and understandable. As a persuasion media, video can be tailored to present the exact image desired for a particular presentation, avoiding any undesirable realities along the way. Video can provide one of the most effective means of learning new information or persuasion: repetition.

Applications of Video

Video is also an effective means of conveying information about:

- Impractical objects - which are hard to demonstrate to the audience on an intimate basis, e.g. forklifts, swimming pools, and grizzly bears

- Special people - who cannot personally converse with all of the target audience, e.g. the President, Albert Einstein, and the corporate Chairman.

- Remote places - which are difficult or impossible to visit for the target audience, e.g. Mount Everest, the Eiffel Tower, and Saturn.

- Processes - which are difficult to explain to a target audience, but may be clear when shown to the same audience, e.g. cell mitosis, video production, and cooking.

- Abstract concepts - which can be conveyed more effectively to a target audience with real-world examples, e.g. light refraction, art composition, and global warming.

Economic Justification of Video Communications

The primary reason to use video as a delivery media is economic: it can, and should cost less than the alternatives, particularly if desktop video technology is used in the production. A videotape makes a much more economic sales or demonstration tool than a salesperson or application engineer. Not only is a video cheaper than a sales visit, but it is now, thanks to desktop video economies, cheaper than a four-color brochure, on both nonrecurring (development) and recurring (duplication) bases. It can also be developed quickly and focused on an particular problem or customer. A video is usually more comprehensible than a manual, particularly for the uninitiated, so it makes an excellent training, demonstration, or coaching tool. At the same time, it costs less to develop, costs less to reproduce on a recurring basis, and can be developed more quickly, again thanks to desktop video.

In the past, it has been assumed that videos are difficult and expensive to develop, ergo they required "experts" and committee decisions, both of which increased cost and decreased timeliness. These assumptions are now out of date, as are the conclusions. The new reality is that videos are neither difficult nor costly to develop, but can be done by practiced non-specialists. This opens up video as a tool to many organizations who had been operating under the old assumptions.

Economic Pressures Leading to Desktop Video

Desktop video is, itself, a result of economic pressures. First, the conventional video industry has allowed itself to be bypassed by newer technology. The primary reason for this has been the reluctance of manufacturers and service bureaus in the industry to adopt new technologies before the old technologies have been amortized. The rate of change in the computer-based technology industry has exceeded the ability of the video industry to keep up without abandoning their investment in older technology. Accordingly, this industry has been caught in a technology gap.

Second, the existing video technology is comprised of primarily proprietary, single-purpose equipment. Today's computer equipment is multipurpose, allowing many functions in a powerful, compact, open structure. The computer can do most, if not all, of the functions performed by the more expensive, specialized gear. It offers the additional flexibility of allowing file interchange between programs, further enhancing its utility.

Third, increased competition and generally tight economic conditions have forced broadcasters and other video professionals to optimize their equipment expenditures. Video professionals have begun adopting desktop video products in lieu of, and supplementing, more expensive conventional studio equipment.

Fourth, the PC manufacturers have saturated the world markets for general purpose products and applications. They have been desperate to find new markets for their technologies and to expand the utility of the existing installed base of products.

Fifth, and perhaps most germane to the current acceleration of product introductions in the desktop video area, is the regulatory and other problems stalling the introduction of HDTV into the U.S. market. The semiconductor manufacturers, in anticipation of HDTV introduction, invested significant sums in digital video technology research and development, resulting in available technology and no market to sell it into. As the encoding and decoding functions in a HDTV tuner is similar to digital video switching, and other technologies necessary for HDTV are equally applicable to desktop video, it was an obvious move for the semiconductor manufacturers to switch their marketing efforts to the desktop video systems suppliers, resulting in the recent deluge of new product introductions. For example, semiconductor products from Philips are central to desktop video products from Matrox and FAST Machines, and Sony developed devices used by Chyron and the Silicon Graphics Indigo.

Desktop Video Economies

Today, for the first time in history, it is possible to completely produce a video presentation on a home or office desktop, hence the term "desktop video". The vast majority of the equipment which makes this possible has come onto the market in the last two years, with more arriving every day. An entire desktop video system, capable of professional-level quality, currently costs under $50,000. Such a system consists of:

- a high-powered personal computer with over 8MB of RAM and 60MB of hard disk

- multiple gigabytes of additional fast, and preferably removable, disk storage

- a 24-bit color monitor, preferably over 17" in size

- a 24-bit graphics adapter *

- a full-motion video capture and compression board *

- a VTR control board or subsystem *

- a video switcher board

- a digital audio board *

- a MIDI controller board *

- a camcorder

- a VTR (or two, or three, depending on the system) **

- edit controller software

- animation software **

- 2D/3D graphics software **

- titling software

- digital audio processing software

- MIDI sequencing software **

- a MIDI synthesizer **

- a microphone

- lighting

- miscellaneous hardware

* sometimes combined into fewer boards or a subsystem

** optional

The key elements of the above list are the large storage elements, the full-motion video input/output/compression boards, the digital audio elements, the video switcher board, the edit controller software, and the VTR controller hardware. The first two of these elements did not exist in any form until the last few years; the latter elements are the result of applying digital technology and miniaturization to existing analog technology.

A desktop video system is further differentiated from a conventional video system in that it:
- performs multiple functions instead of single, specialized ones
- can produce quality output from lower-priced input equipment (cameras)
- usually operates in non-linear mode, resulting in time savings
- is flexible and expandable
- is less complex to use and is more user-friendly than previous equipment
- requires less arcane skills than older systems

The lower initial cost, as well as the lower operating costs arising from ease of use and fewer personnel required for operation, has reduced the effective cost of video presentations from the multiple thousands of dollars per programming minute to the low hundreds. With these economies, a 1-hour presentation or special interest videotape can be produced for $5000 - $10,000, versus previous rates of $50,000 to $500,000.

Today, a desktop video system capable of professional quality output, either in the form of an Edit Decision List (EDL) for export to a studio system, or direct output to videotape, costs between $30,000 and $80,000, depending on configuration. Starter systems are available for much less, but currently have limitations which make them unsuitable for professional quality output, if they are even capable of the entire range of functions required for video production.. Whether the system is intended for on-line or off-line, linear or nonlinear editing or if graphics or animation capability is added to basic editing will determine which end of the pricing scale is appropriate.

The simplest desktop video system is used for off-line editing and/or graphics or animation development, with no device control or nonlinear capability. This means that there is no need for massive magnetic or optical disk drives or expensive VTRs, allowing a cost in the $10,000 range. Adding device control and a VTR deck adds another $15,000. Adding nonlinear capability adds another $5000 or so. Adding extra VTR decks for A/B Roll and other analog transitions, or extra digital storage for nonlinear editing can add $5000 to $30,000. Ancillary equipment, such as camcorders, tripods, microphones, digital audio boards and software, MIDI interfaces, synthesizers and samplers, sound booths, etc. can add between $2000 and $30,000 more to the suite. A typical desktop video suite costs in the $40K to $50K range.

Contrast this with conventional video editing and production suites. The Post Group in Hollywood, CA has editing suites that cost over $1 million. Professional systems in general cost between $500K and $2M. A sophisticated analog editing controller alone costs in the $50K range, and frame-accurate professional-quality VTRs cost between $15K and $50K each. In addition, a studio's inventory of very complex and balky analog gear requires a range of test and calibration equipment and personnel to use it in order to keep it operational. One television station in southern California uses 64 personal computers equipped with desktop video, computer graphics, and business software to run the entire production operation with 96 employees and a $6.5M annual budget, in a 7400 square foot facility. Station management estimates that the competition, employing standard video technology, requires twice the budget and staff and three times the floor space. Further, the ease of use of the equipment allows the use of only 3 engineers versus 45 reporters, versus a conventional ratio approaching 1 to 1.

Desktop Video History

The road to Desktop Video has been long and convoluted. It is important to review some of the past developments to understand where Desktop Video is today, and where it is likely to go in the future.

Analog Video

In the natural world, all things are "analog" in nature. That is, they vary smoothly from one state to another. Water temperature is not "hot" or "cold", but a particular value among the infinite possibilities in the range between 32 degrees and 212 degrees Fahrenheit. Real world devices, such as electronic equipment, also operate in the analog world, at least at the micro level. In the past, video equipment has been entirely analog from acquisition of an image to the eventual television display.

The computer industry pioneers discovered that the real world is far easier to model and manipulate if the continuous variations present in real life could be simulated by gradations. Using the water temperature analogy, digital systems model the infinite number of variations in temperature as a number of finite steps represented by a binary code. If the size, or resolution, of these steps is small enough, it is a sufficient model of the analog system. Binary codes are easily manipulated by digital systems such as personal computers.

The basic specifications behind analog video production have been in effect since the mid-50's. The National Television Standards Committee (NTSC) defined a video signal which, in conjunction with the earlier RS-170 standard from the Electronic Industries Association (EIA), largely defined the video equipment necessary for the fledgling television industry. The NTSC standard, and the similar PAL and SECAM standards for some of the other countries in the world, defined the resolution of compatible video displays as well as the signal characteristics of the composite video signal which produced video images on the display. NTSC encoding specifically defines a video frame of 525 horizontal scan lines, displayed interlaced at 262.5 scan lines per field, with alternating fields displayed 30 times per second (for a total scan rate of 60 fields per second), using a composite video signal with color, brightness, and synchronization information encoded in an analog signal of 1 volt peak amplitude.

Digital Video

This was sufficient for most applications of video until the introduction of computer graphics workstations in the 1970's. These workstations (actually high-resolution graphics terminals connected to mainframes or minicomputers) required higher resolution than that possible from the NTSC standard, so computers and analog video gear began using different video signaling schemes and resolutions. The explosion of the PC industry in the 80's led to a plethora of video standards of varying resolutions and interface schemes utilizing NTSC composite analog video, component analog video with and without separate synchronization, digital component video, and hybrid combinations such as IBM's VGA standard.

Instead of using the analog scan line concept, digital video systems divide a display area into picture elements or "pixels", the smallest addressable area of a video screen. The greater the number of pixels in the horizontal or vertical axis, the greater the resolution of the system. These pixels, in turn, are controlled by stored information in the computer. The greater the number of bits used to describe each pixel, the smaller the variation between each pixel in terms of color and brightness, the more realistically it depicts the real, analog scene it is attempting to reduce. The combination of resolution and bit depth necessary to realistically emulate analog video at a reasonable price has only been available for a very few years.

Component Analog Video

In an effort to capture and reproduce the highest quality signal possible, the analog systems manufacturers began breaking the video signal down into subcomponents, such as "luminance", or brightness information, and "chrominance", or hue information. Higher order systems were developed which could process the luminance and chrominance information separately and then combine the two when necessary to produce video output. Some systems went even farther, and separated the analog information into even more components representing the magnitude of each of the additive primary colors (red, green, and blue) in the video signal, not unlike the way digital signals are represented. These component video signals allowed much higher signal quality than the NTSC composite video signals, although they required more complex equipment to handle them.

24-Bit Digital Video

In the digital world, technology advanced to the point where systems are capable of acquiring, storing, and reproducing images comprised of 24 bits of information, 8 for each primary additive color. This means that each pixel is capable of assuming one of 16.7 million different color values (8 bits of Red = 256 possible values x 256 blues x 256 greens = approximately 16.7 million color combinations) from black to white, including many (but not all, since there is an infinite number) of the variations in between. This granularity in color allows a very good approximation of analog video.

The only problems with 24-bit video are the twin concepts of information flow and storage. To fool the eye into believing that a series of still images are actually moving in a real-world manner, and to prevent flicker of the image, filmed images are captured and displayed at 24 frames per second (where a frame is a single still image). The videotape industry evolved a slightly different standard of 30 frames per second, and there are still other variations. At 30 frames per second, at 24 bits per pixel (3 bytes), and at full screen resolutions of 640x480 pixels (almost a minimum for a full-screen image), each second of video represents approximately 27.6 million bytes of information. This has historically represented the crux of the difficulties with digital video: how to move that massive an amount information around, how to store it or obtain it in real-time, and where to put it?

These difficulties would stymie the industry for some time. While waiting for digital systems with the bus bandwidth and memory speed and capacity to handle the massive amounts of information represented by digital video images, the industry began to rely on the personal computer and other digital systems to control analog systems, in a hybrid arrangement.

Digital Control

Digital computers, as well as other forms of digital systems, provide precise control of connected apparatus, even if that apparatus is analog in nature, assuming that an appropriate interfacing arrangement can be developed. Digital devices began making inroads into the video production industry in the late 70's with the advent of computerized video switchers, the devices which route analog video inputs (cameras or tape decks) to outputs (monitors or other tape decks). The process of editing videotapes was also enhanced by the development of computerized edit controllers at about the same time. Although both the video switchers and edit controllers utilized digital circuitry, they were responsible for controlling analog devices.

Devices evolved to provide character generation, or titling. Other devices evolved which would merge computerized graphics with live video. These devices were all uniformly expensive, so only post-production houses and television studios could afford them.

Nonlinear Editing

Historically, analog videotape editing before the age of desktop video has been "linear" in nature. That is, a tape editor would set up multiple "source decks" (VTRs which will provide the raw video footage), an edit controller, and a single "record deck" (the output VTR) for the edited tape. By "shuttling" or "jogging" the source decks to the appropriate spots in the source material, using the edit controller to generate transitions such as wipes or fades, and by sending the output to the record deck with time code synchronization, an editor laboriously built up a completed videotape.

Because analog VTRs are linear devices, much of the editor's time and effort would be spent waiting for the tape to shuttle to the appropriate spot for the next source footage, or jogging the tape back and forth to the exact frame needed. If there were a means to reduce this idle time and the labor intensity required to fine-tune the edit, it would be a productivity boon to the video editor.

In 1983, one company, Montage introduced the concept of non-linear editing, albeit via a brute force technique. Their $35,000 to $99,000 system (depending on configuration) employed 17 VTRs, sixteen of which were loaded with duplicate copies of the source material, in order to provide the illusion of random access to the individual source clips. An ideal non-linear editing system would allow instant access to any individual source clip for editing and recording to the record deck.

Several other manufacturers implemented non-linear systems based on analog laserdiscs, also known as videodiscs, which provided rapid access to prerecorded source material. The major problem with this approach was that the process of transferring the source material to the videodisc was expensive, thus the applications of this technology were limited to feature films and episodic television programs. In addition, the equipment itself was also relatively expensive; prices would range from just below $100,000 to as high as $200,000.

The Advent of the PC

The 1980's also brought the development of the personal computer, a low-cost, powerful, small, multipurpose, digital computing device. In addition to revolutionizing office work, education, and recreation (i.e. computer games), the PC also brought dramatic changes to the video industry.

In late 1988, EMC introduced a new approach to non-linear editing. They digitized source footage and recorded it to the magnetic "hard" drives of a PC. Although the image size and frame capture rates were limited by the bus bandwidth, disk access times, and storage capacity of the PC, this product began to show the possibilities of non-linear editing, a prime component of desktop video. There were two major benefits to the EMC system and its successors: the cost was significantly lower than analog non-linear systems, and the improvements in productivity and creativity provided by such systems outweighed any limitations in image quality. If the image quality issue could be solved, desktop video would obsolete existing video technology.

Other Uses of the PC

The PC, in the form of the Apple Macintosh versions, the Commodore Amiga versions, the various 80386- and 80486-based versions of IBM PC-compatibles, and even graphics workstations such as the Silicon Graphics IRIS and Indigo, began to insinuate themselves in video production, other than in non-linear editing.

First, they began to take over the character generation, animation, and computer graphics duties from more expensive, dedicated gear. Second, new graphics technologies, such as "morphing", the process of molding one image element into another, made popular by such feature films as "Terminator 2", were created for and implemented with personal computer and workstation technologies. Third, the limitations of personal computers could be overcome if they were used as a "front end" for the more expensive video production studio gear. Personal computers were used for "off-line" editing, which produced an "Edit Decision List (EDL)", or a computerized list of commands to an edit controller defining the sequence of events to occur on the final output. These EDLs would be exported to the studio gear, thereby saving studio time (equivalent to money) and improving the ability for a producer to experiment with different concepts without incurring vast expense.

Also, the PC began to take over the basic functions of video editing and switching, by assuming the control function for the analog equipment. VTR controller boards and edit controller software were among the products in this class.

Desktop Video Arrives

In 1989, Avid Technology introduced the Media Composer line of video editing equipment, which was based on the Apple Macintosh Personal computer. The Media Composer offered larger image sizing and frame capture rates than that of the prior EMC unit. EMC and

Avid leapfrogged each other in the next couple years, adding features such as removable optical storage and JPEG (Joint Photographic Experts Group) compression of the video data.

Compression as an enabling technology really arrived in force in 1991 with the introduction of semiconductor products from C-Cube and others. These compression devices allowed the vast quantities of data required for video to be decreased to the point where existing computer buses, processors, and storage peripherals could handle it. This new technology opened the doors for a number of new video products from organizations such as TouchVision, Montage, Digital F/X, and others. These digital non-linear systems ranged in pricing from about $20,000 to about $90,000, with off-line systems for EDL production at the low end, and full-featured on-line systems at the top.

In the same time frame, the personal computer makers were ballyhooing the introduction of multimedia products to the market. Apple introduced QuickTime, an enabling technology for describing event-based productions. Various innovative products were developed for this technology, including the SuperMac Video Spigot, which began to demonstrate the quickly developing video editing capabilities of this computerized technology. Adobe Systems introduced Premiere, a SuperMac-developed QuickTime editing software package in 1991 and upgraded it to version 2.0 in late 1992. Premiere, or one of its competitors, such as DiVA's VideoShop, plus a suitable video i/o board (e.g. SuperMac's Digital Film or Radius' VideoVision) began to be considered low end production equipment for videotape projects, as well as multimedia ones.

An upstart organization from Topeka, Kansas stunned the video world in late 1990 with the introduction of the Video Toaster, an addin board for the Commodore Amiga PC, which allowed video switching with transitions and some special effects. NewTek sold an estimated 25,000 Toasters in the first nine months of production, feeding the growing demand for desktop video technology.

Avid Introduced the Media Suite Pro in 1992 and began shipping it in early 1993, as the first desktop product which allows true on-line video production. This product is based on the

Apple Mac Quadra PC and includes provisions for both digital video and digital audio editing as well as direct output to a professional quality VTR at full screen sizes and capture rates. Although Avid is the first to the market with such a product, we anticipate that others will be there even before this report is published.

Desktop Video Functionality

The individual elements of a complete desktop video system are as follows. Some of these elements are typically combined into a single product. Different elements are used in different parts of a video production process, from preproduction, to production, to postproduction, and even in distribution.

1) A Personal Computer - which acts as the master controller via outboard systems to handle analog data flow, and/or as the routing and processing device for digital video data.

2) Device Control - hardware, internal or external to the PC, plus software, which controls video input and output devices such as camcorders and VTRs.

3) Video Switcher - hardware, internal or external to the PC, plus software, which chooses the output signal sent to a recording VTR or a video monitor from among video sources, such as cameras, camcorders, or playback VTRs.

4) Special Effects Generator (SEG) or Digital Video Effects (DVE) - hardware or software which works in conjunction with editing hardware or software and the video switcher in order to provide elaborate video switching effects, such as wipes, fades, etc.

5) Frame Grabbers / Still Stores - hardware and software which digitizes analog video input for storage on the PC.   On-line desktop video systems require full-motion frame grabbers. In the past, freeze-frame still stores were used to acquire still images for digitization.

6) Editors - software which allows the indexed retrieval, arrangement, trimming, and playback of video footage. Some editors produce an EDL as output to an on-line system. Most

desktop video editors utilize a graphical user interface. Many allow simultaneous video and audio editing.

7) Video monitors - digital and analog display devices allowing the viewing of video productions before, during, and after the editing process. Digital monitors require a graphics adapter installed in the PC.

8) PC Nonvolatile Memory - typically massive magnetic or optical drives connected to the PC which provide the on-line storage necessary to store digitized video data. Some large percentage of this storage capacity is ordinarily removable, allowing archiving of data and larger video compositions.

9) Digital Audio - hardware and software necessary to acquire, store, retrieve, edit, synchronize, and playback audio information along with video. The audio is digitized and stored to the PC's nonvolatile storage and is retrieved as needed.

10) MIDI Products - hardware and software necessary to compose, store, retrieve, edit, synchronize, and output digital information representing music and sound effects. Devices such as synthesizers and samplers process this information and convert it into audible sound. Some editing products synchronize MIDI commands to audio and/or video. All three may be required for a video production.

11) Print-to-Tape Software - may be required on some systems to allow the system to output video to a recording VTR.

12) Video, Clip Art, MIDI, and Audio Libraries - archived video footage, photographs and computer graphic art, MIDI compositions, soundtrack audio, and audio special effects which can be obtained and used in video compositions.

13) Tape Logging Software - provides the ability to precisely define source footage clips in terms of SMPTE time code for later retrieval.

14) Miscellania - including lighting systems, teleprompting systems, sound booths, microphones, audio amplification, speakers, printers, etc. more commonly used outside of desktop video, but applicable to the video production process with desktop video, as well.

Industry Structure

The desktop video industry has not yet coalesced into a firm industry structure unique to that technology and the array of products and services particular to it. Because it shares many characteristics with the existing professional video and personal computer markets, it is expected that the eventual desktop industry structure will share elements of each. In addition, the disparate professional audio / musical equipment industry market structure will also influence the desktop video market structure because of the overlap of some products.

Personal Computer Industry Structure

In the personal computer industry, products are transferred from manufacturers to consumers, typically called "end users", via a number of marketing channels. The first, more prevalent for higher-end products such as file servers, color printers, bed plotters, etc. is the direct channel, in which the manufacturer employs a direct sales force to locate, qualify, and sell to the end users of the products.

Some manufacturers also sell directly to end users as a supplement to indirect channels, typically as a response to call-in inquiries. The staffing for this function is typically very minimal.

Manufacturers and OEMs

The computer industry structure starts with the manufacturer of the individual components. Although many of the originators of these components sell them into the retail market via the channels described here, most sell the majority of their products to other manufacturers who combine them into larger systems or with other products such as software. In this sense, the vast majority of manufacturers in the computer business can be considered OEMs (Original Equipment Manufacturers), a term which, despite itself, has come to mean an organization who adds value to those of others', selling the end result into the retail or wholesale markets.

Many levels of OEM structures exist. For instance, Fujitsu may sell integrated circuits to Conner Peripherals who may sell drive mechanisms to Wyse Technology who may sell personal computers to Triad Systems, who markets them under their own name. Each of these suppliers may sell essentially the same products to other customers, including the retail market.

Dealers and Mass Merchandisers

Most personal computer industry manufacturers depend on indirect channels in order to deliver their products to the end users. By far the most dominant element of this structure is the computer dealer. These dealerships purchase products at a discount ranging from 15% to 50% off of list price and sell to retail customers, the end users, at prices ranging from suggested list to a 40% discount off of list. The dealers range in size between very small mom-and-pop enterprises to large showroom-oriented operations with twenty to thirty employees.

Some personal computer industry manufacturers have chosen to utilize mass merchandisers such as Costco, Sears, and regional superstores like Fry's, CompUSA, or Whole Earth Access. These operations typically sell a number of other products unrelated to personal computers and act as a form of technology supermarket.

Most dealers offer repair services for the products they sell, although the vast majority provide only board-swapping or other minimal front end services for depot service centers operated by the manufacturer or independent service organizations. Most dealers also operate storefronts in commercial locations, attempting to draw in retail traffic.

Dealer Chains

Some of the major personal computer dealers, such as MicroAge, Computerland, Computer Attic, Connecting Point, Radio Shack, and Egghead Software stores, are franchised locations of regional or national chains. Some of these chains provide centralized product management and purchasing functions, so the manufacturers in effect market to the chain management, who approve and purchase products for the chain stores. Some of these chain operations operate on two levels, where the chain management provides some products to the dealers, yet each individual dealer is free to choose to carry (or not carry) products from other manufacturers.

In the case of the Radio Shacks, the parent organization, Tandy Corp., operates as a manufacturer for some products, an OEM for others, and a chain management organization for all.

Distributors

Many manufacturers without the desire or wherewithal to manage hundreds of individual dealers have chosen to employ two-step distribution by using industrial or commercial distributors such as Hamilton Avnet, Arrow, Pioneer, Merisel, Tech Data, and Ingram Micro to provide inventory and quick delivery to dealers, particularly the smaller ones unable to maintain large quantities of product in their stores. These distributors typically carry inventories from tens to hundreds of manufacturers, purchasing these products at 40 to 75% off of list price and reselling them to wholesale customers at 15 to 50% off of list.

Some distributors also operate retail arms, although this is more prevalent in regional operations than national ones. Most distributors offer credit terms to the majority of their customers, thus providing a form of financing to the smaller dealerships. All distributors operate on contractual credit terms with their suppliers.

Systems Integrators and VARs

A variation on the standard dealer, who provides very little specialized technical knowledge about the products it handles, is the Systems Integrator or Value Added Reseller (VAR). These entities typically offer the functions of a standard dealership, plus enhanced service offerings, such as technical support, repair and maintenance operations, training, software integration, installation, and the like. Often these entities focus on a market niche, such as dental systems or desktop publishing. Some of these entities never take title to products, but only recommend products from other sources, or work with the products already purchased by the end users.

Systems integrators and VARs purchase products from wherever they can get them most effectively. Some purchase directly from the manufacturers or OEMs. Most work with distributors, mail order firms, and other dealers to obtain the needed items.

Mail Order

As products have become more standardized in the personal computer industry, they have tended to become regarded as commodities. These standardized, commodity products can often be obtained without the need for demonstrations, services, or any other added value. A number of mail order operations have developed in the past several years which acquire products at deep discounts, maintain inventories and quick fulfillment mechanisms, market via full-page ads in computer industry publications, and sell to retail or wholesale customers indiscriminately at deep discounts off of list price, typically accepting payment via COD or credit cards. Few mail order forms offer extended credit terms.

Service Bureaus

In some niche markets, such as desktop publishing, it is common for an organization to acquire the products necessary to provide a set of services, such as page layout, to end users. These organizations are known as service bureaus. They typically do not resell personal computer products to the end users.

A service bureau classification that has evolved significantly since the introduction of the personal (versus mainframe or mini) computer is the data processing house, usually focused on accounting and other financial processing for businesses. These organizations were reluctant to adopt the new personal computer technology; as a result, many were forced out of business by those who did. The organizations that acquired personal computers could do the same work with a smaller staff and a smaller capital investment, putting the less agile firms at a competitive disadvantage.

Rep firms

Some personal computer industry manufacturers leverage their sales management efforts with the services of manufacturer's representation firms. These independent sales entities earn commissions by ensuring sales to the manufacturer's defined channels within the reps' territories, typically a defined geographical region.

Rep firms do not take title to the products, but instead act as an agent between the manufacturers and the resellers, or in some cases, the end users themselves.

Use of rep firms is more common with small manufacturers or those who sell to a number of different markets, e.g. stationery suppliers.

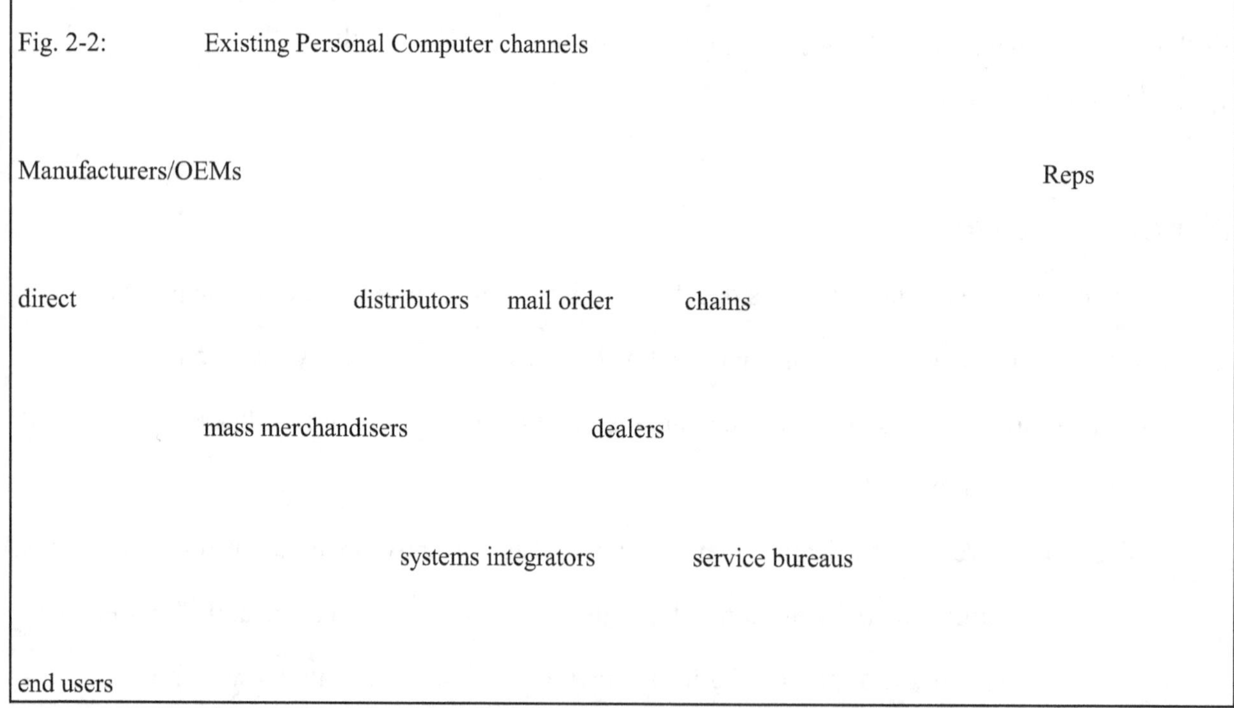

Existing Video Industry Structure

The existing video industry structure is split according to the quality level of the products. Low-end, consumer level products typically follow one route to the eventual end users, home or business consumers. Professional and broadcast-quality video equipment follows an entirely different route to its end users, broadcast organizations such as network and cable television stations, advertising agencies, and commercial and independent video producers.

Manufacturers and OEMs

In the video industry the OEM construct is less prevalent than in the computer industry. Far more prevalent is the differentiation between pure manufacturing and pure marketing organizations, wherein the manufacturer provides very similar products to several different marketing companies, who in turn sell these products into the market. These marketing arms may or may not be owned by the same parent which owns the manufacturing arm. An example of this is the Japanese giant Matsushita Electric, who sells similar products under the brand names Panasonic, National, and JVC, among others.

Video manufacturers have historically relied more on direct sales channels than their personal computer counterparts, mostly because the prices of their products were sufficient to both limit the market size and allow profitable coverage by a direct sales force.

Video Dealers

The key element to the video industry structure is the video dealer. These organizations combine many of the functions of the personal computer distributor and dealer organizations, providing inventory stocking, catalog and direct sales, and some limited services to their customers. Video dealers tend to specialize in the higher-priced professional quality equipment.

Video dealers have tended to specialize in selling to production and postproduction organizations, rather than the mass market. They have also tended to be reactive rather than proactive in selling. They have not classically differentiated themselves on price or services; rather, most differentiate on the basis of geographical territory served.

Mass Merchandisers

At the low end, mass merchandisers provide much of the retail sales for the video industry. Costco, Sears, Target, Montgomery Ward, WalMart, KMart, and a host of other national and regional organizations provide the dominant channel for camcorders, VCRs, and even consumer-quality editing and effects products.

Mail Order

Again, as in the case of the personal computer industry, much of the consumer-level video products are standardized and can be obtained without need for demonstration, comparison, or ancillary services. A number of mail order firms, such as 42nd Street Photo, focus on consumer-quality video equipment and form a growing segment of the distribution for these products.

Rep firms

As in the personal computer industry structure, many manufacturers also employ sales representation firms to leverage their sales efforts. Unlike in that industry, these rep firms tend to focus on end users, such as production and postproduction houses, and commercial television studios, rather than other channel participants.

End Users

Because of the cost of professional video products, the end users have tended to be a relatively small group of highly trained professionals, rather than the general market. The lower end of products, e.g. consumer-quality camcorders and VCRs are marketed to the general public.

Independent Video Producers

The International Television Association (ITVA) boasts membership of 10,000 independent producers, directors, and editors. They are referred to as "independent" because of their lack of affiliation with a major studio or commercial television network. They tend to work on a project by project basis and sell their services to production/postproduction houses, corporations, government entities, and others. They buy services and rent equipment from video rental dealers and postproduction houses. They do not tend to buy equipment and other products from dealers, but rather directly from the manufacturer or via rep firms.

Production & Post-Production Houses

In a manner similar to that of service bureaus in the personal computer industry, production and postproduction organizations have typically obtained professional-quality video products and have delivered services based on these products to their customers, typically independent video professionals, corporations, and government entities. Video equipment has been historically very expensive, as discussed throughout this document, and few organizations have had the wherewithal to obtain these products themselves. The production and postproduction organizations have therefore classically provided a very important intermediary function between the manufacturers and the end users. They have made the investment in products and in the manpower and training necessary to run them, and have in turn amortized these costs by selling services.

These production and postproduction houses have accordingly been a prime marketing target for the manufacturers and the video dealers. Many of these suppliers market exclusively to these service providers, essentially ignoring the end users of the industry. On the other hand, most production and postproduction houses market themselves to the independent and commercial video producers, ad agencies, and others by declaiming not only their past successful output but also the equipment on hand for use in the end users' productions.

Production and Postproduction organizations provide the same function in the video industry structure as the service bureaus in the personal computer industry. Even more telling, they closely resemble the data processing organizations of the pre-PC era in terms of their capital investments and manpower loads. They will be strongly pressured to downsize as desktop video comes to the fore.

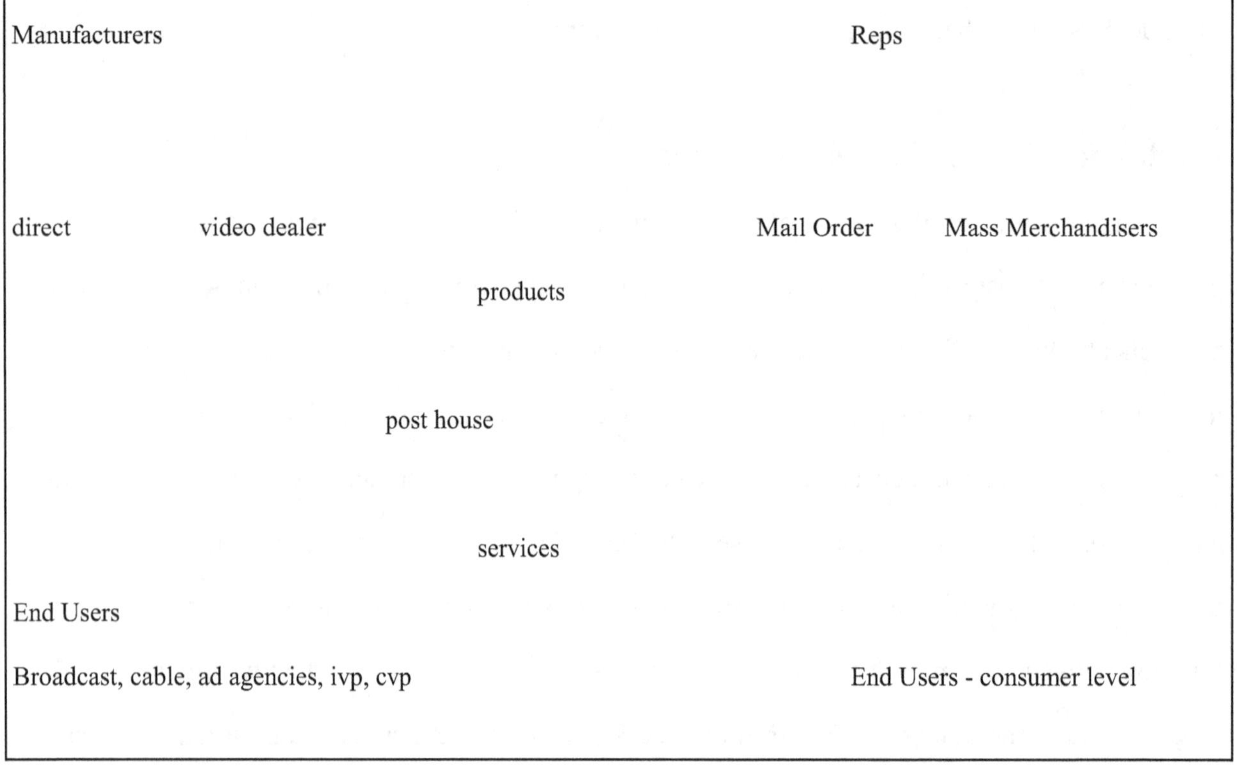

Fig. 2-3:   Existing Video Industry Channels

Manufacturers   Reps

direct   video dealer   Mail Order   Mass Merchandisers

                              products

                    post house

                    services

End Users

Broadcast, cable, ad agencies, ivp, cvp   End Users - consumer level

Broadcast Organizations

At the upper end of the scale in terms of budgets and personnel available for video production are the network television and cable television organizations, such as broadcast networks, local affiliates, and cable television networks. These organizations typically obtain their equipment directly from manufacturers.

Broadcast organizations typically run under tight time budgets, especially for programming like sporting events or news. Desktop video products, because of the productivity gains they allow, will make inroads in these environments increasingly over the future as the technologies improve to meet broadcast quality standards.

Professional Audio & Musical Equipment Industry

Professional quality audio and musical equipment has typically been sold in two simple channels: direct and dealer. Direct sales from equipment and other product manufacturers to the end users, audiophiles, musicians, recording studios, radio and television broadcast studios, and educational institutions, are less prevalent than those via specialty dealers.

Manufacturers are of two classes. There are broad-line manufacturers such as the Japanese firms Sony, Panasonic, Hitachi, and JVC who sell a high end to their consumer products line. There are also dedicated niche firms such as Shure Brothers, Roland, E-mu, Korg, and others, who specialize in a line of professional-quality products for their specialty areas.

Audio-only Dealers

One class of dealer focuses only on audio reproduction. These stores became exceedingly popular during the 70's and 80's by focusing on high-end products such as turntables, receivers, tape decks, and speaker systems. Many also carried sound reinforcement equipment. The advent of digital audio in the form of audio compact discs made high quality audio reproduction feasible on a consumer level and obsoleted much of this channel.

Those audio-only dealers who still exist are small and remain focused on audiophiles as their primary market. They tend to sell at or near manufacturer's suggested list prices.

Musical Equipment Dealers

In the 1980's the musical instrument industry collaborated on the MIDI specification and musical equipment dealers were changed forever. MIDI allows musical instruments and computers to interact, allowing precise composition and reproduction of musical works, even by unskilled musicians. Most of the existing musical equipment dealers began carrying the new

MIDI-compatible product lines, although a few resisted and still do today.

These musical equipment dealers also tend to carry microphones and sound reinforcement

equipment, in addition to MIDI synthesizers and samplers. They also tend to carry the computer

hardware and software necessary to control these synths and samplers and therefore have

acquired at least rudimentary computer skills.

Some dealers provide musical instruction. Others provide equipment service. All sell to

the general public as well as to professional and semiprofessional musicians. The stores which

sell to professional musicians tend to carry the higher-quality and more costly products preferred

by those musicians. These firms have also begun to carry the new digital audio products,

supplementing or supplanting the older analog technology in their catalogs.

Most dealers sell near or at manufacturer's suggested list.

Audio & Musical Equipment Mail Order

As in the personal computer and video industry, a lucrative mail order channel has

evolved in the professional audio and musical instrument industry. These mail order firms

typically publish catalogs and carry professional- as well as consumer-quality products, including

MIDI-compatible equipment and software. They also carry digital audio products.

Mail order firms typically sell at discounts well below manufacturer's suggested list.

Fig. 2-4:   Professional Audio and Musical Equipment Industry Channels

Manufacturers

Audio Dealers   Musical Instrument Dealers   Mail Order

<table>
<tr><td>End Users
musicians, audiophiles, general public</td></tr>
</table>

Current Desktop Video Industry Structure

Desktop video products are currently manufactured by a number of sources, including major corporations such as Sony and Panasonic, smaller established video firms such as Avid Technology, established personal computer firms such as SuperMac, Adobe, Radius, and RasterOps, and upstart firms such as Digital F/X, NewTek, and Matrox. To date, there are very few OEM relationships, although there have been a number of technology transfers among the players.

Desktop video manufacturers are currently utilizing the distribution channels with which they are the most familiar and are trying to pioneer a new channel for the products. Video manufacturers who also build desktop video products are attempting to move these products through their established video dealers. Personal computer manufacturers who are breaking into desktop video (typically via multimedia), are attempting to utilize their dealer networks.

Neither are having much success, partially because the channel participants lack knowledge of the other half of the equation. The computer dealers do not know video; the video dealers do not know computers. Current desktop video solutions require knowledge of both elements.

Evolving Desktop Video Industry Structure

The desktop video industry structure will evolve into a combination of the structures of its three component industries - conventional video, personal computers, and professional audio and musical instruments. There are a number of key reasons for this.

First, the end users for the desktop video market will closely resemble that of the personal computer industry, i.e. diverse sets of individuals and groups with varying skill sets.

Second, the existing industry structures know very little about technologies from the others, e.g. video dealers (generally) know very little about computers, computer dealers (generally) know very little about musical instruments, etc.

Third, production and postproduction houses have significant investments in their existing technologies and will be slow to adapt to the new technologies.

Fourth, video dealers are not accustomed to marketing their products to a diverse end user base.

Fifth, many of the pioneering manufacturers in the desktop video industry have already discovered the problems with existing channels and are working hard to develop new channels for these products.

End Users

Because of the pricing of the products, end users of desktop video technology will more closely resemble those of personal computer products than existing video technology, although there will be some overlap. Further, entrants to the desktop video market will not only include existing video professionals either retained by or leaving their current organizations, but a whole new breed of information producers who could not afford to buy into the old technology. This will expand the potential consumers of desktop video products and services from the 300,000 or so current video production personnel to the tens of millions of computer-literate hobbyists, semiprofessional videographers, and professional communications personnel.

Video Professionals

At the high end of the user scale will be video professionals, those members of independent and commercial video production facilities who choose to adopt the new technologies. They know how to produce video tape programming and understand the limitations and integration issues of VTRs, cameras, switching equipment, character and special effects generators, time code, edit controllers, lighting, etc. Their main issues will be with the integration of desktop video systems with their existing systems and components.

They will also have doubts about the capabilities of desktop video, not unlike the doubts mainframe and minicomputer operators had about the capabilities of personal computers when they first began to infiltrate the corporate world. Many will consider desktop video equipment to be "toys" and will avoid adopting the systems for aesthetic reasons. Others will feel threatened by low-cost technology obsoleting their expensive investments in other equipment.

Still others will deem desktop video sufficient for elements of their productions, such as animations or character generation, but will leave the meat of the production effort to "real" video systems. A more enlightened group will adopt the new technology wholeheartedly and will, no doubt, begin providing stiff competition to their less adaptable peers.

A key problem to overcome with this end user segment is the relative unfamiliarity with computers. This will be more prevalent among the older professionals, who often fear the advent of new technologies.

This segment also includes the semiprofessional (e.g. wedding) videographers already in the business, but who have classically used postproduction houses to finish their projects. Desktop video will allow these individuals complete control over their productions as well as reduced economies.

The key impact of desktop video on small, independent producers has been an increase in the level of control along with the corresponding improvement in creativity provided by that control. To date, video productions have been a committee effort, involving a scriptwriter, a director, a cameraman, an audio engineer, a video engineer, an editor, a graphics artist, a character generator operator, and others, not counting the producer, who often spent most of his or her time raising money to pay for the others and the equipment they needed. The rest of a producer's time was spent coordinating the efforts of this small horde of expensive professionals, rather than developing creative content. With desktop video tools, a trained producer now has the technological ability to reduce this staff to a very few, perhaps the producer only, thus reducing the cost and frustration of coordinating a team of creative individuals.

Communications Professionals

Communications professionals are those industry and government employees who develop print and audio visual materials as part of their work.   They understand the communications process as a science, and they are familiar with the production process for the existing media used in their communications.

Most of these individuals have never produced a video themselves, although they may have had occasion to hire an independent video producer to develop programming for them. With the advent of desktop video technology, these individuals will have the "build vs. buy" choice; that is, they can now choose whether to hire out video production work or do it internally with desktop video products. Those who choose to perform their own video production will have to learn what is required. Contrary to much popular belief, the process is very complicated and will require a learning curve before these relative novices understand the processes of scripting, storyboarding, lighting, shooting, audio production, editing, post production, etc.

These individuals will have to learn about integrating computers and video equipment, as well as all of the technical issues with quality levels, frame accuracy, anti-aliased graphics, sound equalization, etc. that they have formerly left to others. In addition, these individuals may or may not be computer literate and will require some training and support in this area.

Desktop Communicators

Another end user group for desktop video technology will be desktop communicators, those professionals not typically in the print or video communications business, but with occasional need for such output. An example might be human relations personnel responsible for benefits training, or customer service personnel responsible for providing maintenance and repair training. These individuals typically understand the production process for their existing media, typically print publishing, and are generally computer literate.

They know very little about video production and its associated costs.

Home Enthusiasts

A certain number of individuals without a professional requirement to learn video production will become enamored with the technology and become desktop video end users. These early adopters will most likely be very computer literate and will purchase products not for the application, but for the technology itself. They are unafraid to experiment and will work long hours to master a technology.

Some of these individuals will leverage their adoption into new businesses, such as wedding and special event videography.

Novices

These individuals desire the end product of desktop video: a finished videotape production. They are willing to invest a little time and money into the process, but are unskilled in video production, computer/video integration, and possibly even in personal computers, themselves. To date, these individuals have been content with the consumer-quality products out on the market, but we anticipate a growing demand in this segment for more polished productions as well as the products and services necessary to deliver them.

Production and Postproduction Houses

Desktop video will dramatically impact existing production and postproduction organizations, as well as the individuals they employ (see the above section on Video Professionals). Desktop video is forcing a paradigm shift on the conventional video world, not unlike that forced on the publishing world by the advent of desktop publishing. As with all such shifts, they are initially greeted with a great deal of skepticism by the old guard, who are either then forced to adapt or be forced out of business.

Desktop video will do to those who refuse to adapt what personal computers did to the minicomputer manufacturers and service bureaus in the 1980's. The big studios, with their million-dollar investments in standalone, expensive, single-purpose equipment and software will begin facing stiff competition from small basement video "boutiques" who can develop programming of equivalent or near-equivalent quality at one quarter the cost, in one quarter the time, on equipment one tenth or one twentieth as expensive. Those who choose to adapt must learn computer skills and must adapt their processes to reflect the capabilities of the new technologies. This is a non-trivial challenge. Those who refuse to adapt, or are slow to do so, and even some who do so effectively will lose talented personnel who choose to pursue an entrepreneurial path. This implies a great deal of downsizing pressure in this segment of the end user base.

As the financial barriers to entry are lowered, more and more creative personnel will enter the independent video production market, forcing more and more competition on the video establishment. Desktop video is the great equalizer between the "haves" and "have-nots" among video producers. Now, for the first time, the independents will be able to compete on essentially equal terms with the big studios.

Distributors

As desktop video becomes more and more popular, and more and more smaller dealers and VARs begin to carry the products, distributors will carry more of the volume, reselling it to these smaller dealers. The products will be the mid-range, true "desktop" video, products, not the consumer level items or the high end video production products.

Distributors are not really appropriate for the consumer quality items, typically marketed directly to and through mass merchandisers, nor for the high-end video products, which will continue to be marketed through video dealers to the production and postproduction houses.

Video Dealers

Video dealers must evolve one of three directions in order to survive in the age of desktop video. First, they can choose to specialize in high-end products, as implied in the previous section. Second, they can choose to become distributors, without much or any retail focus. Or, third, they must develop the skill sets necessary to become effective retailers of desktop video products.

Those video dealers who choose to specialize in high-end products will be focusing on a small and dwindling niche. This niche is characterized by those who require "broadcast quality" products for use in network television programming, cable television programming, artistic commercial advertising, etc. To date, desktop video does not provide this level of quality, and some believe that it never well. We believe that it is a safe bet that someday, and someday relatively soon, desktop video will provide the quality levels necessary to perform the vast majority of "broadcast quality" functions. Nonetheless, for some time (and perhaps for a very long time if one believes the pessimists) there will be a small market for high-end, analog, "broadcast quality" products. This is the market currently served by these dealers; there's no doubt that some will continue to survive in this niche, but not as many as those there currently.

It is more likely that the video dealers, who tend to operate in a reactive mode anyway regarding sales, will become more like stocking distributors for the small dealers and VARs in the desktop video market. With their knowledge of video processes, they can become a valuable resource for lighting systems, cameras, tripods, microphones, teleprompters, and a host of other specialized video items. In addition, they can provide some value-added services in the form of video production consulting to the novice dealers entering the desktop video market. These distributors will however face stiff competition from established computer distributors who choose to stock and sell the same items.

The biggest challenge, but safest course for the video dealers is to adapt to the new technology and become desktop video retailers. This will force them to acquire technical skills in computer operation, installation, repair, and maintenance, as well as sales skills for penetrating corporate accounts and dealing with the uninformed general public, instead of the highly technical customer base to which they are accustomed. This will allow them to more effectively leverage their accumulated skills in video production processes and to make money off of this knowledge.

Computer Dealers

Existing computer dealers also have choices in how to respond to the challenges of desktop video. First, they can ignore the desktop video market. Second, they can carry the products, but not develop expertise. Third, they can retail the desktop video products, adding value via services, and effectively mutating into a VAR or Systems Integrator.

Those who choose to ignore desktop video will be relatively safe, although they will miss some significant revenue opportunities. They will continue to make money selling products which service other segments of the significantly-sized personal computer market.

Those who choose to carry the products, but not develop the expertise and the attendant value-added services will be at a competitive disadvantage to those who do. They will have to combat the VARs with pricing and availability, the key tools of a volume retailer. These retailers will most likely be large operations, with annual revenues in excess of $____ million per year. Smaller retailers will not survive long in this environment.

Those retailers who add services, such as video production training and consulting, system integration and installation, leasing and rentals, and maintenance and repair, will be most effective in marketing desktop video products.

Fig. 2-5:	Evolving Desktop Video Channels		
Manufacturer			
direct	distributor	chains	mail order
	video dealers	dealers/VARs	
		systems integrators	post houses

Mail Order

For those elements of the desktop video market not requiring value-added services or extensive demonstrations, mail order will be an effective alternative for acquiring some products. Mail order firms, as in the existing personal computer, video, and professional audio and musical instrument markets, specialize in well-known, standardized products which customers request by name. They typically do not have any presales technical support ability and rely on the manufacturers to provide this function.

They do provide discounted pricing and quick deliveries from stock, and will therefore compete strongly with distributors, video and computer dealers who choose not to add services, and even those manufacturers who sell direct.

Direct

Some manufacturers, similar to those existing in the personal computer and video industries today, will sell direct to the end users, either as a primary channel or as an afterthought. They will typically sell at their list price in order to minimize any conflicts with their other sales channels, allowing the other channel participants some latitude in order to discount prices or to add value via services.

The manufacturers who have high-end, expensive components and systems relative to the bulk of products in the market may choose to utilize a direct sales force focusing on the video professionals and communications professionals in the end user market, typically by calling on the production and postproduction houses as well as entities in business and government.

The manufacturers who sell directly as an afterthought typically will do so because of the lack of established sales channels. These will be the smaller, younger firms who are new to the desktop video market.

The midrange desktop video manufacturers will not sell directly to end users, but will focus on developing their indirect channels.

VARs & Systems Integrators

It is anticipated that the strongest channel participants in the desktop video industry structure will be the VARs and Systems Integrators.

Video production is not a simple process. Although desktop video technology simplifies it somewhat, and makes it possible for a single individual to perform all of the functions, there are a number of elements in a successful video production which require specialized skills from the individual or individuals creating the programming. These skill sets currently reside in the 300,000 or so video professionals in the world today. Joe Average, who desires to create his own video masterpiece via the wonders of desktop video, may indeed have the technology at his fingertips capable to do so, but will most likely lack the video production skills necessary to create a satisfactory product.

On the other hand, computers are very complex products and interconnecting them with video equipment is an integration nightmare. People who understand the video production process will usually be baffled by the technological issues of integrating a desktop video system. One will have to know how to configure and operate a computer, how to install and configure video cards, video subsystems, VTRs, camcorders, lighting, MIDI instruments, and audio systems, and how to install, configure, and operate the software which controls the whole array of systems. Then, what will happen when something doesn't work as advertised? Or something goes wrong? Good old Joe Average will have to troubleshoot, repair, or work around the problem, all of which implies that Joe has acquired a significant amount of computer and technological literacy from someplace.

As explored earlier, most of the likely end users of desktop video products are deficient in one or more of these areas of knowledge. Either they know video processes, or they know video equipment, or they know audio engineering and equipment, or they know lighting, or they know computers, but it is likely that they are very familiar with only one or a few of these very specialized areas. This knowledge gap between the end user and the technology calls for a value-added services provider such as a VAR or systems integrator.

It is reasonable to expect that some of the existing personal computer VARs and systems integrators, as well as some of the existing production houses, postproduction houses, and dealers in the video industry, will evolve into desktop video VARs and systems integrators. Some will retail the products; some will only provide services and will not take title to the products.

The most significant of these will be the VARs who acquire product lines directly from the manufacturers, or via distributors, mail order providers, and even other dealers, for resale directly to desktop video end users. They will have sales forces focused on specific niches, such as ad agencies or corporate service departments, and will have structured consulting, integration, training, installation, maintenance, and repair programs, as well as leasing services and service bureau functions in some cases.

In most cases, these VARs will bundle the services with the products they sell, such that the products are effectively priced at manufacturer's suggested list and the supplementary services constitute between 20% and 80% of the bundle's price.

Industry Organizations

The desktop video industry, as such, is in its infancy and no specific organizations have evolved with a focus exclusively on desktop video. Its component industries, professional video, professional audio, and multimedia, have evolved and continue to evolve a number of industry organizations whose purview overlaps desktop video. These include the following:

The International Television Association, or ITVA, an association of over 12,000 professional videographers primarily providing video production services to business and industry. The ITVA holds an annual trade show and convention.

The National Association of Broadcasters, or NAB, a U.S.-based association with international offices, focused on TV and Radio professionals. The NAB convention, held every spring in Las Vegas, is a major announcement opportunity for key manufacturers and other participants in the broadcast and allied industries.

The Society of Motion Picture and Television Engineers, or SMPTE (pronounced Simm-Tee) is a technical society for video engineers from broadcasters, manufacturers, and other industry groups. It provides a technical forum for film and video personnal, sets standards, and holds an annual trade show. SMPTE is a U.S. organization with international branches and has within its structure a number of committees which make recommendations to the CC!R (the UN regulatory body covering all froms of communications).

The National Television Systems Committee, or NTSC, a U.S. broadcast engineering advisory group responsible for defining the composite color television signal used in video transmissions.

The CCITT (an acronym for the French designation) and the International Standards Organization, or ISO, are two key international groups responsible for defining key telecommunication standards. MPEG and JPEG, the two groups chartered with developing video compression standards, are joint projects of the CCITT and ISO.

The Electronic Industries Association, or EIA, is a group comprised of representatives of the electronics industry in the United States. It is a combination information services bureau, offering such data as current sales of VCRs and television sets, as well as a standards development organization. The EIA is responsible for the development of the "RS" or "Recommended Standard" family of specifications, such as RS-170, RS-232C, and RS-422.

The National Association of Music Merchants, or NAMM, is the U.S. counterpart to NAB for the musical instrument and professional audio industry. It holds a trade show every summer which presents a key product introduction opportunity to the manufacturers of audio equipment and musical instruments.

The International MIDI Association, or IMA, is a organization comprised of MIDI musicians and representatives of musical instrument manufacturers who have defined and maintained the MIDI standard.

The MIDI Manufacturers Association, or MMA, is the leading U.S. organization focused on MIDI products and systems, and is comprised predominantly of representatives of MIDI product manufacturers.

The Association of Independent Video and Filmmakers, or AIVF, is a 5,000 member organization of independent producers. It offers various discount programs to members, on products such as indurance, car rentals, and technical books, plus publishes The Independent, a journal of independent video development.

More important at this time than the establishment of formal industry organizations is the development of open aggregations of manufacturers around established technology standards. Again, few of these standards and the organizations supporting them can be considered to be focused on desktop video. Rather, they have evolved from the personal computer industry, the multimedia industry, or the professional audio and video industries.

First among these are manufacturers that have aligned themselves with the various hardware/software standards for personal computer platforms. The hardware vendors focusing on storage, graphics adapters, graphics peripherals, and CPU engines, as well as the software manufacturers focusing on operating systems, word processing tools, spreadsheets, accounting packages, graphics packages, and video-oriented packages comprise a set of informal industry organizations centered on the primary desktop video platforms. A group of vendors is focused on ISA, EISA, and MCA bus computers (the so-called "PC-compatibles") as well as the supporting operating systems (MSDOS, OS2, Windows, and to a lesser extent, UNIX). This aggregation has been supplemented by those working on video-specific tools for these platforms, using such standards as Microsoft's Multimedia Extensions for Windows, Media Control Interface specification, and Video for Windows , Intel and IBM's Audio Video Kernel, Intel's DVI compression standard, and even Apple's QuickTIme for Windows.

The Apple-centric manufacturers have focused on the Apple NuBus platforms, including the Quadra family, the System 7 operating system, and Apple's QuickTime framework. Another group of manufacturers have focused on the Commodore Amiga platform and the NewTek Video Toaster, developing a series of products which are compatible with these base products. A last group is forming at present around the SGI Iris Indigo platform, consisting of both hardware and software vendors providing supporting products for the Indigo system.

On the audio side, the MIDI Manufacturers Association is a loose group of competitors and collaborators who develop and market products based on the Musical Instrument Digital Interface specification.

These various groups, though loosely structured, very informal, and internally competitive, are defacto industry organizations helping to guide the future of desktop video.

A more formal collection is the Open Media Framework (OMF) standards organization, led by Avid Technology. OMF is a group of digital video and digital audio product manufacturers who have collected together to define a standard for interchanging data among hardware and software products in order to create seamless systems.

Although they are not industry organizations in a normal sense, industry periodicals provide a forum for information interchange, for product announcements and advertisements, for technical discussions and tutorials, for product evaluations, and for a host of other functions usually associated with trade organizations. Various periodicals address desktop video from the perspective of the component industries. General purpose computer publications such as Infoworld, PC Week, Mac Week, and MacWorld cover desktop video from the perspective of multimedia and computer graphics, as do Computer Graphics World, Animation, Presentation Products, New Media, and Computer Pictures. SMPTE Journal, Broadcast Engineering, Film & Video, Videomaker, Millimeter, Producer, Videography, Video Systems, AV Video, American Cinematographer, Backstage-Shoot, and others approach desktop video as a subset of conventional video technologies and markets. High Color, Publish, EC&I, Imaging, and similar magazines cover desktop video as a sideline to their main focus of color imaging, and such audio-oriented magazines as Mix, Keyboard, and Electronic Musician focus on the audio aspects of desktop video.

Video Toaster User magazine was the first dedicated desktop video publication, followed in early 1993 by Desktop Video World. Whereas Video Toaster User is focused on the NewTek products and the Toaster support family from other vendors, Desktop Video World surveys the entire spectrum of desktop video.

Industry Issues

There are a number of technological, distribution, end user, application, and standards issues yet to be resolved in the growth of the desktop video industry.

Technological Issues

The central technological issue for desktop video is the trend toward online, nonlinear editing resulting from widescale use of digital video technologies. Without the continued development of these digital technologies, desktop video will never realize the full economies which will make it affordable to the mass market. Digitized video and audio is easier and faster to edit, does not degrade over time or during processing, and allows the use of low-cost, general-purpose computer equipment versus the more expensive, special-purpose, analog equipment used in current professional applications.

The problem with digitization of video and audio is the sheer volume of data which must be manipulated, stored, and retrieved in real time. An analysis of this data volume is worthwhile just to demonstrate the magnitude of the challenge

Video Data Rates

NTSC color video supports 525 lines of vertical resolution. Although VHS videotape supports only 240 lines of resolution, and this is acceptable to the majority of consumers, professionals prefer higher resolutions for crisper details. S-VHS and Hi-8 formats support just over 400 lines of resolution and this is deemed "marginal" for many applications. Most professional videotape organizations prefer to utilize Betacam SP formats, which support around 500 lines of resolution.

Assuming a target of Betacam SP resolution, and a video aspect ratio on most systems of 4 horizontal pixels for every vertical pixel, in order to produce a rectangular picture as is common today on both televisions and computer graphics terminals, a digital representation of a

Betacam-like image will require a screen resolution of something like 670x500. It so happens that standard VGA resolution, common on many PC-compatible and Macintosh computers is 640x480. Close enough.

Analog signals can present an essentially infinite variety of colors for each of the image elements on a video screen. In order to emulate this successfully, the digital pixels must be able to represent a near-infinite range of colors. For practical purposes, this requires 24-bit video representations for each pixel on the screen, allowing approximately 16.7 million color combinations for each pixel.

Twenty four bits is three bytes. Three bytes times 640 horizontal pixels times 480 vertical pixels is 921,600 bytes (almost a megabyte) of data for every fixed video image, or "frame" of video.

Standard NTSC video is presented at 30 frames per second. Thirty times 921,600 equals 27.65 million bytes of data per second.

Audio Data Rates and Overhead

The above figure represents the video data only. Most video programs require stereo audio, also, and this information must be stored, manipulated, and retrieved simultaneously with the video data. Consumers have become accustomed to the sonic quality of audio compact disks and expect this quality in all of their audio presentations. Audio CDs provide two channels (stereo) of 16-bit audio (2 bytes per channel), sampled at a rate of 44.1 kHz (or 44,100 samples per second).

Two channels times two bytes times 44,100 equals 176,400 bytes of data per second. Added to the video data, this totals 27.83 million bytes per second.

Unfortunately, this is not the only data which needs handling. Overhead data, associated with error detecting, addressing, and other housekeeping will add another 5 to 10 percent on top of this, depending on the techniques used. For the purposes of this discussion, the magnitude of digital video and audio data to be handled is in the range of 30 MB (megabytes) per second.

What to Do?

Thirty of megabytes per second, in any kind of sustained period as is common in video presentations, is a phenomenonal amount of data for personal computer systems to handle, given current technologies. Not only must a system find a storage place for the incredible volumes of data which will accumulate for even the shortest presentations (5 minutes equals 9 GIGABYTES!), but the flow rate itself is also excessive for both personal computer bus structures and storage device interfaces. There are four basic approaches, used singularly or in combination which manufacturers are currently using and will likely continue to use to address this challenge.

The first technique is the simplest approach but the most difficult technologically: Ignore the difficulties, damn the torpedoes, brute-force the problem into submission. I.e., handle the 30 MB in real time.

The second technique is to divert the data into specialized hardware, capable of handling the data in real time. The limitations of the personal computer bus thruputs are bypassed by this technique.

The third technique is to utilize advanced mathematical algorithms implemented in dedicated hardware devices to "compress" the data so that less data is handled in real time and the data rates are within the range of capabilities of personal computer platforms. Other systems combine hardware and software compression techniques to further reduce the storage requirements.

The fourth technique is cheating, either regarding image sizes, horizontal or vertical resolutions, or video bit depth, audio bit depth, and audio scanning frequencies, or a combination of the above.

The following paragraphs address each approach.

Brute Force

Current personal computer structures are clearly unable to handle the massive volumes and flow rates of data generated by digitizing full-screen, full-motion video. Even the high end Silicon Graphics Indigo systems are unable to move data around this fast. This notwithstanding, there are currently no storage systems capable of storing and retrieving data at 30 MB/s sustained rates, nor any affordable 50+ GB storage systems (in personal computer terms).

In short, the brute force technique cannot be implemented today with desktop video systems. There are workstations and larger computing engines capable of handling these data rates, but the costs of such systems far exceed the costs of conventional analog equipment, thus causing the cure to be more painful than the disease.

If the desktop video industry were more similar to the conventional video or conventional audio industries, with their slow rates of change, this technique would perhaps never be viable. Instead, it is driven largely by the digital electronics and personal computer industries in which complete technological revolutions occur within the span of ten or fewer years.

It is now early 1993. Ten years ago, the state of the art in personal computers was an 8-bit machine (the IBM PC-XT) operating at 4.77 MHz, producing 320x200 pixel color images, equipped with a 10MB hard disk, and producing less than 1/4 of a MIP in computing power. This report was developed on a 32-bit machine (a 80486 "clone") operating at 33 MHz, producing 800x600 pixel color images, equipped with a 205 MB hard disk, and producing nearly 20 MIPS in computing power. It is not even a state-of-the-art product today as there are hundreds of other personal computer platforms on the market with higher performance, more storage, or better graphics. But it is indicative of the technology curve in the personal computer market. The personal computer of 1993, described above, is 50+ times more powerful than the PC of 1983, yet it cost over $1000 less on the open market.

In 1983, the state of the art for personal computer disk storage was a 10MB magnetic Winchester drive. It was able to pass data to and from the PC at about 100 kilobytes per second. In 1993 it is common to find 2GB drives who can store and retrieve data in excess of a megabyte per second. Furthermore, the street price of today's 2GB drives not much more than the 10MB ones were ten years ago.

Some day, and probably some day in the next ten years, the brute force technique of handling video data will be feasible. For today, however, manufacturers have to be a little more clever.

Specialized Hardware

It is clear that the power and storage abilities of today's personal computers are sufficient, if not excessive, for the majority of applications to which they are applied. This is not to say that all applications can be accomplished with the existing personal computer structures; digital video, as explained in the preceeding paragraphs, is an application which requires extra capabilites. Others are continually being developed.

Most applications, however, require only the base capabilities available in the various personal computer families. For instance, word processing applications do not require the horsepower of a 80486 or 68040 or R4000 microprocessor, nor do they require 1280x1024 graphics or 2GB disk drives. Manufacturers have chosen to follow the proverbial 80/20 rule and focus their platforms around the 80% of all possible applications rather than the 20% in the market fringes. Accordingly, most personal computer platforms are optimized for general purpose applications, thereby reducing costs and expanding the available market for PC products.

Those applications which require extra power, e.g. digital video, often discover the limitations of a general purpose platform. For instance, in the interest of backward compatiblity, ISA-bus platforms operate at a bus speed of 8 Megahertz and with 16-bit data transfers, even if the microprocessors and other peripherals typically operate at higher speeds and with 32-bit transfers. Some manufacturers have included supplementary bus structures within these platforms to circumvent the limitations of the general bus structure and to take advantage of higher-performance hardware.

This technique is often used in desktop video products to mate video acquisition and playback boards with compression boards (discussed in a following paragraph). It is also used to mate graphics boards with microprocessor units and RAM in many systems.

A variation of this technique is to remove those components requiring higher speed transfers to a separate chassis, with a separate, faster bus structure, and to interconnect this expansion chassis to the base platform so that they can exchange less time-critical data at normal bus speeds (or even slower). This is the technique employed by such vendors as Digital F/X and Immix in order to somewhat isolate their video processing functions from the limitations of the Macintosh NuBus bus structure.

This has both advantages and disadvantages from the perspective of the user. The advantages are the increased performance available if the limits of the standard platform are circumvented, as well as the increase in other expansion capability allowed by getting the video processing cards out of the primary chassis. The disadvantages include the extra space and power required by a secondary chassis, as well as the investment required in special purpose hardware, which somewhat defeats the purpose of a general-purpose platform.

To some extent this approach has led to desktop video systems employing a personal computer platform primarily as a controller of other, specialized hardware.

Compression

A far more clever, less expensive, and more technologically feasible method of dealing with the data storage, manipulation, and retrieval challenge is by using mathematical algorithms to reduce the amount of processed data which represents a set of raw data, e.g. digital video images. This technique is called "compression" and can result in 100-to-1 decreases in the amount of data required to represent video and audio images. Three megabytes per second is a lot easier to handle than thirty, and the storage required for 30 or 60 minutes of compressed video is a lot less expensive than that for the uncompressed equivalent.

Compression techniques are applicable on information in which large portions of the data remain unchanged from preceeding data. Consider the following sequence of characters: "AAAAAAAABBBBBBBCCCCCCDDDDDDDEEEEEEEE". Suppose a "compression algorithm" exists which counts the number of identical characters in a sequence and replaces it with a "flag character", a single character describing the number of repeated characters, and the character to be repeated. If so, our sequence will reduce to something like: "!8A!7B!6C!7D!8E", where "!" is used as a flag character. Our "uncompressed data" consists of 36 characters; our "compressed data" consists of only 14, a 2.57:1 compression factor.

Note that this compression algorithm has some builtin limitations. First, it can't handle data that includes the "!" character unless some extra rules are added. Second, it can't handle more than 10 contiguous similar characters unless some coding technique, such as hexadecimal is used. It is also less than useful on some other forms of "data", i.e., the Gettysburg Address's "Four score and seven years ago" requires just as much data to represent in our "compressed" format as in the original uncompressed structure.

Fortunately the algorithms employed for video compression are a bit more powerful than that in our example, and the very nature of video information also plays a strong hand in the utility of compression for reducing the amount of digital data needed to represent video images. Video images are replete with spacial redundancy, meaning relatively vast spaces in an image are typically the same color, allowing the compression algorithms to implement duplication functions like in our example. Also, video programs vary with time, but they also include a great deal of temporal redundancy, meaning that the majority of an image does not change from frame to frame of a video program. To illustrate, if someone were making a videotape of you reading this report now, how much of the scene would change every 1/30th of a second? Not much, right? Typically, less than 25% of any given image changes from frame to frame, excepting those occasions in scenes are "cut" together in an abrupt transition.

Video compression algorithms, discussed in the Standards section later in this Chapter, make use of the temporal and spacial redundancies in video to reduce the data required to represent the images by significant amounts. Depending on the algorithm used, and the degree of compression employed, some of these techniques introduce data losses and "artifacts" or temporary image abnormalities. As with most things in life, one can rarely get something for nothing. However, since the majority of the video viewing public seems content with the limitations of VHS resolution, an occasional artifact at S-VHS or Hi-8 resolution seems acceptable for most applications. Digital video vendors, and indeed the majority of desktop video manufacturers, are gambling on the acceptance of compressed video quality by the viewing public, even as better algorithms are being developed.

Most of these algorithms are implemented in VLSI hardware which is incorporated into the video circuitry between the video inputs and outputs and the personal computer bus. This means that the data arriving at the personal computer bus to be manipulated, stored, and retrieved comes in at a volume and flow rate which is more reasonably handled by the personal computer CPU, peripherals, and storage systems. Some desktop video systems also employ software compression algorithms to further compress the incoming data, or to implement the compression functions without hardware when combined with some of the "cheating" techniques described below.

Cheating

When all else fails, cheat. This seems to be the motto of many of the digital video manufacturers, particularly those focused on the multimedia market. Realizing that the brute force technique is not economically possible, the specialized hardware approach is undesirable, and that compression requires both dedicated hardware and a very powerful and moderately expensive computer system to implement a desktop video system, some vendors have implemented digital video systems by cutting corners.

The first cut corner eliminates some digital video products from desktop video use, except for some preproduction functions as described in Chapter 4. Recognizing that the data volume and rates are the problem area, some vendors have arbitrarily limited the image size which can be digitized, processed, stored, retrieved, and displayed, to less than a full screen of video. By reducing a screen size to, say, 160x120 pixels is in itself a 16:1 compression of the data required to represent the image. Postage stamp, playing card, or even post card-sized video images may be suitable for multimedia applications but are clearly unsuitable for professional-quality video presentations.

The second cut corner is often used by these same manufacturers who reason that if their users don't need full-sized images, they don't need full-motion images. So, instead of digitizing and playing back 30 frames per second, they operate at 5, 10, 15, or some other lower frame per second rate. This results in jerky, distracting images, again perhaps acceptable for multimedia applications, but again clearly unacceptable for videotape work. Some vendors combine the two techniques described above to further decrease the data volumes and rates required for representing live video. By combining a 160x120 screen size with a 5 frame per second frame rate, one can reduce the data needed to describe an image by almost 100 to 1. Thirty megabytes per second are impossible to handle with current personal computer technologies; 300 kilobytes per second are child's play.

It is also common for the practitioners of the above techniques to also employ software compression techniques to further reduce the data rates and volumes.

The third technique is typically employed by those vendors making significant attempts at digitizing and reproducing full-screen, full-motion video images. Reasoning that most video consumers are satisfied with VHS resolutions of 240 lines, they have implemented techniques of pixel-doubling or scan-line doubling, or both, to reduce the 640x480 target resolution to a more viable 320x480, 640x240, or 320x240. In this technique, the digital video hardware digitizes and stores only every other horizontal or vertical pixel, or both, effectively reducing the data to be handled by 50 or 75%. These techniques, in combination with hardware compression products, allow the marketing of so called "full-screen, full-motion" video boards and reasonable facsimiles of live video.

Of the variations, the 640x240 scan-line doubling technique is used by the better digital video products, such as the Avid Media Suite Pro and the SuperMac DigitalFilm because it more accurately represents NTSC video than those which reduce the horizontal resolution by pixel doubling.

Even Silicon Graphics cheats. The low-end Indigo systems, which are priced like high-end personal computers, employ 8-bit color graphics systems in order to emulate 24-bit graphics workstations. In order to implement the 24-bit color necessary for desktop video, these systems must be upgraded with expensive graphics adapters, thus increasing the effective price of the systems well above $10,000, long considered the threshold for "personal" computer systems. In fairness, SGI's Indigo also has a lot of positive features, including internal CD-quality audio processing and a very powerful processor system, which somewhat offset this liability.

Digital video isn't the only area in which there is room for cheating. Many vendors fudge on the stereo, 16-bit, 44.1 kHz requirements of CD-quality audio needed for professional video presentations. Some vendors offer no audio at all and force the buyers to integrate audio products from 3rd parties. Some vendors offer only mono audio. Many more provide 8-bit audio functionality which is again more applicable to multimedia or games than to high-quality videotape presentations. Even otherwise impressive products such as the SuperMac DigitalFilm fudge on the audio by offering only 10 bits of resolution.

Wheras cutting corners on the audio bit depth reduces the fidelity of the recorded and reproduced audio, reducing the sampling rate to values like 22 kHz lowers the bandwidth of the audio. According to a mathematical rule called the Nyquist Sampling Theorem, the sampling rate should exceed the highest frequency being sampled. A 22 kHz sampling rate allows a maximum reproducable frequency in the 11 kHz range, cutting off almost all of the treble in audio programs. This is clearly unacceptable for video programming, from which consumers expect to receive Hi-Fi audio programming comprising frequencies between 20 Hz and 20 kHz (20,000 cycles per second).

Combinations

Most of the desktop video manufacturers seriously attempting to cultivate the desktop video market have employed, and are likely to continue to employ, a combination of the above techniques. One can limit the products that fall into this range as those which at least claim "full-screen, full-motion" video capabilities, meaning their images fill an entire video screen and operate at full 30 frame per second rates. Further, horizontal pixel-doubling seems to be less acceptable than vertical scan-line doubling.

Likewise, one can limit the real desktop video products to those which offer stereo, CD-quality audio capabilites, either integrally or part of an overall package. These two factors leave a limited range between what is acceptable for desktop video applications and what is technologically and economically possible at the present time.

As of early 1993, the only vendor shipping a product which meets these criteria is Avid, with the Media Suite Pro. Even it includes compromises, including a lossy motion-JPEG compression algorithm implemented via C-Cube hardware and scan-line doubling resulting in an effective 640x240 resolution. Others come close and still others are announced but are not yet shipping as of press time. Examples include SuperMac's DigitalFilm system and Immix's Video Cube.

All of these systems require a significant amount of processing power and storage from their base personal computer platforms. The current generation of personal computer systems, including the 80486-based ISA, EISA, and MCA machines, the 68040-based Apple Macintosh Quadra family, and even the low-end, R3000-based Silicon Graphics Iris Indigo platforms are hard pressed to handle even highly-compressed, full-screen, full-motion video.

Desktop Video Platforms

The desktop video revolution is focused on four primary personal computer families. The majority of the current installed base is centered on the Commodore Amiga family because of the success of the NewTek Video Toaster system.

The Amiga family includes the powerful 4000 unit, based on a 25 MHz Motorola 68040 microprocessor. It offers an ISA bus, allowing it to use hardware developed for the PC-compatible market, in addition to a proprietary "Zorro" bus. The dominant feature which was most important to the development of desktop video products on the Amiga was its ability to process and output NTSC video signals

The shortcoming of the Amiga system is its relatively low stature in the personal computer industry in terms of available applications, installed base, and future prospects. A significant industry has grown up around the Video Toaster, thereby injecting some life into Amiga sales, but the longterm prospects for the Amiga line are less rosy as the growing desktop video industry focuses on the more popular PC-compatible and Macintosh platforms.

The PC-compatibles break into three camps from a hardware perspective and three to four camps from a software perspective.   All are based on the Intel 80x86 microprocessor families. IBM is the dominant proponent, among a very few, of the Micro Channel Architecture bus structure and the OS/2 operating system. The ISA (Industry Standard Architecture, also known as the AT-bus) bus structure, created by IBM with the PC-AT in the early 80's, is the dominant base for this class of computers. The EISA bus structure is an enhancement to the ISA system, allowing the use of ISA or EISA cards almost interchangeably. Both the EISA and ISA families rely primarily on operating systems from Microsoft, either MS-DOS or Windows. A variety of manufacturers make the base platforms, compatible hardware, and applications software. A huge industry has grown up around the PC-compatible framework.

Current state of the art in PC-compatibles is the 80486 microprocessor, operating at up to 50 MHz, although there is an impressive installed base, as well as continuing sales, of less capable units. The processing power of the 80486 unit is comparable to the 68040 used in Apple Macintosh and Commodore Amiga platforms, as well as the R3000 used in low-end SGI Indigo workstations.   Despite this processing power, the bandwidth of the popular ISA bus limit its utility in digital video applications. The MCA and EISA bus each offer higher bandwidths and may be more appropriate to future demands on the platform.

The Apple family is based on the Motorola 680x0 family of microprocessors. The Quadra family of 68040-based products is most often specified for desktop video systems. As with the 80486-based PC-compatibles, this family is only marginally appropriate for desktop video and will likely be underpowered for future requirements. Apple personal computers are quickly securing more and more of the desktop video platform sales, primarily because of the success of Avid, Digital F/X, SuperMac, Radius, and RasterOps.

Silicon Graphics is a bit of a wild card in the world of desktop video. Their Indigo platform has impressive horsepower as well as CD-quality audio and graphics processing capabilities, but its price range is significantly above that of competing products. Nonetheless, a number of desktop video and computer graphics manufacturers have ported their products to the Indigo platform. Its processing power is above that currently available for Macintosh, Amiga, and PC-compatible platforms, making it more appropriate for the processing demands of desktop video.

Apple and IBM are working on a project deemed the Power PC for the next generation of Apple products, and perhaps creating the merger of the Macintosh and PC-compatible product structures. Intel is developing the Pentium as its next generation processor, offering even more processing capabilities over the impressive 80486 family. Microsoft is working hard to release Windows NT, a next-generation operating system capable of operating on a number of different platforms, perhaps even further unifying the software application interfaces of the future. A number of vendors have collaborated on improvements to the UNIX operating system, including such formidable players as SCO, improving its credibility as a legitimate operating environment. It is safe to say that desktop video platforms will continue to evolve for at least the forseeable future.

Silicon

Underpinning the board development from vendors in the desktop video industry are a number of developments in semiconductor devices oriented toward video processing. Products such as the Matrox Studio and the FAST Video Machine are based on VLSI devices from Philips, who was among the first to market with full-motion video devices.

Digital Signal Processing (DSP) devices from SGS Thompson, Motorola, TRW, and Sony are also fueling some of the growth in digital video. Companies such as C-Cube Microsystems, IIT, TI, Intel, and Brooktree have focused on perfecting compression devices which are in turn integrated into dedicated compression boards or integrated systems. ICS, Yamaha, Kurzweil, and others have miniaturized digital audio and music synthesis devices into a few ASICs. Other companies, including NewTek, have developed their own custom ASICs for their products..

Now that the market is growing and the semiconductor houses are beginning to see returns on their investments it is reasonable to expect continued development in this area. Of particular interest are the companies, such as C-Cube, who are working on MPEG compression hardware. This next generation of hardware should increase the interoperability of digital video products (current systems are based on a plethora of incompatible compression formats) as well as improve the throughput of video to and from storage, thereby making full 640x480, 30fps video viable for a number of products.

Standards Issues

Standards, either *de jure* or *de facto*, are important in any industry for focusing the efforts of both manufacturer and consumers around certain levels of performance and for encouraging the development of compatible products from a number of suppliers. Without standards, a development organization is required to provide all of the functionality associated with a given technology, something few organizations have the financial, engineering, manufacturing, and marketing resources to accomplish.

De jure standards, those developed by force of law or general agreement among participants, typically lag industry development. It is far more common for standards to be established on a de facto basis wherein a leading product emerges around which the industry congregates. The IBM PC is an example of such a standard-setting product; an entire industry grew around the basis of being "PC-compatible".

Desktop video is young enough that few de facto standards have arisen, with the possible exception of the Video Toaster from NewTek. A number of organizations have adopted the Toaster as the center of their development efforts, providing "Toaster-compatible" hardware and software to the desktop video market. Others will no doubt soon appear.

Desktop video is also too young to have established much in the way of de jure standards. OMF, the interchange standard from an industry consortium led by Avid Technology, is among the first of these, although few OMF products have yet to hit the market. As they do, the OMF standard will begin to influence both buying decisions from consumers as well as future development decisions from manufacturers.

It is more common for desktop video to borrow usage of standards from its parent industries of personal computers, multimedia, professional audio, and professional video. Many of these are detailed in the succeeding paragraphs.

Video Signals

The first key area in standardization to discuss is the electrical representation of video signals, since the acquisition, manipulation, transmission, reception, and viewing of video images is largely an electrical process.

Prior to 1953, television was a monochrome technology, resulting in "black and white" television sets and programming. Nonetheless, a large number of consumers acquired this new technology, forever transforming the American families and the very fabric of American life. Broadcast networks were established along with local stations in almost every major city.

In the early 1950's, engineers developed a means to broadcast and receive color video signals. This presented a dilemma: how to broadcast color video signals that would be downward compatible with the installed base of "black and white" televisions. Televisions at the time were significant investments for the average family, and it was not viable to expect families to discard their expensive sets for new technology. So the manufacturers and broadcasters had to determine a way to send color information in the same signal used by the existing monochrome devices.

In 1953, the National Television Systems Committee (NTSC) agreed on a system which defined a video signal usable by both existing "black and white" televisions as well as the emerging color televisions. The NTSC standard called for a video signal comprised of "luminance" (brightness, or monochrome) and "chrominance" (color) information. This signal was then decoded as a video display consisting of 525 lines in an interlaced format, presented at 30 frames per second, or 60 "fields" of 262.5 lines per second. The NTSC standard is used primarily in the USA, Canada, Japan, American territories, and some of Latin America.

Although it was the first color transmission standard, and the one today with the largest user base, it is not the best. The British followed with the PAL (Phase Alternating Line) standard as an improvement on the NTSC standard as well as a system which would work with their 50 Hz electrical supply. The PAL standard is used extensively throughout Europe and in various other places around the world. It defines a 625 line signal which is displayed at 25 frames per second interlaced, resulting in 50 fields of 312.5 lines per second. Because of the higher bandwith allowed for each of the "color difference" signals from which chrominance is decoded, as well as a technique of inverting the phase of the reference color on alternate fields, some annoying hue shift problems in the NTSC signal are avoided. PAL televisions and monitors cost slightly more than equivalent NTSC devices because of the extra hardware required for this inversion, as well as the lower demand for these devices versus the Japanese and American markets.

Ever independent, the French developed the SECAM standard as an alternative to both NTSC and PAL. SECAM, which stands for Sequential Coleur a Memoire, is used in France, the former USSR, Eastern Europe, Greece, Luxembourg, former and present French territories, and much of the Middle East. The SECAM standard employs 625 lines like the PAL standard, but uses a different scheme to eliminate the hue shift problem in the NTSC signal.

Most desktop video devices are manufactured explicitly for one of these three standards. Some devices have switchable capabilities allowing compatibility with two or more different systems.

Although the NTSC standard defines the signal content for video signals in the U.S., the gross electrical and mechanical characteristics of hardwired connections carrying these video, as well as audio, signals were defined by the Electronic Industries Association in its RS-170 standard.

Tape Formats

The output of desktop video products is a programmed videotape cassette, either as the final end product or as an intermediate product for use in other forms of distribution. Today, desktop video systems are used primarily with Hi-8, S-VHS, VHS, and Betacam formatted tapes and recording/playback devices. These are but a few of the variations available in videotape formats.

The vast majority of past and present videotape formats are analog in nature. That is, analog information is recorded to the tape and can then be retrieved for playback. In recent years, there has been a trend to digital formats, which offer superior performance and less degradation, but systems capable of all-digital recording are extremely expensive and are likely to remain so at least for a few years.

Analog formats are very subjective in nature. Machines which record and playback analog formats require constant calibration and examination. Identical machines often have significant variations in performance. They often require extensive operator expertise for setup. Tracking, head equalization, and audio and video signal levels require constant monitoring. In reel-to-reel systems, loading tape requires a complex theading procedure. In almost all analog formats, audio quality is a secondary concern, never matching video quality. In short, analog formats have been difficult to use.

In recent years, some of these difficulties have been eliminated, at least for consumer-quality formats. In the last several years, higher quality analog formats have become available in easier to use consumer and prosumer-quality systems. The professional-quality systems for these formats are still very complex.

In order to understand where videotape formats for desktop video are going, it is worthwhile at this point to explore where all commercial videotape formats have been and what is currently in use for both desktop video and conventional video applications.

Analog Formats - 0.75" to 2"

The first videotape format, known as "Type A", used 1" wide open-reel tape. Type A is now obsolete and has been so for some time. Its successors, Types B and C, are still used in professional broadcast applications, although they are gradually being replaced by more current, and more convenient, formats. Types B and C appeared in succession, employing 1" metal oxide tape, and allowing a playing time of 3 hours. Type C arrived in 1978 in order to add "stunt" capabilities such as slow motion and stop action. Types A, B, and C pioneered a technique of recording video called helical scanning, in which the record heads are mounted at an angle to the direction of tape movement, thereby allowing utilization of more of the tape width for recording. Also, each of these types were composite video devices; that is, they input and output composite video signals.

Two 2" formats, "Quad" and "Quad Cartridge", using the wider oxide tape were used for some applications in the broadcast industry, but never were accepted on a wide scale. Quad Cartridge did add a dimension of portability, key to such applications as Electronic News Gathering (ENG), but its 5-minute maximum play length was a severe limitation.

In the early 1980's the U-Matic format appeared. This format utilized 3/4" oxide tape in a cassette package. It was the first widely accepted videocassette format, being particularly popular in ENG and industrial environments. U-Matic tapes could record up to 75 minutes of video and audio, employed two linear audio tracks, and exhibited the high level of quality required for broadcast applications. U-Matic devices also input and output composite video signals. An upgrade appeared in the late 80's, adding Dolby C noise reduction, better resolution, better signal to noise ratio, and other features. U-Matic SP machines offered 1 hour of play time, 330 lines of video resolution, and downward compatibility with U-Matic tapes. U-Matic SP machines are still common in many video production facilities, local television stations, and industrial environments.

Analog Formats - Consumer

In the late 70's, two analog videocassette formats dueled for supremacy in the consumer market. Betamax, or "Beta", was a technologically superior 1/2" cassette format championed by the Sony Corporation, also a prime proponent of the U-Matic and U-Matic SP formats in professional environments. VHS, the Video Home System format championed by the Matsushita organization (Panasonic, JVC, et. al.) was the technologically inferior format, but one which offered a 2.5 hour play duration compared to Beta's 90 minute limit. Since feature films were among the primary programming recorded to these consumer formats, the VHS format soon proved more popular with the buying public. Today, it is difficult to find either Beta VTRs or Beta programming due to the market dominance of the VHS format.

Analog Formats - Matsushita Family

VHS videotapes, while acceptable to the public as a distribution means for entertainment and special interest video programming, is actually one of the lowest quality tape formats available. When it first came out in 1976, it only offered the "Standard Play" duration of 150 minutes, two mediocre-quality audio channels, and 240 lines of resolution. Later enhancements added "Extended Play" and "Long Play" durations, two channels of high fidelity audio, and higher output resolutions.

Despite its faults, the VHS system remains extremely popular. Most desktop video presentations will eventually be recorded to VHS videocassettes, as VHS players are the most common form of VTR/VCR in the world today.

In 1987, Matsushita announced a significant enhancement to the basic VHS system. The S-VHS format offers over 400 lines of resolution, topping even the U-Matic SP standard commonly in use in broadcast applications. S-VHS uses high-density, metal oxide tape, allowing a higher recording frequency bandwidth, and resulting in higher signal to noise ratios S-VHS also allows component video input and output signals, via a S-Video connection, thereby further improving resolution and picture quality. The S-VHS format has become quite popular in industrial and low-end broadcast applications and will be quite popular with desktop video enthusiasts. S-VHS, like U-Matic SP, is downward compatible with its predecessor format. Most S-VHS VTRs will play and record in VHS format.

One problem with both VHS and S-VHS formats is the relative bulk of the videocassette and therefore the mechanism required to drive it. This is not a major difficulty with fixed units such as VTRs, but for portable applications, such as a recording format for camcorders, it is a major limitation for the formats. Matsushita solved this difficulty by introducing the VHS-C, and later the S-VHS-C, formats. These smaller format cassettes utilize the same 1/2" oxide tape, recording techniques, resolution, and other features of their larger brethren, but sacrifice playing time (30 minutes max.) in order to reduce the cassette size.

Matsushita also is making an attempt to field a professional-quality 1/2" videocassette format. The "M" format is based on an upgrade of VHS, employs two linear audio tracks, and records 20 minute tapes using component video inputs. An upgrade of M, called "MII" or "M-two", extends the recording time to 90 minutes, adds two high-fidelity audio channels, and improves the bandwith and signal to noise ratio of the M format to the broadcast-quality range. M an MII use 1/2" cartridges about the size of VHS cassettes; MII employs high density metal particle tape.

Matsushita has fought a running battle at all quality levels with another Japanese giant, Sony. Sony fielded Betamax; Matsushita fought back with VHS, and won. Sony offered 8mm; Matsushita countered with VHS-C. Matsushita enhanced VHS to S-VHS; Sony countered with Hi-8, and Matsushita parried with S-VHS-C. Sony burst out with Betacam, and later Betacam SP; Matsushita followed with M and MII. The war rages on: Matsushita appears to won a decisive battle at the consumer-quality range (VHS vs. Beta), Sony appears to have an edge at the broadcast-quality range (MII vs. Betacam), and the dust hasn't cleared in the prosumer/industrial battle (S-VHS an S-VHS-C vs. Hi-8).

Analog Formats - Sony Family

The Betamax or "Beta" format was introduced by Sony in the early 70's as the first mass-market videocassette format. The 1/2" cartridges offered 90 minutes of video programming, two standard audio and two high-fidelity audio tracks, and composite recording. When Matsushita countered with the VHS format, offering over two hours of program duration, more applicable to the emerging video rental businesses focused on feature film entertainment, Beta began losing ground, never to recover.

Conceding that market to VHS, Sony attacked the shortcomings of the VHS format on two fronts, size and quality. As camcorders became popular in the mid-80's, the size and bulk of the VHS cassettes translated into heavy, bulky camcorders. Sony introduced the 8mm format (also called Video8), based on a small cassette containing 8mm-width metal particle tape. This format offered the performance range of Beta in a smaller size and also allowed a two-hour recording time in SP mode. 8mm format provides approximately 240 scan lines of resolution and uses composite inputs and outputs.

8mm became very popular among camcorder owners because it allowed significant reductions in the bulk of the recording apparatus, thereby making palm-sized units possible. The downsides to 8mm were its lack of technical superiority over the current VHS iteration and the fact that 8mm tapes would not play in VHS machines. Sony short-circuited both shortcomings by increasing the performance of the 8mm format by introducing Hi-8.

The Hi-8 evolution much resembled the VHS/S-VHS revolution in that Hi-8 provided increased video frequency bandwidth and signal to noise ratios over 8mm, resulting in improved video resolution. Hi-8 systems will play and record 8mm tapes, thus solving the obsolescence problem in the same manner as VHS/S-VHS. Hi-8 systems offer long play times (2 hours SP, 4 hours LP) and over 400 lines of video resolution.   Hi-8 systems can typically input and output either from a composite port or a S-Video connection. Although they offer a superior solution for video acquisition, since they produce S-VHS or U-Matic SP performance in a compact package, Hi-8 systems have proven less than ideal for editing purposes.

Hi-8 uses high-density, metal partical tape. The tape itself is 8 millimeters wide and does not offer a large adhesion area for the metal particles. Accordingly, after several passes, some Hi-8 tapes begin to lose some of this metal particle coating, resulting in "dropouts" in the recorded video images. Dropouts are momentary image flaws, typically white dots or smears. Some Hi-8 tapes are less susceptable to dropouts than others, but in the main, Hi-8 not been widely used as an editing media because of the wear tapes receive in that application. It has, however, proven quite acceptable for video acquisition applications such as ENG.

For professional video acquisition and editing applications Sony introduced the Betacam system in the late 80's, and followed it with the Betacam SP upgrade. Betacam systems utilize component video input, output, and recording and 1/2" tapes. The original version had a 30 minute recording length, used oxide tapes, and had only two linear audio channels, but the SP format improved to 90 minute recording lengths, metal particle tapes, and an additional two high-fidelity audio channels. Like the 8mm/Hi-8 and VHS/S-VHS formats, Betacam SP units can play and record standard Betacam tapes. The Betacam SP high fidelity audio tracks utilize Dolby C noise reduction.

Today, Betacam SP is the dominant acquisition and editing media in professional broadcast-quality applications.

Digital Formats

All of the above systems are analog formats, suffering from the maladies of the analog world including data deterioration, generational losses, noise, and troublesome recording and playback equipment. In recent years, following the general trend to digitization throughout the video and audio industries, there has been a move to digital videotape formats.

Although recording of digital data to tape is nothing new, and not particularly complex, recording realtime high-resolution video data in a digital format to anything is no trivial matter. Current digital videotape equipment is very expensive and only marginally less complex than its analog predecessors. It does, however, offer superior performance characteristics. As such, digital videotape devices and the tapes themselves are found today only in high-end production studios such as those for the broadcast networks.

This is not to say that this will always be the case. The trend in conventional video, and certainly in desktop video, is to digitize everywhere. It makes little sense to acquire an image with a digital device (a CCD camera), record it to an analog media, edit it on another digital device (online, disk-based desktop video system), and record the output back to another analog device. To keep the video data in a digital format as long as possible will reduce the overall performance degradation throughout the system, as well as simplify the electronic interconnections between video devices.

The original digital videotape format, defined in 1985, is called "D1", logically enough. It utilizes 19mm oxide tape in three different sized cassette cases. Component video is sampled according to a 4:2:2 algorithm and is recorded to tape along with 1 longitudinal audio track and 4 FM high-fidelity tracks. The "4:2:2" refers to the sampling rate of the luminance signal and each of the color difference chrominance signals in terms of a reference rate of 3.375 MHz. D1 machines are all-digital; their inputs and outputs, as well as the recording mechanisms are digital in nature. They are therefore applicable only to a completely digital recording suite.

D2 systems are digital recording and playback systems intended for conventional suites. The inputs and outputs are analog component video ports, but the tapes are recorded in a digital format. Since D2 devices fit in existing suites, the format has been more widely accepted than the D1 format and has essentially replaced 1" formats in professional production and postproduction facilities. D2 offers 220 minute recording times on cassettes filled with 19mm oxide tape. Like D1, the D2 format offers 1 longitudinal audio track and 4 FM high-fidelity tracks, recording 8-bit digitized video signals to tape at about 127 Megabits per second..

The prime mover of D2 systems has been Sony. Recently, Matsushita introduced the D3 format in order to compete with D2. The war rages onward.

Desktop Video Formats

What does all of this mean for desktop video? Desktop video is focused on industrial and commercial applications between the mass consumer market and the high end broadcast market. It is also focused on economics, i.e., creating video presentations of adequate quality in the most cost-effective way possible.

There's little doubt that some desktop video products will be used in conjunction with Beta(max), Betacam, M, VHS, VHS-C, 8mm, 1", Quad, D1, D2, and D3 videotape formats. If for no other reason, someone will use desktop video products with these formats just to prove it can be done. However, it is unlikely that a great deal of work will ever be done with the somewhat obsolete 1" and Quad formats, given their scarcity and cost, and the greater relative availability of U-Matic SP, MII, Betacam SP, and even digital devices. It is also unlikely that much desktop video work will be done in conjunction with D1, D2, and D3 devices because of the high cost of these items. Beta units are very difficult to find, so they can be disregarded for desktop video work. VHS-C is primarily an acquisition media, and it has been superseded by S-VHS-C, anyway. Likewise, 8mm has been bypassed by Hi-8, M by MII, and Betacam by Betacam SP.

This leaves VHS. The authors of this report believe that VHS VCRs and televisions will be the dominant delivery media of video programming for some time, because of the low cost of the combination, the vast supply of programming already available, and the acceptable quality of the output. VHS, however, is not a very acceptable acquisition or editing media (for those systems not using disk-based editing), so it is more likely to be used only as an output media. Even then, VHS output is likely to be produced from an S-VHS VTR.

The great midrange between the consumer quality formats and broadcast quality formats of today and tomorrow is the domain of desktop video. Formats such as S-VHS, S-VHS-C, Hi-8, MII, and Betacam SP will fight it out for dominance in the desktop video arena. At the present time, Betacam SP holds an edge over MII in professional, broadcast- or near-broadcast quality applications. Hi-8 is preferred over S-VHS-C as an acquisition media, although S-VHS is preferred over both for editing purposes.

As desktop video goes more and more away from analog videotape editing and toward online, disk-based systems which reduce the overall video degradation from input to final output, look to Hi-8 to dominate the acquisition formats, S-VHS to dominate the mastering formats, and VHS to remain strong as a distribution format. Betacam SP, while technically superior to all of these, is incompatible with any. Its superior performance is not needed for most desktop video acquisition applications and it cannot produce VHS distribution media, although it can produce superior-quality masters. The economic costs far outweigh the performance gains over S-VHS, and S-VHS devices can create VHS tapes, so there is little longterm place in desktop video for Betacam SP.

Time Codes

In video production and postproduction processes, it is necessary to keep track of exactly where events occur in the various source material. A given piece of source videotape may contain dozens or even hundreds of "clips" of video or audio which must be pieced together along with clips from other source tapes, voiceover audio, music, sound effects, transitions, and other video data to create a finished program. This function has classically been accomplished by used of "Time Code".

Time Code, or more properly SMPTE Time Code, is the glue which holds conventional video development processes together. Time Code is a sequence of electronic data recorded to videocassette tapes and used to provide positioning and control information for accessing and editing videotapes. Typically, TIme Code of a given format is applied to a tape prior to any video or audio being recorded. After the video and audio is acquired, the Time Code information provides frame-accurate location information for all video and audio on the tape. Editors use this Time Code information to determine starting and stopping points of clips to be used in the final program, generating Edit Decision Lists either by hand or electronically to define the location, duration, and sequence of each piece of source material to be assembled into the output program.

Time Code can be thought of as an address. Each address refers to a given frame of video. In the NTSC scheme, there are 30 frames of video per second, 60 seconds per minute, 60 minutes per hour, and 24 hours per day, so there are 30x60x60x24 or 2,592,000 uniquely addressable frames. Time Coding simply applies one of these unique addresses to each frame in a videotape program.

SMPTE, the industry organization which formalized Time Code, defined two different recording techniques for the addressing information. The first, and simplest, is called Longitudinal Time Code or LTC for short. In this format, the Time Code information is laid down longitudinally on an audio track as the tape is recorded. LTC can be "post-striped" or applied after the video signal is recorded, if necessary. VITC, pronounced "Vitt-See" for Vertical Interval Time Code is recorded to tape along with the video signal for each frame, during the vertical interval blanking period of the video signal. VITC allows recording and playback devices to keep track of the Time Code associated with a given frame even when tape is not moving, e.g. during a "Pause". LTC requires normal tape movement at full speed before it will indicate accurate timing.

.

Drop Frame Time Code

In the early days of video only monochrome signals were recorded to tape. Monochrome signal timing was derived from the power frequency of exactly 60 cycles per second (Hz), resulting in exactly 30 frames per second with each frame having a duration of 33.33 milliseconds.

In 1953, the NTSC introduced color into the video equation. As discussed previously, it was necessary to modify the existing video signal being transmitted only slightly so that existing black and white television systems would not be made obsolete by the new technology. Engineers developed a technique for adding color information to the previous monochrome signal by adding a color subcarrier, a special frequency associated with each television channel used to convey the color information. This subcarrier was set at a very specific frequency, from which all other frequencies in a video system were to be derived.

The horizontal and vertical scanning frequencies for NTSC video were thereby modified slightly, resulting in a vertical scanning frequency of 59.94 Hz, versus the previous 60.00 Hz. This doesn't seem like a large change, but it has significant impact over a long program. If the vertical scanning frequency is decreased to 59.94 Hz, then the frame rate is decreased to half that, or 27.97 frames per second.

.   SMPTE Time Code easily incorporated this change, since the new frame rate was less than the 30 maximum frames per second allowed. The only problem is that now each frame of video requires 33.3667 milliseconds (the inverse of 27.97 frames per second) versus the original 33.33 milliseconds. One hour of programming recorded to tape would not indicate the final 01:00:00:00 Time Code value expected, but instead would indicate 01:00:03:18, or a 3.6 second differential.

This situation is analogous to recording a 1 hour videotape of a overly fast clock. The clock recorded to tape will indicate a time duration greater than the real elapsed time. In video editing, 3.6 seconds in an hour is a significant period of time.

Drop Frame timing corrected this problem. Since the 29.97 Hz frame timing adds extra time, Time Code versus real time, SMPTE developed a means to eliminate occasional addresses for frames of video in order to resynchronize the Time Code address with real elapsed time. The Drop Frame technique drops the first two frame addresses (00 and 01) of each minute to be dropped, except every tenth minute. This amounts to dropping 108 frames, or 3.6 seconds, per hour. Note that only the addresses are dropped (on the fly), not the video frames themselves.

Other SMPTE Time Code Information

The even numbered Time Code frame numbers always correspond to the first frame of a color frame pair; the odd Time Code frame numbers correspond to the second frame of the color frame pairs. Color frame pairs are used to calibrate the color response of video systems.

Time Code information consists of 80 bits of digital data encoded in an analog format to tape. 32 of the 80 are defined as "User Bits" and are available for other purposes, such as defining cassette numbers, scene and take numbers, program information, and other data important to cataloguing video information. These User Bits are often accessed during editing to speed access to the proper clips.

Time Code and Desktop Video

Conventional video, due to its reliance on analog, linear recording and editing devices, relies on Time Code to provide accurate information about each clip acquired for a video production. As digital video processes become more prevalent, thanks to the emergence of desktop video systems, some of the requirements for Time Code and Time Code-compatible equipment disappear.

Random access editing systems operating on data stored on personal computer hard disks allow frame accuracy without use of Time Code. As these systems become more powerful and applicable for professional video applications, the need for Time Code is lessened significantly. Since Time Code-compatible equipment is both expensive and complicated, this represents another boon to the user base for desktop video. Instead of $5000 to $10,000 mastering decks, $1000 VTRs will do. Instead of $5000 cameras or camcorders, $1000 camcorders will do, etc.

MIDI

Musical instruments began as mechanical devices. Instruments produced musical tones by being plucked, hit, or being blown through, either directly by human beings or via complicated mechanical assemblies, as in the case of pianos and pipe organs. In the 1940's a means of amplifying a guitar was developed, leading directly to the creation of Rock and Roll music in the mid-50's. Smaller, electrical keyboards, such as organs also began appearing around the same time. In the early 70's, some pioneers developed a new series of musical instruments in which the musical tones were electronically generated. These early synthesizers were enormously expensive and complicated devices.

By the late 1970's synthesizers had become smaller and more capable, and at the same time less complex for users to operate. They became popular in the newer forms of music, adding new "voices" to musical compositions and supplementing or replacing popular acoustic instruments like flutes and violins. Other devices, called "samplers" also appeared on the music scene. These devices allowed a user to "sample" any sound and reproduce it at will at different frequencies by merely playing a note on a piano-like keyboard. Other devices, known as "sequencers" could be connected to synthesizers and samplers in order to produce sequences of musical notes, thereby allowing a synth or sampler to act as backup to live musicians or as a musical composition tool.

The increasing use of VLSI electronics allowed these synthesizers, samplers, and sequencers to become more and more portable and less and less expensive. This combination of factors led to unprecedented popularity in these "artificial" musical instruments by the early 80's. The only problem was that a sequencer from a given manufacturer would not necessarily control a synthesizer or sampler from another manufacturer. This lack of standardization slowed the acceptance of these electronic devices by many musicians because it forced limitations on them.

Creation of MIDI

In the early 80's a group of electronic musical equipment suppliers, led by Sequential Circuits and Roland Corporation, got together and defined a interface standard for interconnecting these instruments from different manufacturers. MIDI, the Musical Instrument Digital Interface, was born.

The original MIDI specification defined the electrical interface and an original set of commands allowable over the interface. MIDI has been continually updated since then and has acquired a substantial set of new commands and features.

MIDI Connections

MIDI instruments are connected together with three wires, leading to and from 5-pin circular DIN connectors. These wires convey digital serial data at a data rate of 31,250 bits per second. MIDI devices have MIDI IN ports for incoming data, MIDI OUT ports for outgoing data, and MIDI THRU ports for data passed from the IN port to downstream devices. MIDI circuits do not carry audio signals; rather, they carry commands from "controllers", e.g., sequencers or keyboards, to sound generation devices such as synthesizers or samplers. Note that this structure allows the separation of keyboard controllers from synthesizers, allowing both lightweight, simple keyboards and rack-mounted, hidden synthesis devices connected via MIDI.

Sequencers, originally separate hardware devices, have now been integrated into computer programs wich run on personal computer systems. PCs have MIDI interfaces which allow them to communicate with downstream electronic instruments. The Roland MPU-401 quickly became the standard interface for ISA-bus personal computers to MIDI instruments. Most manufacturers for the ISA-bus market follow this standard. Apple products implement MIDI interfaces via connection to one of the PC's serial ports. Commodore Amiga PCs have builtin MIDI ports.

MIDI Software

The storage and data manipulation capabilities of PCs also make them ideal for storing and manipulating "patch" information, "patches" being the set of parameters necessary for a synthesizer to define a particular set of sounds. A tuba patch allows a synthesizer to sound like a tuba, etc. More importantly, sequencers developed editing capabilities when they were implemented on PCs. Products such as Opcode Systems' Vision and Studio Vision products, Mark of the Unicorn's Performer, Twelve Tone Systems' Cakewalk and Cakewalk Pro, and a host of other products have been developed to allow PCs to act as MIDI sequence editing, recording, and playback devices

MIDI command structures include such basic functions as turning a given note on or off, setting instrument parameters, or reporting instrument setup information. MIDI functions also implement System Exclusive commands, allowing each manfacturer to define proprietary data structures and pass this information over MIDI to the connected instruments, thus reconfiguring them as desired. Using System Exclusive commands a PC-based librarian program for, say, a Korg M1 synthesizer can retrieve a special M1 "glockenspiel" patch and send the parameters for it down to a connected M1, in the middle of a song, if necessary. The M1 would accept this information as a command to load the patch parameters into its circuitry, so that when the next "note on" command was received, it would play a "glockenspiel" note of the appropriate value.

MIDI is limited to 16 channels of information. Many synthesizers and samplers are also multichannel devices and can be configured such that the data arriving on channel 1 is assigned to a "piano" patch, the data on channel 2 is assigned to a "bass guitar" patch, channel 3 to a "drum kit" patch, etc. In this way, a suitable polytimbral, multichannel synthesizer coupled with a suitable sequencer program can form an extremely powerful musical creation device for both professional and amateur musicians, as well as video producers.

Most synthesizers have historically implemented their instrumentation patches differently. A Kurzweil synthesizer might define patch 27 as a "clarinet" sound, whereas an E-Mu unit might define patch 27 as a "cowbell". Needless to say, before MIDI sequences could be interchangeable by various synthesizer devices some standardization was required. In the last couple of years the MIDI Manufacturers Association defined General Midi Mode, defining a standard set of voice mappings. Products compatible with standard agree on the general nature of each patch number (e.g., patch number 27 is always a "electric guitar" or whatever), no matter what synth is used. This allows MIDI sequences developed for one synthesizer to be used on another with ease.

Some sequencer programs are configured for use by professional musicians interested in creating music. Others are more oriented toward those who merely wish to play back compositions created by others. Most allow cut-and-paste editing, tempo changes, instrumentation reallocation, and other functions allowing non-musicians to adapt MIDI sequences to their needs. In a desktop video environment, a set of MIDI sequences, a synthesizer, and a PC-based sequencer/editor allow a video producer to adapt a given MIDI sequence to the video and provide background music for the video program.

The MIDI applications of today are far more complex than the applications prevalent when the standard was developed. It is common today to see MIDI systems controlling effects processors, power amplifiers and preamps, mixing consoles, recording decks, and even lighting, in addition to synthesizers, drum machines, and samplers.

MIDI Limitations

Despite its immense power, MIDI has limitations which limit its utility in large configurations, such as those prevalent in professional studios and in popular music concerts. The first problem is the limitation of 16 controllable channels. When attempting to control racks full of polyphonic synthesizers, samplers, effects devices, mixers, amplifiers, recording decks, and lighting systems, sixteen channels are not nearly enough. Some hardware providers have developed channel expanders, multiport interfaces, and MIDI patch panels to allow expansion and dynamic routing of the available channel information, thus allowing single controllers to handle many devices.

A bigger problem has been the fact that MIDI is a serial interface; that is, the commands are sent one after the other on the cabling. If a controller unit, e.g. a sequencer, is attempting to send 16 channels of commands at one time, and the commands themselves consist of multiple note on or note off commands, program change commands, and even patch dumps, the bandwidth of the interface is exceeded and all information is no longer sent in effectively real time. In live music applications, this is a disaster, since notes no longer appear where they're supposed to, the timing of songs is destroyed, etc.

In the late 80's some manufacturers have proposed implementing high speed LAN connections between MIDI notes, allowing dramatic increases in response times and well as solving the channel expansion problems. The MMA and other MIDI organizations are considering adopting these LAN recommendations into the MIDI standard.

Multimedia Sound Cards

Another development in the MIDI area is the growth of multimedia sound cards for the growing multimedia market. These cards typically employ an 8-bit, FM-synthesis music synthesizer, limited audio digitization and playback capability, and an external MIDI interface for connection to external, professional-quality synthesizers. Although these systems have little utility in desktop video or professional music applications, they have helped an entire new market get into the realm of electronic music generation, thereby whetting their appetites for better quality audio/MIDI products.

It is anticipated that desktop video market participants will gradually adopt more and more MIDI technology for their productions, for many of the same reasons that they adopted desktop video technology, itself. MIDI allows a single person, not even necessarily a musician, to emulate the musical efforts of many different individuals, thus reducing the time, effort, and cost associated with creating music.

Computer File Structures

Another set of standards to be considered for desktop video are the plethora of file structures associated with personal computer audio, MIDI, graphics, and moving video files. Since a large benefit of desktop video is the ability to store, modify, and retrieve computerized representations of the live video and audio to be included in desktop video productions, the interchangeability of these files among various software applications and hardware products is paramount.

Audio

Digitized audio is becoming more common in professional audio and music applications such as radio production, television production, and musical recording, as well as in desktop video. Compact Discs employ digital audio to produce outstanding fidelity in a playback-only media. Other media, such as computer disk drives, employ standardized file structures allowing one software program to record audio data to disk, another to edit and "sweeten" it, and a third to play it back.

Pioneers in the Macintosh-based digital audio industry, such as Farallon and Digidesign, established file format standards such as SoundEdit, SoundDesigner, SoundDesigner II, and Dyaxis. A standardized format, AIFF for Audio Interchange File Format, evolved out of the industry and has become the most common interchange structure. Most programs can import or export AIFF files in addition to their own proprietary file structures. Of the remaining Mac file structures, SoundDesigner II has garnered a significant amount of third party support and will likely remain strong. Both AIFF and SoundDesigner II files support CD-quality, 16-bit, 44.1 kHz digital resolution.

The Multimedia Personal Computer specification, defined byMicrosoft and adopted by a number of multimedia manufacturers, calls out the use of WAV files for digital audio. WAV files are therefore important for ISA-bus and EISA-bus personal computer platforms and for the software which run on them.

MIDI

Several file structures have also become important for MIDI data files. First among these are the Standard MIDI File (SMF) formats, defined for storage of sequence information.

SMF Type 0 format is the simplest of the three and provides single channel storage for simplistic, single-instrument melodies. It cannot handle tempo changes, instrument changes, and other higher functions. As such, it is appropriate only for storage and playback of simple melodies, such as children's music. SMF Type 1 is widely used to store MIDI sequences. It adds multichannel support, allowing more complex musical structures, as well as increased functionality over Type 0. More often than not, when someone refers to "Standard MIDI" files, they are talking about Type 1 files. Type 2 formats are rarely used. They store music as blocks of information along with instructions for ordering and repeating the blocks.

Samplers also utilize a standardized file format for interchanging sample information. The SDS, or Sample Dump Standard format, allows a sampled segment of information, say a grand piano note, to be recorded on an Akai sampler and played back on a Yamaha unit.

Still Video

There are hundreds of "standard" file formats for describing still video data, such as computerized graphics or digitized photos. Some of these have evolved into de facto standards. Graphics file formats break into two basic types: bitmapped and vector-based structures. Bitmapped formats describe images by defining each pixel in an image. Vector-based formats break each image into a series of line segments of defined length, width, and color. Vector graphics formats are typically used for applications such as CAD, Computer Aided Drafting, in which the images are comprised predominantly of lines. They are also common in animation programs. Bitmapped formats require more storage space (in general) than vector formats, but allow finer detail. They are more common in photographic applications.

Fig. 2-6:	Example Bitmapped Graphics File Formats

BIT	A monochrome bitmap file
BMP	Windows bitmapped file.
CLP	Windows clipboard file
DIB	Device Independent Bitmap
FAX	Fax file format produced by computer-based fax systems
GIF	Compuserve's graphics interchange file format
ICO	Windows icon file
IMG	GEM bitmap file
PCC	PC Paintbrush clipboard file
PCL	Hewlett-Packard bitmap file
PCX	A PC Paintbrush file.
PIC	PC Paint files, Dr. Halo graphics files, and others
PICT	Mac bitmap file (either PICT1 or PICT2 versions)
RLE	Compressed Windows graphics file (Run Length Encoded)
TGA	Images generated on a system equipped with a Truevision TARGA board.
TIFF	Tagged Image File Format.
WPG	WordPerfect bitmap file

A veritable alphabet soup is used to describe these file formats. Some of the more common bitmapped formats are listed below in Figure 2-6.

Of the above file formats, TIFF is among the most common for desktop video applications, along with PICT and IMG formats. PCL is common for describing graphics information sent to laser printers.

Common vector file formats include those listed in Figure 2-7.

Fig. 2-7:	Example Vector Graphics File Formats
AI	Adobe Illustrator file
CDR	Corel Draw file
CGM	Computer Graphics Metafile
DRW	Micrografx Designer file
DXF	AutoCAD binary output file
EPS	Encapsulated PostScript file
GEM	GEM Draw file
GRF	Micrografx Charisma file
HPGL	Hewlett-Packard graphics language format
MET	OS/2 Presentation Manager File
PIC	Micrografx Draw file or Lotus picture file
PIF	IBM picture interchange format

PS	PostScript file
WMF	Windows Metafile
WPG	WordPerfect clip art file

Of the vector formats, Adobe's PS and EPS formats are common, as are those of the key vector graphics manufacturers, including Corel's CDR and Autodesk's DXF. The GEM format is common in the Amiga environment, since the Amiga platform is based in the GEM operating system.

A number of vendors have discovered the plethora of file formats and the attendant confusion among users as to which products are compatible with which formats. These vendors have developed conversion utilities for converting images, both still and moving, from one format to another. Some even have image processing functions builtin which allow users to touch up, crop, rotate, and otherwise manipulate images converted from one file format to another. A partial list of these applications is given in Figure 2-8.

Fig. 2-8:	Example Graphics File Format Conversion Programs
Conversion Artist	North Coast Software
DeBabelizer	Equilibrium Technologies
Hijaak for Windows	Inset Systems
ImagePrep	HSC Software
SnapPRO!	Window Painters, Ltd.
Image Alchemy	Handmade Software

Animations / Moving Video

For animations and other time-dependent data like video capture and playback, the existing graphics file formats are insufficient. Graphics file formats express images in terms of 3 dimensions: length, width, and color. Animations and video require the addition of a fourth element, time.

Some animation packages adapted existing still graphics formats in order to develop the PICS, FLI, FLC, and DIB formats. These will continue to be important in animations, although several new developments will take precedence in the area of desktop video.

The first major development was the announcement of QuickTime by Apple in early 1992. This standard created a new file type, the QuickTime Movie, which stores the time-dependent elements in QuickTime-based presentations. QuickTime also supports an enhanced version of PICT files for static images. In late 92, Apple also announced QuickTime for Windows, bringing new file standards to the Windows-compatible PC market.

Microsoft countered Apple with the announcement of Video for Windows. Video for Windows uses the AVI file format to perform the same function as QuickTime's Movie format.

It is anticipated that Microsoft's and Apple's offerings will dominate the file format interchanges used for multimedia applications for the rest of the decade. Some of these applications will extend upward into the realm of desktop video, in the form of animatics and even completely digital presentations as the technologies supporting these environments matures

Avid's OMF framework performs essentially the same functions as QuickTime and Video for Windows, but for higher-end digital video products.   The OMF standard specifies three types of digital media data file formats: common interchange formats, public interchange formats, and private interchange formats. The common formats include AIFF and WAV files for audio, TIFF for still images, and a variation on TIFF for moving video and animations. The TIFF files further support 24-bit and 8-bit RGB pixel bitmaps, JPEG's JFIF format for compressed video, and the JPEG YCC compressed video format. The private and public file formats supported by OMF are yet to be determined.

Avid Technology announced the formation of OMF, the Open Media Framework, in April of 1992 and to date over 100 organizations have agreed to produce compatible products. The OMF is designed to provide a structure wherein all of the information required for digital media, including video, animations, graphics, still images, MIDI, audio, etc., can be combined, stored in either compressed or uncompressed forms, and presented via heterogeneous platforms and applications. An OMF interchange file contains three basic types of information: media data (the raw data, including MIDI sequences, or audio samples), media source information (to identify the physical source of the media data), and compositions (the information required to play back an integrated program). Although OMF was developed for desktop video and other high-end digital video applications, the standard also allows for integration with multimedia structures, such as QuickTime. In fact, Apple and Avid have agreed to work together to provide links between OMF and QuickTime.

Edit Decision Lists

In the professional video market there is no reliance on file formats to store actual video and audio data. Rather, there is use of a number of computerized index file formats to describe source material contents, starting and ending time codes, transition description and duration, and other factors. These Edit Decision List (EDL) standards vary from manufacturer to manufacturer. Typically the name of the EDL standard format is the name of the professional equipment manufacturer and system on which that EDL standard was first implemented, as in the case of CMX 340, 3400, 3400A, and 3600 EDLs, Grass Valley Group GVG I EDLs, and Sony 900, 910, 5000, and 9000 EDLs.

EDLs are important only in offline systems, in which preliminary editing is done on a lower cost (e.g. desktop video) system and the results of this editing are transported to a more capable and expensive online editing suite. The intent of digital video applications is to remove the offline/online dichotomy, thereby reducing the need for EDL standards as digital video becomes more and more applicable for high-quality video editing. At such time, digital video standards such as OMF, QuickTime, and Video for Windows will become more important for desktop video (and by extension, conventional video) applications.

Compression

As discussed previously in this Chapter, compression is the enabling technology which allows the massive data quantities and flow rates of digitized video to be pared down to a level capable of being handled by personal computing platforms. There are a number of compression standards already in the market and more are arriving every year.

The current dominant desktop video compression standard is not even a single "standard" at all. Rather, it is a set of mutually incompatible enhancements to a still-video standard developed by the Joint Photographic Experts Group, or JPEG, an advisory group formed jointly by the CCITT and ISO. The JPEG standard applies to still video and graphics compression and does not define file formats, audio compression, audio/video synchronization, and systems integration issues necessary for motion video implementations. A number of manufacturers have developed hardware and software based around JPEG VLSI circuitry which implement the so-called "Motion JPEG" compression standards. These mutually incompatible Motion JPEG implementations typically provide real-time video compression and decompression at 25:1 to 100:1 ratios.

The CCITT and ISO also formed a second committee to address the requirements of motion video. The MPEG, or Motion Picture Experts Group, has not yet announced their final specification, which is due in late 1993. Depending on the exact form of the specification, MPEG implementations may or may not be fully applicable to desktop video editing applications, as the compression technique may be asymetric, or unable to handle real-time data.

Although JPEG and MPEG lend themselves to hardware implementations, some compression can be accomplished via software. For example, Apple's QuickTime includes several different software compression algorithms including Compact Video Compressor and Apple Video Compressor. These compressors can work in real-time with limited image sizes and frame rates, but as both increase, the compression algorithm becomes asymmetric and unable to compress images in real time. Compact Video Compressor is capable of compressing 320x240 windows at 15 to 24 frames per second into 30 MB/minute. AVC can only handle 160x120 windows at 12-20 frames per second into 25 MB/minute.

Intel provides both hardware and software compression tools for ISA-bus, EISA-bus, and MCA-bus personal computer systems. Intel's Indeo is a real time compression algorithm suitable for low quality applications, and storage rates commensurate with the quality level selected among several choices. Indeo can operate in a software-only environment or can utilize hardware acceleration products to enhance its performance. Indeo is also cross-platform compatible. Intel also provides the i750 chip set, collectively known as DVI, a programmable video processor forming the basis of a number of hardware and software products for PC-compatible platforms. Intel and IBM are working together to continue to develop this technology.

Other compression schemes, both hardware-based and software-based are also available. RTV, Real Time Video, provides reasonable video quality, adjustable data rates, and cross-platform compatibility. PLV, Production Level Video, provides high quality video and 16-bit audio compression, but is highly asymmetric, requiring an outside service bureau to perform the file compression. CEC True Motion is reported to provide both real-time and asymmetric compression at near-broadcast quality.

Distribution Issues

As discussed earlier in this Chapter and elsewhere within this report, the distribution channels for desktop video are just begining to evolve away from their bases in other market structures. Some other issues, other than industry structure, will have impact on how desktop video products are distributed.

Production and Postproduction Facilities

For some time in the conventional video industry, as well as in the professional audio industry, it has been common for service providers such as production and postproduction facilities to differentiate themselves by three major factors: location, quality (as proven by previous work), and equipment available. The latter factor is evident in the marketing efforts of these organizations. A video production facility, for example, will claim ownership, and presumably competence, with an entire laundry list of expensive, complicated equipment. More so, the identities of these very organizations are wrapped up in this equipment, with some facilities being known as "Grass [Valley Group]" houses, and others as "Avid", "Sony", or "CMX" facilities.

Marketing efforts from manufacturers, at least in terms of brand recognition, must therefore be applied at two different customer sets: the actual users of the products (the production and postproduction facilities), as well as the end consumers, the contractors for services based on these products. The end consumers of video services often do not know a time code from a microphone, much less the reason why they should prefer a "Grass" facility over a "Sony" facility, or vice versa. They want to understand features and benefits, not technical details. The production and postproduction facilities, on the other hand, do want to know technical details, since their purchase decisions are influenced by predominantly by technical capabilities of the products they acquire.

In desktop video environments more of the actual end users/consumers will own and operate the equipment. These individuals will be generally less technical than the inhabitants of professional audio and video production and postproduction facilities and must be marketed to on a less-technical level than the professionals. The professional staffers, on the other hand, will often influence purchases by consumers (at least while desktop video is in its infancy), and are underwhelmed by the gross generalities and oversimplifications in most end user marketing campaigns. To reach these people and convince them of the merits of desktop video products, manufacturers must state clearly the functionality and performance specifications of their products and not rely on glossy, feel-good types of campaigns. As the desktop video market matures, the influence of the video and audio professionals on the market will decline, and manufacturers can focus on more mass-market oriented campaigns.

Cost Ceilings and Leasing

Although desktop video products are significantly less expensive than conventional video products performing the same functions, they are not yet in the "pocket change" category. Fully configured desktop video systems cost in excess of $30,000 today and will likely remain above the $10,000 threshold for some time. Not every potential consumer has the up-front capital necessary to acquire these systems.

One alternative is leasing. Manufacturers and their distribution channels will be well served by implementing leasing programs, allowing financially stable but capital-limited personnel to take advantage of this new technology. Leasing will overcome one significant barrier to entry for these individuals, thereby expanding the number of market entrants beyond the monied few able to overcome the initial purchase hurdle.

Conventional Market Segmentation

Prior to the advent of desktop video, the conventional video market was segmented by both manufacturers and consumers into four discrete submarkets. This segmentation was based on the performance level, therefore complexity, and therefore cost, of the products in the video market. These products broke well into four categories.

The lowest category, offering the lowest performance for the lowest cost, was the consumer segment. Consumer products included such items as VHS VCRs, 8mm camcorders, and the like. Next in the chain was the prosumer segment, offering slightly more complex products, with greater performance, and at greater cost. Examples of prosumer products included low-end S-VHS VCRs,Hi-8 camcorders, etc. The third segment was the industrial quality segment, differentiated by additional features and cost over the prosumer segment. Examples include high-end S-VHS VCRs with time code capability, 3-CCD Hi-8 camcorders, etc. The final level was the broadcast segment, including professional VCRs, cameras, editing equipment, etc.

Today, this segmentation has changed dramatically via the evolution of existing products and the emergence of the desktop video technologies. First, the differentiation between consumer and prosumer quality has blurred considerably, effectively erasing the prosumer category. Second, industrial-quality products have become less expensive, often competing with consumer-quality products at slight cost differentials. Third, industrial-quality products have also become more capable, often exceeding the capabilities of what was once considered "broadcast quality". Finally, the broadcast segment has been pushed upward, in terms of both cost and performance from previous levels. This is due to pressure from industrial-quality desktop video gear as well as the evolution of more powerful digital systems such as D1 and D2 VTRs.

Desktop video technologies today lie somewhere between the upper range of consumer products and the upper range of industrial products.

End User Issues

Training

Desktop video users will follow classic new-technology adoption trends. The people who are utilizing the new technologies today fall under the broad range of "early adopters". They are comprised mostly of video professionals adopting the new technologies within their existing workplaces, or branching out on their own. Over time, more and more of the communications professionals and less video-skilled personnel will adopt the newly evolving desktop video technologies.

Although much of the advertising in the desktop video industry to date has fostered the notion that creating video presentations is easy, the reality is quite different. Desktop video has simplified the process somewhat, but video production still requires skills in many areas, some technical and some artistic, which are not prevalent in today's populace. The desktop video producer will have to effectively acquire at least reasonable proficiency in a number of very complex fields, typically performed in conventional video productions by skilled professionals such as executive producers, producers, directors, scriptwriters, storyboard artists, camera personnel, video engineers, audio engineers, lighting directors, grips, gaffers, scene designers, logistic planners, set builders, acting and voiceover talent, computer specialists, editors, graphics artists, among others. This proficiency will not come overnight.

Individuals without the requisite skill sets, or unable to obtain them on contract bases, will find themselves frustrated at their inability to produce professional-quality presentations. Such frustration will of course lead to customer dissatisfaction and to slow market growth unless significant efforts are taken by the manufacturers of desktop video products, as well as their chosen distribution channels, to offset their customers' lack of skill with appropriate training and support. Just selling products, at least in the short term, will not be sufficient for success in desktop video. There must be a real commitment to providing video development skills along with the products, at least until technological advances offset the skills required.

Artistic skills, as well as purely technical ones, must also be developed in the newly emerging users of desktop video. For example, most people are not used to thinking visually - how to get a concept across in a visual manner. Most novices writing their first scripts or developing their first productions will find them lifeless, distracting, confusing, or even silly when the final output is delivered. Professional lighting directors can work magic creating interest or even moods with proper application of lighting. Amateurs can make a mess of shadows, sharp contrasts, improper coloration, and reflections. Skilled audio engineers and musicians can compensate for the quietest and loudest of sounds, in poor or excellent acoustical conditions, and mix in music to heighten moods or emphasize key points. Amateurs can easily amplify noise as well as desirable sounds or misjudge the effects of music or sound effects on the material being presented.

Integration

End users will encounter the nightmare of interfacing digital computer technology with analog video and audio systems. One of these elements, or perhaps all three, will be beyond the technical experience of the average end users, so getting all to work together will be a time-consuming, frustrating process, at least until upcoming desktop video systems further integrate the various component systems, thereby simplifying the current maze of cabling and connections required to implement a system.

It will be the function of the manufacturers and their sales channels to make this integration as painless as possible. Unfortunately, it is a fact of life that the technology which creates the need for integration will be held responsible for the operation of the whole system. That is, if the audio system develops a hum or the computer's printer stops working, it is the fault of the desktop video components (at least in the minds of the users). Sorting through these difficulties will require patience on the parts of all involved.

Sources of Desktop Video Users

From where will all of the people expected to acquire desktop video equipment come? Intitially, as briefly noted above, these people will come from the ranks of the trained video professionals and other technically skilled individuals. Computer literacy in the professional communicator user segment will allow some of these to adopt the new technologies. What about the rest? The video and communication professionals are the only ones with a legitimate job-related reason, at present, to obtain this new, still-expensive technology.

Clearly, if desktop video users are limited to these two primary classes, the overall market will remain small. To penetrate the general market beyond the professional presenters will require developments in several areas. First and foremost, the training and integration issues described above will have to be conquered, either through advancing technology, improved support, or a combination of the two. Second, applications for video presentations, hence the number of people requiring them, will have to expand beyond those currently and commonly used.

The authors of this report believe that the former issue is being actively addressed and the latter will take care of itself. There are thousands of potential video applications and millions of individuals interested in exploiting them in the general market. The decreasing complexity and cost of desktop video systems will put the necessary tools in the hands of these individuals and the individuals themselves will develop creative applications for video presentations beyond any currently in use.

Application Issues

Video Programming Development

The development of video programming occurs in four phases: preproduction, production, postproduction, and distribution. Conventional video, and consequently desktop video, products are usually focused on one or two of these phases, although some products span more.

The preproduction phase includes the activities which occur before the cameras start rolling. To date, this has been a predominantly manual process including scriptwriting, storyboarding, budgeting, casting, funding, and set and site preparation. Few tools have been historically used in this environment, although personal computers have made incursions into the areas of budgeting and scriptwriting. Desktop video tools will continue to automate the activities in the preproduction phase of video development. The preproduction phase is discussed in Chapter 4 of this study.

The production phase includes the activities required to capture live action and audio footage for the video presentation. Production is very labor intensive and has tended to require expensive and elaborate lighting, prompting, camera, and audio equipment, as well as the skilled personnel to use it. Desktop video allows the use of smaller and less expensive lighting and audio setups, force the development of less expensive teleprompting equipment, and allow use of lower quality camera equipment than is common in conventional video production. The production phase of video development is detailed in Chapter 5 of this study.

The postproduction phase will be affected most by the incursion of desktop video products. It is the phase in which the activities occur that are neccessary to transform the captured live action video and audio, as well as supplementary graphics, music, voiceovers, sound effects, titling, and other elements, into a finished video program. Postproduction requires the most expensive and complex equipment of all of the video phases as well as the most skilled professionals. Desktop video allows a single individual to perform almost all postproduction tasks on a relatively inexpensive, personal computer-based platform. The postproduction phase of video development is detailed in Chapter 6 of this study.

The distribution phase of video development is the process of conveying a completed video presentation from the studio to its intended viewers. Obviously, this phase uses a multiplicity of vehicles to accomplish this task, including broadcast and CATV organizations, VHS and other format videotapes, multimedia presentations, etc. Each of these vehicles has its own structure and needs. The distribution phase is beyond the scope of this report and is mentioned here only for the sake of completeness.

Services

This study is also focused on products, in the sense of goods, tangible hardware and software. Each of the phases of video development also foster (and sometimes require) the utilization of a number of services, provided by either groups or individuals. The use of these services is common in the conventional video market, and will be less so (although nonzero) in the desktop video market.

Services are available for practically every element of video development and for the operation of practically every piece of video hardware and software in existence. If a desktop video producer has subject material, but cannot write scripts, there are scriptwriters who will contract to perform this service. Artists, actors, camera operators, lighting specialists, audio engineers, musicians, animators, editors, tape duplicators, entire production facilities or postproduction facilities (and crews) are available on a number of different arrangements.

The services market associated with conventional video development is quite substantial. The services associated market associated with desktop video will be less so, since desktop video automates many of the functions performed by service providers in the conventional video domain, but there will always be some demand for specialists in particular service areas. The desktop video services market is beyond the scope of this study.

Time and Cost Effects

Desktop video can be thought of as the digitization of an analog world. Digital video processes, and the equipment which allows them, will revolutionize the way video programming is created, developing it faster, cheaper, and more efficiently than ever before. The current disparity between the film-based technology in use in feature films and the like, and the technology used in videotape production is disappearing rapidly.

As desktop video becomes viable for broader and broader applications, the economic effects become more apparent. Current video professionals without the funds to own a conventional studio have been forced to lease time from those that do. Typically, studio time costs between $150 and $500 per hour, although some suites charge upwards of $1000. Desktop video studio time, in contrast, is currently averaging between $80 and $150 an hour.

This delta alone is substantial but ignores the time effects of desktop video. Independent producers have observed a 50-75% decrease in time required to create a program on desktop video equipment as opposed to conventional studio gear. Time in a studio equates directly with a producer's cost, so desktop video productions can be completed with 10 to 30% of the budget of an equivalent program developed on conventional equipment. The flexibility of desktop video systems also allows more experimentation and creativity, since the cost of studio time is low compared with previous means.

Even a short video, such as a 15-second commercial, can easily run up a production bill in excess of $10,000. Producers have been quick to notice that they can recoup their investment in desktop video gear in short order, as well as improving their control over the video editing process.

Future Costs

It is important to realize that desktop video is in its infancy. Functionality that costs $80,000 today will likely cost $30,000 in three years. Functionality that costs $35,000 today will be under $10,000 in 1995. Why?

Reason 1: As a technology, desktop video is very low on the learning curve. As more vendors get involved, competition will force prices down.

Reason 2: The semiconductor industry will continue to push desktop video because it represents a marketing avenue to the estimated 125 million personal computer platforms in the world and the over 86 million in the U.S. Capturing even a small segment of an addon market to this installed base is a significant business.

Reason 3: Existing video production professionals are converting to the newer technology, adding to the demand. There are over 300,000 video professionals in the U.S. alone, and some 20,000 have already obtained elements of desktop video solutions.

Reason 4: desktop video demand has been small to date, because the output quality has been sub-professional. With the advent of products like the Avid Technology Media Suite Pro, and other midrange-quality systems, the objections to output quality have abated. Semiconductor manufacturers will likely pursue this midrange market, since it represents both volume and quality (translation: price) opportunities. Ergo, technological development in this segment will be faster than that at the low or high end, blurring the distinction between prosumer, industrial, and broadcast quality distinctions and elimating the quality objections.

Reason 5: The advance of technological improvement continues unabated in the personal computer market. There has been a dearth of new applications; desktop video is one. The massive personal computer industry has begun to target desktop video with new applications and devices. desktop video is poised for the explosive growth of such prior application areas as desktop publishing.

Reason 6: Desktop video focuses on digital processes, which allow nonlinearity and zero signal degradation through multiple edits. Conventional equipment is overdesigned, allowing for gradual degradation in signal quality from acquisition, to editing, to duplication and distribution. Digital processes allow lower quality signal acquisition and transfer, which translates to lower peripheral costs. Since most desktop video systems are currently used in off-line editing, this distinction is unimportant and unutilized, but as the systems become viable in on-line editing, this will allow acquisition and duplication using S-VHS and Hi-8 videotape equipment, versus the 3/4" U-Matic SP, MII, and BetaCam SP more prevalent today. Today's consumers are paying for higher priced cameras and VTRs that will not be necessary at some point in the future.

Reason 7: Desktop video relies on the processing power of a personal computer. Today's machines are barely capable of the intensive data manipulation and transfer tasks associated with moving video data. The power of personal computers are increasing dramatically at an ever increasing rate, while holding costs relatively stable for a state-of-the-art system. desktop video systems requiring expensive compression, DSP, and other video acceleration hardware will soon be supplanted by simpler, equally powerful systems relying on new personal computer hardware, more on the order of today's desktop workstations. The net effect will be lower pricing and greater reliability for equivalent or greater functionality.

Real World Programming

Desktop video, because of the economies it offers to potential video developers, makes financially viable a whole new range of video programming, both for general and specific markets. In general markets, topics which are not appealing to mass markets, e.g. fly-tying, pool maintenance, or soybean cultivation, can be effectively and profitably presented using desktop video tools to develop appropriate programming. In specific markets, such as business or government, where the target audience is a smaller, focused group, desktop video makes viable video programming as a tool to small and medium-sized groups, as well as to larger organizations who are perhaps already using conventional technologies.

Directed communication, such as video programming, is used to provide one or more functions to the viewers: to inform, to persuade, or to entertain them. Figure 2-___ is an example list of video programming applications achievable on a wide scale through the use of desktop video tools.

Fig. 2-9:	Example Video Programming Applications

Topic	Information	Persuasion	Entertainment
Career Information Education	X		
Consumer Awareness Education	X		
Corporate/Group Presentations	X	X	
Employee Communication	X		
Employee Motivation	X	X	X
Exercise	X		X
Fashion Videos	X	X	X
General Training	X		
Health and Nutrition Education	X	X	
History/Current Events Education	X		
Infomercials	X	X	
Language Education	X		
Legal Documentation	X		
Medical Education (General)	X	X	
Medical Training	X		
Music Videos			X
Nonprofit Fund Raising		X	
Performance/Visual Arts Education	X		
Point of Purchase Presentations	X	X	
Product Demonstrations	X	X	
Promotional Videos	X	X	
Public Relations	X	X	
Public Service Information	X		
Recruiting	X	X	
Science and Math Education	X		
Social Sciences Education	X		
Specific/Technical Training	X		
Sports Highlight Videos			X
Sports Training/Coaching	X		X
Technical Information Report	X		
Travel Videos	X	X	X

Incursions in Conventional Video

Desktop video has already made significant incursions into the conventional video industry as production studios have begun using desktop video systems to supplement or supplant elements of their existing systems. One such application is the use of desktop video systems for video storyboarding or animatics. A producer can rough out a commercial or entire video production using animation, graphics, and editing tools on a desktop video system, saving the massive costs of creating a hand-drawn storyboard and/or workprint in order to demonstrate concepts and try out creative ideas.

Another application of desktop video systems in conventional video production is as a replacement for expensive, dedicated character generation systems used for titling and other graphic lettering. Character generation is the most vital graphic element of video production, used for everything from opening titles, lower-third IDs (such as the names of speakers in the video), and rolling credits at the end of a production. desktop video systems offer the antialiasing and 3D effects of existing systems, plus expanded font availability and the capability of importing and exporting data to and from other applications, such as page layout software, unlike existing systems

Other applications include PC-based VTR control, recursive compositing of graphics, automated video switching, and graphics composition and rendering. As desktop video systems become more powerful, more and more of the functionality within conventional suites will be replaceable or supplementable with the newer technologies.

Editing: A Paradigm Shift

The biggest impact of desktop video systems on conventional processes will be in the realm of video editing Editing is the process of assembling all of the component parts of a video program into a coherent whole. It involves selecting and trimming source material, synchronizing audio from live action, voiceovers, music, and special effects, selecting and implementing scene transitions, mixing and setting audio levels, and a host of other functions.

There are three basic levels of editing. The lowest level involves technical details of how various edits are performed, including techniques for assemble, split, and insert editing. The next highest level involves whether the editing is based on linear media, such as videotape, or nonlinear media such as digital data stored on a computer's hard disk. The highest level involves the purpose of the editing, whether it is to create a finished product (online) or an Edit Decision List (offline) for later use in creating the finished product.

Offline vs. Online

Offline editing is performed because of the cost of utilizing online equipment and personnel. Offline equipment is typically lower-cost, and lower quality, than the online equipment in professional video suites. Offline systems are used to emulate the capabilities of online suites and create an Edit Decision List, or EDL, which is a series of instructions to the online system for duplicating the offline work and producing higher quality output.

There are two immediate problems with this approach to editing. First, the output of a typical offline system is inappropriate for anything other than for feeding an online system. This forces use of a second set of equipment instead of completing the edit process on the original equipment. Some desktop video systems address this situation by offering moderate-quality online output and producing an EDL for those applications in which broadcast-quality output is required.

The second problem is the general inability for EDLs to completely convey the edit information for functions performed on the offline suite to the online suite. As such, there is rarely a 1-to-1 correspondance between the edited output seen on the offline suite and the final product. This reduces the creative control of a small producer (who may do the offline edits) and increases the input of postproduction service bureau personnel, producing occasional conflicts and dissatisfaction.

A perfect solution would be to implement a high-quality, low-cost online system, thereby removing extraneous personnel from the creative process. Such is one of the aims of the desktop video movement, although many of the existing systems are applicable only (at the present time) for offline applications.

Linear vs. Nonlinear

Linear editing employs linear media, i.e. videotape. Nonlinear editing employs random-access storage media such as hard disk drives. As such, nonlinear editing is a digital process, most likely under computer control, and therefore in the domain of desktop video. Linear editing can employ either digital or analog media, but because of the cost of digital VTRs, most linear editing suites employ analog VTRs and videotape.

In either case, VTRs are less than optimal devices for editing purposes. Ideal editing would allow instant access and playback of any selected video or audio segment; since VTRs are linear devices, they require significant time to locate source footage (jog, shuttle times) and prepare to play or record (preroll). Nonlinear editing therefore requires the edit personnel to spend a significant time waiting on the VTR decks to find desired footage and prepare to play it.

Another problem has been that analog systems, which dominate the nonlinear market, suffer degradation throughout the editing process. Tape gradually wears out during the shuttling required for editing, producing dropouts or other forms of video and audio noise. Successive generations of analog media exhibit decreasing quality levels in terms of injected noise.

A third problem is that the revision process in linear editing systems is slow and painful, thereby reducing creative options and increasing time (therefore cost) in the edit studio. To change a simple transition between two scenes on some linear systems require an entire reassembly of the output tape, a process that may take several hours.

Nonlinear systems, in an ideal world, solve all of these problems. First, they employ random-access media, offering near-instantaneous access to any desired source footage, and cutting hours or days off of editing sessions. Second, they utilize digital media which does not suffer the degradations common in the analog world, providing less of a change between the recorded video/audio quality and that which appears in the final program. Third, revisions are quick and simple, allowing more creative freedom at lower cost.

The problem with nonlinear systems has been in the area of price vs. quality. High-quality systems have been available for a number of years, albeit at high cost. Low-priced systems, such as those commonly available through desktop video technology, offen suffer from inability to produce sufficient quality output for professional purposes.

As digital video matures, desktop systems employing this technology will increase their output quality, thereby removing the majority of objections against them and bringing nonlinear editing to the fore as a technique.

Editing Techniques

The lowest level of editing involves the explicit details of how source material is patched together into a composite product. These techniques differ considerably depending on whether the system is linear or nonlinear in nature, and to some extent if the system is offline or online.

Linear processes require the use of time code to provide precise location data for both source and record footage. Tapes must be "striped", either before recording audio and video data, or during the process, in order to lay down time code information uniquely identifying each frame of the data. Pains must be taken during editing in order to preserve this "striping" so that precise edits can occur.

Transitions occur when one video or audio segment or "clip" ends and another begins. The simplest transition is a "cut", or a hard transition from one segment to the next. Another form of transition is a "dissolve", or a more gradual, softer change between segments. An advanced form of a dissolve, called a morph, has become popular in music videos and some feature film entertainment in recent years. More involved transitions, called wipes or DVE moves, are also possible. It is the role of the editor to select appropriate transitions for both the audio and video segments comprising the source material for a program.

Video and audio edits do not need to occur at the same time. It is common for the vocal portion of a segment to continue under alternate video segments. This is called a "split edit". Insert edits are used to add segments of audio and/or video in the middle of a program. Assemble edits are used to append new material to the end of a program. A/B Roll editing is a nonlinear technique allowing a transition between source material from one source VTR to material from a second VTR.

Although they may be implemented differently on conventional video systems, almost all desktop video postproduction systems are capable of performing the editing functions outlined above.

Chapter 3
Forecasts of the Total U.S. Desktop Video Products Market

Market Definitions and Overview

In Chapter 2 of this report, desktop video was defined as "the technology which facilitates the production of video presentations destined for final or intermediate output via videotape using personal computers and other microprocessor-based desktop equipment". This, by its very nature excludes some elements which others might consider parts of the desktop video market, e.g. the delivery mechanisms for video programming, whether that be broadcast transmission, CATV, videotape distribution, CD-ROM, or any other method.

Also, in an effort to limit the scope of the report, the authors focused on "products", i.e. goods, and ignored the considerable value of the services associated with desktop video and the programming content produced by the combination of goods and services. Each of these elements adds significant value to the overall desktop video market and will perhaps be analyzed in later revisions of this report.

Finally, this report is limited in geographical scope, covering only the U.S. market. Significant markets, no doubt, exist in Asia and Europe and elsewhere on the globe; it was beyond the scope of this initial research to cover these areas. Also, due to the relative youth of the desktop video market and the general dominance of small, U.S.-based suppliers, the international markets are probably insignificant in size, today, compared to the U.S. market, although this may not be the case for long.

Market Segmentation

Any market can be segmented in multiple ways. Some markets naturally segment themselves along price lines, along user bases, along technological divisions, or along any number of other possible boundaries. The desktop video market is no exception, and because of its youth and current rate of evolution, it offers a multitude of possible segmentation choices.

Goods vs. Services vs. Programming

One obvious way to segment the desktop video market is to look at the three major elements: goods, services, and programming. This was essentially done in this report, with the focus being placed on the goods, both "hard" and "soft" tangible products, and the services and programming elements ignored.

A products segment would include the various hardware and software elements defined in Chapters 4, 5, and 6 of this document. A services segment would include the labor from desktop video specialists, such as producers, directors, editors, camera personnel, audio personnel, graphic artists, animators, video engineers, computer specialists, acting talent, voiceover talent, scriptwriters, marketing personnel, and on and on. A programming segment would define and discuss the various final outputs of a desktop video development process, including "how-to", training, corporate presentation, sales demonstration, educational, and other videotape applications.

Quality

The desktop video market can also be segmented along the lines of quality and sophistication. At one end of the quality spectrum are the so-called "broadcast" quality products, services, and programming. These are typified by the use of extremely expensive, complex equipment, requiring the use of trained, experienced professionals, and producing programming of the highest audio and video resolution, content, and production values possible. There are uses for desktop video technologies in this environment, although such uses tend to be ancillary in nature.

At the other end of the spectrum is "consumer" quality. Home and other occasional video consumers have acquired zillions of camcorders, VCRs, and recorded special moments, thanks to the explosion in the low-cost, low-quality video technology market in the 80's. Some percentage of these people will consume desktop video products and services in an effort to improve the output of their home videography.

In between are the key users of desktop video systems, in the "prosumer" and "industrial" quality ranges. The goods and services in this quality range are substantially better than the amateur efforts of the consumer market, yet not quite up to the high standards of the broadcast market. For most of the applications of low cost video productions, such as those produced by desktop video technologies, these quality ranges are sufficient. Accordingly, desktop video will see the most penetration in these quality ranges.

Where Consumed

Another way to look at the desktop video market is to look at the consumption of the final output, the programming. Some percentage of desktop video-produced programming will end up in the home. Other programs will end up being consumed in business, both for-profit and nonprofit, environments. Still others will be used in governmental or educational markets.

Where Produced

Along the same lines, one can segment the desktop video market along the lines of the personnel who will utilize it. There are video professionals, including independent videographers, whose occupation is the creation of video programming. There are communications professionals, whose occupation is communicating specific messages, sometimes in a video format. There are desktop communicators, whose occupation is in an area other than communications, but who sometimes have needs for communicating messages via video programming. There are home enthusiasts, who produce video presentations as a hobby, or as a prelude to a career as a videographer. And, of course, there are the home users, non-professionals who merely want to catalog and clean up their home movies.

All of these users are potential consumers of desktop video technology.

Purpose

Another split of the market can occur along the lines of the intended purpose of the final output produced by the desktop video technology. Is it to entertain the consumer? If so, elements such as special effects, dramatic lighting and audio, and complex scenery becomes more important. Is it to educate the consumer? If so, closeup shots, simple sets, and voiceovers become important. Is it to persuade the consumer to buy or take some other action? If so, this requires a combination of the elements of the educational and entertainment programming.

Desktop video is most applicable currently to the latter two applications, although elements can certainly be used in entertainment programming, also.

Sales Channels

Another way to segment the desktop video products market is by the channels used to convey the products from supplier to consumer. Some manufacturers sell their products direct to the end users, via direct sales forces. Others use mail order catalogs. Most desktop video products are moved through dealers, a class of retailer specializing in a particular product area, whether it be video equipment, musical instruments, or computer systems.

Because of the inability of these channels to provide high levels of focused support for technologies such as desktop video, suppliers and consumers often turn to VARs (Value Added Resellers) as a primary channel. VARs often buy their products through distributors, or direct from the suppliers.

As products become more standardized and mainstream, mass merchandisers like major department stores, electronics superstores, and warehouse stores are often used.

Some suppliers manage these channels via direct supervision; others employ agents, called manufacturer's reps to manage their sales efforts. Most who use reps also integrate them with direct supervision channels.

All of these sales channels are appropriate for elements of desktop video.

By Project Phase

Perhaps the most applicable segmentation when dealing with the "products" piece of the overall market is to break the products out according to when they are used in the video program development. There are four phases of video programming development. The first is "preproduction", defined as the phase between the initial concept and the beginning of acquisition of video and audio footage for development of the concept into a finished piece. "Production" is the phase of development in which the live audio and video necessary to complete a project is captured. "Postproduction" begins after the last footage is captured, when the video and audio is edited into a final "master" tape. The final phase of a video development is "distribution", or the duplication and delivery of the finished program to its consumers.

In this report, the desktop video products market is segmented according to project phases. The distribution phase is not covered. So, to recap, this report covers desktop video products, sold to the U.S. market, and segmented according to their use in the preproduction, production, and postproduction phases of video development.

Preproduction

Preproduction is the phase of video development between the genesis of a program concept and the acquisition of video and audio source material to develop that concept. A program concept can be inspired by a number of stimuli: a customer request, an interesting anecdote, an enjoyable book, a business need, or a host of other possible causes. The producer of a video program is responsible for taking this concept and developing a "treatment" of it.

Such treatments typically involve the creation and revisions of a "script", a written guide to the casting, action, audio, scenery, and possibly lighting and camera movement desired in the final production. A "storyboard" is often used as a visual representation of a script in order to develop effects, props, stunts, and to sell the concept to investors. Scripts and storyboards typically undergo many revisions before a final consensus is obtained and a project will move forward.

Some of the remaining preproduction tasks include budgeting and scheduling the production and postproduction processes. Video production typically requires the assembly of sets and the collection of all of the footage associated with each set before moving on to the next set. This requires a producer to break the script into a "shooting script", which defines all of the actions to be undertaken on an individual set before it is "struck", or disassembled, and the next set is constructed. Also, the postproduction process may involve the creation of animations or complex graphics, audio, or video effects, and the talent and tools for these elements must be scheduled. Since all projects require at least some funding, the producer must also define a budget for personnel and equipment, arranging financing, and other monetary matters.

Other preproduction tasks include the hiring of "talent", including actors, actresses, voiceover artists, doubles and stunt personnel (if necessary), and "crew", including camera personnel, lighting directors, grips (assistants), gaffers (electricians), set builders, artists, video engineers, audio engineers, directors, caterers, production assistants, drivers, makeup artists, and a whole range of potential specialists. Also any necessary equipment must be purchased or rented, supplies for set creation and other purposes must be obtained, housing and transportation for cast and crew must be secured (on location shots), leases must be negotiated, etc.

Desktop video preproduction efforts typically require fewer personnel, less equipment, and far less hassle than the ones described above, thanks to the less grandiose programming expected from desktop video producers, but some of these same elements will still apply in desktop video preproduction. Preproduction planning often sets the stage (pardon the pun) for the quality of the overall effort; diligence here can make the difference between a profitable, professional masterpiece and an overbudget mediocrity.

Production

After all of the planning has occurred it is time to gather the source material for a video project. A director arranges for the sets to be assembled, the cast to be prompted, and the crew to begin acquiring live video and audio footage. In conventional video productions, this requires multiple cameras and camera operators, lighting and lighting specialists, microphones, audio recorders, and audio engineers, and a host of other professionally trained personnel. Desktop video technologies allow the reduction in personnel and equipment complexity in this phase of development, as most systems can be operated with very little crew, and most productions can be done with simple sets and small casts. Often, a single individual will act as producer, director, audio engineer, camera operator, video engineer, lighting specialist, electrician, and set builder in small, simple productions.

Multiple repeats of each scene are often taken in the production phase until the director is sure that at least one meets the requirements of the script. The shooting script is followed until all of the scenes required have been "shot", and the video and audio footage is "in the can", meaning recorded and stored away. When all of the shooting is complete, and all of the video and audio footage is gathered, the cast and crew are dismissed and the project moves to the postproduction phase.

Postproduction

Postproduction is the most capital-intensive phase of video development, as it requires the most complex equipment and most specialized personnel. In this phase, the captured video and audio footage is combined with still graphics, titling, music, special effects, and transitions to create a "master" tape.

The video and audio footage must often be "sweetened" or "corrected" in order to match colors and lighting, to change tonal qualities, to add reverb or echo, or to change volume. The spoken audio must be combined with recorded music or special sonic effects, like gunshots or footsteps, in most productions. These elements must be "mixed" in the proper proportions.

Sections of live video and audio footage are often intercut with "stock" footage, such as pieces of old television shows or commercials, old movies, news clips, graphic art, or recorded speeches. Graphic art elements, animations, and titling effects add professionalism and spice to live programs, especially those involving complex subject material. DVE moves and other transitions make interesting scene changes and add variety over simple "cuts", or abrupt changes between scenes. Transitions also allow for gradual blending of audio and video material between scenes. Music is often created specially for a given production; a "score" is created by a composer, who works with musicians to implement it, following the instructions of a director and the output of the video editing process. In desktop video applications, existing recorded music is often tailored to the program by an audio editor.

Postproduction efforts are the domain of video and audio editors, who work under the direction of the producer and director to produce the final output as defined in the original concept and as modified by the producer and director as the project developed. Good editing can save a bad concept; bad editing can destroy a good concept.

Desktop video techologies allow the combination of the director, producer, video editor, audio editor, animator, and graphic artist into a single person, assuming that that individual has the requisite skills.

Organization of the Report

The primary sections of this report are Chapter 2 through Chapter 6. Chapter 2 is an overview of the desktop video market and technologies. Chapter 3, which you are now reading, is an analysis of the overall U.S. desktop video products market, excluding any products used exclusively during the distribution phase, as noted in the explanation above.

Chapters 4 through 6 are indepth analyses of each phase of the video development process, focusing on the desktop video products available to accomplish the tasks of the phase. Chapter 4 covers the preproduction phase, Chapter 5 the production phase, and Chapter 6 the postproduction phase.

Revenues and Revenue Growth Rates

The desktop video products market is a very new phenomenon, essentially beginning with the advent of personal computer-based control mechanisms and graphics software used in conjunction with conventional video equipment in the latter 80's. The advent of the Video Toaster, 24-bit graphics adapters, and full-motion digital video products has led to the explosion of desktop video products in the early 90's. As personal computers become more powerful, and as digital video and audio technologies mature, the desktop video market is poised to grow dramatically throughout the 90's.

In 1989, about 21 thousand desktop video units, including both discrete elements and bundles of products from all phases of video development, were shipped, accounting for over $87 million in revenues. By 1992, this figure had risen to 475,000 units and $1.17 billion in revenues. Revenue growth for the three intervening years was over 100%, peaking in 1991 at 210.2 percent. Much of the early growth was based on the emergence of NewTek's innovative Video Toaster product and the platforms, peripherals, accessories, and software necessary to support it. By 1992, a number of Macintosh- and PC-compatible-based desktop video systems had emerged, bringing video development capabilities to most of the rest of the personal computer user base.

By 1995, the desktop video market is expected to grow to $4.8 billion, based on sales of over 7.2 million units. By 1999, total revenues are anticipated to reach almost $20.4 billion, on shipments of almost 18.4 million units.

Fig. 3-1:	Total U.S. Desktop Video Products Market Unit Shipments and Revenue Forecasts, 1989-1999		
Year	Units (000)	Revenues ($M)	Revenue Growth (%)
1989	21	87.2	-
1990	62	177.9	104.1

1991	210	551.8	210.2
1992	475	1,171.7	112.3
1993	829	1,963.0	67.5
1994	1,460	3,174.3	61.7
1995	2,551	4,798.3	51.2
1996	4,354	7,064.2	47.2
1997	7,253	10,229.6	44.8
1998	11,761	14,616.7	42.9
1999	18,368	20,379.8	39.4
CAGR			*50.4%*

Unit Shipments and Pricing Trends

Unit shipment growth began the decade at extremely high levels, nearing or exceeding 200% for the first two years surveyed. By 1992, following the initial penetration of new products in the market, the growth rate had declined to a more sedate 74.4 percent.

Unit growth rates are anticipated to hold steady through 1995 in the mid-70 range, and then begin a gradual decline for the rest of the decade, reaching 56.2 percent for 1999. Unit shipment CAGR for the period survey is forecasted at 68.6 percent. The high sustained growth rates are anticipated for several reasons. First, video programming is a new application area for personal computers, of which there are over 125 million in the world. Suppliers are hyping the technology since there are few other innovative applications for personal computers helping them move hardware and software. Second, world economies have forced businesses and governments to seek more economical ways of communicating; video is among the most cost-effective techniques for delivering information, education, or entertainment. Third, video development has the allure of Hollywood; everyone wants to be in the movies.

The dramatic unit growth is not always reflected, at least to the same extent, in revenue growth, due to pricing pressures. In the early years of this survey, a number of evolutionary changes occurred in the product categories associated with desktop video. Powerful graphics-based operating systems became more prevalent for a new generation of powerful personal computer platforms. New graphics software tools became available. U-Matic SP VTRs were replaced by Betacam, S-VHS, and Hi-8 units. These product lines offered equivalent or superior functionality at equivalent or lower pricing than the previous generation of products, so desktop video adopters quickly shifted to the newer technologies. The net effect was a substantial reduction in the cost of products associated with desktop video.

In the next several years, 1991 through 1993, the continued evolution in these product areas, and the attendant pricing effects, was somewhat mitigated by the advent of powerful, but expensive, desktop video postproduction systems. Pricing continued to erode, but at a substantially slower rate, with the delta between unit shipment growth and revenue growth pegged at about 7 percent for 1993.

Price erosion for the period between 1993 and 1997 is anticipated to rise again, to a peak of 13.7 percent in 1995, as the new desktop video technologies begin to mature and competitive pressures force pricing battles among similar product lines. By the 1998 timeframe, the market is anticipated to settle out somewhat, and pricing is expected to continue to decline, although less steeply than in the previous period. Pricing is expected to drop 10.7 percent from 1998 to 1999 and it is reasonable to expect continued moderation after 2000 in a mature market. For the survey period, pricing is anticipated to drop at a CAGR of -10.8 percent, reflecting the difference between the CAGR of unit shipments (68.6 percent) versus revenues (50.4 percent).

Market and Technology Trends

Trends by Market Segment

In 1989, the beginning of the survey period, the desktop video products market, as defined by unit shipments was split with approximately 50 percent of the revenues associated with postproduction products, and the remaining 50 percent split essentially equally between preproduction and production products. The low price of preproduction products, thanks to a preponderance of software items, allowed it only 2.6 percent of the 1989 revenues, however. Production products included an array of relatively low-priced hardware items, which also contributed to its low share of the 1989 revenues (13.6 percent) relative to its share of units shipped. Postproduction products, on the other hand, included expensive VTRs, animation software, personal computer hardware, and other items, which contributed to its 83.8 percent share of the 1989 revenues for desktop video products.

As the market emerged, several trends became apparent. First, the preproduction products garnered higher percentages of the revenues while making lower percentages of the overall unit shipments. This is because of the evolution of special purpose concept development tools, which commanded higher prices than the previous general purpose tools, and the emergence of digital video hardware and software, leading to a net pricing increase in this segment of the market.

Second, the unit shipment and revenue percentages garnered by the production segment remained fairly constant, plus or minus a few percentage points, indicating segment growth rates approximately the same as the overall market growth patterns.

Third, unit shipment percentages for postproduction products rose slightly, while revenues dropped slightly, indicating higher than average unit sales and strong pricing pressures in this segment. This is due to the advent of digital video Integrated Systems and Components, allowing use of lower-cost VTRs and other Recording and Playback Systems in this segment. The emerging technologies spurred purchases of Graphics Software Products units, additional Personal Computer Platforms, and the other ancillary products in the postproduction products market. At the same time, the prices of these items were being reduced by both evolutionary (normal competitive pressures) and revolutionary (replacement of technology) processes.

In 1992, preproduction products garnered 14.1 percent of the shipments and 4.3 percent of the revenues in the desktop video market. Production products accounted for 25.4 percent, and 15.7 percent, respectively, and production products took 60.5 and 80.1 percent, respectively.

By 1995, preproduction products are expected to obtain 17.0 percent of the market shipments and 13.3 percent of the revenues, indicating the continuance of the upward pricing trend as well as increased availability of desktop video preproduction tools where none were available before. The applicability of low-end digital video products to video postproduction in this period also contributes to this growth. Production products are anticipated to garner 30.6 percent of the unit shipments, indicating growing use of these items, including lighting and teleprompting systems, in desktop video environments. 1995 revenues from production products are expected to gather approximately 14.8 percent of the market, indicating pricing pressures, particularly in teleprompters, in this market segment. Postproduction products are expected to account for 52.4 of the 1995 shipments and 71.9 percent of the revenues. The declines in both categories are attributed to the anticipated growing use of desktop video in the other segments, rather than any problem in postproduction.

Fig. 3-2:	Total U.S. Desktop Video Products Market Percent Projections by Shipments & Market Segment			
Year	Preproduction Products	Production Products	Postproduction Products	TOTAL
1989	22.5%	25.4%	52.1%	100.0%
1990	22.4%	18.9%	58.7%	100.0%
1991	15.0%	22.7%	62.3%	100.0%
1992	14.1%	25.4%	60.5%	100.0%
1993	16.0%	25.2%	58.8%	100.0%
1994	17.1%	27.0%	55.9%	100.0%
1995	17.0%	30.6%	52.4%	100.0%
1996	16.8%	32.5%	50.7%	100.0%
1997	16.6%	33.7%	49.7%	100.0%
1998	16.7%	34.5%	48.8%	100.0%
1999	17.1%	35.2%	47.7%	100.0%

By 1999, preproduction products are expected to hold 17.1 percent of the overall product shipments and a 25.4 percent shares of the overall revenues. The stabilization in growth of the unit shipment share indicates a period of product maturity and the increasing revenue percentage indicates pricing stability, versus the overall trend of downward pricing. Production products are expected to hold 35.2 and 16.0 percent shares, respectively. The growth in unit shipments is anticipated to be caused by desktop video's intrusion into more complex studio environments, requiring more cameras, lighting, and microphones, but the revenue share indicates continued strong pricing pressures for the products in this segment. Postproduction products are expected to garner 47.7 and 58.6 percent, respectively, as VTRs are effectively obsoleted, graphics software becomes more affordable, groupware becomes more common, pricing pressures remain strong, and the other segments continue to grow relative to postproduction products.

Fig. 3-3:	Total U.S. Desktop Video Products Market Percent Projections by Revenues & Market Segment			
Year	Preproduction Products	Production Products	Postproduction Products	TOTAL
1989	2.6%	13.6%	83.8%	100.0%
1990	3.5%	12.9%	83.5%	100.0%
1991	2.4%	15.2%	82.4%	100.0%
1992	4.3%	15.7%	80.1%	100.0%
1993	7.4%	14.0%	78.6%	100.0%
1994	10.6%	13.9%	75.5%	100.0%
1995	13.3%	14.8%	71.9%	100.0%
1996	15.9%	15.6%	68.5%	100.0%
1997	18.4%	16.1%	65.6%	100.0%
1998	21.5%	16.2%	62.4%	100.0%
1999	25.4%	16.0%	58.6%	100.0%

Trends by Product Type

This report covers the period between 1989 and 1999, with actual shipment and revenue numbers available for 1989 to 1992, and forecasts made for 1993 through 1999. In Chapters 4, 5, and 6, the overall U.S. desktop video products market is divided into 13 discrete subsegments, 3 applicable to the preproduction phase, 4 for the production phase, and 6 in the postproduction phase.

The overall market separates roughly into three different periods: the emergence of the market, the transition period, and the beginning of maturity. The market emerged in the period between 1989 and 1991 and began to settle down in 1992. 1992 saw, and 1993 through 1996 will see, continued rapid growth in the market caused by users adopting the new technologies to supplant existing ones. After 1997, the market is anticipated to begin maturing, with more price competition and supplier consolidation.

Growth rates and pricing trends within the individual 13 subsegments of the desktop video market differ from the overall trends. In the market emergence period, products in some categories were created where none existed, such as in postproduction's Integrated Systems and Components subsegment or preproduction's Concept Development Tools - High Range. Growth in these categories tended to exceed the average values, where growth rates in other, more conventional categories tended to fall below the growth of the overall market. Examples include Video Acquisition Products in the production phase, and Machine Control Products and Recording and Playback Systems in the postproduction phase, where new technologies obsoleted or brought new economies to existing conventional technologies.

In the transition period, desktop video begins to enter the mainstream of video development instead of being only a fringe element. New users adopt the technology and existing video developers convert, at least partially, in order to take advantage of the economic advantages of the new products. Some subsegments are expected to perform exceedingly well during this period, including the Concept Development Tools - High Range subsegment, which contains much of the digital video hardware and software expected to lead the desktop video revolution during this timeframe. Other subsegments, such as Lighting Products (production) and Audio Systems (postproduction), are expected to grow at moderate rates as users gradually become more cognizant of the need for quality peripheral elements in order to create quality video presentations. Still others, like Machine Control Products (postproduction) or Concept Development Tools - Low Range (preproduction), are expected to decline precipitously in terms of relative segment shipments, as their functionality is incorporated into other, more powerful products.

As the market begins to mature in the late 90's, some segments will begin to dominate the others in terms of growth rates and therefore relative market shares. One example is Graphics Software Products (postproduction), whose importance will grow stronger throughout the decade as video development moves from an all-analog process to a predominantly digital one. Graphics Software is necessary for manipulation of this digital video data, so as the market evolves, the importance of this subsegment will grow. Also, as the market matures and desktop video both becomes more endemic in all video development environments and engenders new cost consciousness, previously insignificant segments such as Teleprompters (production) and Project Management Tools (preproduction) will obtain more importance.

Distribution Trends

In almost any newly emerging market, one can find two initial trends. First, as the technologies are developed and products emerge, there are no established distribution channels tailored to the new product lines. Suppliers adapt existing channels to the new products. Second, the knowledge necessary to utilize the new product technologies are not existent, in total anyway, in either the potential consumers or the distribution channels. Much confusion exists until the suppliers figure out a way to transfer knowledge and usage skills down the distribution channels and eventually to the consumes.

Both trends are currently evident in the desktop video market. The established channels for moving the component elements of desktop video are not really appropriate for the evolving market. There are at least three major distribution channels of these component elements currently, and none has much expertise in the product areas outside of those it is specifically chartered to sell. For example, professional video dealers tend to know a great deal about conventional video technologies, some of which are used in desktop video applications, but very little about computer equipment. Computer dealers tend to know less about video products, and so on.

Broad knowledge and skill sets are important to channel elements in desktop video, since the potential users of this new technology are typically even less skilled than the resellers. The channels for desktop video products will have to convey expertise in computers, audio, and video, provide integration services, and train potential users, in order for the market to truly grow and mature. New channel participants are beginning to emerge who combine these skill sets, and as these resellers evolve, more and more of the product volume will begin to move through them.

End User Trends

New, low-cost technology replacing older, more expensive products inevitably spur at least three new trends among the adopters of this technology. First, the lower cost allows growth in potential users from the ranks of those who could not afford the older technology. Second, the products arising from the new technology engender new applications, including some perhaps unforeseen by the suppliers. Third, the new technology both allows productivity gains as well as time and money for experimentation, since the new products typically improve the time and cost required to accomplish necessary tasks.

Again, all of these trends hold for the desktop video market. New video developers are emerging every day, thanks to the affordability of desktop video products. Not all are computer-literate, and most are video- and audio-illiterate. Giving a user a tool is not the same as giving him or her the skill to use it. For example, an amateur can operate a hammer and a saw, but does not necessarily have the skills to build a house. Many of these new users will have to be trained in computer operation. Others will have to learn the complexities of video creation, including camera placement and operation, scriptwriting, graphics for video, lighting, and editing. More will have to learn audio skills.

Video programming has been a relatively expensive media for communication, at least until the emergence of desktop video. Because of the economies of desktop video, video programming can now be used for applications for which video has never been used before. An example is the use of video presentations to replace 35mm slide presentations. Video offers movement, sound effects, and eye-catching visual effects not available in static slide presentations. If one has 5 minutes to impress an audience, which will work better?

Lastly, the productivity improvements engendered by desktop video do more than merely reduce the cost and time it takes to create professional-quality video presentations. They also allow room for experimentation, much in the way spreadsheets allowed the creation of "what if?" analyses among personal computer users. Video developers can now try out story concepts, inexpensively and quickly, before deciding on a final approach to a particular message. Businesses can create rough drafts of a desired presentation before sending it off to a professional video producer for actual development. Advertising agencies can create "animatics", or animated storyboards, instead of the conventional hand-drawn representations used to obtain client approval for commercial advertising development.

Another productivity gain is in the reduction of the numbers of people required to create a video presentation, above and beyond the cost benefits of this reduction. When a number of people are involved in a project, communication and coordination become primary concerns of a project manager, instead of the desired output. The same is true in video development. A conventional video producer often has to worry more about coordinating the efforts of a team of personnel rather than concentrating on the product he or she is trying to develop. Creativity suffers from this, as well as from the inevitable moderating effects of decisions-by-committee. Desktop video gives a single individual most of the tools necessary to create video presentations, thereby improving the level of control that individual has over the project, freeing him or her from a great deal of coordination, and allowing more creative exploration in the project.

Qualitative Trends

Desktop video is bringing computers to an area which as been isolated from them in the past. The incumbent users of conventional video technology are not typically computer-literate, and hence often fear the intrusion of this new technology. This trend will only continue because the economics of the intrusion are obvious, so the incumbent video professionals will have to adapt and learn new skills or be replaced by new entrants into their domains. At the same time, desktop video systems bring the tools for video development to vast new range of potential users, the owners and users of personal computers. Some of these will acquire enough video skills to go along with the tools and will begin to compete with the incumbent professionals with small, inexpensive desktop video suites costing less than a tenth of conventional suites.

Desktop video systems also replace numerous, expensive, specialized pieces of equipment with few, inexpensive, generalized pieces. This reduces the size and complexity, as well as the cost, of a video production facility, and eases the financial burden of hardware obsolescence. Desktop video systems will continue to decrease in size, cost, and complexity as the market matures.

The all-analog world of conventional video is slowly, but surely, going digital. Part of this is due to the desktop video revolution. Digital technologies allow less noise, better fidelity, better editing and control capability, and a host of other features, leading to less complex and expensive video suites. In the same way that the digital technologies of CD players revolutionized recorded music, digital video technologies will revolutionize the way video presentations are created and viewed.

The addition of computers into the video has also made possible a number of concepts previously unavailable in the video development environment. The first is the possibility of cross-phase integration, where elements developed for one phase are used on others. For example, there is no reason why a script cannot be reused as material to feed a teleprompter during production, assuming proper formatting. The use of the computer allows storage and manipulation of this and other material in ways that improve the labor productivity throughout the entire video development process.

Second, the continuing development of artificial intelligence may allow desktop video systems to eliminate some of the tedium from video development. Systems may become smart enough to suggest plot developments, lighting changes, production schedules, and edit transitions which reduce the cost of the overall presentation while maximizing production efficiency.

Third, despite the advent of desktop video, some video developments will remain group projects. There may be several scriptwriters, multiple unit directors, dozens of graphic artists and animators, and hundreds of crew personnel in some environments. Some of these people will need to share ideas and information. Computerized desktop video systems will allow the use of networking and groupware to facilitate this exchange.

Competitive Analysis

Competitors in the desktop video market range the gamut between 1-man moonlighting organizations to multibillion dollar international corporations. Of the approximately 500 market participants listed in Figure 3-4, almost 90 percent compete in only one segment of the market. The remainder consists of 55 companies who compete in two segments and a single competitor who competes in all three.

The dual-category competitors tend to fall in 5 general classes. Slightly over a dozen competitors provide software for both the preproduction and postproduction market segments. Slightly over a dozen provide both audio acquisition products like microphones and mixers, as well as postproduction components such as speakers, headphones, or synthesizer devices. Another dozen or so make both low-end and high-end digital video hardware. About half a dozen are major Japanese electronics corporation, including the three corporations who practically own the camera and VTR markets, both at consumer and higher levels. Another half dozen or so are miscellaneous competitors like Hewlett-Packard, who makes both personal computer products and instrumentation used in calibrating video signals. The remaining two are IBM and Commodore, who make both personal computer platforms and multimedia components used in preproduction.

The sole competitor in all three categories is Comprehensive Video Supply. Comprehensive is actually a marketing organization who acts as a distributor and dealer for products made by its subsidiary, CV Technologies, and other suppliers, including many of the ones listed here. Comprehensive OEM's many products made by other suppliers and sells them under its brand name.

Fig. 3-4:   U.S. Desktop Video Market Participants

Company	Preproduction	Production	Postproduction
A+ Development			X
Abaton			X
Abbate Video			X
Abvent			X
Acoustic Research			X
Acoustical Solutions		X	
Activa International			X
ADA		X	X
Adaptec			X
ADDA			X
Adobe	X		X
Advanced Digital Imaging (ADI)			X
Advanced Digital Systems			X
Aegis			X
AIM Graphics			X
AimTech	X		
AirCraft			X
Aitech International Corp.			X
AKG Acoustics		X	X
Al Giddings Images Unlimited			X
Aldus	X		X
Aldus/Silicon Beach	X		X
Alesis		X	
Alias			X
ALR			X
Altec Lansing			X
American Lighting		X	
Antex			X
Anton Bauer		X	
Aphex Systems		X	
Apple			X
Archive			X
Archive Films			X
Aris Entertainment			X
ARRI		X	
ART		X	

ARTI				X	
ASDG				X	
Associated Production Music				X	
AST				X	
Asymetrix	X				
AT&T GSL				X	
ATI Technologies	X			X	
Atlas/Soundolier			X		
Audio Logic			X		
Audio Technica			X	X	
Aurora				X	
Austin Computer Systems				X	
Autodesk				X	
Avid				X	
AVR Technology				X	
AXA Corp.				X	
Aydin Controls				X	
Azden			X		
Bag End				X	
Barco				X	
BCD Associates				X	
BDL AutoScript			X		
Bencher			X		
Best Shot				X	
Beyer Dynamic			X	X	
Big Noise Software				X	
Black Belt Systems				X	
Bogen Photo Corporation			X		
Borland	X				
Boss			X		
Brilliant Media		X			
Broadcast Television Systems					X
Broderbund				X	
Brown-Wagh				X	
Byte By Byte				X	
CalComp				X	
Camera Support Intl.			X		
Canon				X	
Canon			X		
Cardinal Technologies					X
Carvin			X		
Cayman Graphics				X	
CBS News Archives				X	
CEI				X	
Centaur Development				X	

Chase Technologies					X	
Chyron					X	
Cine 60, Inc.			X			
Cinema Products			X			
Cinenet					X	
Claris	X					
Classic Images						X
CMS					X	
Coda					X	
Collaborator Systems	X					
Colortran			X			
Commodore International	X				X	
Communications Specialties					X	
Community					X	
Compaq					X	
Compix Media						X
Comprehensive Video Supply		X		X		X
CompuAdd Computer					X	
Compunic Electronics					X	
Computer Associates	X					
Computer Friends	X				X	
Computer Modules					X	
Computer Prompting Corp			X			
Computer Specialties					X	
Conquest Sound			X			
Corel Systems, Inc.					X	
CoSA	X				X	
Costem					X	
Countryman Associates			X			
Covox					X	
Creative Labs	X					
Crown International			X		X	
Crystal Graphics					X	
Cubicomp					X	
DacEasy	X					
Data Translation					X	
dbx			X			
Dedotec USA, Inc.			X			
Dell Computer					X	
DeSisti Lighting			X			
DeWolfe					X	
Diamond Computer					X	
Diaquest					X	
Digidesign					X	
Digital Arts					X	

	Col A	Col B	Col C	Col D
Digital Audio Labs			X	
Digital Creations			X	
Digital F/X			X	
Digital Micronics			X	
Digital Processing Systems		X	X	
Digital Vision			X	
Digitech		X		
Digivox			X	
Disney Software			X	
Display Research Lab			X	
Display Tech			X	
DiVA	X			
DNF Industries			X	
DOD		X		
Dolby Labs		X		
Dr. T's Music Software			X	
Drawmer		X		
Dreamlight Images			X	
Dubner				X
Dynaware			X	
E-Machines			X	
E-Mu Systems			X	
Eastman Kodak			X	
Echolab			X	
Eclipse Technologies			X	
Educorp			X	
Electric Image			X	
Electro-Voice		X	X	
Electronic Arts			X	
Electronic Script Prompting		X		
EMC			X	
Emulex			X	
Energy Productions			X	
Ensemble Designs			X	
Envisio				X
Epson			X	
Equilibrium Technologies			X	
Everex Systems			X	
Exabyte			X	
Fabulous Footage			X	
Fast Electronic			X	
Fast Forward Video		X		
Film Bank			X	
FirstCom Broadcast Service			X	
Fish Films			X	

	Col 1	Col 2	Col 3
Focus Graphics			X
Folsom Research			X
FOR.A		X	
Fostex		X	
Fractal Design			X
Fresh			X
Frezzolini Electronics		X	
Fujitsu			X
Furman		X	
Future Video			X
Gene Michael Productions			X
General Electric Lighting		X	
Generation Systems			X
Genoa Systems Corp.			X
Gitma		X	
Gold Disk Software	X		X
Graphisoft			X
Grass Valley Group			X
Great Valley Products			X
Greatsounds			X
GTE/Sylvania		X	
Hal Leonard Publishing			X
Halland Broadcast Services			X
Heifner Communications			X
Hewlett Packard		X	X
High Res Technologies			X
Hitachi		X	X
Homrich Communications			X
Horita		X	X
Hot Shots & Cool Cuts			X
Hotronic			X
Houston Insts./Summagraphics			X
Howtek			X
HSC Software	X		X
HyperPro	X		
I-Den Videotronics Corp		X	X
IBM	X		X
Idek			X
IEV International			X
Ikegami		X	X
ILC Technology		X	
Image Bank			X
Image Logic			X
Image North Technologies	X		X
ImageWare			X

Company			
Imageways			X
Imagine Multimedia	X		
Imaging Technology, Inc.			X
Immix			X
Impulse	X		X
In-Motion			X
InnoVision			X
Instant Replay	X		
Intel	X		
Intelligent Environments	X		
Intelligent Resources			X
Intelliprompt		X	
Interactive Image	X		
Interactive Media Technologies			X
Interactive Solutions	X		
International Video Network			X
Intuit	X		
Invisible Touch			X
ITE		X	
J.L.Cooper			X
JBL			X
John Morley	X		
Jovian Logic	X		X
JVC		X	X
Kalieda	X		
KDI			X
Kesser			X
Key Tronic Corp.			X
Klark-Teknik		X	
Klipsch			X
Korg			X
Koss			X
Kurzweil			X
Lake Compuframes	X		
Lapis Technologies			X
Lazerus			X
Leader		X	
Leitch		X	
Lenel Systems	X		
Lexicon		X	
Light Source Computer Images			X
Linker Systems	X		X
Listec Video		X	
Logitech			X
Lotus Development	X		X

Company				
Lowel Light		X		
LTM Corporation		X		
Lyon Lamb			X	
MacGillivray Freeman				X
Mackie Designs		X		
Macproducts			X	
Macromedia	X		X	
Magic Teleprompting		X		
Magni		X	X	
Mark of the Unicorn			X	
Mass Microsystems	X		X	
Masterclips			X	
Mathematica	X			
Matrox			X	
Matthews Studio Equipment		X		
Maxoptics			X	
Maxtor			X	
McQ Productions			X	
McRoberts Software			X	
Media Pedia			X	
Media Vision	X		X	
Merkel Films			X	
Micro Frontier			X	
Micro Technology Unlimited			X	
MicroGrafx			X	
Micropolis			X	
Microsoft	X		X	
Microtime		X		
MidiSoft			X	
Military Channel			X	
Miller		X		
Mirror Technology			X	
Mitsubishi		X	X	
Mole-Richardson Company		X		
Motion Works			X	
Mouse Systems			X	
Mus-art			X	
Musco Moble Lighting, Ltd.		X		
Musicator			X	
Nady Systems		X		
Nanao			X	
NEC			X	
Neil Research Laboratories	X			
Network Music			X	
New Media Graphics			X	

Company	Col 1	Col 2	Col 3
New Video	X		
NewTek			X
Nikon			X
Nissei Sangyo America			X
Northern Media			X
Northgate Computer Systems			X
Nova Systems		X	
NRG		X	
Nucleus Electronics			X
Nutmeg Systems			X
O'Conner		X	
Octree Software			X
Olduvai Corp			X
Omnicomp			X
Omnimusic			X
Opcode Systems			X
Optibase			X
Orban		X	
Orchid Technology			X
Owl	X		
Oxxi			X
Pacific Gold Coast	X		
Pacioli	X		
Paltex			X
Panasonic		X	X
Parker Adams Group			X
Passport			X
Paul Mace	X		
Peavey		X	X
PEP			X
PG Music			X
Philips			X
Phoenix			X
Photron			X
Pinnacle Micro			X
Pioneer		X	X
Pipeline Digital			X
Pixar			X
Pixel Resources			X
PM Ware	X		
Presentation Graphics Group			X
Presentation Technologies			X
Prime Image		X	
Profusion Group			X
Promusic			X

Company	Col 1	Col 2
Prosonus		X
QSI Systems	X	
QTV	X	
Quantum		X
Quark		X
Questel		X
QuickSet	X	
Quik-Lok	X	
Radius	X	X
Rainbow Software		X
Ramsa	X	X
Rane	X	
Rapid Technology		X
Raster Graphics		X
RasterOps	X	X
Raxxess	X	
Ray Dream		X
Redlake Corp		X
Reliable Communications		X
Relisys		X
Reply Corp.		X
RGB Computer & Video		X
RGB Dynamics		X
RGB Spectrum	X	X
Ricoh		X
Roctec		X
Roland	X	X
Ron Sawade Cinematography		X
Rosco	X	
Ross Systems	X	X
RTG Music		X
Sachtler	X	
Sampo		X
Samson Technologies	X	
Samsung		X
Samtron		X
San Francisco Canyon Co.		X
Sanyo	X	X
Screenplay Systems	X	
Seagate		X
Seiko Instruments		X
Selectra		X
Sennheiser	X	X
SFV International		X
Sharp		X

Shure		X		
Sigma Designs					X
Sigma Electronics		X		
Signature				X	
Silicon Graphics				X	
Smith Audio Visual				X	
Software Publishing Corp.	X			X	
Sonic Solutions				X	
Sony		X		X	
Sound Ideas				X	
Sound Source Unlimited				X	
Soundcraft		X			
Soundtech		X			
Spectral Innovations				X	
Specular International				X	
Steinberg/Jones				X	
Storage Solutions				X	
Strand Lighting		X			
Strata				X	
Sundance				X	
SuperMac Technology	X			X	
Symantec	X				
Symetrix		X			
Syndesis				X	
SyQuest				X	
Tandy Corporation				X	
Tannoy				X	
Tascam		X		X	
Taxan				X	
Teatronics		X			
TEC				X	
Technical Aesthetics Operations				X	
Technical Necessities		X			
Tekskil			X		
Tektronix		X		X	
Telescript		X			
Television Program Enterprises				X	
Texas Instruments				X	
Texture City				X	
Theatre Vision International		X			
Time Arts				X	
TOA				X	
Toshiba		X			
TouchVision Systems				X	
Travelview				X	

	1	2	3	4	5
Trompeter				X	
Truby's Writer's Studio	X				
Truevision	X			X	
Trycho Music				X	
Turbo Music				X	
Turtle Beach Software				X	
Twelve Tone Systems				X	
Ultimate		X			
United Pixels and Lines				X	
Universal		X			
Universal City Studios					X
Urei		X			
Ushio America			X		
VAC		X			
Valentino				X	
Vantage Lighting		X			
Vega		X		X	
Vestax				X	
VICON		X			
Video Tape Library				X	
VideoLake	X				
VideoLinx				X	
VideoLogic	X			X	
Videomail	X			X	
Videomedia				X	
Videotek		X			
Videssence		X			
VIDI				X	
ViewSonic				X	
Vinten		X			
Virtus				X	
Vision Imaging	X				
Vision Software				X	
Visionetics				X	
Vividus				X	
Voyager Co.				X	
Voyetra				X	
Wacom Technology				X	
WangDAT				X	
Wangtek				X	
Waveframe				X	
Wavefront Technologies				X	
Western Digital				X	
Will Vinton				X	
Willow Peripherals				X	

Wolfetone			X
WordPerfect	X		
Workstation Technologies	X		
Worldwide Television News			X
WPA Film Library			X
Wyse/Amdek			X
Xaos			X
Yamaha		X	X
Zenith Data Systems			X
Zoom		X	
ZSoft			X

All of the competitors listed in Figure 3-4 are also broken out by specific product categories supplied, and sometimes by product names, in Chapters 4, 5, and 6. Most of them are also listed in Chapter 9, along with addresses and phone numbers.

Chapter 4
Forecasts of the U.S. Desktop Video Preproduction Products Market

Total U.S. Preproduction Products Market

Market Definitions and Overview

Video preproduction is the process of defining the concept (content and purpose) and planning of the final video production. It includes such elements as developing a script outline and preparing a script for the program, developing a storyboard for the program, and determining the budget and schedule for the entire project.

The preproduction segment constitutes approximately 14.1 percent of the $1.17 billion desktop video products market as of 1992 and will grow to approximately 17 percent of the overall market in 1999, accounting for $5.17 billion in revenue. Revenues in this segment come from sales of software and hardware products which improve the productivity of the historically manual processes of preparing to create a video production. Units are defined as individual copies of software programs, or individual hardware/software bundles consisting of one software product mated with a compatible hardware (typically a personal computer circuit board) device, which are purchased or used primarily for preproduction tasks.

Before investigating the product families in detail, it is useful to define some key concepts in video preproduction:

The Script

A script is a written guide to the production. It defines the verbal and physical actions of the actors and actresses, or "talent", in the program. It may even define specific characteristics for each of the cast talent, such as:

"Bill is a middle-aged, balding, slightly overweight, Caucasian man. He's opinionated, grumpy, brusque. He's wearing gray cuffed trousers with a thin belt, a white shirt (a little frayed around the collar), black socks, and black wingtip shoes."

The script also includes instructions for voiceovers, or those verbal passages which will not emanate from the on-screen talent, but from an unseen speaker. Voiceovers are used to explain still or live video footage or graphics, to introduce scenes, and for a number of other purposes.

The script includes definitions of the video stills, footage, graphic art elements, and titles which accompany the voiceovers or the live action. A director's script may even contain information about camera angles, lighting, closeups and wide shots, and other technical information for the camera operators. The script contains information about visual and special effects and background music.

A script, like most written documents, should start with an outline. It should end up as a sheaf of multicolumn pages, with each column directing an element of the production in chronological order. These written script representations have historically been manually generated. Desktop video tools are now emerging which automate this process, thereby improving the productivity of scriptwriters and others who rely on the script to generate video productions.

The Storyboard

A storyboard is a visual representation of the major elements of a script. It consists of a series of graphic panels which represent major events in the script, allowing the viewer to interpolate the intervening actions. In this manner, it resembles a comic book both in presentation and in content. A storyboard is typically used by the project producer and/or scriptwriters to "sell" the concept of the script. It is more effective than a script for this purpose, because most people think visually and cannot visualize what a completed production will look like from the script only. An analogy of this is the architect's model vs. a set of blueprints. The storyboard is the equivalent of a model, whereas the script is more like a blueprint.

Storyboarding, like scriptwriting, has been a manual process requiring the talent of a graphic artist who would laboriously draw the individual storyboard panels. The advent of graphics software on the various personal computer platforms provided improved tools for these artists, and the ever-improving multimedia and emerging desktop video preproduction tools are adding further refinements.

The Budget

As with all involved projects, a video production will require a budget. The budget is a guideline for forecasting and tracking the financial costs of the production from inception to completion. The success or failure of commercial ventures in video production and almost every other field is largely determined by the ability of the participants to accurately forecast the costs of the endeavors and to control these costs, bringing the project in at or under budget.

A typical budget for a desktop video production might include the following line items in the preproduction phase: Script Development (time and materials), Storyboard Development (time and materials), Site/Scenery Development (time and materials), and Budget/Schedule Development (labor). In the production phase, the budget might include line items for: Equipment (video and audio equipment rentals or amortization), Lighting (rentals or amortization), Location Fees (leases, utility charges, licenses, etc.), Materials (videotape, props, etc.), Crew (labor: wages and per diem fees), Meals (for cast and crew), Lodging (for cast and crew on remote sets), and Travel (air/train/taxi fare, mileage, car rentals, etc.). The cast and crew will typically include an audio engineer, camera operators, on-screen talent, voiceover talent, and directors and assistants. In small productions, several functions will be combined into single individuals. As the project progresses into postproduction, the budget must anticipate charges for: Tape Transfer (time and materials), Graphics Development (time and materials), Tape Stock (audio and video materials), Graphics Transfer (time and materials), Audio Transfer (time and materials), Off-line Edit (time and materials and/or lease fees), Off-line Mastering (time and materials, List Cleaning (time and materials, preparing for the final edit), On-line Edit (typically time and materials in a studio), Audio Layover (labor and possibly licenses for music), Special Effects Creation (labor and materials, possibly licenses), Audio Sweetening and Mixing (labor), and Audio Layback (labor).

Historically, video productions have relied on written budgets (if any). The advent of spreadsheet programs and accounting software on the various personal computer platforms have made small inroads into the video preproduction market, and special purpose tools for video preproduction budgeting are beginning to appear. As the video industry becomes more computerized, and as more computer literate individuals enter the video market, these tools will become more prevalent.

The Production Schedule

The production schedule is the chronological guideline for collecting the source materials for the project, including live video footage, animation graphics, still photographic or graphic art, audio effects, and voiceovers. As the adage "time is money" is very applicable to the video production cycle, the production schedule will tie closely with the budget, as well as with the script. A director may choose to shoot sections of the original script out of sequence in order to minimize costs and time during production. For example, imagine a script that requires 3 sets, A, B, and C. Action involving each of these sets is scattered through the script. If the director were to shoot in sequential order, the crew would have to assemble set "A", light it appropriately, set the audio levels, shoot the scene, tear down or "strike" the set, build the "B" set and configure it, shoot the scene, tear it down, and so on. Normally, the director will shoot all of the "A" scenes at one time (and "B" and "C" scenes similarly), in order to minimize setup and teardown time and cost, and the costs of having the talent stand idle. The scenes will then be rearranged in the proper order during the post-production editing process.

The Postproduction Schedule

The postproduction schedule is the chronological guideline for assembling all of the source materials into a finished product. It normally is not a separate item, but an extension of the "master" production schedule.

Tools for automating the production and postproduction schedules are just beginning to emerge in the video preproduction market.

Revenues and Revenue Growth Rates

Revenues from the total U.S. desktop video preproduction market are shown in Figure 4-1. Revenues from this market are derived from the sale of products in the desktop video, multimedia, and general purpose computer and video products markets, but count only those items used specifically for desktop video preproduction efforts. In 1989, revenues from this market were $2.3 million and grew to $50.0 million in 1992, although the desktop video market in general, as well as its components, are in the very early stages of development. Revenues from the total U.S. desktop video preproduction market are forecasted to increase throughout the next decade as technologies make the concept of desktop video more viable to the mass market and more palatable to the professional video market. In 1995, revenues are forecasted to be $638.3 million and should increase to almost $5.2 billion by the end of the 90's.

Revenue growth rates were 175.9 percent for 1990 as the desktop video market began to emerge and existing products began to be used for desktop video preproduction efforts. Strong growth was seen through 1992 and is expected through 1995 as vendors develop both products specific to desktop video and products targeted at the simultaneously emerging multimedia market but applicable to desktop video preproduction tasks. 1992 revenue growth was 281.3%, indicative of the introduction of a number of preproduction oriented products, and is expected to remain above 100 percent for the next several years. In 1995, as the overall desktop video market begins to mature following penetration with early adopters and video professionals, is growth rates will slacken as both unit growth and pricing begins to drop off. Revenue growth is anticipated at a healthy 89.3 percent for 1995, gradually declining, but staying quite strong

through 1999, resulting in an overall revenue CAGR of 117.8 percent for the period surveyed.

Fig. 4-1:	Total U.S. Market for Preproduction Products Unit Shipment and Revenue Forecasts 1989-1999		
Year	Units (000)	Revenues ($M)	Revenue CAGR (%)
1989	4.8	2.3	-
1990	13.9	6.3	175.9
1991	31.5	13.1	107.8
1992	66.9	50.0	281.3
1993	132.8	144.7	189.5
1994	249.9	337.2	133.0
1995	434.4	638.3	89.3
1996	731.5	1125.0	76.2
1997	1202.5	1877.6	66.9
1998	1961.4	3136.8	67.1
1999	3129.4	5169.2	65.8
CAGR			*117.8%*

It is essential to note that some product classifications which began the decade as

"preproduction" products only will end the period performing many more functions within the

video development process. In addition, in the first years covered by this survey, most

preproduction products are single-purpose (e.g. scriptwriting tools), requiring an individual end

user to purchase 2 or 3 separate items in order to cover the range of preproduction tasks. It is

anticipated that many of these products will be integrated together to provide more

comprehensive preproduction tools as well as with functions necessary for later in the production

or postproduction phases. For instance, it is reasonable to expect the integration of scripting and

storyboarding tools together, as well as merged with teleprompting tools used in the production

phase. The high revenue growth rates in the preproduction phase will therefore somewhat offset

the growth rates in the later phases as preproduction tools become more capable.

Unit Shipments and Pricing Trends

In 1989, there were 4.8 thousand units of preproduction products shipped to the U.S. market. A unit is defined as a single software or hardware package which will independently perform single or multiple preproduction tasks, or the combination of two or more items which together function to perform such tasks. The high growth years of 1990 through 1992, as described in Chapter 2, culminated in 66.9 thousand units shipped in 1992, a 112.7 percent growth over the preceding year. Unit growth is anticipated to remain quite strong for the remainder of the decade, gradually declining from the peak growth rate in 1990. 1999 unit growth is estimated at 59.6 percent and the compound annual growth rate for the preproduction products shipped to the U.S. market for the survey period is forecasted at 81.8%. Unit shipments are expected to reach 434.4 thousand by 1995 and 3.13 million by the end of 1999.

The average price for units in this category is derived from the weighted average of all preproduction products analyzed in this study, including high- and low-end concept development products and project management tools.

Average pricing declined slightly in 1990 and 1991 as there were few entrants to the market and little pricing pressure, except that from other markets served by the same products, which are beginning to mature. The onslaught of new entrants to the market in 1992 forced a net increase of 79.3 percent in product pricing, and this upward trend is anticipated through the rest of the decade. Average pricing is expected to grow significantly through 1994 as more powerful products are introduced to the growing market. Prices will continue to grow at single-digit rates until after 1999, when they will begin to decline in a mature market. The overall pricing trend is forecasted to rise at 19.8 percent for the survey period. Much of this upward trend is because of the continued introductions of new and more powerful products anticipated for the years of 1993 and 1994. The remainder is due to the expectation, as evinced by prior history, that vendors of these products will attempt to hold the prices of existing products steady by continually adding features and new improvements. Post-maturity, in the years following 1999, the preproduction market is expected to receive strong downward pricing pressures as products become more standardized and available, and as the low-cost manufacturers enter the market in force.

Market and Technology Trends

As the overall desktop video market is still in its infancy, there are few historical trends in either the market or the technology, but there are a number that can be reasonably forecast. The same holds true for the preproduction elements of the overall market.

Trends By Product Type

The preproduction products segment of the U.S. desktop video market has been further segmented into 3 separate areas, the low range and high ranges of products used to develop the concept and content of video productions, and the products used to plan and manage the schedule and budget of the process.

In 1989, due mostly to the relative dearth of high range concept development tools and project management tools, the low range concept development tools constituted 96.5 percent of the overall preproduction products segment. The explosion of products in the high range concept development tools subsegment in 1992 allowed that subsegment to capture 11.1 percent of the overall market, dropping the low range products to 83.6 percent. Project management tools constituted 3.1 percent of the preproduction market in 1989 and experienced a small spurt in growth, culminating in 5.4 percent in 1992. Project management tools are not forecasted as a significant portion of the overall preproduction products market for the rest of the decade, holding relative shares from 3.5 to 4.3 percent of the whole.

On the other hand, the high range concept development tools subsegment is expected to explode, mostly thanks to the introduction and growth of digital video products. In 1992, this subsegment constitutes 11.1 percent of the whole, and this portion is expected to grow steadily throughout the decade, culminating in 67.1 percent in 1999. Low range products will decline to 29.0 percent and project management tools will hold 3.9 percent in 1999.

Distribution Trends

Product Knowledge

In any new technology area there is a problem connecting small developers operating with limited resources with the small portions of the populace who are interested in obtaining these new, exciting products. In terms of the desktop video preproduction products, developers are conceiving great new products and prospective end users are demanding new and improved performance, potentially delivered by these great new products, yet the two groups are having trouble making connections. Some of this difficulty will soon disappear, as the desktop video market arises from the "noise level" and attains recognized status as a major technology market, a transformation occurring today. This will convince some existing resellers to carry desktop video products, including those used for the preproduction phase, for sale to these early adopters.

Integration Complexity

A bigger difficulty is in providing the services, including technical support and training, that these new desktop video customers will require. To date, there are very few entities capable (much less actually doing so) of providing the computer expertise, the video equipment expertise, and the video production process expertise necessary for successful resale of desktop video products. Value Added Resellers, or VARs, are becoming an important part of this technology transfer function and will continue to be important for some time.

Low Software Margins

Another distribution trend we can expect is a resistance to carrying software on the part of both existing computer and video dealers. This has been a trend in the personal computer retail market, since software occupies precious shelf space, produces small revenues per unit, and is often sold around the dealer by mail order firms. Video dealers have classically shunned low-price, high-support items like software. Accordingly, VARs will have to fill the gap with these products until they become commodities, whereupon mail order, direct mail, and catalog sales will provide the bulk of these products to the market.

Bundling

A final trend to be expected will be bundling by both resellers and manufacturers of preproduction products with complementary products from all phases of the video development process. For instance, most digital video hardware manufacturers are currently including digital video editing software with their products (e.g. SuperMac Digital Film and Adobe Premiere 2.0). It is reasonable to expect complementary products such as scriptwriting packages and teleprompting packages to be bundled, prior to the merging of such products by enlightened manufacturers.

End User Trends

Prospective Users

The key end user trend, already underway, is the increasing number of prospective users as desktop video technology is introduced and matures. The increasing sophistication of the products have made it more and more feasible for novices as well as those with limited experience and expertise to begin developing video presentations. The sophistication of these prospective end users is also increasing, since most of the new entrants to the market are already at least partially computer literate, improving over the existing video professional user base.

Productivity & Creativity Improvements

It is reasonable, as evinced by recent history, to expect order-of-magnitude jumps in the sophistication, capability, and user friendliness of new products and new product versions in the overall desktop video market. These performance improvements will translate directly into productivity improvements and indirectly into creativity improvements, as producers now have the ability to experiment with concepts without destroying their budgets.

Computer Literate Users

Another trend, mentioned above in another context, is the influx of computer literate individuals into the professional video market. These individuals are more inclined to embrace computer-based technologies such as desktop video, and less inclined to rely on historical and technological precedents. It would be unexpected to find a scriptwriter today who does not use a word processing software package on a personal computer; it will be equally difficult in several years to find a producer who budgets on paper, or a storyboard artist who works in pen and ink.

In-House Experimentation

In general industry, it is common for communications professionals and desktop communicators to outsource to independent producers much of the preproduction work necessary for a video project. The advent of personal-computer based preproduction tools allows industry professionals the ability to perform this work themselves before committing resources to outside agencies, thus saving themselves cost and time.

Qualitative Trends

There are two very key qualitative trends for preproduction products. The first is the overall concept of introducing a personal computer into the workflow where none had existed before.

New Computerization

The professional video business has proceeded to the current date largely without the benefit of computerization. Where the personal computer has made inroads, it has done so as a general purpose machine with general purpose products, such as word processing or accounting software. Accordingly, many of the people who are accustomed to doing video preproduction work, e.g. scriptwriting or storyboarding, have historically done so with manual tools. Over the last ten years, this has gradually begun to change, with scriptwriters leading the way.

Over the last five years, storyboard artists have begun to use general purpose graphics tools in order to develop their hard-copy output. Producers and other personnel have largely ignored computerization to date and have relied on their manual methods of project management and budgeting.

It is clear that desktop video is forcing the computer to become endemic in the preproduction process. Younger video professionals are familiar with computers and are more likely to adopt them than resist them like their older counterparts. Simultaneously, focused tools are now hitting the market which improve the productivity of the entire preproduction process. The paradigm shift is underway, in terms of the existing video professionals and those likely to join that end user segment.

This trend is less important to the far larger, and far more important, end user segment in terms of growth rates and pricing pressures. That segment is the general public, led by computer-literate early adopters, who have limited awareness of the previous technology of video development, and hence have no conditioned resistance to the concept of desktop video as a computerized process.

Generalized Functionality

The second major trend is an ongoing trend away from specialization toward generalization. Desktop video itself is fueled by this trend on a macro scale; one of the reasons for desktop video to exist is the economies afforded by the utilization of a single multipurpose tool in lieu of a number of special purpose tools, as was the case in the conventional video market. On a micro level, applications which currently provide discrete functions will begin to manifest functionality applicable in several, and perhaps all, phases of video development.

It is reasonable to expect the combination of scriptwriting, storyboarding, and teleprompting tools, as mentioned above. It is also reasonable to expect the digital video tools applicable today only for the preproduction phase of video development to evolve into full-function postproduction tools, allowing a producer to storyboard and edit on the same platform. It may be reasonable to expect the same tools to perform a number of functions, e.g. script development, animatic storyboarding, final animation development, teleprompting and camera direction, MIDI composition, audio, video, and MIDI editing, character generation, and special effects/transitions, all within the same application having a common user interface.

Dynamic Storyboarding

Other trends include a continued rise in the use of animatics versus static storyboards for "selling" projects. In the same way that visual information conveys more content than written text, thus providing the impetus for storyboards to supplement scripts, full-motion visual information conveys more content than static or still-motion graphics. The advent of powerful new animatics tools, driven largely by the multimedia market, combined with the increasing computerization of the video process, will help drive this trend.

Artificial Intelligence

Another anticipated trend is the inclusion of artificial intelligence in both concept development and project management tools used in the preproduction process. It is reasonable to anticipate character development tools, camera direction tools, automatic budgeting tools, and the like, with builtin error checking and the ability of offering suggested alterations to the user. Some of these functions are beginning to appear in applications even today.

Applications themselves will tend to help make some of the creative and cost decisions based upon the availability of certain equipment used in the production and postproduction phases of the development process. Today, content developers must keep in mind both the message to be conveyed to the audience and also the capabilities of the technology to be used in developing the programming. For example, a desktop video postproduction system based on a Macintosh enables the script to include more graphics than a script prepared for a non-graphics, cuts-only edit suite.

Groupware

The video production process has always been people-intensive, and there is little reason to anticipate that one person will develop video productions by him/herself, at least in professional environments. Although the desktop video tools will make this technically feasible, there are training and talent issues to overcome before single individuals can perform all of the functions required for a professional presentation. In the meanwhile, it is reasonable to expect the advent and development of groupware products allowing multiple individuals in a workgroup to share information and produce a joint output. This implies the rise of networking in desktop video environments.

Competitive Analysis / Market Share
Competitive Environment

Generally, there are few manufacturers at this time who focus their products *specifically* for the desktop video preproduction market. The products in this segment are typically general purpose, or multimedia-focused, products which have been adapted for use in video preproduction. The products which *are* focused on this segment tend to come from small companies who have recognized a viable niche. There are both opportunities to succeed and to fail for these small niche exploiters; the upside is the rapidly growing market. The downside is the requirement for marketing, distribution, and sales efforts to capitalize on their early entries into the market before a larger competitor focuses its significant resources on the segment.

Small organizations typically have very limited marketing and sales capabilities and may be capital limited in attempting to develop them. They typically have inefficient and ineffective distribution channels, often relying on direct sales for the bulk of their product movement. They are frequently unaware, or at least undereducated, of the capabilities and presence of significant competitors or potential competitors. These factors make these organizations extremely vulnerable and unstable since they can easily be blindsided by a major competitor while attempting to develop the user base for their products.

At the same time, potential consumers for these products have difficulty in locating the small suppliers because of a lack of public information, e.g. advertising or shelf space in retail organizations. They often opt for a more generic solution available from a known vendor instead of searching for a better solution from an unknown, and hard to find, supplier.

Structure

As of 1992, there are over 100 competitive products in the preproduction segment of the U.S. desktop video market. More competitors are being added almost daily as the market grows along with the developing technologies. The competitors range in size from multibillion dollar international corporations like IBM and Apple to single-entrepreneur development firms. The vast majority of competitors in the desktop video preproduction market are small to medium sized firms, yet the largest market shares in each subsegment are controlled by the larger, better capitalized firms with the strongest marketing presence. No firm has been in the desktop video market for more than three or four years, since the market itself is so new.

Figure 4-2 shows the major participants in the desktop video preproduction market and the subsegments in which they compete.

Few companies participate in more than one subsegment of the desktop video preproduction products market. Those that do, fall into two general categories. The first includes such organizations as Microsoft, Borland, Computer Associates, and Software Publishing Corp., who produce general purpose products which can be adapted for use in preproduction functions. The second includes various multimedia product developers, e.g. Adobe, VideoMail, VideoLake, Neil Research, and Macromedia, with a range of products spanning both the high and low ranges of tools applicable for desktop video concept development.

Of the various segments of the preproduction products market, the Concept Development Tools (Low Range) segment offers the largest selection of competitors. There are several reasons for this. First, this segment includes general purpose word processing packages, allowing Microsoft, Borland, Computer Associates, and other software giants to compete with their general purpose products. Second, the price range (under $1000) is appropriate for the majority of products emerging for the multimedia market, yet appropriate for desktop video concept development. The multimedia market has received a great deal of marketing hype over the last several years, increasing developer interest and attracting funding from capital providers, resulting in a flood of new products. Third, one of the key desktop video purposes for these tools is the development of animatics, or animated storyboards. These are merely applications of long-existing computer graphics programs to a new market. There are a number of these graphic development and animation programs in the market today, typically falling into the defined price range.

Fig. 4-2: Preproduction Market Participants

Manufacturer	Concept Development (Low Range)	Concept Development (High Range)	Project Management
Adobe	X	X	
AimTech		X	
Aldus	X		
Aldus/Silicon Beach	X		
Asymetrix	X		
ATI	X		
Borland	X		X
Brilliant Media	X		
Claris	X		X
Collaborator Systems	X		
Commodore	X		
Comprehensive Video Supply	X		
Computer Associates	X		X
Computer Friends	X	X	
CoSA	X	X	
Creative Labs		X	
DacEasy			X

DiVA		X		
Gold Disk Software		X		
HSC		X		
HyperPro/Mass Micro		X		
IBM		X		
Image North Technologies	X			
Imagine Multimedia		X		
Impulse		X		
Instant Replay		X		
Intel			X	
Intelligent Environments		X		
Interactive Image		X		
Interactive Solutions		X		
Intuit				X
John Morley		X		
Jovian Logic			X	
Kalieda		X		
Lake Compuframes		X		
Lenel Systems		X		
Linker Systems		X		
Lotus Development				X
Macromedia		X	X	
Mass Microsystems			X	
Mathematica		X		
MediaVision		X		
Microsoft		X		X
Neil Research Laboratories		X	X	
New Video			X	
Owl		X		
Pacific Gold Coast		X		
Pacioli				X
Paul Mace		X		
PM Ware		X		
Radius		X	X	
RasterOps			X	
RasterOps/Truevision			X	
RGB Spectrum			X	
Screenplay Systems		X		
Software Publishing		X		X
SuperMac		X	X	
Symantec		X		
Truby's Writer's Studio		X		
VideoLake		X	X	
VideoLogic			X	
VideoMail		X	X	
Vision Imaging		X		
WordPerfect		X		
Workstation Technologies			X	

The High Range of Concept Development Tools is much less populated with competitors, mostly due to the very recent development of high-quality digital video products. The number of competitors in this segment should grow significantly between now and 1995 as the digital video technology becomes more cost-effective and applicable to postproduction, as well as preproduction, tasks in the desktop video environment.

There are very few competitors in the Project Management Tools segment. Those that are listed are general purpose project management, accounting, and spreadsheet tools which can be adapted easily for use by desktop video users. No dedicated desktop video packages, to the knowledge of the authors of this report, have yet emerged for this segment.

Issues

There are two key competitive issues for the preproduction market, as for the other major segments of the desktop video products market.

Differentiation vs. Existing Video Tools

The first is differentiating the product from the existing video market substitutes. In many cases, this is a non-issue, since the video market has long done without computerized tools. The emerging desktop video preproduction tools are often competing with existing manual techniques. The key competitive factor then becomes ease of use; the new adopters of the technology must be able to quickly realize the increased productivity offered by the new tools, or else they will not bother to adapt their existing processes to them.

Differentiation vs. Existing Computer Tools

Those new entrants into the video market have the option of reverting to manual techniques, using the newly emerging specific-purpose tools, or adapting common computer tools (e.g. Excel, WordPerfect, Quicken, etc.) to video preproduction tasks. This points out the second key issue for the emerging preproduction products market: differentiation from existing computer tools. Existing computer users entering the video development field will choose new tools based on functionality over substitute tools with which they are more familiar. The new tools must offer incremental benefits over the generic word processing, graphics, spreadsheet, project management, or budgeting tools already available and familiar to the new entrants to the desktop video market.

The successful vendors in the preproduction market will note both requirements and provide incremental functionality over generic computer tools in an easy to use format, as well as increased productivity vis a vis the option of not using the desktop video tool in the first place.

Price

The basic reason for the growth of desktop video as an overall market is an economic one: desktop video allows the development of video programming at a cost lower than that possible via established technology. Accordingly, a key competitive factor in all segments of the desktop video market, including preproduction, will be the price paid by the end user for the products necessary to complete his or her video program. Those vendors able to provide sufficient functionality and performance at a low price will compete more effectively than those offering superior functionality and performance at a higher price.

Breadth of Knowledge

Many of the current participants in the desktop video market are major participants in either the personal computer industry or the professional video industry. These two industries, while sharing much with the emerging desktop video industry, are very different. They have different underlying technologies, different processes, different required skill sets, different distribution channels, and on and on. The successful vendors in the desktop video industry, and specifically in the preproduction products segment, will be those who acquire the complementary knowledge from the "other" parent industry; i.e. the computer products manufacturers who acquire video knowledge, or the professional video manufacturers who acquire personal computer wherewithal.

Those manufacturers who underestimate the complexity of the "other" side, e.g. a personal computer manufacturer who underestimates the complexity of the video production process or a video manufacturer who disregards the rate of change of technology in the personal computer industry, will be doomed to fail. Those who will be successful will integrate elements from both industries into a cohesive whole. Some will do this via personnel practices, e.g. hiring talent from the "other" industry. Others will merge with or acquire complementary organizations. An example of this is the recent acquisition of DiVA, a digital video software manufacturer, by Avid Technology, a pioneer in desktop video postproduction well integrated in the professional video industry. Another is the recent acquisition of E-Mu, a professional music products company by Creative Labs, a personal computer/multimedia products manufacturer.

Concept Development Tools (Low Range)

Total Concept Development Tools (Low Range) Market

Market Definitions and Overview

Concept development products include those desktop video products which assist in the development of a project script and storyboard. They include scripting software, storyboarding software, presentation software, multimedia authoring software, and digital video hardware and software, as well as existing word processing systems employed for this purpose. Products in this category tend to break into two separate segments: those products costing above $1000 and those below. The Low Range products tend to include the dedicated scripting and storyboarding products, the existing word processing software used for concept development, presentation software used for storyboarding, and the low end of multimedia authoring and digital video products.

Percentage Contribution

In 1989, the revenues contributed by the low range concept development tools subsegment constituted 96.5 percent of the entire preproduction products market. In 1992, this relative proportion dropped to 83.6 percent, largely due to the impact of the introduction of the digital video products into the high range concept development tools subsegment. This share of the preproduction products market is expected to continue to decline throughout the remainder of the decade to an eventual share of 29.0 percent in 1999, as the high end tools subsegment grows rapidly. Although the relative percentage of the preproduction market revenues is forecasted to drop, the absolute contribution in terms of revenues will grow substantially, as described later in this section.

Elements

Low range concept development tools include a number of subcategories of products, some intended for other purposes, all applicable to the process of creating scripts and storyboards on desktop video platforms:

Scripting Software

Scripting software helps the script writer prepare the production script in the format required for the production. This software may either stand alone as a complete tool or may be an add-on to a generic word processing package.

Storyboarding Software

Storyboarding software incorporates pictures or artist sketches to enable the production concept to be conveyed to the client visually, typically via a computer screen or a series of printed color graphics panels or slides.

Presentation Software

Presentation software products, normally used to create overhead slide presentations for business meetings, can also be used to create storyboards. The portion of these products used for desktop video production has been included in this accumulation.

Multimedia Authoring Software

Multimedia authoring software, while not explicitly developed for use in desktop video, can also effectively be used to develop storyboards. It also can develop a type of storyboard called an "animatic", which adds animation and audio to a basic storyboard concept. With these multimedia tools, the storyboard is no longer static, but can be a computer-generated model of the live production to come. The lower range of these products is included in this category.

Digital Video Hardware and Software

Digital video products now entering the market, as well as those on the market for the last two years, are being portrayed by their manufacturers as desktop video postproduction tools. Examples of such hardware and software products include SuperMac's DigitalFilm and VideoSpigot, Adobe's Premiere, DiVA's VideoShop, Radius' VideoVision, etc. The current reality is that none of these products are truly applicable to professional quality desktop video postproduction; they all have limitations which currently limit their utility, mostly because of screen resolutions and sizes as well as video capture and playback rates, in video productions. Many are also incapable of supporting high-quality audio capture, editing, and playback, or of exporting Edit Decision Lists, or of controlling VTR decks.

These products are very applicable for multimedia applications such as kiosks or CD-I interactive video presentations. They are also currently applicable in the desktop video arena as preproduction products. A QuickTime movie developed and played via VideoSpigot and Premiere makes an excellent animatic, replacing a conventional storyboard. Many high end production facilities are already using these products for this purpose, speeding and decreasing the cost of preproduction creative planning such as "what if" scenario developments, thereby improving the productivity and creativity of the project personnel.

General Purpose Word Processing & Graphics Software

Some concept developers will choose to utilize existing general purpose computer tools such as word processing or graphics software packages instead of special purpose products designed for video preproduction. Only those sales of general purpose software packages in which the use for video preproduction concept development is the primary goal, or the actual dominant use, is included in the following market projections.

Revenues and Revenue Growth Rates

Revenues from the low range of concept development tools sold to the U.S. desktop video preproduction market are shown in Figure 4-3. Once again, these products include dedicated scriptwriting and storyboarding tools developed specifically for desktop video preproduction work, as well as to that portion of general-purpose and other-purpose products (e.g. multimedia development software, presentation software, and word processing packages) used specifically for desktop video preproduction efforts. In 1989, revenues from this market were $2.1 million and grew to $19.7 million in 1992. A unit of this category typically consists of a single software package or the bundle of a software package plus a hardware card.

Revenues arising from sales of low range concept development tools are forecasted to increase throughout the decade as desktop video, led by preproduction products, revolutionizes the video development process. In 1995, revenues are forecasted to be $80.5 million and should increase to over $259 million in 1999.

Fig. 4-3:	Concept Development Tools - Low Range Unit Shipment and Revenue Forecasts 1989-1999			
Year	Units (000)	Revenues ($M)	Revenue Growth(%)	Unit Growth(%)
1989	4.6	2.1	-	-
1990	12.8	5.2	152.0	180.0
1991	28.9	10.8	107.0	125.0
1992	55.9	19.7	81.9	93.5
1993	98.6	33.3	68.9	76.3
1994	163.5	53.4	60.5	65.8
1995	254.1	80.5	50.9	55.4
1996	373.0	115.0	42.8	46.8
1997	520.0	156.2	35.8	39.4
1998	698.9	204.7	31.0	34.4
1999	907.2	259.3	26.7	29.8
CAGR			55.5%	60.7%

Revenue growth rates were 152.0 percent for 1990 as the desktop video market began to emerge and most of the products available for the market were low-end preproduction products. Strong growth was seen through 1992 as more vendors introduced concept development tools, mostly for the multimedia market, but with application to desktop video. 1992 revenue growth was 81.9%, indicating the beginning of a drop in demand levels of the relatively higher priced digital video products, mostly because of the advent of their more powerful (and more costly) siblings. At the same time, introductions of low priced scriptwriting and storyboarding tools helped offset the decline in growth of the digital video products. A continued decline of revenue growth in this area is expected throughout the decade, although with somewhat stronger unit growth, because of the change in product mix. Revenue growth is anticipated at 50.9 percent for 1995, gradually declining, but staying quite strong through 1999 (at 26.7 percent), resulting in an overall revenue CAGR of 55.5 percent for the period surveyed.

Unit Shipments and Pricing Trends

Unit growth started out at over 100 percent, in part because of the relative dearth of installed base prior to 1990, and grew at a solid rate to 1992. A unit again is defined as a single package of software or the combination of a single hardware unit with an accompanying unit of software. The growth rate in 1992 declined to 93.5 percent, and continued decline is forecast throughout the rest of the decade.   The unit CAGR for the survey period is forecasted at 60.7%.

Pricing for the survey period is anticipated to hold reasonably steady, for several reasons. First, some proportion of this market segment's products are comprised of mature word processing and animation programs. Their manufacturers tend to hold prices relatively steady by periodically introducing significant product upgrades via new versions. Second, manufacturers of most of the multimedia-focused as well as the emerging desktop video-specific products in this category will most likely follow a similar strategy. They will attempt to stabilize prices by adding specific features and improvements needed by their chosen target markets. As this occurs, some general purpose products will become less applicable to desktop video and will lose whatever market share they have obtained; others will become more useful and will gain market share without having to erode pricing substantially. The forecasted CAGR delta of only 5.2

percent between unit shipment growth rate and revenue growth rate reflects the anticipated steadiness in pricing as the market grows.

Market and Technology Trends

Qualitative Trends

Many of the general trends listed for the overall U.S. preproduction market are applicable to its components, including this one. Of particular note are the trends towards computerization and generalization/integration, which will help the low-end concept development tools attain and retain market share.

Presentation Products

Presentation software products, while mostly geared toward static presentations, will become more and more like multimedia authoring tools and will probably merge with that class of products. In the meanwhile, one significant application for desktop video tools is the conversion of existing and planned 35mm and overhead slide presentations into videotape presentations. These presentation development tools can facilitate this conversion.

Scripting and Storyboarding Tools

Some developers will continue to bring to market dedicated scriptwriting and storyboarding tools; others will focus on providing utilities and add-on products to general purpose products such as word processing, animation, or graphics programs. Some multimedia products will become so specialized for multimedia applications that they become unsuitable for desktop video work

.

Cross-Platform Tools and Groupware

It is reasonable to expect vendors to develop cross-platform concept development tools, allowing interchange of information across multiple platforms. An artist who prefers to work on a Macintosh platform with existing tools should be able to do so, yet share data with the desktop video producer who is operating on a Windows-based PC or SGI Indigo workstation.

It is also reasonable to expect that content development is a prime candidate for groupware applications. Script development or storyboard development can performed by a group faster, and at times more creatively, than by a single individual.

Competitive Analysis / Market Share

Competitive Environment

As in the overall preproduction market, this subsegment is populated by both extremely large and powerful organizations as well as small entrepreneurial outfits, and all forms of organizations in between. The emerging status of the desktop video industry has opened many technological niches for organizations to exploit. The low barriers to entry have encouraged many small organizations to enter the market, typically with low-range concept development tools, since these are relatively less time- and capital-intensive to develop. These smaller organizations typically lack the resources or knowledge to successfully market their products. On the other hand, the larger organizations often enter the desktop video market with preconceived notions about what is needed, spend enormous sums missing the target, and flounder. The successful firms in this market will determine the market needs, develop products to meet these needs, and have sufficient marketing resources and capabilities to bring these products to the growing number of devotees to desktop video.

Structure

Figure 4-4 shows the companies who provide low range concept development tools to the desktop video preproduction market.

The low range of the desktop video preproduction concept development tools market has today attracted the most competitors in the overall desktop video market. The reason for this is the applicability of products developed for multimedia, presentations, or even the general business market, for the functions of concept development. Many desktop video users are

satisfied with the near fit of off-the-shelf products developed for these other tended uses. Also,

the customization of products for desktop video use in this subsegment have not required

massive time or capital investments, enabling new entries into the market with ease.

<table>
<tr><td colspan="2">Fig. 4-4:   Concept Development Tools (Low Range)
List of Selected Vendors and Products</td></tr>
<tr><td>Company</td><td>Products</td></tr>
<tr><td>Adobe</td><td>Premiere *</td></tr>
<tr><td>Aldus</td><td>Persuasion</td></tr>
<tr><td>Aldus/Silicon Beach`</td><td>SuperCard</td></tr>
<tr><td>Asymetrix</td><td>ToolBook; Make Your Point; MediaBlitz!</td></tr>
<tr><td>ATI</td><td>Authology Multimedia</td></tr>
<tr><td>Borland</td><td>Applause, Full Impact</td></tr>
<tr><td>Brilliant Media</td><td>Storyboarder Professional</td></tr>
<tr><td>Claris</td><td>HyperCard; Hollywood</td></tr>
<tr><td>Collaborator Systems</td><td>Collaborator II</td></tr>
<tr><td>Commodore</td><td>AmigaVision</td></tr>
<tr><td>Comprehensive Video Supply</td><td>Script Master</td></tr>
<tr><td>Computer Associates</td><td>Cricket Presents</td></tr>
<tr><td>Computer Friends</td><td>Movie Producer *</td></tr>
<tr><td>CoSA</td><td>Egg / PACo Producer *</td></tr>
<tr><td>DiVA</td><td>VideoShop *</td></tr>
<tr><td>Gold Disk Software</td><td>HyperCard</td></tr>
<tr><td>HSC</td><td>Interactive; Santa Fe Media Manager</td></tr>
<tr><td>HyperPro/Mass Micro</td><td>VideoAuthor</td></tr>
<tr><td>IBM</td><td>StoryBoard Live!; Storyboard Plus</td></tr>
<tr><td>Image North Technologies</td><td>ImageQ</td></tr>
<tr><td>Imagine Multimedia</td><td>MediaStation</td></tr>
<tr><td>Impulse</td><td>Foundation</td></tr>
<tr><td>Instant Replay</td><td>Instant Replay Professional</td></tr>
<tr><td>Intelligent Environments</td><td>Crystal</td></tr>
<tr><td>Interactive Image</td><td>HyperCase</td></tr>
<tr><td>Interactive Solutions</td><td>MovieWorks</td></tr>
<tr><td>John Morley</td><td>Scriptwriting Tools; Scriptwriting for Hi Impact Videos</td></tr>
<tr><td>Kalieda</td><td>MediaScript</td></tr>
<tr><td>Lake Compuframes</td><td>Showscape</td></tr>
<tr><td>Lenel Systems</td><td>Media Organizer</td></tr>
<tr><td>Linker Systems</td><td>Animation Stand</td></tr>
<tr><td>Macromedia</td><td>Director; Magic; MediaMaker *; Action</td></tr>
</table>

Mass Microsystems	ColorSpace FX
Mathematica	Tempra Media Author; Tempra Media Show
Media Vision	Pro Movie Spectrum
Microsoft	Powerpoint, Word
Neil Research Laboratories	MovieStudio *
Owl	Guide
Pacific Gold Coast	Take-1
Paul Mace	Grasp
PM Ware	UltraScript
Radius	Digital Media, RadiusTV
Screenplay Systems	Dramatica
Software Publishing	Video Player
SuperMac	VideoSpigot
Symantec	More
Truby's Writer's Studio	Storyline
VideoLake	VideoFusion *
VideoMail	VideoBase
Vision Imaging	Media Master; Multimedia Studio
Word Perfect Corp.	Word Perfect

* Also listed under High Range Concept Development Tools

Issues

More products from small organizations can be expected to arrive to the market, some to compete and fail, some to find niches and survive, and fewer still to grow and become industry standards. This subsegment, like the entire desktop video industry, presents opportunities for innovators to develop exciting new products, perhaps to become de facto industry standards.

In addition, major products providers such as Sun, Apple, Adobe, Silicon Graphics, IBM, Microsoft, and Computer Associates have introduced products in this area or are likely to do so. The marketing clout of these large organizations is both an opportunity and a threat to the smaller, more prevalent developers. They are threats to develop or acquire a reasonably innovative product and become de facto industry standards through marketing clout alone. They are opportunities for the same reason; a small developer with an innovative product stands a reasonable chance of being bought out by one of the giants.

Market Shares

As of 1992, five companies hold the largest market shares of the concept development tools (low range) subsegment of the desktop video preproduction market. The first is Adobe, with a 19.3 percent share as of the end of 1992, based mostly on sales of version 1.0 of Premiere. The vast majority of copies of Adobe Premiere were bundled with SuperMac Technology's Video Spigot systems, which gathered 15.8 percent of the market. Aldus, with Persuasion, a leading presentation software package, contributed 9.6 percent market share, and Microsoft's Powerpoint, another leading presentation software package, added 7.9 percent. Macromedia's Director, the leading multimedia authoring package, captured 6.6 percent of the market in 1992.

The largest contribution by a focused desktop video competitor was Lake Compuframes, whose storyboarding software package Showscape garnered 0.9 percent of the whole low range concept development tools market segment in 1992.

```
Fig. 4-5:        Concept Development Tools (Low Range)
                 1992 Market Shares

Company                         Share

Adobe                           19.3 %
SuperMac                        15.8 %
Microsoft                        9.6 %
Aldus                            7.9 %
Macromedia                       6.6 %
Lake Compuframes                 0.9 %
Others                          39.9 %
                                --------
                               100.0 %
```

The remaining contributors, including word processing vendors, presentation software vendors, multimedia authoring package developers, as well as digital video providers, and emerging scripting and storyboarding tools vendors comprised the remainder of the market, with no vendor capturing more than 5 percent market share.

__Highlights of Selected Vendors__

IBM

IBM Storyboard Live v1.0 and Storyboard Plus v2.0 are two multimedia authoring packages which double as desktop video storyboarding applications. Both packages let users create screen presentations that incorporate text, graphics, video, sound, and animation. Storyboard Live supports MIDI and includes a library of 34 animation routines. It retails for $495. Storyboard Plus has more image manipulation tools and can control still frame grabs. It includes several modules, including Picture Maker, a image manipulation package plus clip art libraries, Story Editor, a multimedia editing package, Picture Taker, frame grabbing software, and Text Maker, a text editing package. Storyboard Live works with the IBM Music Feature, imports PCX and TIFF files and exports TIFF files. Each runs on IBM or compatible personal computers.

Macromedia

In late 1991, Macromind (now Macromedia) introduced Magic, a Mac-based low-end multimedia authoring tool. Magic has a simple, graphic user interface which makes it easy to use and reduces the time required for new users to get productive with the product. It provides powerful animation capabilities. Macromedia's Action, a presentation software package, began shipping in the fall of 1992. As of early 1993, version 2.5 is now shipping, for a retail price of $495. It supports Microsoft's Video for Windows, Apple's QuickTime for Windows, and Intel's DVI 2.5 video formats in the PC version. Action 1.0 is also available for the Mac platform. Action offers drawing and text tools, file import and export ability, and the ability to merge with AIFF or SoundEdit audio files. It also offers a playback only package for output-only applications.

Director is another Macromedia product, and the leading multimedia authoring tool, which allows users assemble 2D animations, antialiased text, artwork, full motion video, audio, and scripts into interactive, animated presentations. Director includes 24-bit paint tools, synchronization modules for adding audio and transitions, a scripting programming language, cross-platform playback-only modules, dual audio channels, animation controller support for output to videotape, and a MIDI interface. Director consists of two modules, Overview and Studio. Overview allows the user to create a slide-like presentation from various media files and Studio focuses on the animation functionality of Director. Director is designed for operation on the Apple Macintosh.

Macromedia's MediaMaker is a digital video editing package similar to Premiere, retailing for $695. MediaMaker provides serial control of VTR decks, multiple sound channels, QuickTime and Director compatibility, and TitleMaker titling software. Version 1.5 offers support for Sony VISCA, Sony Vbox, plus RC time code-compatible devices and QuickTime movie files.

SuperMac

SuperMac has developed an extensive line of digital video products, beginning with the innovative VideoSpigot and its derivatives. The VideoSpigot is a hardware card which plugs into a Macintosh personal computer and allows video digitization to disk, retrieval, and playback. It was one of the very first tools developed to support Apple's QuickTime standard for event-based data storage and retrieval. The VideoSpigot family includes versions which support audio digitization (via MacRecorder and SoundEdit Pro from Macromedia), high and low graphics support levels, and the different bus structures in the Macintosh family. All of the Mac versions are bundled with Adobe's Premiere, a product which originated within SuperMac as Reeltime. There is also a PC/Windows version of the VideoSpigot, which is bundled with Microsoft's Video for Windows and Asymetrix's multimedia authoring suite, including Make Your Point, ToolBook, and MediaBlitz!.

Others

Owl International, Inc. offers Guide, a Windows-based, hypermedia authoring package. It includes a development language and a configurable user interface and supports and device for which a Windows driver exists. Guide, although suitable for simple storyboarding, really shines in the area of interactive multimedia development because of its hypermedia capabilities, allowing the use of "buttons" for selection of various functions.

A longtime veteran of the video industry, Comprehensive Video Supply offers a broad range of products for all phases of the video production process, including a 4-column scriptwriting package called Script Master. Script Master retails for $345 for the basic version and for $395 with a spelling checker utility built in.

Commodore Business Machines released AmigaVision in 1990 as an icon-based multimedia authoring package for the Amiga platform. It is currently bundled with many of the Amiga configurations and contains a number of internal editors. Expression Editor creates variables and conditional statements for program scripting, Object Editor creates graphical objects such as circles and polygons, Videodisc controller manipulates video sequences, and Database Editor creates, imports, and modifies database information.

Concept Development Tools (High Range)

Total Concept Development Tools (High Range) Market

There are products in the multimedia authoring and digital video areas which are more capable than those in the low end of the spectrum. These products typically cost well above $1000 per unit (or combination in the case of digital video). We have broken these products into a separate category for two reasons: first, the cost, and second, because of the rapid advances occurring in the digital video area which will radically alter the utility of these products in the desktop video postproduction market.

Market Definitions and Overview

The high range of concept development tools constituted only 0.4 percent of the total desktop video preproduction market in 1989, mostly because of a relative lack of products in this area. As of 1992, several high end multimedia development tools had emerged as well as the first high end digital video hardware and software bundles for general purpose personal computers. This pushed the 1992 market share to 11.1 of the whole, and began a growth trend which is anticipated to last throughout the decade. By 1999, the contribution of the high end of concept development tools to the overall preproduction market is expected to rise to 67.1 percent, mostly due the increasing applicability of these tools throughout the video production cycle, from preproduction to production to postproduction.

There are two major components of high range concept development tools for the desktop video preproduction market, the most capable of the multimedia authoring tools, and digital video bundles comprised of software packages like DiVA's VideoShop and Adobe's Premiere, plus digital video hardware cards for the Mac, PC, or other platforms.

Multimedia Authoring Tools

Multimedia authoring tools in the high range typically include more powerful animation tools than those in the low end. They may or may not include print-to-tape capability. These products will be hard pressed to maintain their price deltas over low end products as the less capable products gain functionality. The high range products will have to add functionality well in excess of that available in less costly products in order to survive.

Digital Video

High end digital video products, such as the combination of Adobe's Premiere 2.0 and RasterOps' MoviePak bundle or SuperMac's DigitalFilm, are currently not quite appropriate for desktop video postproduction work, despite the claims of their manufacturers. It is clear that within a couple of years, and possibly within the upcoming year, this class of products will be very appropriate for this purpose, providing the desktop video market with a series of low-cost, off-line editing systems capable of providing professional quality output. It is reasonable to expect that such products will form the basis of an integrated platform used for preproduction, production, and postproduction efforts. In the meanwhile, while the technology is being advanced to this point, these products are excellent multimedia development tools as well as excellent preproduction tools. Because of the relative price of these hardware/software bundles, they are grouped in the high range of concept development tools.

Revenues and Revenue Growth Rates

Revenues from the high range of concept development tools sold to the U.S. desktop video preproduction market are shown in Figure 4-6. These products are limited to high-end multimedia authoring software such as Macromedia's Authorware, as well as the high end of digital video hardware/software combinations. One unit in this category is defined as a single dedicated software package or a hardware/software bundle which is primarily used for video preproduction concept development functions. In 1989, revenues from this market were nearly nonexistent, but grew to \$29.3 million in 1992. It is important to note that only one high-end digital video combination was available in 1992; over a dozen will be on the market by the end of 1993.

Revenues arising from sales of high range concept development tools are forecasted to rise dramatically in the near future as the technology improves and the overall desktop video market begins its rapid growth phase. In 1995, revenues are forecasted to be \$553.7 million and should increase to \$4.88 billion in 1999.

Fig. 4-6:	Content Development Tools (High Range) Unit Shipment and Revenue Forecasts 1989-1999			
Year	Units (000)	Revenues (\$M)	Revenue Growth(%)	Unit Growth(%)
1989	0.0	0.2	-	-
1990	0.1	0.8	380.0	540.0
1991	0.4	1.6	110.6	170.0
1992	7.4	29.3	1701.7	1995.0
1993	28.5	109.9	275.2	284.8
1994	77.2	281.4	156.0	170.9
1995	165.1	553.7	96.8	113.9
1996	332.3	1003.1	81.2	101.3
1997	636.4	1709.7	70.4	91.5
1998	1184.9	2912.9	70.4	86.2
1999	2100.8	4880.5	67.5	77.3
CAGR			*107.7%*	*124.1%*

Revenue growth rates were 380.0 percent for 1990, mostly from the sale of Authorware into the newly emerging desktop video environment. In late 1992, several organizations shipped their digital video hardware products and bundled them with digital video editing software, resulting in a phenomenal 1992 revenue growth of 1701.7 percent. These products, and others already introduced are planned for 1993 introduction will lead to three exceptionally strong years of revenue growth, followed by a period of slackening growth caused by some price cutting and saturation effects in the last few of years of the decade. As discussed in Chapter 2 of this document, the introduction of digital video products capable of professional quality output will revolutionize the video industry and make video production tools available to the mass market. These tools are just now arriving in 1993; 1993 through 1995 should see a tremendous increase in available professional-quality digital video products, satisfying pent-up demand as well as expanding the market dramatically for such products. Revenue growth is anticipated at 156.0 percent for 1995, gradually declining to 67.5 percent in 1999, resulting in an overall revenue CAGR of 107.7 percent for the period surveyed.

Unit Shipments and Pricing Trends

Unit growth started out very high, in part because of the relative dearth of installed base prior to 1990, and experienced a 1995 percent spurt in 1992, due mostly to the introduction of the high-priced digital video products. The growth rate in 1993 is expected to decline to a more reasonable 284.8 percent and continue a gradual descent throughout the rest of the decade, ending 1999 at 77.3 percent. The unit CAGR for the period 1992-99 is forecasted at 124.1%.

Pricing is anticipated to hold relatively steady until 1995 as digital video products with increasing functionality and performance levels are introduced, superseding older, less capable products. After 1995, pricing is anticipated to begin a fairly sharp decline as competition increases and volume manufacturers enter the market. High-end multimedia product pricing and unit shipments are anticipated to decline throughout the survey period because of the emergence of lower-end products with features suitable for desktop video. Overall unit shipment CAGR exceeds revenue CAGR by 16.4 percentage points, indicating the pricing changes in the latter part of the survey period.

Market and Technology Trends
Qualitative Trends

Many of the trends applicable to the overall preproduction market are also applicable to the high end of concept development tools subsegment. Also, some of the trends specific to low-end concept development tools also apply to their more expensive siblings. In particular, we can expect use of computerized products based on these tools where computers have never been used, we can expect continued evolution of the products wherein manufacturers attempt to hold up street prices by adding functionality and performance, and we can expect product entries from both large and small organizations.

Applicability to Postproduction

The major trend to expect in this category is the pursuit of applicability for video postproduction editing, which should be realized within the next two years. When digital video products are capable of supporting full-motion digitizing and playback of full-screen video without scan line doubling, pixel interpolation, bit depth reduction, or significant compression-induced image artifacts, and when such products can include such functionality as recording, editing, and playback of multiple channels of CD-quality audio, integration with MIDI, time code compatibility, and VTR control, digital video technology has truly arrived to the desktop video market. These products will have enormous impact on video production processes and will serve as the cornerstones of true desktop video suites.

Increasing Functionality and Performance

As the functionality and performance of these high-end products are improving, it is reasonable to expect reductions in the prices of obsoleted products and use of these products to replace existing low-end entries. It is also reasonable to expect that the replacement high-end products will carry much the same price tag as the original items, allowing the vendors to offset pricing pressures with improved functionality and performance.

Groupware and Cross-Platform Applications

These high-end products, because of the acquisition costs, are prime candidates to acquire groupware and cross-platform functionality. These functions will allow these relatively expensive products to be shared by more users, improving the cost/benefit tradeoff.

Competitive Analysis / Market Share
Competitive Environment

The fact that their products are being used for desktop video preproduction no doubt comes as a surprise to many of the multimedia authoring software and digital video hardware and software manufacturers. Most of the multimedia products developers are marketing their products at the growing multimedia market, believing their output to be destined for CD-ROMs and other interactive media. Most of the digital video hardware and software vendors are pushing their products as appropriate for "videotape editing", i.e. desktop video postproduction, for which they are currently less than applicable.

The reality is that most of the multimedia authoring tools are being used for their intended purposes, but some are actually being used in the desktop video environment, largely because of a lack of better tools. The digital video products, while inappropriate for professional-quality video postproduction, are very applicable for animatic storyboard development during the desktop video preproduction phase. All of the tools in this segment allow a client to visualize a completed production, a necessary step since few can visualize a finished product based only on a script, much in the way few can visualize a completed house based on blueprints.

The high costs of production and postproduction will continue to force more emphasis on the planning elements in preproduction as competitive pressures grow in those environments. Ergo, there will be continued market pressures to develop better concept development tools in order to minimize costs down the line. Although the segment is currently populated by redirected products from other markets and a few dedicated products from smaller manufacturers, the firms which will compete best in the longterm environment will be those who are able to develop the most productive tools which integrate best with production and postproduction tasks.

As of now, the digital video vendors compete mostly on the bases of price/performance and distribution availability. Performance is less important for the concept development task than for the postproduction tasks for which they are being marketed. Price is the larger issue here as animatics require significantly less performance in terms of frame sizes, rates, and bit depth, as well as audio resolution and sampling frequencies, than live video. Price, of course, is irrelevant if a product is unavailable to a consumer; distribution is a key differentiator in market acceptance. Companies such as SuperMac and Radius, with established channels of distribution, are likely to perform better than, say, New Video or Computer Friends, whose products are harder to find.

Structure

The number of competitors in this category has grown rapidly in 1991 and 1992, and continues to expand in 1993, as more and more high-end digital video products come to market. As time goes on, the high end multimedia tools in this segment will become less noticeable among the wave of digital video hardware and software products expected to evolve here.

As of early 1993, there are approximately 20 competitors in this market segment, with more arriving every day. Some are graphics hardware suppliers who have developed full-motion capture and playback boards as additions to their lines. Examples include SuperMac, Radius, and RasterOps, plus its newly acquired subsidiary, Truevision. Others are small organizations who have developed specific hardware for the multimedia and desktop video markets, including Creative Labs, Jovian Logic, New Video, and VideoLogic. The final group of competitors produce software only. Their products work in conjunction with hardware solutions to provide edit control, special effects, graphics integration, and other functionality. These include Adobe, AimTech, CoSA, and Macromedia.

As this is a newly emerging technology, the competitors are of all sizes and forms, from software giants like Adobe and Macromedia, to established hardware companies like Radius and SuperMac, to smaller firms like CoSA, Neil Research, and VideoLake.

<table>
<tr><td colspan="2">Fig. 4-7:   Concept Development Tools (High Range)
                 List of Selected Vendors</td></tr>
<tr><td>Company</td><td>Products</td></tr>
<tr><td>Adobe</td><td>Premiere</td></tr>
<tr><td>AimTech.</td><td>IconAuthor</td></tr>
<tr><td>Computer Friends</td><td>Movie Producer</td></tr>
<tr><td>CoSA</td><td>Egg / PACo Producer</td></tr>
<tr><td>Creative Labs</td><td>Video Blaster</td></tr>
<tr><td>Intel</td><td>ActionMedia II</td></tr>
<tr><td>Jovian Logic</td><td>Olivia</td></tr>
<tr><td>Macromedia</td><td>Authorware Professional, MediaMaker</td></tr>
<tr><td>Mass Microsystems</td><td>ColorSpace IIi</td></tr>
<tr><td>Neil Research Laboratories</td><td>MovieStudio</td></tr>
<tr><td>New Video</td><td>EyeQ</td></tr>
<tr><td>Radius</td><td>VideoVision</td></tr>
<tr><td>RasterOps</td><td>24STV, 24MxTV, 24XLTV, MoviePak, MediaTime</td></tr>
<tr><td>RGB Spectrum</td><td>Videolink 600</td></tr>
<tr><td>SuperMac</td><td>DigitalFilm</td></tr>
<tr><td>VideoLake</td><td>VideoFusion</td></tr>
<tr><td>RasterOps/Truevision</td><td>VideoTime; Bravado</td></tr>
<tr><td>VideoMail</td><td>VMC-2</td></tr>
<tr><td>VideoLogic</td><td>DVA-4000, Mediator</td></tr>
<tr><td>Workstation Technologies</td><td>MoonRaker</td></tr>
</table>

Issues

The dominant issue for this category is that most of the vendors in this market are unaware that their products are being used for video preproduction. Many are marketing their products for the multimedia market; others are making claims about suitability for video postproduction. Those that take notice of this rapidly growing subsegment of the desktop video market have the opportunity to optimize their products for it and emerge as market leaders.

The second key issue is the fact that someday, and someday soon, many of the digital video products will be suitable for at least industrial quality, and perhaps broadcast quality, video postproduction. They will continue to be used in preproduction concept development, but their primary use, and the one for which they will be purchased, will be postproduction.

The high end multimedia packages will face strong pressures from lower-level products adding functionality, and from the digital video products, at least in their application to desktop video preproduction tasks. It is anticipated that the impact of these products on this market segment will decline over the next 2 to 3 years. On the other hand, the digital video products will become more and more important, with hardware having 1 to 2 year life cycles and software having 3 to 5 year lives. The hardware will be replaced by successively higher iterations as the technology grows and matures, but the software will tend to last longer as users are slow to adapt to new features, functions, and user interfaces.

The market remains very fragmented with a number of small vendors. It is likely that some of these manufacturers will choose to merge with competitive or complementary vendors in order to provide a broader product line and more stable organizational structure. Some of these mergers and acquisitions have already occurred, with RasterOps acquiring Truevision, and Avid Technology acquiring DiVA.

Market Shares

As of 1992, this category is dominated by RasterOps, largely because they were out early with powerful high-end digital video solutions in the form of their MediaTime product (bundled with Adobe's Premiere), plus a range of other 24-bit full-motion video cards. These products captured 81.0 percent of the high range concept development tools market in 1992 by themselves; the addition of the MoviePak bundle (also known as Editing Aces) added another 1.4 percent to the market. Although Adobe Premiere was a component in many of these sales, its contribution is not counted here because it was bundled with higher-value products.

The only other significant player in this market segment was Macromedia with Authorware, its top-of-the-line multimedia authoring package. Authorware accounted for 2.7 percent of the 1992 shipments.

Although they did not ship until 1993, and thus did not appear in this breakout, SuperMac sold a large number of its DigitalFilm products (also bundled with Premiere) in early 93. A number of other vendors including Radius also shipped significant quantities of digital video products in 1993. In addition, as of 1992, desktop video was predominantly the domain of the Commodore Amiga and Apple Mac personal computer platforms. Major vendors such as Intel and Truevision, although quite popular in other markets such as graphics development and multimedia, had quite small market shares. Their shares will, no doubt, also grow in the future, and will change the 1993 market share composition significantly.

<table>
<tr><td>Fig. 4-8:</td><td>Concept Development Tools (High Range)
1992 Market Shares</td></tr>
</table>

Company	Share
RasterOps	81.0 %
Macromedia	2.7 %
RasterOps	1.4%
Other	1.4 %
Other	13.5 %

	100.0 %

Highlights of Selected Vendors

Macromedia

The leader of the high-end multimedia authoring packages is Authorware Professional from the Authorware division of Macromedia. It is oriented toward interactive applications, and is therefore overkill for videotape applications, but it offers features similar to those available in low-end products such as Macromedia's Director, so it is used somewhat in animatic storyboard creation. Authorware includes a multimedia database manager, media clips, powerful text manipulation features, graphics drawing and paint tools, stereo sound manipulation tools, animation tools, digital and analog video support, and an extensible environment. Both Mac and Windows versions are available.

SuperMac

In early 1993, SuperMac began shipping DigitalFilm, a high-range digital video system being sold as a video production system. It claims 30 frame-per-second acquisition and retrieval of digitized video at full-screen sizes, albeit with some trickery involved. It is both NTSC and PAL compatible, as well as S-Video compatible, and provides JPEG frame-accurate image compression. Variable compression ratios up to 70:1 are supported. DigitalFilm supports SMPTE time code, 24-bit color, and audio digitization and playback. It supports enhanced keying and optical effects and provides a Postscript-based character generation function. In 1993 the company plans to offer DigitalFilm as components, including DigitalFilm Player, DigitalFilm Recorder, and DigitalFilm Encoder and Breakout Box. Every DigitalFilm system is bundled with Adobe Premiere.

Adobe

SuperMac sold its Reeltime digital video editing software to Adobe Systems in September of 1991, and licensed the product, now known as Premiere, for bundling with its digital video hardware systems. Since then, the two companies have executed several agreements to continue this relationship indefinitely.

Premiere, which began as a $495 editing package with some special effects capabilities, but with a number of limitations, was greatly enhanced in late 1992 with the release of version 2.0. Premiere 2.0 includes support for full-size video screens, improved editing features, chroma keying, rotoscoping, animated titles, SMPTE time code, Edit Decision Lists, and machine control. It also supports several digital audio cards and 24-bit graphics cards. The combination of Premiere 2.0 with suitable digital video hardware is an extremely powerful desktop video preproduction system, and is very close to being the nucleus of a cost-effective postproduction system. Adobe sells Premiere 2.0 for $695 by itself, but it is bundled with digital video hardware from several vendors, including SuperMac and RasterOps.

RasterOps

RasterOps has an entire line of high end graphics boards, including the 24STV, 24XLTV, and the 24MxTV, and the MediaTime board, which adds CD-quality audio to a 24-bit video adapter. The MediaTime board uses Digidesign's AudioMedia chip set to provide stereo, 16-bit, 44.1 kHz audio, plus 640x480 video resolution. The 24xxTV series provide varying ranges of video resolution over that of the MediaTime board, but no audio. All of the boards are compatible with the MoviePak compression adapter, allowing the storage and retrieval of full-motion video. All also are compatible with the Video Expander II, an outboard encoder which converts interlaced RGB signals into NTSC composite, S-Video, and RS-170 RGB signals.

RasterOps provides MoviePak, MediaTime, and the Video Expander II in a $4700 bundle also called Editing Aces.

Others

AimTech offers IconAuthor as a high-end multimedia authoring package available on multiple computer platforms, including UNIX systems and PC/Windows. The PC version was first shipped in 1989.

New Video offers the Eye Q board for $4495 (authoring) as well as a playback only version for $2495. The Eye Q board is a video capture and playback system, similar in many ways to the SuperMac Digital Film product, but offering different compression algorithms with correspondingly different quality levels and capture rates. One of the video compression algorithms employed by the Eye Q product is PLV, which offers superior video quality, but requires an off-line production service to perform on the raw data. The playback-only version of the Eye Q board can then retrieve and output the compressed video files. Eye Q also offers 16-bit audio capture and playback and graphics overlay capabilities.

Project Management Tools

Total Project Management Tools Market

Putting together even the simplest of video productions requires managing multiple people and skills over time. If any one element is not available when needed, that loss will tend to delay the project and increase the cost. Computerized project management systems tend to reduce this risk, as well as providing the ability to monitor progress while a project is underway.

Market Definitions and Overview

Project management software allows the user to define the individual tasks in the production and postproduction schedules and allocate time budgets, as well as to schedule the individual tasks. Products in this category include dedicated video planning tools as well as those generic project management tools (e.g. Microsoft Project) which are used for this purpose.

For purposes of this study, budgeting tools are lumped in with project management tools, since both sets of products are used to plan and control projects, one set from the financial side and one from the scheduling side. Dedicated video budgeting tools are just now becoming available and many video producers are using generic tools such as spreadsheets and accounting/finance packages such as Quicken for this purpose. As dedicated, special purpose, applications become available, more producers will opt for the video-specific applications.

Project management tools constituted 3.1 percent of the total desktop video preproduction market in 1989 and grew to around 7 percent in 1990 and 1991 as the video industry began accepting computer tools into general use. By 1992, the explosive growth of the other subsegments of the preproduction market shrank the product management tools share back to 5.4 percent. This subsegment, while growing in absolute size as the desktop video production market becomes more competitive and producers look to improved methods of tracking and budgeting projects, will shrink relative to the other segments, particularly high range concept development tools, by the end of the decade, ending at 3.9 percent of the preproduction market in 1999.

Revenues and Revenue Growth Rates

Revenues from project management tools sold to the U.S. desktop video preproduction market are shown in Figure 4-9. These products include dedicated project management, scheduling, or budgeting software programs specifically designed for video preproduction, as well as any general purpose project management tools. In 1989, revenues from this market were nearly zero, due to low adoption in the professional video market, but gradually grew to $1.0 million in 1992. A unit of this category consists of a single copy of a software package purchased explicitly for use in video production as a project management tool, including any incremental purchases of general purpose software which are intended primarily for video production use.

Fig. 4-9:	Project Development Tools Unit Shipment and Revenue Forecasts 1989-1999			
Year	Units (000)	Revenues ($M)	Revenue Growth(%)	Unit Growth(%)
1989	0.1	0.0	-	-
1990	1.0	0.3	514.7	547.1
1991	2.2	0.7	115.1	131.3
1992	3.6	1.0	53.0	62.8
1993	5.7	1.6	55.0	59.0
1994	9.2	2.5	59.0	61.4
1995	15.3	4.0	62.8	65.3
1996	26.2	6.8	68.1	71.5
1997	46.2	11.7	72.7	76.4
1998	77.6	19.3	64.5	68.1
1999	121.4	29.4	52.4	56.5
CAGR			*61.9%*	*65.3%*

Revenues arising from sales of project management tools are forecasted for moderate growth over the rest of the decade as professional video producers gradually acclimate to computerization and as new computer-literate producers begin acquiring desktop video systems. This subsegment is the smallest of the three surveyed, accounting for forecasted revenues of $4.0 million in 1995 and rising to $29.4 million in 1999.

Revenue growth rates were 514.7 and 115.1 percent for 1990 and 1991, reflecting the injection of new technology into existing video production businesses. In 1992, revenue growth dropped to 53.0%, and are anticipated to rise gradually to 1997 as more products enter the market and project management tools ride the desktop video surge. After 1997, in a mature market, the revenue growth rates will decline the rest of the decade. Revenue growth is forecast at 62.8 percent for 1995, rising gradually to 72.7 percent in 1997, and declining to 52.4 percent in 1999, resulting in an overall revenue CAGR of 61.9 percent for the period surveyed.

Unit Shipments and Pricing Trends

Unit growth started out very high, in part because of the lack of installed base prior to 1990, but tapered off to 62.8 percent in 1992. The unit growth rate is expected to gradually rise until 1997 and then descend throughout the rest of the decade, ending 1999 at 56.5 percent. The unit CAGR for the period 1992-99 is forecasted at 65.3 percent.

Unit shipments for 1989 were negligible, but 3.6 thousand units were shipped in 1992. 1995 shipments are forecasted at 15.3 thousand and 1999 shipments are expected to reach 121.4 thousand units. A unit is again defined as a single piece of project management software purchased for, or used predominantly for, the process of video preproduction. Project management software includes specific-purpose packages as well as general-purpose spreadsheets, accounting programs, and project managers.

Pricing is anticipated to remain very stable for the survey period. The delta between the unit shipment CAGR of 65.3 percent and the revenue CAGR of 61.9 percent indicates the minimal pricing drop expected for the period. Pricing is expected to remain stable because of the maturity of existing general-purpose tools, which have obtained fairly stable price points, and the pressures these substitute products will put on specific-purpose tools being developed.

Market and Technology Trends

Qualitative Trends

Again, many of the trends already discussed in other sections related to the remainder of preproduction products also apply to project management tools. The key trends, again, are the advent of computerization into non-computerized video development organizations and the integration of multiple functions into a single application. Also expected are groupware applications for project management, allowing key contributors to collaborate on development and tracking of project schedules and budgets.

Perhaps the biggest trend in this area is the increased emphasis on cost and schedule control resulting from increased competition in video development, caused in turn by the economies of desktop video. With this emphasis comes a need for better planning during preproduction, allowing better control during the latter phases, as well as tighter adherence to planned schedules and budgets. The tools in this subsegment are focused directly on this need.

Competitive Analysis / Market Share

Competitive Environment

Though a few products have emerged to provide project management functions for motion pictures and film, the authors are unaware of any which have been developed explicitly for video production. The motion picture products are generally inapplicable for video development, so video producers tend to use generic project management tools, selected for their ease of use and adaptability to the tasks of planning video development.

General purpose packages, including spreadsheets, accounting packages, and project management packages, have been available in the personal computer market for a number of years. These products generally compete on the basis of price/performance; products applicable to desktop video project management fall on the low range of both categories, except in the area of user friendliness. Because of the relative computer illiteracy of the existing video producers, the simplest and easiest to use packages are being used in the video development environment.

As software developers discover the emerging desktop video market, dedicated products will begin to appear for project management. The most obvious, and probably the most acceptable, product category will be templates for existing general purpose spreadsheets. It is also reasonable to expect stripped-down project managers and accounting packages developed specifically for video preproduction, but these products will face significant competition from existing general purpose products.

Structure

Although there are hundreds of applicable general-purpose software packages which could be used for the tasks in desktop video preproduction project management, only a few are actually used. These tend to be the most common spreadsheets and low-end accounting packages.

Fig. 4-10:	Project Management Tools List of Selected Vendors
Borland	Quattro Pro
Computer Associates	Supercalc, Superproject
DacEasy	DacEasy Accounting
Intuit	Quicken
Lotus Development	123
Microsoft	Project, Excel
Pacioli	Pacioli 2000
Screenplay Systems	Movie Magic Budgeting, Scheduling/Breakdown
Software Publishing Corporation	Harvard Project Manager
Symantec	Time Line, On Target

The spreadsheets are available from the big three software vendors of Microsoft, Borland, and Lotus Development, who provide broad ranges of products for the Macintosh and PC-compatible platforms. The low-end accounting packages are from lesser-known vendors such as

Intuit and DacEasy. These vendors tend to specialize in single products or single market niches, i.e., accounting for small businesses.

The more elaborate project managers from Microsoft, Software Publishing Corporation, et. al., and the high end accounting packages have made few inroads into the realm of desktop video, although they may become more common as competitive pressures grow in the preproduction segment. Figure 4-10 provides a partial list of the products and vendors serving this segment.

General purpose software products are sold through computer dealers, mail order, and to a far lesser extent, direct sales to end users. The growing use of these products by the desktop video market participants is not anticipated to affect this structure.

Issues

Product lifecycles in the general purpose tools area are very long mostly because their generality allows application to a number of changing environments. Specific purpose tools developed for desktop video preproduction project management should also have long life cycles as long as enough flexibility is built in to allow the products to adapt to the evolution of the desktop video market.

This market area, project management, is ideal for integration with the remainder of the preproduction functionality. That is, budgets and schedules can be closely tied to shooting scripts and storyboards, which are in turn tied to teleprompters, edit lists, and graphics. An integrated product may evolve which competes with the products in each of these categories by offering a cost effective implementation to all or many of these functions.

A third issue in this area is the fact that creative video development personnel are not currently computer literate (in the main), nor do they have a particular liking for the strictures of schedules and budgets. This, coupled with the lack of video-specific tools, indicates that there will be little correlation initially between budget and schedule plans and actual performance.

Competitive pressures will, however, force better compliance on these creative producers, as well as improve the tools available to them.

Market Shares

Microsoft's Excel dominates this small market with a 47.4% share in 1992, mostly because of its ease of use and applicability on both Macintosh and PC-compatible platforms. Lotus follows with its venerable 123 spreadsheet at 26.9%. Lotus's market share is shrinking as many PC users have switched to the more powerful Excel program for their general purpose spreadsheet work. This switch is also affecting use of these products for desktop video project management.

Over time, it is reasonable to expect the market shares for both Excel and 123 to decline and for new products to emerge for this application.

<table>
<tr><td>Fig 4-11:</td><td colspan="2">Project Management Tools
1992 Market Shares</td></tr>
<tr><td> </td><td></td><td></td></tr>
<tr><td>Company</td><td colspan="2">Share</td></tr>
<tr><td> </td><td></td><td></td></tr>
<tr><td>Microsoft</td><td></td><td>47.4%</td></tr>
<tr><td>Lotus Development</td><td></td><td>26.9%</td></tr>
<tr><td>Others</td><td></td><td>25.7%</td></tr>
<tr><td> </td><td></td><td>-----------</td></tr>
<tr><td> </td><td></td><td>100.0%</td></tr>
</table>

Highlights of Selected Vendors

Lotus

Lotus Development introduced its award-winning spreadsheet, 123, in the early 80's as a competitor to the then-dominant VisiCalc from VisiCorp, as well as Microsoft's Multiplan and several other competitors. It took over the spreadsheet market and brought one of the first major applications to the emerging personal computer market. 123 was originally developed for MS-DOS personal computer platforms only, although versions for Microsoft Windows, UNIX, the Apple Macintosh, and other operating environments exist now. Lotus was slow in developing a graphical user interface for 123, making it appropriate for the Windows and Macintosh markets opening in the latter 80's, thus opening the window (pardon the pun) for Microsoft's Excel.

Microsoft

Excel was developed at a time when Lotus owned the spreadsheet market. Microsoft first created the Mac version and then ported it over to the new Windows environment, where it has now overtaken Lotus 123 as the dominant PC-compatible spreadsheet. Lotus countered with its Mac and Windows versions, but the lead had been lost, and Microsoft remains the dominant player in these markets today. Excel offers a powerful point-and-click graphical user interface, multiple font styles, sizes, and colors, on-line help, data portability with other Windows or Mac applications, and powerful graphing functions. Excel is suitable for rudimentary accounting, "what-if" planning, and even simple project management and database functions. As such, it is used in a number of environments, including desktop video preproduction, as a general purpose tool.

Chapter 5
Forecasts of the U.S. Desktop Video Production Products Market

Market Definitions and Overview

Video production is the process of collecting the raw video footage and field audio, and creating the animated graphics called for by the script generated during the preproduction process. The footage and audio may be collected by traveling to a location, where equipment portability is important, or may be collected in a sound stage, where sound proofing, lighting, and sets are important.

The production segment constituted 25.4 percent of the overall desktop video market in 1989 and dropped the following year to 18.9 percent, due mostly to the rapid growth of the postproduction segment. By 1992, this segment returned to 25.4 percent of the whole and by 1999 is expected to represent 35.2 percent of the $20.4 billion desktop video products market.

The video production segment of the desktop video market is further subdivided into subsegments representing the major product families employed during the production stage of video development. These subsegments are: Video Acquisition Products, Audio Acquisition Products, Lighting Products, and Teleprompters.

Revenues and Revenue Growth Rates

Revenues from the total U.S. desktop video production market are shown in Figure 5-1. Revenues from this market are derived from sales of video acquisition, audio acquisition, lighting, and teleprompting products for use specifically with desktop video systems. Where such products may be sold to multiple markets or for other purposes, only the portion applicable to desktop video production has been counted.

In 1989 production products accounted for $11.8 million in revenues, mostly from sales of cameras and camcorders. In the explosive growth years of desktop video, 1990 through 1992, the revenue growth rate jumped as high as 265.3 percent and ended 1992 at 118.9 percent. 1992 revenues were $183.6 million.

By 1995, production products revenues are anticipated to reach $711.0 million, although revenue growth for the period is forecasted to drop to 61.3 percent. The same trend is expected to hold through the rest of the decade as declining camera, camcorder, and teleprompting prices are expected to reduce the revenue growth to 37.7 percent by the end of 1999, when total revenues produced by the production segment are expected to reach $3.3 billion.

Fig. 5-1:	Total U.S. Market for Production Products Unit Shipment and Revenue Forecasts 1989-1999		
Year	Units (000)	Revenues ($M)	Revenue CAGR(%)
1989	5.4	11.8	----
1990	11.7	23.0	94.0
1991	47.6	83.9	265.3
1992	120.9	183.6	118.9
1993	208.7	275.5	50.1
1994	394.2	440.9	60.0
1995	779.3	711.0	61.3
1996	1413.5	1102.6	55.1
1997	2445.6	1644.6	49.2
1998	4058.4	2365.6	43.8
1999	6472.9	3258.3	37.7
TOTAL			*56.5%*

The explosive growth in 1991 and 1992 was caused predominantly by the emergence of desktop video and the application of expensive broadcast-quality video acquisition products in conjunction with personal computer-based editing systems. The increasing role of nonlinear, digital processes, as discussed fully in Chapters 2 and 6 of this report, allow lower quality video acquisition devices (e.g., camcorders) at correspondingly lower costs. This leads to an anticipated precipitous drop in 1993 in terms of revenue growth as the expensive professional-quality equipment is supplanted by lower-cost industrial quality products, even as the market continues to grow. At the same time, the movement of desktop video out of the professional studio environment into the mass market implies fewer multi-camera installations associated with desktop video systems, thereby having a negative effect on unit growth in 1993, also. As the decade wears on, the revenue and unit growth numbers are anticipated to follow a more normal growth pattern, mirroring the general desktop video market.

Unit Shipments and Pricing Trends

Units of production products are defined as individual hardware products, such as cameras, camcorders, tripods, microphones, or mixers, packages of products intended for a single purpose, e.g. lighting packages, or integrated hardware/software systems in the case of teleprompters. Only those units destined for utilization in productions centered on desktop video products are included in this segment.

1989 shipments were 5400 units, growing to 120,900 by 1992. By 1995, unit shipments are expected to grow to over 779 million and are expected to approach 6.5 million by the end of 1999. Unit shipment growth rates for 1990 and 1991 were 117.4 and 307.0 percent per year, respectively, as desktop video systems became more common and more and more corresponding production products were required to provide input to them. By 1992, the rate had dropped to 154.0 percent and is expected to continue a gradual decline to 59.5 percent by 1999, for a cumulative growth rate of 84.9 percent for the period surveyed.

Pricing for production products is expected to decline substantially over the period surveyed. Average prices in 1989 were $2200, declining at approximately 10 percent per year to $1518 in 1992, due mostly to the technology improvements and competitive environments for professional quality camcorders and audio mixers. Prices are anticipated to accelerate in their decline throughout the remainder of the decade as significant pricing decreases in lighting and teleprompting systems is expected with the advent of new technology. Overall, prices are expected to decline at 15.3 percent for the period, ending 1993 at an average of $503 per unit.

Market and Technology Trends
Trends By Product Type

The production market is broken into four subsegments: video acquisition products (including cameras, camcorders, and ancillary equipment), audio acquisition products (microphones, mixers, and ancillary equipment), lighting products, and teleprompters. In 1989, video acquisition products constituted 51.8 percent, audio acquisition products constituted 38.9

percent, lighting products were 6.0 percent, and teleprompters were 3.2 percent of the total.

These relative percentages are expected to change considerably throughout the period surveyed, with video acquisition products declining relative to the others and audio acquisition products rising. Lighting products and teleprompters are forecasted to maintain small, relatively constant market shares relative to the other categories. Video acquisition products are expected to decline in relative share because of the rapidly declining costs of cameras and camcorders, due in part by improving camera technologies, but mostly from the impact of digital processes on requisite input quality as discussed above and elsewhere in this report. Audio acquisition products are expected to grow because of relatively stable technologies leading to stable pricing at the same time demand for such products is expected to grow rapidly. Lighting and teleprompting equipment segments are expected to maintain (within a few percentage points) their relative shares because anticipated unit growths largely offset any pricing declines in those product areas.

By 1999, video acquisition products are expected to hold 31.2 percent of the production market, audio acquisition products 53.4 percent, lighting 10.2 percent, and teleprompters 5.1 percent. The 1989 production market totaled $11.8 million and grew to $183.6 million by 1992. The market is anticipated to grow to $711.0 million by 1995 and to end the decade at $3.3 billion.

Distribution Trends

Products sold into the production segment of the desktop video market are the least differentiated from those sold to the consumer and professional video markets, so the distribution means will tend to reflect these similarities. The consumer-quality items will be sold direct through magazines and catalogs and through mass-market music and video dealers. The professional-quality items will be sold through professional video dealers, desktop video value added resellers, and professional audio dealers.

There is generally both significant pricing and quality differences between consumer items and professional items. Professional equipment, in the main, will be priced at retail 2 to 20 times more than corresponding consumer equipment. Lower-range professional video and audio equipment, often called "prosumer" or "industrial" quality products, will be most applicable to desktop video environments; therefore, their distribution channels will be most important to the development of the desktop video market, at least until dedicated desktop video channels develop.

As in the preproduction area, companies developing new products specifically focused on the desktop video market will have some difficulty in finding an appropriate channel to direct these items to the end users until the VAR organizations are sufficiently developed. The reason, as explained elsewhere in this report, is the lack of breadth of knowledge in the existing channels for professional audio, professional video, and personal computer equipment of the technologies in the other market areas.

End User Trends

Desktop video's economic effects, mostly seen in the postproduction phase, will result in a lower overall cost of completing video productions, thus spurring more production from existing video developers as well as encouraging projects from new entrants to the market. The increased demand for video productions will translate indirectly into an increased demand for production equipment.

Along with this increased demand for production products will be an increased demand for knowledge in operating these products. Although the technology itself is quite available for the novice, and will become more so over time, the skills required to perform set lighting, camera work, and audio production cannot be purchased off the shelf. The lack of training in these areas among the general public will hamper their efforts to develop satisfactory video presentations. There will be a significant opportunity in the production area for VARs and other independent services suppliers to provide training in video production skills.

Qualitative Trends

The major qualitative trend in the production segment of the desktop video market will be the reduction in size, scope, complexity, and cost of existing systems to meet the demands of the new, untrained entrants to the video production market. Products in all four subsegments will tend to become physically smaller and less complex in order to be more useful in the hands of less technically skilled personnel, much in the way 35mm cameras have done so, opening the high-quality photography market to the general public. The capabilities of the products will increase in order to offset the limited skills of the users and to produce a higher quality output.

The scope of these items will become narrower; for instance, lighting systems will be developed for portability and for a limited range of applications, thus reducing their complexity and cost, but also reducing the bewildering options of professional lighting systems to a more manageable few. As the scope, complexity, and size of these systems decrease, the demand for desktop video production products increases, and more competitors enter the market, the once narrow, insulated, niche video equipment market will incur competitive pressures leading to lower costs.

The second most expensive phase of video development (after postproduction) is the production segment since it requires high capital investment and high personnel costs. Desktop video's impact in this area will be significant since it both lowers capital costs and decreases the number (hence cost) of personnel required to create a video presentation.

From a video acquisition product manufacturer's perspective, desktop video creates a whole new demand for the middle of their product lines, between the consumer quality equipment and broadcast products. In the past, the manufacturers have tried to segment their product offerings between the consumer and broadcast markets by leaving out key professional capabilities on their consumer products. However, since Sony and Matsushita (Panasonic and JVC) have experienced some shrinkage in their broadcast video business, and the demand for lower cost professional production products from the desktop videographers will encourage the adoption of broadcast/professional capabilities on the consumer and prosumer level production tools. This will result in lower costs for improved hardware and a more aggressive introduction schedule than pf a given camcorder's tapes "can play in my VCR", clearly a shot at the popular Hi-8 format and a plug for the VHS family.

As discussed in Chapter 2 of this study, the Hi-8 format exhibits a number of advantages for video acquisition purposes, particularly in portable or small-installation applications as found in desktop video environments. The format is less applicable in postproduction applications such as editing or mastering, but will most likely become the dominant video acquisition media in the desktop video environment, over the Matsushita family and the more expensive Betacam products, because of its acceptable resolution, compact size, playing/recording time, and popularity in the consumer marketplace.

Upgrades

Much of the anticipated growth in the desktop video market will come from consumers who own camcorders and have taken hours of footage. Desiring to catalog and organize this footage, editing it along the way, these consumers will acquire desktop video postproduction systems. Purchases of postproduction systems will whet appetites for better quality cameras and camcorders, thereby driving new sales of video acquisition equipment in the prosumer/industrial quality range.

This trend is already evident. Video Toaster customers, among the earliest desktop video advocates, are regularly upgrading their video acquisition systems as they become familiar with the capabilities of the "Toaster", a postproduction switching system.

Market Shares

As of 1992, Sony held a commanding market share lead in the video acquisition products subsegment of the desktop video production market, primarily via sales of their Hi-8 camcorders, but also from bleedover sales of U-Matic SP, Betacam SP, and even 8mm products into the emerging desktop video environments. Panasonic, the dominant Matsushita trading company, contributed another 15.2 percent market share, followed by JVC at 4.9 percent, mostly through sales of S-VHS cameras and camcorders, but also via sales of limited numbers of VHS, VHS-C, S-VHS-C, and MII products into the desktop video environment. Panasonic, JVC, and Sony also sell a range of video monitors which supplement the sales of their camera equipment.

Mitsubishi, the only other competitor in this market with a greater than one percent share, is known mostly for its video monitors. Well recognized in the computer products market as a video monitor vendor, Mitsubishi commands a smaller portion of the composite/component monitor market suitable for video acquisition uses. In 1992, Mitsubishi garnered 1.8 percent of the video acquisition products market.

The remaining manufacturers in the video acquisition products category collectively acquired 29.8 percent of the market in 1992. None garnered more than one percent.

Fig. 5-5:   1992 Market Shares
                Video Acquisition Products

Company	Share
Sony Corporation	48.3%
Panasonic	15.2%
JVC Corporation	4.9%
Mitsubishi Corporation	1.8%
Others	29.8%

TOTAL	100.0%

Highlights of Selected Vendors

Sony

The Sony Corporation, one of Japan's industrial giants with annual sales approaching $30 billion per year, is a leading supplier in several segments of the desktop video market. Most of the products manufactured by Sony and applicable to desktop video environments are the responsibility of the Business and Professional Group, headquartered in Montvale, NJ, and one of the three major divisions of Sony's U.S.A operation, the Sony Corporation of America. The avowed charter of this division of the Sony Corporation is to "meet the business communication needs of the broadcast and production industry, corporate America, and the government, education, and medical markets." [source: Sony corporate backgrounder]

Sony B&PG sells directly to end users and via a network of authorized resellers, typically of the professional video dealer variety. Some of these resellers utilize mail order sales, but most sell directly to their chosen markets, the professional video developers in network and independent video production studios.

Sony produces a number of professional- and consumer-quality products oriented toward the video development market. These include cameras, camcorders, and video monitors, as well as editing systems, audio equipment, color printers, machine control products, VTRs, and a broad range of other products. Video acquisition products include the EVO-150TR and EVW-300 Hi-8 camcorders, the PVM-1340, -1341, and -1344Q 13" video monitors, and the GVM-2020 20" multiscan video monitor. Sony offers a broad range of products compatible with their 8mm, Hi-8, Betamax, Betacam SP, and U-Matic SP formats, as well as equipment for the VHS family of formats. Sony offers color monitors in sizes from 5" to 34".

Panasonic

Panasonic is actually several organizations, each of which is a 100 percent-owned subsidiary of the giant Japanese conglomerate Matsushita, or more properly the Matsushita Electric Industrial Company. Matsushita, which also owns controlling interest in the Victor Corporation, the parent of the JVC brand, reported sales in excess of $45 billion for 1992. The several divisions of Panasonic serve as trading organizations for Matsushita with the Panasonic Broadcast and Television Systems Company responsible for video acquisition products.

Panasonic and Sony compete head to head in a number of product areas, including cameras, camcorders, and video monitors, plus audio equipment, videodisc equipment, VTRs, editing equipment, video projection systems, machine control products, and consumer audio and video products. Another division of Panasonic produces and markets computer equipment, including laptop personal computers, printers, and computer monitors.

Panasonic's video acquisition solutions include the AG-3 3-CCD S-VHS-C camcorder, the AG-460 2-CCD S-VHS camcorder, the BT-S1360Y and BT-S1370Y 13" color video monitors, and the DT-2700MS 27" multiscan color video monitor. Panasonic offers VHS, VHS-C, S-VHS, S-VHS-C, MII, and D3 formatted video acquisition products, as well as recording and playback systems.

JVC

JVC is a group of subsidiaries of the Victor Company of Japan, which is in turn owned primarily by Matsushita Electric Industries of Kabota, Osaka, Japan. Matsushita is a giant conglomerate and also is the parent organization of the various Panasonic trading companies also known for both desktop video and conventional video systems. JVC, in the guise of the JVC Professional Products Company, produces a broad range of audio and video equipment at both consumer and professional quality levels, including video acquisition products such as cameras, camcorders, and video monitors. Other JVC products include video editing equipment, audio products, and consumer quality televisions, VCRs, camcorders, and audio systems.

JVC's desktop video products include the KY-25U, a professional quality 3-CCD color camera and the GY-X1TCUL 14, a 3-CCD S-VHS-C camcorder. The BY-10U series is a single-CCD camera, offering over 450 lines of resolution, and mating capability with a VTR docking unit, the BR-S411U. JVC also offers a broad range of color and black and white video monitors, including the TM-R14U 14" monitor with composite inputs, the TM-1400SU 14" color monitor with S-Video inputs, the VM-R190SU 19" color monitor, a series of 9" and 13" monitors, and a line of monitor/receivers.

Mitsubishi

The Mitsubishi Professional Electronics Division of Mitsubishi America, a fully owned subsidiary of the Japanese industrial conglomerate Mitsubishi Electric Corporation, is responsible for producing and marketing the video acquisition products under the Mitsubishi brand name. Unlike its competitors Sony and Matsushita, Mitsubishi is not focused solely on electronic products and systems, choosing instead to offer products for a number of markets, including automobiles, trucks, airplanes, and industrial machinery, among others.

Mitsubishi Professional Electronics is particularly known for wide screen televisions and video monitors. Their DiamondScan products are among the most popular wide screen systems in the world and include the AM-2751A and AM-2752A 27" multiscanning monitors, the AM-3151A 31" and AM-3501R 35" multiscanning video monitors, and the AM-1480 and AM-1490 14" monitors. Mitsubishi also offers a line of color video printers, editing VTRs, video projection systems, consumer audio equipment, and a line of small and large-screen monitor/receivers.

Cinema Products

Cinema Products Corporation of Los Angeles, California offers the Steadicam series of mechanical camera stabilization equipment, which has quickly become the standard for portable image stabilization. Steadicam products have earned both Emmy and Oscar awards for their technical contributions to the professional film and video industry.

Cinema Products offers a line of Steadicam products, from the low-end ($499) Steadicam JR, to the larger Steadicam SK ($12,500), to the high-end Steadicam EFP ($26,000). All utilize a unique battery-powered gyroscopic and pendulum-based mechanical stabilization system to remove the sway and jitter common in handheld, portable camera applications. Most desktop video environments will be based on lightweight camcorders, which are suitable for use with the Steadicam JR product. Heavier camcorders and cameras will require the EFP or SK models.

Others

Prime Image, of Saratoga, CA is a leader in standalone and board-based Time Base Correctors, offering over 25 models ranging in price from $1000 to $12,000. Digital Processing

Systems, of Scarborough, Ontario, Canada, offers a series of ISA-compatible option boards which provide vectorscope, waveform monitor, and TBC functions. The VT-2500 is a card-based TBC supporting either S-Video or composite inputs. The VM-2000 is a digital waveform monitor and vectorscope pattern generator which accepts composite video waveforms and displays it on a PC monitor over a blank background or any input video program. Tektronix, the instrumentation and graphics workstation organization out of Beaverton, Oregon, offers the 1740A, 1750A, and 1760 series of analog waveform/vector monitors. These units can either be configured as tabletop instruments or mounted in a standard rack. They start from about $4200 and range upwards of $7000, depending on capabilities. Tektronix also supplies test signal generators. Magni, another Oregon organization, offers a rackmounted chassis containing waveform monitor and vectorscope circuitry which utilizes a separate NTSC video monitor. It lists for about $1500.

Audio Acquisition Products

Total Audio Acquisition Products Market

Market Definitions and Overview

Audio Acquisition Products are those elements necessary for acquiring live audio for integration with video, specifically in those productions developed using desktop video systems. These products are identical to those in the professional musical instruments market; only the items specifically used in desktop video productions are counted for purposes of this study. In 1989, Audio Acquisition Products accounted for 38.9 percent of the total video production products revenues. This relative share dropped slightly the next two years as the Lighting Products subsegment experienced a spurt of growth, then grew back to 39.8 percent by 1992. The audio acquisition products segment is forecasted to grow at a slightly increasing rate for the rest of the decade, reaching 53.4 percent of the overall $3.3 billion desktop video production products market by 1999.

Microphones & Accessories

Audio for desktop video will tend to be acquired directly into the camcorder or VTR record deck in the case of separate camera/deck setups. There will usually not be a separate audio deck. The audio quality of most camcorder microphones does not meet most professional standards, so most higher-quality desktop video productions will employ additional microphones. Smaller desktop video installations will employ only a single microphone for voiceover work; larger installations will utilize multiple microphones, at time simultaneously, for different applications.

Lavalier mics are the most common for desktop video situations employing "talking heads", or on-screen commentators. Lavalier mics are small, lapel-mounted, condenser microphones which do not interfere with a scene's visuals. "Lav" mics are not appropriate for all applications as they tend to pick up noise from clothing movement and are usually visible, as opposed to boom mics and shotgun mics.

Boom mics will be employed on some of the more sophisticated sets. Boom mics are sensitive area mics which are physically lowered to a point just above camera view in a scene via a long pole called a boom. Boom mics are suitable to pick up sounds from one or more people in a tight location and where it is not desirable to see the microphone.

Shotgun and parabolic microphones are used to pick up sounds from long distances, again typically out of camera view. Shotgun mics have tighter pickup patterns, allowing the user to focus in on individual sound sources from as far away as 50 yards. Parabolic microphones utilize the same principle as the human ear, the reflecting telescope, and the satellite receiver. They employ a parabolic dish to focus sounds from a particular direction into a sensitive pickup. Parabolic mics are common for sporting event applications and nature shots.

More common in desktop video will be handheld and stand-mounted professional vocal microphones. These come in two major categories: ones intended for handheld applications such as singing, and the more delicate, fixed position microphones intended for professional voiceover and other recording work in studio applications. Professional quality vocal microphones are available in the $100 to $400 dollar range; studio microphones are as much as ten times those figures.

All microphones can be connected back to signal processing equipment such as mixers via either cables or wireless connections. Cable connections are far more common and less expensive, but wireless connections are becoming more common where mobility is a major concern.

There are also a number of accessories common in use with microphones. The first of these are the items used to control wind noise, either from natural sources or from human breath. These are called windscreens or pop filters and tend to be fairly inexpensive. Microphones also require mounting apparatus, including shock mounts, fixed mounts, hand booms, stand booms, and mic stands, in all applications except handheld (such as Electronic News Gathering) or body-mounted (e.g. lavalier). Direct connected microphones and/or wireless receivers must be connected to recording equipment or mixers via suitable cabling, and in some cases preamplifier circuitry or impedance matching transformers. The sum total of all accessories required for each microphone installation will typically require between $50 and $200.

Mixers

Mixers are electronic devices which provide a variety of functions beyond the mere mixing of audio signals. First, they provide a means of interconnecting several different inputs to several different outputs. Second, they provide a means of adjusting the absolute level of each input signal and each (typically) output signal. Third, they provide a preamplification function, matching microphone signal levels to standard audio "line" levels. Fourth, they typically provide a metering function for input and/or output audio levels, helping to prevent audio distortion or inadequate signal levels. Fifth, they provide headphone output amplification. Sixth, they provide at least some level of frequency equalization, or tone control. Other features are also available.

Mixers vary in terms of quality, as measured by signal/noise ratio and other technical factors, as well as number of input channels, number of output channels, and channel functions. Most small desktop video applications will require a 4-6 input mixer providing at least two output channels (for speakers and for the recording device). Tone control is desirable in most applications in order to optimize the frequency response of the microphone and room to the audio information being recorded.

In desktop video applications, the interconnection and preamplification functions are key. Although some desktop video users will not use a separate external mixer, but will rely instead on switching cables for interconnections and on separate preamplifiers for line level matching. They will then utilize digital audio software to provide the mixing, equalization, and gain control functions. At the present time, this software is not entirely adaptable to production mixing, and the interconnection and preamplification functions alone make an external mixer worthwhile for desktop video suites.

Revenues and Revenue Growth Rates

Revenues from audio acquisition products in 1989 totaled only $0.6 million, again due to the extreme youth of the desktop video market. As in many other segments of the desktop video market, revenue growth rates for 1990 through 1992 neared or exceeded 100 percent, reaching a high of 273.0 percent in 1991. Total revenues for 1992 reached $11.3 million in 1992 as the initial surge of these products into the desktop video market began to subside somewhat.

Revenue growth is expected to remain strong throughout the period surveyed, due mostly to fairly stable pricing (audio acquisition products are also components of the vastly older and more stable professional audio and musical equipment markets) and the strong growth of desktop video. In a manner similar to video acquisition products profiled in the preceding section of this report, revenue growth is anticipated to drop off rapidly in 1993 after the initial surge, then rise gradually to a peak in 1995, and then decline gradually for the rest of the decade. Revenue CAGR for the period is anticipated at 77.7 percent. The reason for the anticipated slump in 1993 is the movement of desktop video from the early adopters in the professional studio environments, where multiple microphone and complex mixing arrangements are common, to the home and small production studio environments with simpler setups. The performance of revenue growth for this subset is then expected to mirror the overall growth of the desktop video market for the rest of the decade.

1995 revenues of audio acquisition products are anticipated to reach $82.5 million. Revenues are anticipated to continue to grow throughout the remainder of the decade and close 1999 at $632.8 million.

Fig. 5-6:   Audio Acquisition Products
              Unit Shipment and Revenue Forecasts 1989-1999

Year	Units (000)	Revenues ($M)	Revenue Growth(%)	Unit Growth(%)
1989	2.1	0.6	----	----
1990	4.3	1.1	93.0	106.4
1991	17.1	4.3	273.0	296.8
1992	48.1	11.3	165.0	180.4
1993	87.1	19.4	72.1	81.2
1994	181.6	38.7	99.1	108.5
1995	403.0	82.5	113.0	121.9
1996	751.3	148.4	79.9	86.4
1997	1309.5	250.9	69.1	74.3
1998	2165.9	404.6	61.3	65.4
1999	3456.7	632.8	56.4	59.6
TOTAL			77.7%	84.2%

Unit Shipments and Pricing Trends

Units of audio acquisition products are single hardware items. Only those utilized in desktop video applications are counted in this segment.

Unit growth largely mirrors revenue growth in the audio acquisition products subsegment because of the stability of pricing. Prices are anticipated to remain stable for several reasons.

First, the same products used in this segment are used in greater quantity in the professional audio and musical products markets. Second, microphone technology is nearly 100 years old and few truly significant innovations have occurred in the last 20 years. Third, the vendors of microphone products are large, established firms with quality products, discouraging new competitors in the markets they serve. Fourth, mixers are currently priced about as low as economically possible given current technologies. To improve the pricing further will require a revolutionary leap in technology not anticipated at this time.

Unit growth began the period surveyed at 106.4 percent in 1990 and ended 1992 at 180.4 percent, reflecting shipments of 48,100 units. By 1995, shipments are anticipated to reach 403,000 units and shipment growth is expected to rise to a peak of 121.9 percent, following the expected slump in 1993 and slight recovery in 1994. By 1999, shipments are expected to exceed 3.4 million units and the growth rate is anticipated to drop to 59.6 percent, approximating the revenue growth rate at the time. Overall unit shipment CAGR is forecasted at 84.2 percent, only slightly higher than the 77.7 percent forecasted for revenues.

The slight difference between the unit growth rate and the revenue growth rate for every year in the survey period indicates a lack of dramatic pricing changes expected. Audio acquisition technology is relatively stable, and pricing is driven predominantly by other markets, so pricing is anticipated to remain stable throughout the period, thereby allowing unit shipment changes to map directly into revenue changes.

Market and Technology Trends
Qualitative Trends

Mixers

In this study mixers are listed in the production segment of the market. In reality, audio mixing is employed in both the production and postproduction phase. In the era of desktop video, the audio mixing function is typically performed by software and digital signal processing hardware in a pure digital format, whereas production audio mixing remains analog only. It is reasonable to expect that the trend to all-digital mixing will move into the production phase like it has in the postproduction phase.

In the meanwhile, desktop video will continue to rely on all-analog mixing during production. These audio mixers will continue to increase in quality and functionality while decreasing in price and size. Functions available today via external effects devices, including compression, limiting, echo, reverb, and improved equalization, will become more common in low-cost, small, multichannel mixers.

Recording Environments

The increasing use of desktop video systems will entail that most voiceover tracks will be developed outside of conventional studios with their soundproof recording rooms. Given that most home and office environments have noise levels unsuitable to high-quality recording, there will be an increasing demand for suitable audio recording space. This demand will most likely be filled, not by renters of studio time, but by products providers who solve the ambient noise problem in normal environments. Portable sound booths, active noise damping systems, voiceover helmets, etc. are possible responses to this problem.

Several vendors already produce portable recording and/or musical practice booths. Some postproduction systems employing digital audio editing techniques allow digital signal processing techniques to help eliminate or reduce intermittent or constant noise recorded during production. It is far better to prevent (An ounce of prevention ...) noise from getting recorded that to try to correct it in postproduction (...a pound of cure.), despite the improving capabilities of these digital audio editing products.

Competitive Analysis / Market Share
Competitive Environment

The audio acquisition products submarket, unlike the its video counterpart, is not controlled by a small group of manufacturers. Instead, each specific product area within the submarket has a medium-sized set of preeminent suppliers, often very well established, who compete with specific products for specific applications. Some of these suppliers provide products in several product areas; others focus only on a single area.

Structure

The direct-connect microphone market is very stable with established manufacturers providing a wide range of products. Vendors serving the professional end of the spectrum include Shure Brothers, Electro-Voice, Sennheiser, Beyer Dynamic, Sony, AKG, and AudioTechnica. It will be very difficult for any new manufacturers to break into this established market.

Fig. 5-7:   List of Selected Vendors
                Audio Acquisition Products

Company	Product Lines
Acoustical Solutions	portable audio booths
ADA	signal processing equipment
AKG Acoustics	mics, accessories
Alesis	mixers, signal processing equipment
Aphex Systems	signal processing equipment
ART	signal processing equipment, mixers
Atlas/Soundolier	accessories
Audio Logic	signal processing equipment
Audio Technica	mics, mixers, accessories
Azden	mics, accessories
Beyer Dynamic	mics, accessories
Boss	mixers, signal processing equipment
Carvin	mics, mixers, accessories
Comprehensive Video Supply	mics, mixers, accessories
Conquest Sound	accessories
Countryman Associates	mics
Crown International	mics, accessories
dbx	signal processing equipment
Digitech	signal processing equipment
DOD	mixers, signal processing equipment
Dolby Labs	signal processing equipment
Drawmer	signal processing equipment
Electro-Voice	mics, mixers, accessories
Fostex	mixers, signal processing equipment
Furman	signal processing equipment
JVC	mixers, accessories
Klark-Teknik	signal processing equipment
Lexicon	signal processing equipment
Mackie Designs	mixers
Nady Systems	mics, wireless mics, accessories
Orban	signal processing equipment
Panasonic	mics, mixers, accessories
Peavey	mics, mixers, accessories

Quik-Lok	accessories
Ramsa	mixers, accessories
Rane	signal processing equipment
Raxxess	accessories
Roland Corporation USA	mixers, signal processing equipment
Ross Systems	mixers
Samson Technologies	mics, accessories
Sennheiser Electric Corp.	mics, accessories
Shure	mics, mixers, accessories
Sony	mics, accessories, mixers, signal processing equipment
Soundcraft	mixers
Soundtech	mixers
Symetrix	signal processing equipment
Tascam	mixers
Technical Necessities	accessories
Ultimate	accessories
Urei	signal processing equipment
Vega	mics, wireless mics, accessories
Yamaha	mics, mixers, accessories, signal processing equipment
Zoom	signal processing equipment

The wireless microphone market is a different situation. The technology allowing low-cost, radio-frequency microphone and instrument connections is fairly new, and the market includes most of the traditional microphone manufacturers, plus newcomers like Nady, Samson, and Azden. It will be easier for new manufacturers to break into this subsegment of the microphone market than in the more traditional direct-connect market.

The professional-quality, as opposed to the consumer products available from sources like Radio Shack, mixer market has been divided for years into two major segments: 4-8 input, low-cost, powered mixers used for sound reinforcement and expensive, 8-64 input "studio" mixers. The increasing componentization of the professional musical instrument business and the growth of the electronic keyboard segment of that business have led to the development of a middle range of products ideal for desktop video applications. They are 4 to 16 input, unpowered, medium-featured, low-cost mixing boards. The makers of these products tend to be musical products specialty manufacturers like DOD, Alesis, Mackie Designs, Roland, and Fostex, in addition to larger and more established firms like Shure, Electro-Voice, Sony, Panasonic, and Tascam.

Other companies specialize in accessories such as wind screens, cables, pop filters, transformers, preamplifiers, and the like. Still others specialize in electronic equipment which processes audio signals by removing noise, compressing or limiting, providing equalization, adding reverb or echo, or other functions. In total, there are perhaps 100 companies who offer audio acquisition products suitable for use with desktop video systems. A selected list of these organizations is shown in Figure 5-6.

Issues
Microphone Selection

Desktop video microphones are differentiated on the bases of quality, pickup pattern, application , pickup pattern, and cost (typically a function of quality).

Quality has both subjective and objective components: the subjective component is reflective of the construction and durability of the product, the objective is a function of the frequency response and sensitivity of the product. Microphones have two construction elements: case composition, element mounting, and element type. The microphone element can be one of several different types, each with different sonic and durability characteristics.

The pickup pattern is a geometrical representation of the microphone's response to sonic events in its proximity. Some respond only to sounds from a single direction (unidirectional) and others respond to events from all directions (omnidirectional), without discrimination. Pickup patterns of specific types (cardoid, supercardoid, hypercardoid, figure 8, etc.) are available in different microphones, each appropriate for different acquisition applications.

Microphones are often tailored for specific applications and perform best when matched for their designed applications. Live vocal microphones, the most common variety, are typically general purpose, rugged, lightweight, dynamic element microphones suitable for stand or boom mounting. Instrument amplification microphones vary according to the characteristics of the instruments being amplified and may resemble either live vocal mics or studio vocal mics. Studio vocal mics are typically less rugged, more sensitive, larger, heavier, and more expensive than live vocal mics.

Clip-on lavalier mics are used for interviews and other "talking head" applications. They are usually very lightweight, offer moderate quality and durability, and utilize condenser elements. Shotgun and parabolic mics are used in applications where it is important to detect, amplify, and record sonic information from a distance. They tend to be expensive, large, moderately rugged, and very sensitive. Wireless microphones are typically live vocal or lavalier microphones with attached FM radio transmitters, coupled to an appropriate receiver unit, which is in turn connected to the recording or sound reinforcement system. Wireless mics are typically used when the application is for amplifying sounds from rapidly moving subjects, such as rock musicians or aerobics instructors.

Cost, the final element of microphone selection, is predominantly a component of the other elements. Some "name" manufacturers are able to demand higher prices for their products than those of competing, equivalent, but less well known suppliers.

Mixer Selection

Desktop video mixers are differentiated mainly on cost, although some basic features are required and others are desirable. Required features include 4-8 inputs with independent gain controls, microphone preamplification for 2 channels, headphone amplification, and output level monitors. Many of these features are capable of being integrated in digital audio products, and have been done so. Some users will opt for the software-based mixers along with some outboard interconnection and preamplification devices instead of the hardware-based products.

Mergers, Acquisitions, and Cooperation

Several of the key competitors in the audio acquisition products subsegment are in fact subsidiaries of larger organizations. Electro-Voice, one of the oldest and most established vendors in this segment, is a subsidiary of the Mark IV Corporation, owner of several other sound products providers, including Vega and Altec-Lansing. Sony is, of course, a very diversified organization with products in multiple segments of the desktop video market, as is Panasonic. Panasonic also owns Ramsa and uses that brand name to market professional-quality audio acquisition systems and speakers.

Sennheiser and Neumann, two smaller but well respected microphone manufacturers have combined U.S. operations in Old Lyme, Connecticut. Likewise, JBL, Urei, Seck, and Soundcraft are part of the same organization out of Northridge, California, which is in turned owned by Harman International, who also owns DOD Electronics, who in turn owns DigiTech. Soundcraft makes and markets mixers, DOD makes signal processing equipment and small mixers, and the other two organizations focus mainly on audio reproduction, covered in Chapter

6 under Audio Systems. AKG Acoustics, another smaller microphone manufacturer, also owns dbx, a leading noise reduction products manufacturer.

Market Shares

Market shares for audio acquisition products are shown in Figure 5-7. Shure has captured the largest share of the desktop video audio acquisition market via its broad product line and excellent distribution, including video dealers, music stores, electronics ships, and mail order. Electro-Voice follows close behind, for many of the same reasons. Both companies produce a range of direct-connected and wireless microphones, from consumer-quality to studio-quality, including shotgun, lavalier, condenser, and dynamic varieties, as well as small mixers and various microphone accessories. Electro-Voice also manufactures speakers and speaker components. Shure is better known in the professional music industry and Electro-Voice is more recognized in the Electronic News Gathering environment. Their visibility in these environments and with these product lines have led directly to their leading positions in the desktop video market, with 19.7 percent and 14.8 percent shares, respectively.

Two other microphone manufacturers, AKG Acoustics and Sennheiser, have also claimed respectable stakes in the desktop video audio acquisition subsegment. Both have a high-quality line of microphones in addition to a line of professional-quality headphones. AKG has garnered 4.9 percent of the audio acquisition products market, followed closely by Sennheiser at 3.5%.

The remaining three competitors who gathered more than 1 percent of the audio acquisition products market as of 1992 did so because of their mixers. Mackie Designs, a small company out of Washington, holds the largest share at 3.1 percent. Tascam and Yamaha, two larger and more established organizations, follow with 2.3 percent and 1.6 percent, respectively. Tascam is better known for its recording equipment, such as 4- and 8-track analog audio recorders and DAT tape recorders. Yamaha is a conglomerate known best for its motorcycles, grand pianos, synthesizers, and other products. All three organizations also make very fine, small audio mixers. Mackie's are particularly suited for desktop video because of their configurations and low prices.

The remaining vendors in the audio acquisition products market split the remaining 50.1 percent of the market with no vendor acquiring more than 1 percent.

Fig. 5-8:   1992 Market Shares
Audio Acquisition Products

Shure	19.7%
Electro-Voice	14.8%
AKG	4.9%
Sennheiser	3.5%
Mackie Designs	3.1%
Tascam	2.3%
Yamaha	1.6%
Others	50.1%

TOTAL	100.0%

Highlights of Selected Vendors
Shure

Shure Brothers, Inc., of Evanston, Illinois, is the world's best known microphone manufacturer. They produce a broad line of mics, mixers, and microphone accessories including both cable-connected and wireless products and powered and unpowered mixers. Shure mics include the SM57 and SM58 dynamic stage microphones, two of the most popular microphone designs ever produced, the Beta 57 and Beta 58 enhanced models, the SM7 studio mic, the SM81 and SM87 condenser mics, lav mics, low profile mics, stereo mics, area mics, and shotgun mics.

Shure offers a line of powered and unpowered audio mixers for audio acquisition, ENG, and other field applications. Most are not equipped with equalization controls and other advanced features. Shure's line includes the FP31 and FP32 3-channel mixers and the FP410 automatic 4-input mixer.

Electro-Voice

Electro-Voice Corporation, a subsidiary of the Mark IV corporation and headquartered in Buchanan, Michigan, has been in business for over sixty years and produces a broad range of audio products including some of the world's most popular microphones. The 635A, RE-10, RE-11, RE-15, and RE-50 mics are popular in Electronic News Gathering Applications. The RE20 and RE27N/D mics are common in recording studios and radio stations. The N/D series, including the N/D857B, are popular stage microphones for live vocal applications. Electro-Voice also manufacturers a broad range of other microphones, including dynamic and condenser live vocal and studio mics, podium and lavalier mics, shotgun mics, and wireless mics.

Electro-Voice also manufacturers the BK-42 series of 8- to 24-channel audio mixers, a line of graphic equalizers, and a line of powered mixers for live stage applications. EV is also known for its speaker systems, ranging from small studio monitors and speaker components up to large sound reinforcement speakers. EV also manufacturers a line of accessories for its speaker systems, mixers, and microphones.

Electro-Voice utilizes a series of regional representative firms to market its products direct to end users and through a series of audio and video dealers.

AKG and Sennheiser

AKG Acoustics, of San Leandro, California and Sennheiser Electric Corporation, of Old Lyme, Connecticut are the next most popular manufacturers of microphones for desktop video applications and for professional live vocal applications in musical environments. Both companies also manufacture lines of headphones used by recording engineers worldwide to ensure proper audio mixes. The AKG C414B-ULS is a popular studio vocal microphone and the AKG D112 is a common microphone used for stage miking of bass drums and other bassy instruments. Its C-460B, C-451E, C-568EB, and D-310 are also popular models for different applications. AKG manufactures a broad range of microphones including headset mics, condenser handheld mics, lav mics, and dynamic stage mics. AKG also owns dbx, a leading manufacturer of noise reduction systems, also used in desktop video applications.

Sennheiser's parent organization is located in (West) Germany and has been manufacturing top quality audio products since 1945. Sennheiser is best known for the venerable MD421 ($469) dynamic microphone equally suited to stage and studio applications. Its other products include the MD422 and MD441, the MKH series of studio mics, the MKE4032, and the MD5xx series of stage microphones, and the EK line of wireless mics.

Both companies also manufacture and market accessories for their microphone and headset products.

Mackie Designs

Mackie, a four year old Seattle-area firm, has taken the low-end mixer market by storm. At recent audio/video trade shows Mackie units have been more prevalent in the booths of other manufacturers than any other line of mixers. Bands and other live audio users have adopted Mackie's low-cost, feature-rich, compact, and high-quality products, as have desktop video producers, home audio studios, and even professional recording studios.

Mackie's flagship product, the CR-1604, is a 16-channel stereo mixer with professional features at a very reasonable price ($1099). Although the CR-1604, and the larger LM-3204, are probably excessive for desktop video applications, the smaller Microseries 1202 is not. This 8-channel (4 mono, 4 stereo) stereo mixer is ideal for desktop video applications, offering balanced and unbalanced inputs, tape monitors, effects sends and returns, level monitoring, headphone amplification, stereo panning, equalization, phantom power, +4db signal levels, and a host of other professional features in a unit available for under $400. All Mackie products are built to withstand physical abuse, electromagnetic interference, and "hot" input signals.

Mackie also offers a line of accessories including mixer mixers (mixer expansion & combination units), cabling, remote fader units, and MIDI automation units.

Tascam and Yamaha

Tascam, of Montebello, California, is a division of TEAC America Inc., itself an American subsidiary of a Japanese conglomerate. Yamaha's Professional Audio Division, also in Southern California (Buena Park), is a division of Yamaha Corporation of America, the American subsidiary of the Japanese giant Yamaha Corporation, better known for making motorcycles, snowmobiles, grand pianos, saxophones, synthesizers, and a broad range of other products. Tascam and TEAC are better known as manufacturers and marketers of audio recording systems, including DAT tape decks.

The two organizations are also leading small, professional-quality mixer manufacturers. The Tascam M108 is a 8-channel rack-mountable mixer, as is the more capable M1508. The MM-1, M1516, M2516, and M2524 are larger units beyond the scope of most desktop video applications. Yamaha's MC802, MC1202, and MC1204II mixers are all appropriate for desktop video use. Yamaha also makes the larger MC1602, MC1604II, MC2404II, MC3204II, PM1800A series, and PM1200 series of professional mixers for larger studio applications.

Yamaha also makes a line of signal processing equipment including the SPX1000 and SPX900 digital multi-effect processors, the REV5 reverb unit, the Q2031A stereo equalizer, and

the GC-2020BII stereo compressor/limiter. It also manufactures a line of low-range
microphones appropriate for live audio acquisition purposes.   Tascam also makes a line of
audio patch panels.

Lighting Products

Total Lighting Products Market

Market Definitions and Overview

Lighting Products include both stationary and portable lighting systems intended to
provide illumination for desktop video productions. Units are only counted for the incremental
sales arising for desktop video applications. Lighting Products represented 6.0 percent of the
total video production products revenues in 1989. This percentage grew to 11.2 percent in 1992
as the growing ranks of desktop video devotees discovered the impact of poor lighting on their
fledgling efforts. The relative share is forecasted to peak in 1993 and then begin a slight decline
through the rest of the decade, ending 1999 at 10.2 percent of the whole production market. The
reason for the relative decline is that some lighting systems are anticipated to be shared by
multiple desktop video systems in larger studios as desktop video continues to invade
conventional video suites.

Lighting systems employed for desktop video purposes will take several forms:

Stationary Lighting Kits

By far the most common form of lighting in conventional video applications are the
stationary lights employed on sound stages. These systems range in total cost from $5000 to
over $100,000 and are typically hardwired to the studio's electrical system. The lighting includes
individual spot and fill lights, gels and gel holders, barn doors, stands or mounts, and reflective
or diffusive screens.

In desktop video, these stationary lighting kits will be utilized in production facilities
which convert from conventional video systems to the computer-based desktop video systems.
Most corporate or home desktop video users will not employ stationary lighting, but will rely on
the less costly, and more flexible, portable lighting kits.

Larger desktop video installations, typically those who convert over from conventional technologies, will continue to rely on the larger fixed lighting installations. It is anticipated that these larger installations will grow in relative percentage as the desktop video market grows.

Portable Lighting Kits

Still photographers were the first users of portable lighting kits. They were followed by film and video developers working "on location", where lighting could be expected to be less than optimal for video acquisition. These portable kits consisted of stands and tripods, spot and fill lights, diffusers and umbrella reflectors, as well as gels and gel holders, all designed to improve the ambient lighting conditions of the shooting location, eliminating or softening shadows and highlighting the on-screen talent.

Desktop video users will be key consumers of portable lighting kits. The kits are relatively lightweight and compact, provide the majority of basic lighting functions, are relatively inexpensive, and use standard electric outlets for power. They are not sufficient for broadcast studio effects, but most desktop video productions will not require that level of quality, anyway. They are sufficient, and necessary, to elevate desktop video productions from the quality range (re lighting, anyway) of home videos to that acceptable to the majority of commercial and other non-broadcast uses for which desktop video is appropriate.

Accessories

Lights, themselves are only components of a lighting kit. A kit will typically consist of a number of different light assemblies, consisting of lamps of various power levels, lenses to gather and focus the light produced by the lamp, and enclosures for the lamps and lenses, as well as to attach gel holders and barn door assemblies.

Gels are colored pieces of plastic which are placed in a lamp's beam, thereby coloring the light produced. Gel holders hold the gels in place on the light assembly. Barn doors are mechanical devices constructed to limit the horizontal and vertical spread of the light produced by a given assembly.

Each light assembly must be physically mounted and directed toward a scene. The mounts are usually fixed tripod assemblies, although they may be movable in studios.

Diffusers are translucent screens which are placed in a light beam in order to diffuse the light produced, thereby creating a "softer", less-direct light on the subject. Reflectors, such as umbrellas, often accomplish the same purpose or direct light into shadows such that harsh contrasts are avoided.

Camcorder Lights

In many desktop video productions, the only lights used will be the ambient (room or outside) lighting, plus a fixed light mounted on the camcorder. This form of lighting produces an improved picture in low-ambient conditions, but often results in harsh shadows. It is appropriate for electronic news gathering applications where there is little time to setup more elaborate schemes. It is also extremely portable and can be used in places where other lighting systems are inappropriate. It produces reasonable, but less than professional, results for many applications.

Revenues and Revenue Growth Rates

Revenue growth in the lighting products subsegment, like that in the other parts of the production products segment, was over 100 percent for each of the years between 1989 and 1992, due again to the emergence of desktop video as a market and the application of existing lighting products to this emerging market. Revenues in 1989 were only $0.4 million, but grew rapidly to $13.5 million in 1992.

Revenue growth peaked in 1991 at 355.9 percent, fell to 118.0 percent for 1992, and is anticipated to decline slowly throughout the rest of the period surveyed. The growth rate is expected to decline to 71.6 percent by 1995 and descend to 51.7 percent by the end of 1999. Revenues for these years are forecasted at $78.3 million and $476.8 million, respectively. Revenue CAGR for the period is forecasted at 66.4 percent.

Fig. 5-9:   Lighting Products
              Unit Shipment and Revenue Forecasts 1989-1999

Year	Units (000)	Revenues ($M)	Revenue Growth(%)	Unit Growth(%)
1989	0.3	0.4	----	----
1990	1.2	1.4	243.2	273.0
1991	5.9	6.2	355.9	385.0
1992	13.5	13.5	118.0	129.5
1993	26.5	25.4	88.4	96.3
1994	49.5	45.6	79.2	86.7
1995	88.5	78.3	71.6	78.8
1996	152.7	128.3	63.9	72.5
1997	254.5	203.2	58.4	66.7
1998	414.3	314.3	54.7	62.8
1999	661.6	476.8	51.7	59.7
TOTAL			66.4%	74.4%

Unit Shipments and Pricing Trends

Units of lighting products consist of aggregated bundles of lights and accessories necessary to illuminate a scene to be captured and processed by a desktop video production suite. Only those sales of lighting systems for desktop video applications are counted in this segment.

Unit growth rates track, but exceed, corresponding revenue growth rates for the period surveyed, due mostly to reasonably stable pricing in this market segment. Lighting systems employ technologies largely unchanged over the last fifty years, and therefore are not prone to learning curve pricing effects, although a few innovations are anticipated during the forecast period which will reduce the average price somewhat for these products.

Unit growth peaked in 1991 at 385.0 percent during the emergence of desktop video as an application area for lighting products. Unit growth for 1992 dropped to 129.5 percent and is anticipated to drop gradually throughout the rest of the decade. 1995 growth is forecasted at 78.8 percent; 1999 growth is pegged at 59.7 percent. Unit shipment CAGR is anticipated at 74.4% for the period surveyed.

Market and Technology Trends
Qualitative Trends

Downsizing

Although lighting technology is very mature, there is still a little room for some innovation. It is reasonable to expect lighting systems to continue to decrease in size and weight, and somewhat in cost. This trend has been underway for some time in the lighting market, thanks to new materials and technologies which have vastly reduced the bulk and weight of older systems. Quartz halogen lamps have improved the efficiency of the lights themselves, allowing smaller packaging and producing less heat. Improved materials for reflectors and diffusers have also decreased the weight of these items. The decreased weight and size of these primary tools has allowed the support members to decrease in size and weight, also, thereby allowing portability of multilight systems.

Distribution

A second trend to be expected in lighting products is improved distribution. Professional-quality lighting products are hard to find outside of the video business. They will be in demand as desktop video emerges as a market, and the same suppliers who provide the bulk of desktop video production products will be expected to carry lighting systems, as well.

Competitive Analysis / Market Share
Competitive Environment

Most of the lighting products vendors who produce products for the conventional video market have a smaller subset of their lines which are applicable for desktop video purposes. These vendors are yet to recognize the growth of the desktop video market and have continued to market their products via their conventional video channels.

These channels include both direct sales and sales through video dealers. Accordingly, from the perspective of the desktop video user, distribution of lighting products is a major limiting factor, since many of the emerging desktop video devotees are not familiar with the conventional video industry and its distribution channels. From the perspective of the manufacturers, differentiation via distribution will be a major competitive factor in the ability to obtain market share among desktop video users. Lighting products manufacturers will have to adapt their distribution channels to include the evolving desktop video channels in order to take advantage of the growth of the desktop video market.

Also, the vast majority of the lighting products subsegment is comprised of complicated, powerful, and expensive units and systems. Most desktop video environments are and will be smaller systems in which cost is a major factor. It will behoove the lighting products suppliers to tailor lines of products toward these smaller, less costly, and less complex installations. Those who do will have a competitive advantage over those who don't.

Structure

There are over 30 individual organizations providing lighting products to the desktop video market. With the exception of the giants GTE/Sylvania and General Electric, who supply bulbs for the fixtures built by the other organizations, the remaining manufacturers are small- to medium-sized organizations focused primarily on the commercial video and film production lighting markets. Some, like Sachtler and Anton Bauer, also make products for other segments of the video production market. The ubiquitous Comprehensive Video Supply also competes in this market segment with lighting products from several vendors, as well as participating in almost every other conventional and desktop video market segment with other products.

Figure 5-9 contains a list of selected vendors of lighting products and a general description of the products offered.

Fig. 5-10:   List of Selected Vendors
                Lighting Products

Company	Product Lines
American Lighting	stands, accessories
Anton Bauer	camcorder lights
ARRI	lighting systems
Cine 60, Inc.	mobile lighting systems, camcorder lights
Colortran	lighting systems
Comprehensive Video Supply	lighting systems, accessories, stands
Dedotec USA, Inc.	lighting systems
DeSisti Lighting	lighting systems

Frezzolini Electronics	lighting systems, camcorder lights, accessories
General Electric Lighting	bulbs
Gitma	lighting systems
GTE/Sylvania	bulbs
ILC Technology	lighting systems
Lowel Light Manufacturing Company	lighting systems, accessories
LTM Corporation of America	lighting systems, accessories
Matthews Studio Equipment	accessories
Mole-Richardson Company	lighting systems
Musco Mobile Lighting, Ltd.	mobile lighting systems
NRG	lighting systems, camcorder lights, accessories
Rosco	gels, accessories
Sachtler Corporation of America	lighting systems, accessories
Strand Lighting	lighting systems, accessories
Teatronics	lighting systems
Theatre Vision International	lighting systems
Ushio America	bulbs
Vantage Lighting	lighting systems
Videssence	lighting systems

Issues
User Awareness & Training

Thanks to the marketing efforts of the camcorder and other desktop video suppliers, many more users have access to video acquisition equipment than know how to properly use it. Most new desktop video users will have at least some experience making "home movies" with inexpensive equipment. They are generally unaware of the requirements of moving to the next level of video quality. One of these requirements will be improved lighting, both in the form of products and technique.

These neophyte desktop video consumers are unaware of their ignorance in the area of scene lighting and will therefore be somewhat dismayed by their early efforts. The desktop video industry will have to educate these individuals on the need for lighting, first, and then follow with specific training in lighting techniques. These efforts will both increase customer satisfaction and improve sales of ancillary products, i.e. lighting systems.

Low-Light Cameras
As camera and camcorder technologies have improved, specifically via lower lux CCD systems, the quality of video acquired from unlighted targets has improved. This effect will

reduce, but not eliminate, the need to acquire professional lighting in desktop video environments.

Distribution

As discussed above, a major factor in the acquisition of lighting products by desktop video consumers is the availability of those systems in common distribution channels. The current distribution channels for these products are not sufficient to get them to the new desktop video market entrants. The rapidity at which lighting products vendors develop alternate channels suitable for desktop video consumers will determine both the market penetration of these suppliers as well as the early acceptance of lighting solutions in general by these consumers.

Market Shares

Several established, mid-sized, conventional video lighting suppliers control the largest market shares in the desktop video lighting products market. The leading shares are controlled by Lowel and Sachtler at 21.6 percent and 18.6 percent, respectively.

Lowel and Sachtler are followed by NRG, known best for batteries and battery charger systems, but also a leader in camcorder lights. NRG commands 11.3 percent of the desktop video lighting products market. NRG is followed by two conventional video lighting suppliers: Strand Lighting and Colortran, with 6.8 and 5.1 percent, respectively, and Comprehensive Video Supply, the combination manufacturer, OEM, and distributor of general video products with 4.5 percent.

No other supplier captured more than 1 percent of the remaining   percent of the desktop video lighting products market.

Fig. 5-11:   1992 Market Shares
               Lighting Products

Lowel Light   21.6
Sachtler   18.6
NRG   11.3
Strand Lighting   6.8
Colortran   5.1
Comprehensive Video Supply   4.5
Others   32.1

TOTAL   100.0%

Highlights of Selected Vendors

Lowel Light

The Lowel Light Manufacturing Company of Brooklyn, New York, offers both standalone lighting units as well as kits, focusing on the more portable systems which will tend to be utilized by desktop video producers. Their Tota-Light, Omni-Light, V-Light, and Pro-Light units can be combined with a number of accessories in order to create small to midrange portable kits, priced from around $600 to over $3000.

Lowel is an established supplier of lighting products who introduced their first product in 1959. They market through a network of authorized dealers, typically professional video dealers.

Sachtler

Sachtler Corporation of America is a subsidiary of Sachtler AG, a German video products firm in business for over ten years. Sachtler's U.S. headquarters are based in Freeport, New York. Sachtler is best known for camera mounts, tripods, and other camera support systems, but they also make and market studio, portable, and camcorder lighting systems.

Sachtler lighting systems range in price from about $300 for camera/camcorder-mounted lights to over $30,000 for complete studio systems. Sachtler markets its products through professional video dealers.

NRG

NRG Research, Inc., of Grants Pass, Oregon provides lighting and power solutions for portable videographers. Their products include camera-mounted portable lights, portable lighting kits, lighting accessories, batteries, battery packs, and battery charging systems.

The 51000 and 51500 Photoflood kits and 51200 and 51800 Focusing Quartz kits are high-quality, low-cost portable studio lighting kits which retail for $400, $525, $455, and $570, respectively. These kits can be enhanced with a number of accessories and upgrades, including gels and gel holders, barn door kits, umbrellas and mounts, light stands, etc. The Mite Lite, Highlite, Versalite, and Versalite Professional lines of camera/camcorder-mounted portable lights are priced from $120 to $190.

NRG markets its products through authorized dealers.

Strand, Colortran, Mole-Richardson

Strand Lighting, of Rancho Dominguez, California, is known for their Pulsar, Ianebeam, and Iadi lighting fixtures, their portable lighting kits, and their professional dimming systems. Their Location Kits range in size and price from $1450 to $2700.

Colortran, Inc., of Burbank, California, makes individual theater fresnel fixtures, location lighting kits, and Soft-Lite fill/flood lighting fixtures. Their portable lighting kits, the Mini-Pro Kit and the Pro-Kit IV, are priced at $1260 and $1470, respectively.

Mole-Richardson, of Hollywood, California, makes a line of studio lighting products, most of which is intended for fixed studio installations. Their Molequartz line of portable lights is applicable to desktop video environments. It consists of several 600 to 1000 Watt quartz halogen fixtures suitable for mounting on stands and connecting to 120 volt AC power. They also produce several small lighting kits, including the Tweenie II Kit ($2445), the Baby Softlite Kit ($2653), the Mighty Mole Kit ($2820), and the Teenie-Weenie Mole Kit ($1376), which are suitable for desktop video environments.

Comprehensive Video Supply

Comprehensive Video Supply Corporation, of Northvale, New Jersey, is the video industry equivalent to a J.C. Whitney (automobile supplies), a Black Box (computer communications), or even a Sears, Roebuck (general merchandise). That is, they are a catalog-based, mail-order supplier of a broad range of products, some manufactured internally, some distributed under the suppliers' brand names, and many OEM'd or remarketed under the Comprehensive brand name.

Comprehensive offers products for practically every phase of video production and for practically every segment of the desktop video market, including lighting products. Comprehensive's lighting products include light meters, spot and fill fixtures, stands, accessories, gels, kits, camcorder lights, umbrellas, batteries, and bulbs. Lighting kits are available from $539 up.

Comprehensive sells directly to end users and through subordinate authorized dealers.

Teleprompters

Total Teleprompter Market

Market Definitions and Overview

Teleprompters are devices which allow on-screen talent to read script lines while appearing to look at the audience through the camera lens. Teleprompters are very common in conventional video studio applications, and as desktop video begins to take over some of these functions, teleprompters are becoming more common in desktop video suites. Only those teleprompting systems which are used with desktop video production suites are included in this category.

Teleprompters represented 3.2 percent of the total video production products revenues in 1989. This percentage remained relatively constant through 1992 as the desktop video market emerged. Teleprompting systems are forecasted to rise by the 1995 time frame to 5.6 percent of the overall desktop video production market, peak at 5.7 percent in 1996, and decline slowly to 5.1 percent of the $3.3 billion overall desktop video production market by 1999 as prices fall dramatically in the latter years of the decade.

Teleprompting systems are generally comprised of a character generation system attached to a video monitor. The monitor's images are reflected via an apparatus of clear panels such that the images appear to the on-screen talent directly in front of a primary camera's lens. These systems must be firmly attached to the primary camera, typically via an elaborate mechanical apparatus including the camera's tripod. Other systems are detached from the main camera, but have the disadvantage of forcing the eyes of the on-screen talent away from the camera's lens.

Revenues and Revenue Growth Rates

Revenues from teleprompter sales in 1989 were only $0.7 million, reflecting the newness of the desktop video market and the inapplicability of teleprompters to most desktop video productions at the time. Revenues grew sharply in the next three years, with 1992 ending at $14.4 million. Growth rates for these years exceeded 100 percent as the desktop video market emerged and productions requiring teleprompting systems increased in quantity as well as percentage relative to the whole. Growth rates for teleprompter revenues peaked in 1991 at 293 percent and are expected to decline over the rest of the decade.

Revenues are anticipated to reach $117.7 million in 1995 and climb to $331.8 million by the end of 1999. Revenue growth rates for this period are expected to remain positive, but decline rapidly along with the pricing for teleprompting systems. These systems in 1992 are special-purpose, overpriced, dedicated systems; as the desktop video market matures, and products are developed which integrate functions from the various phases of video development, some of these products will replace the dedicated teleprompters with functionality from a general purpose, integrated, desktop video system.

Fig. 5-12:   Teleprompters
Unit Shipment and Revenue Forecasts 1989-1999

Year	Units (000)	Revenues ($M)	Revenue Growth(%)	Unit Growth(%)
1989	0.2	0.7	----	----
1990	0.4	1.6	127.0	130.5
1991	1.6	6.1	293.0	299.0
1992	3.8	14.4	135.0	138.6
1993	9.0	32.1	122.9	137.1
1994	20.6	65.5	104.0	129.2
1995	43.6	117.7	79.7	111.4
1996	80.8	176.5	50.0	85.2
1997	134.4	231.9	31.4	66.3
1998	214.0	284.3	22.6	59.2
1999	332.9	331.8	16.7	55.6
TOTAL			56.5%	89.5%

Unit Shipments and Pricing Trends

A teleprompter unit is an integrated system providing visual prompting cues to on-screen talent in desktop video productions. Only those units destined for productions dominated by desktop video systems are counted in this segment.

Unit shipments in 1989 were almost negligible, but grew to 3800 by 1992. Growth rates during the period were in excess of 100 percent per year, peaking at 299.0 percent in 1991 and dropping to 138.6 percent in 1992. Growth rates are expected to decline slowly the remainder of the decade to an eventual rate of 55.6 percent in 1999. Unit shipment CAGR for the period is forecasted at 89.5 percent, well in excess of the revenue CAGR of 56.5 percent. This is indicative of the anticipated strong downward pressure on teleprompter pricing throughout the period surveyed.

Pricing is expected to drop dramatically for teleprompters in the 1994 and 1995 time frame as computer technologies take over for the existing analog video-based systems. As the desktop video industry grows and matures in the years between 1994 and 1999, pricing of these systems is expected to continue to drop as the currently inordinately expensive projection systems are replaced by suitable alternatives.

Market and Technology Trends

Qualitative Trends

Teleprompting systems currently retail for between $3000 and $5000. It is clear that in the age of desktop video, these prices are out of line. Teleprompters will be driven by notebook or other personal computers with text extracted from word processing or dedicated scripting programs. The PC's monitor will provide the teleprompter operator with a control monitor, and other monitors can easily be connected for viewing by the onscreen talent. Assuming that a PC is already part of the overall desktop video suite, there is no reason why the additional hardware (single monitor) should cost more than $500. It is reasonable to expect strong downward pressure on teleprompting systems in the near future.

Also, conventional teleprompting systems are bulky and heavy. With the focus in desktop video production on small camcorders and their attendant portability, it is counterproductive to attach large, heavy teleprompting systems when they are needed. It makes far more sense to arrange either lighter, smaller systems, or to develop a means to detach the teleprompter from the camera. Developments in this area should also be anticipated in the short term.

Competitive Analysis / Market Share

Competitive Environment

There have been historically very few suppliers of teleprompting systems as the market for conventional fixed studios is very limited. With the advent of desktop video, every desktop video user will have a studio, dramatically increasing the number of potential homes for teleprompting systems. In addition, a large number of special interest and corporate videos, those expected to be commonly produced on desktop video systems, will require the use of "talking heads", personnel standing or seated and reading script material from a teleprompter system.

Because teleprompting systems have been such a small segment of the conventional video market, the few suppliers have not faced significant pricing or technological pressures. This is about to change. The suppliers in this market in 1995 are expected to differ greatly from the ones listed today, since new suppliers can be expected to penetrate the market, and some existing suppliers can be expected to not adapt quickly enough to the technological and pricing pressures of the new entrants.

Structure

This is a niche market at present. Teleprompters are typically used in programs shot on a sound stage where actors or the main speaker must read information rather than recite. As desktop video programs become more diverse, these units will be needed in many different forms of video presentations, growing the market substantially.

As a niche, the teleprompting market is served by several small, single-line suppliers as well as one "supermarket" supplier.

Fig. 5-13:   List of Selected Vendors
              Teleprompters

Company	Product Lines
BDL AutoScript	hardware, software
Comprehensive Video Supply	hardware, software, display systems
Computer Prompting Corp.	hardware, software, display systems
Electronic Script Prompting	software
Intelliprompt	hardware, software, display systems
Listec Video	hardware, software, display systems
Magic Teleprompting	software
Q-TV	hardware, software, display systems
QSI Systems	hardware, software, display systems
Tekskil	hardware, software, display systems
Telescript	hardware, software, display systems

Issues
Integration

A key issue for desktop video teleprompting systems suppliers, as opposed to conventional video systems suppliers, will be the degree of integration allowed with other desktop video preproduction and postproduction products. Those vendors able to integrate a teleprompting package with a scriptwriting package, an editing package, or even a graphics software package will have a decided advantage over those who choose to keep their products segregated.

Application to Corporate Video

As the use of video in corporate presentations grows, the use of teleprompters in corporate videos will grow, primarily because the "talent" in corporate presentations is generally comprised of company personnel, not professional actors. These personnel, including the corporate president or chairman, are not accustomed to memorizing and delivering script lines to a camera. A teleprompter solves the memorization problem as well as focuses the "talent's" eyes on the camera lens.

Barriers to Entry

There are few significant technological, financial, or other barriers for new participants in the teleprompting subsegment. Developing teleprompting systems requires neither extensive research and development efforts nor massive capital investment in manufacturing equipment or inventories.

The one effective barrier has been the limited market size. With desktop video expanding the available market for teleprompting systems, there should be no remaining barriers to new, innovative solutions from new and existing suppliers to this market segment.

Market Shares

Market shares for teleprompting systems in 1992 are very difficult to determine. Reasons for this include the small size of the market, the lack of a dominant market leader, the application of these systems in conventional video suites, and the tendency for users to integrate parts of several systems together, e.g. a Listec display system with a Comprehensive software package. Nonetheless, the market shares in Figure 5-13 are presented as a best approximation of the state of the desktop video teleprompting market as of 1992.

Listec Video, Telescript, and Comprehensive Video Supply have achieved early leads in this market segment with 29.1, 22.9, and 17.5 percent of the market, respectively. They are followed by Q-TV, Computer Prompting Corporation, and Intelliprompt with 8.7, 3.4, and 2.6 percent shares, respectively. No other competitor could be identified as holding more than 1 percent of the 1992 market. Other organizations comprise the remaining 15.8 percent.

Fig. 5-14:   1992 Market Shares
                       Teleprompters

Listec Video	29.1%
Telescript	22.9%
Comprehensive Video Supply	17.5%
Q-TV	8.7%
Computer Prompting Corp.	3.4%
Intelliprompt	2.6%
Others	15.8%

TOTAL	100.0%

Highlights of Selected Vendors
Listec Video

Listec Video of Hauppage, NY produces both PC-based and independent prompting systems, in addition to various sizes of display units which attach to camera mounts or stand alone. PC-based hardware and software systems range from $2400 to $3150 and prompting software is available independently for $1995. Independent hardware is available for $4500 to $5850, depending on capabilities. A 9" display unit is available for $2095, 12" units for $2300 and $2395, and 15" units for $2400 and $2495.

Listec sells predominantly via video dealers.

Telescript

Norwood, New Jersey-based Telescript, Inc. offers two PC-based systems, TeleScript PC and TeleScript LT. TeleScript includes three software modules: a script manager, a script editor, and a script prompter. The software translates Word Perfect, Microsoft Word, or ASCII files and is available alone for $2830. Telescript PC is a PC-based system (minus the PC) available for $4210 to $4810. Telescript LT includes a notebook PC and a VGA/NTSC converter for $7210 to $7910. Display systems are also available separately, as are components and accessories.

Comprehensive Video Supply

CVS, the distributor/OEM/manufacturer profiled elsewhere in this Chapter, offers the Autoprompter Deluxe, a $550 software package which turns an Apple II into a teleprompter. The product provides a hand-held controller and an integral word processor. The Cue Master system runs on PC-compatibles and lists for $995. Neither of these systems include a monitor and mounting apparatus for a camera stand. Comprehensive offers such an apparatus, the CP-1200VGA for the VGA-output devices and software, such as the Cue Master system, for $2449.

Q-TV, Computer Prompting Corp., Intelliprompt

Q-TV, out of New York City, offers the QCP LT PC-compatible software with WordPerfect, MS Word, and ASCII file import capability for $2650. Variations are available for up to $4450. On-camera prompter hardware is available for $1950 to $3250, depending on the size and construction, and freestanding hardware is available from $1975 to $2810.

Computer Prompting Corp., of Washington, DC, developed the first PC-based prompting system, the CPC-1000 software system. The CPC-1000 has been refined over the years and now boasts a flat screen prompter display using electroluminescent technology and accepting either RGB or NTSC video input.

Intelliprompt, from Los Angeles, markets the Intelliprompter II PC-based software at a list price of $2995 and display assemblies from $2350 to $4195

Chapter 6
Forecasts of the U.S. Desktop Video Postproduction Products Market

Total U.S. Postproduction Products Market

Market Definitions and Overview

The postproduction phase of the video production process is the key focus of the desktop video movement. It is the phase which has historically been the most costly, depending on extremely complicated special-purpose systems and the highly trained and talented personnel needed to operate them. Video postproduction is the process of editing together visuals, graphics, voices, music, sound and visual effects together into an "edit master" tape for duplication and distribution.

Before desktop video, a typical postproduction suite consisted of a video switcher, an edit controller, an audio mixer, graphics "paint" systems, character generators, still stores, VTRs, video monitors and speakers, in addition to patch bays, cables, test instrumentation, and personnel. With the advent of desktop video into the postproduction process, many of these components can be integrated into a single system, thus reducing the overall cost and complexity of the postproduction suite. Some desktop video postproduction systems merely control the analog elements in the suite; others operate completely in the digital domain. Still others are hybrid systems with both digital and analog elements.

Postproduction Market Shares

The postproduction segment constituted 52.1 percent of the desktop video products market in 1989. By 1992, following the introduction of several innovative products offering analog desktop video editing, this segment had grown to 60.5 percent of the overall market. 1993 is a key year for this market as Avid Technology and others will deliver true digital desktop video editing systems to the market. Additionally, vendors in the preproduction and production segments will add significant new products to their markets, growing these segments and expanding the whole desktop video market substantially, but correspondingly shrinking the relative contribution of the postproduction segment. By 1999, the postproduction segment is expected to represent 47.7 percent of the $20.4 billion desktop video products market. It is important to note that many of the digital video products listed in Chapter 4 will have significant application in the postproduction phase, also. The postproduction revenues listed here do not include the contribution from these products.

Postproduction Subsegments

For purposes of this study, the postproduction products segment has been broken into six discrete subsegments. They are: Integrated Systems and Components, the heart of desktop video functionality; Personal Computer Platforms, the multipurpose base of the all the desktop video technology; Machine Control Systems, the devices and software which allow a personal computer to control outboard devices such as VTRs, laserdiscs, and film recorders; Recording and Playback Systems, a general grouping of VTR and laserdisc products; Audio Systems, the hardware and software necessary to create (as opposed to record), modify, and output audio for video productions; and, Graphics Products, the software and hardware necessary to import, create, modify, and output computer graphics images on desktop video systems.

Of these categories, the Integrated Systems and Components grouping is the one which drives the consumption of the others in the desktop video market. Indeed, without this category, there is little need to separate desktop video from its component technologies of personal computation, multimedia, professional audio, and professional video. It is also the most difficult category to adequately describe, since it comprises a very fluid set of functionality. Some of the products in this segment provide only one function; others provide hundreds. It is difficult to find two products in this segment with the same set of functionality, yet all of the products in this category contribute to the acquisition of full-motion, full-size video, the processing (including editing) of this video, and the preparation for and/or execution of output of the processed video (with or without audio) to a recording device.

Conventional Functionality

To better understand the subsegmentation of the postproduction products market, it is perhaps germane to explore what elements are required for this functionality in a conventional video editing suite. In a conventional suite, the functions listed below are typically implemented in discrete, special-purpose devices, whereas, as we shall see, in desktop video configurations, these functions are typically grouped and are performed by multi-purpose elements.

Video Switcher

A video switcher in a conventional postproduction suite is a device which routes video signals from the various sources, e.g. VTRs or SEGs, to the outputs, video monitors and a record VTR. In a "linear" desktop video postproduction system, this is typically a circuit board which plugs into a personal computer, plus some external connectivity devices. The circuit board is under the control of the personal computer, which is in turn controlled by the edit controller software and the operator. In a "nonlinear" system, all of the video switching effects are performed via hardware and software internal to the PC in a purely digital format; there is no external device control needed for this purpose.

Edit Controller

In a conventional system, the edit controller is a human being who selects the various video clips, editing effects, and transitions in real time and implements them via the video switcher and edit controller. Software in a desktop video postproduction system implements the actions of the human operator in a repeatable, defined manner. These actions include cuts between different sources, as well as automating the selection of other transitions, plus some digital video effects, titling and other graphics.

Special Effects Generators

A special effects generator is a device which provides for elaborate editing transitions and other effects. In recent years, a series of very powerful digital special effects generators, or DVEs for Digital Video Effects, have become the standard in conventional suites. In a desktop video system, the DVE typically is integrated with the edit controller and video switcher.

Audio Mixer

An audio mixer in a conventional suite is used to normalize the signal levels of the various source devices as well as mix in voiceovers, background music, and audio special effects. Although a discrete, analog audio mixer is still useful in the production phase for desktop video systems, it has been supplanted in most desktop video postproduction suites by audio editing software integrated in the edit controller/switcher/DVE package.

Many of the functions available via digital signal processing software in a desktop video suite must be provided by extra discrete components in a conventional video suite.

Graphics System or "Paintbox"

In conventional systems, any graphic art needed for the video output was developed on a special purpose paintbox system. In recent years, many postproduction suites have begun using dedicated personal computers for this purpose instead of other proprietary systems. In true desktop video suites, the personal computer which provides the basis for the postproduction edit controller also is the graphics generation system. Graphics software provides the same functionality as the classic "paintbox", yet allow exchange of data with other programs, and do not require specialized hardware.

Character Generator

In the conventional video world, a character generator, or "CG", is a standalone device which generates titles and other text for keying into the video output. In a desktop video postproduction system, this standalone device has been implemented in software which is installed in the personal computer acting as the central desktop video edit controller. Character generator quality is measured in terms of edge resolution timing. Broadcast standard is 35 nanoseconds. Desktop video systems typically offer much better performance.

Computer to Video I/O

In the desktop video postproduction suite, it is necessary to import and export video information to and from the personal computer system in order to accept video images from cameras, camcorders, and source VTRs and to output the edited product to video monitors and record VTRs. The formats of the electrical signals used to convey the image in analog video equipment and in computer graphics systems are quite different and several electronic devices may be necessary in desktop video systems in order to implement these conversions.

Frame Grabbers

Single image digitization hardware and software has been available in the conventional video market for some time. These products are typically known as "still stores". In the desktop video environment, it is more common to implement full-motion video digitization and playback. This function is typically included in an integrated system, or in a full-motion video component. Full-motion systems are also typically able to store still images.

Personal Computer Platforms

In a conventional video system, little or none of the functions are implemented via the control of a personal computer, although this has gradually changed in recent years. In a true desktop video postproduction system, the personal computer platform is the basis of the overall system. A personal computer platform includes the CPU (central processing unit), base memory and input/output functions, power supply, and chassis, floppy and base hard disks, computer monitor and/or projection system, keyboard, mouse or trackball, and ancillary input devices such as scanners, jog/shuttle controllers, and digitizing tablets.

A personal computer platform forms the locus of control for the remainder of the functions in a desktop video suite. Many of these functions are implemented in computer software only; others require hardware "cards" which are plugged into the personal computer CPU unit. Still others are attached via outboard interface structures.

Integrated Systems

Integrated desktop video postproduction systems, based on personal computer platforms, implement some or all of the above functions in a single workstation. For example, the Video Toaster system from NewTek includes a video switcher element, a special effects generator, a graphics program, a frame grabber, and a character generator. It does not, however, provide edit control or audio processing. These functions must be supplied by other products. The Video Toaster is a combination hardware/software package which is installed in and on a Commodore Amiga personal computer platform.

The Avid Media Suite Pro is another integrated system, based on an Apple Macintosh Quadra platform. It includes digital video switching and editing, special effects generation, a character generator, a full-motion frame grabber, computer to video I/O, and CD-quality audio processing. It integrates easily with graphics programs and additional audio processing.

Other products in this category may only implement pieces of this functionality and must be supplemented by other products. Some, like the Media Suite Pro, require little supplementation in order to be effective postproduction tools.

Revenues and Revenue Growth Rates

Revenues from the total U.S. desktop video postproduction market are shown in Figure 6-1. Revenues from this market are derived from sales of integrated desktop video postproduction systems and the individual components necessary to complete a postproduction suite based on the central desktop video system.

Revenues from all postproduction sales in 1989 totaled $73.1 million. Although postproduction products were among the first desktop video products to be developed, and this accounts for the rapid start in terms of revenue generation, this segment benefited from the tremendous growth in the market in the years between 1990 and 1992, achieving growth rates in excess of 100 percent for all three years. The growth rate for this segment peaked in 1991 at 206.0 percent with the introduction of a number of key desktop video systems.

Revenues on sales of desktop video postproduction products reached $938.1 million in 1992. Revenue growth for 1992 slowed somewhat to 106.3 percent and is forecasted to continue drop significantly until 1994, when it is anticipated to reach 55.3 percent, and then drop more slowly for the rest of the survey period. The steep growth rates between 1989 and 1994 are due to the emergence of the new market; the decrease in growth rates will be caused by the beginning of market stabilization, a drop in the rate of new product introductions, continued market growth, and the beginning of some price erosion due to competition.

Revenues are forecasted at $3.4 billion for 1995 and $11.9 billion for 1999. 1995 revenues are expected to grow at 43.9 percent and 1999 revenue growth is anticipated at 31.1 percent. The revenue CAGR for the period is pegged at 50.7 percent.

Fig. 6-1:	Total U.S. Market for Production Products Unit Shipment and Revenue Forecasts, 1989-1999		
Year	Units (000)	Revenues ($M)	Revenue CAGR(%)
1989	11.0	73.1	----
1990	36.4	148.6	103.4
1991	130.6	454.8	206.0
1992	287.4	938.1	106.3
1993	487.5	1542.8	64.5
1994	815.8	2396.2	55.3
1995	1337.0	3449.1	43.9

1996	2208.9	4836.6	40.2
1997	3604.6	6707.3	38.7
1998	5741.4	9114.2	35.9
1999	8765.8	11952.3	31.1
TOTAL			*50.7%*

Unit Shipments and Pricing Trends

A unit of desktop video postproduction products is defined as a single hardware product, a single hardware/software bundle, or a single system of hardware and/or software products providing a postproduction function or functions for a desktop video system. Only those items intended for use in desktop video suites are counted in this segment as similar items may be employed in multimedia or conventional video production.

In 1989, 11 thousand units of postproduction products were shipped to the desktop video market. The years of 1990, 1991, and 1992 saw explosive growth in unit shipments, with growth rates of 229.7, 259.3, and 120.0 percent, respectively. In 1992, 287,400 units were shipped.

Growth rates in unit shipments are expected to drop off significantly in 1993 and then gradually decline for the rest of the survey period, as the extraordinary growth of the early years of desktop video applications cools and the digital video products (listed in this report as preproduction items) come to the fore. Unit shipments are anticipated at 1.3 million for 1995 and 8.8 million for 1999, evincing the substantial growth of the postproduction segment of the desktop video market. Unit shipment CAGR for the period is anticipated at 66.5 percent, outstripping the substantial revenue CAGR of 50.7 percent.

Pricing is anticipated to decline at an overall CAGR of -9.5 percent per year for the period surveyed. This pricing figure is derived from the fact that the postproduction segment is comprised of both mature and evolving technologies. The overall pricing for the segment is therefore a mix of the stable pricing of the mature technologies and the 15-30 percent decreases expected from evolving high technology markets.

Market and Technology Trends

Trends By Product Type

The postproduction segment of the desktop video market breaks into six discrete subsegments. The first, and most important longterm is Integrated Systems and Components. Also included are Personal Computer Platforms (including peripherals), Graphics Software, Audio Systems (including MIDI products), Recording & Playback Systems, and Machine Control Products.

At the beginning of the survey period, in 1989, the largest subsegments of the postproduction market in terms of shipments were the Recording and Playback Systems at 42.0 percent and Personal Computer Platforms at 33.3 percent of the whole. The remaining subsegments contributed the remaining 25 or so percent. By 1992, following the initial growth phase of the market, the contribution of Recording and Playback Systems had dropped to 27.2 percent, in a virtual tie with Personal Computer Platforms (25.7 percent), and the rapidly growing category of Graphics Software (25.3 percent). The next two largest segments, Integrated Systems and Components at 12.3 percent and Machine Control Products at 8.9 percent comprised the majority of the remainder of the postproduction products market.

By 1995, Recording and Playback Systems are expected to decline to 17.7 percent of the whole, primarily because of a decreasing need for VTRs as postproduction systems become predominantly non-linear and disk-based, and because of desktop video's ability to utilize less complicated and costly VTRs than conventional processes.   Machine Control Products will convert from mostly hardware products to mostly software products, gradually becoming integrated with other systems, ending 1995 at a forecasted 5.9 percent of the postproduction market. Graphics Software (23.3 percent) and Personal Computer Platforms (38.4 percent) are anticipated to be the dominant subsegments, with Integrated Systems and Components contributing 12.6 percent.

By 1999 and the end of the survey period, Graphics Systems will comprise 46.4 percent of the total desktop video postproduction products market, followed by Personal Computer Platforms at 32.6 percent, Integrated Systems and Components at 10.7 percent, and the other three categories contributing less than 5 percent each to the whole. Audio Systems, while never constituting a significant segment of the total, is forecasted to grow steadily throughout the period to a maximum share of 4.1 percent in 1999. On the other hand, Recording and Playback Systems, the largest shareholder in 1989, is expected to decline significantly in importance throughout the period, as is Machine Control Products.

Distribution Trends

Integration Complexity

Desktop video postproduction systems are complicated structures integrating complex computer and video technologies. Conventional video dealers lack the computer expertise to effectively market, support, and service these products. Conventional personal computer dealers lack the video production process expertise of their video counterparts. Value Added Resellers, or VARs can and will help fill this gap by acquiring expertise from both fields and by conveying this to the growing desktop video customer base.

Low Software Margins

Both video and personal computer dealers pursuing the desktop video market can be expected to be resistant to carrying unbundled software, due to the low margins available on these products, the shelf space requirements, the high support requirements, and the typical availability of such items through mail order competitors. VARs will provide these products until they become commodities, whereupon mail order, direct mail, and catalog sales will become the main distribution path for software products.

Bundling

Although postproduction products will tend to be the central products in a desktop video suite, it is reasonable to expect vendors and resellers to bundle postproduction products with complementary products supporting other phases of the video development process. It is also reasonable to assume some integration of preproduction and production functions into postproduction products, thereby allowing the purchase of truly integrated, self-contained production systems.

Evolving Distribution Channels

Many vendors providing postproduction products have been servicing the conventional video market for some time. The channels established for this market have been effective at connecting the consumers of the products with the suppliers. As the desktop video market evolves, a totally different set of end users will develop for these and any new entrant vendors to the market. The previously structured channels, e.g. direct sales and video dealers, will not be effective in matching the supply of products with the demand. These manufacturers will have to develop alternative channel structures in order to meet the growing desktop video demand.

End User Trends

Prospective Users

As discussed elsewhere in this document, desktop video technology allows an entirely new class of prospective users the tools to develop video productions. The key end user trend is therefore the evolution of the end user base from non-computer-literate, skilled video professionals, to partially computer-literate, unskilled (in video) masses. This shift in end user demographics will constitute challenges for the product developers, marketing channels, and the video establishment as new concepts and participants revolutionize video production.

Productivity & Creativity Improvements

The order-of-magnitude decreases in postproduction costs afforded by desktop video systems will have much the same impact on video development as spreadsheets had on financial planning. "What if?" experimentation will become more common, improving the creative output of video developers, given the lower costs and improved ease of developing alternative scenarios.

At the same time, the technological improvements in the postproduction process will dramatically improve the productivity of video developers, allowing them to produce better and quicker output, improving time to market and overall output flow.

Computer Literate Users

The professional video production community, long an isolated enclave of very specialized technical knowledge, is nonetheless relatively computer-illiterate. Desktop video postproduction efforts will require significant computer skills among both existing participants in the professional video market as well as new entrants. The new entrants will likely have a sufficient set of these skills; it is obvious that the incumbent professionals will have to adapt to this new skill set requirement or lose their positions to the new breed.

Video Skills

At the same time the existing video community will be challenged with learning computer skills, the new entrants to the desktop video market, presumed to be largely computer literate, will be challenged with learning the non-trivial skills necessary for professional video creation. The magnitude of this task should not be underestimated; elements such as proper lighting, effective video editing, audio engineering, camera angles, scriptwriting, and the like require specialized skills unfamiliar to the general public. There will be a significant opportunity in this area for organizations and individuals offering training in these specialized skills.

Qualitative Trends

New Computerization

A key general trend brought on by desktop video technology is the introduction of personal computers in an area where they were previously nonexistent. This will force new techniques, products, and skills on the existing video community. New entrants into the professional video market will be less computer-averse than the incumbent professionals and will therefore adapt more quickly to the new technology, forcing the incumbents to adapt or become obsolete. Existing postproduction suites, some of which are not yet fully amortized, will become in part obsolete. This will place extreme financial hardships on some elements of the video postproduction community, thus opening some doors for new entrants to this market.

Generalized Functionality

Existing video technologies focus on point solutions with special-purpose hardware. Desktop video brings general purpose platforms into this environment. The special applications necessary for video postproduction will be integrated into a single multifunction system with a common user interface, requiring fewer trained professionals in order to support and operate the system. Along with the integration will come increased automation of previously manual tasks and adjustments, thus simplifying the complete postproduction process.

Cross-Phase Integration

As desktop video matures as a technology, more functions from all the various phases of video development will be incorporated into the central system. A system whose primary purpose is the postproduction function of video editing will also serve as the preproduction script and storyboard development system, will maintain shot logs and provide teleprompting during production, will serve as the animation and graphics development workstation, and will provide all audio mixing and sweetening during both production and postproduction. The obvious benefit to this is that a single system will be both less costly and far easier to use than a collection of interconnected devices when performing video development, thereby reducing both the time and budget required to create video presentations.

Networking and Groupware

As desktop video systems become more powerful and prevalent, it is reasonable to expect the networking of multiple systems and the sharing of data through groupware functions. This will remove the single-workstation serial access bottleneck and will allow different functions such as video editing, audio sweetening, and graphics development to occur simultaneously for the same project in larger installations. Groupware will also allow multiple individuals to collaborate on single elements, such as animation development or scriptwriting.

Digital Domain

A key trend which will both revolutionize conventional video development as well as make video production available to the mass market, is the trend away from analog, linear editing to digital, non-linear editing. This is really the core technology of desktop video: it will obviate the expensive, high-quality analog devices needed for current video production, such as Betacam VTRs, vectorscopes, video switchers, and genlocks. It will eliminate the requirement for SMPTE time code compatibility, since frame accuracy is always assured in the digital domain, thus eliminating thousands of dollars from both production and postproduction suites. It will place new demands on the digital mass storage industry, who will be required to develop higher capacity and thruput storage devices for use in this new market.

Audio

Audio acquisition, processing, and output have been traditional problem areas for the conventional video market. The advent of 16-bit, CD-quality, digital audio processing on desktop video systems will help improve the overall quality of audio for video as well as dramatically improving the ease at which it is manipulated. Digital audio DSP functions such as mixing, gain control, equalization, noise gating, compression, and cut-and-paste editing are revolutionary improvements over the existing analog audio processing techniques.

Competitive Analysis / Market Share

Competitive Environment

Competition in the postproduction segment continues to become more and more intense as large organizations like Sony, Panasonic, and JVC, spin-offs like Matrox and Immix, and small startups like Abbate Video spend significant R&D money developing and introducing postproduction products based on personal computers. The competition among Personal Computer Platforms suppliers has been intense for several years and will likely continue to be so, even without the effects of the desktop video revolution.

To date, most of the competition in the segments other than Personal Computer Platforms have focused on functionality in order to differentiate themselves from each other, and price to differentiate themselves from conventional video technologies. As desktop video matures as a market, pricing will be used more to differentiate competitors in each segment.

Competitors who are entering the desktop video market from the conventional video orientation are focused on those customers who are currently in the business of doing video productions. Competitors who are entering the market from the personal computer, professional audio, or other orientations are focused on those customers who want to get into video production, e.g. corporate trainers, sales departments, etc. The existing video producers tend to have allocated budgets for acquisition of new systems; the "wannabes" tend to have to justify new purchases in terms of investment payback. Therefore, the early growth in the desktop video market has come from the video-familiar users while some competitors have struggled with educating those who would like to get into video production.

Structure

The structure of the postproduction products market is vary diverse, as the distribution channels and means of competition tend to take the forms of the component industries from which each category arises. For instance, the video-related products tend to be distributed through professional video dealers, the Audio Systems through professional audio and musical instrument dealers, and the computer-based products through computer dealers. A new structure to this market will arise as the desktop video market matures.

Competitors in the postproduction products market are shown in Figure 6-2.

Fig. 6-2: Postproduction Market Competitors						
Company	Integrated Systems & Components	Personal Computer Platforms	Machine Control Systems	Audio Systems	Recording & Playback Systems	Graphics Software Products
A+ Development						X
Abaton		X				
Abbate Video			X			
Abvent						X
Acoustic Research				X		
Activa International						X
ADA				X		
Adaptec		X				
ADDA	X					
Adobe						X
Advanced Digital Imaging (ADI)	X		X			
Advanced Digital Systems	X					
Aegis						X
AIM Graphics						X
AirCraft				X		
Aitech International Corp.	X					
AKG				X		
Al Giddings Images Unlimited						X
Aldus						X
Aldus/Silicon Beach						X
Alias						X
ALR		X				
Altec Lansing				X		
Antex				X		
Apple		X		X		
Archive		X				
Archive Films						X
Aris Entertainment				X		X
ARTI			X			
ASDG	X					X
Associated Production Music				X		
AST		X				
AT&T GSL			X			X
ATI Technologies		X				
Audio Technica				X		
Aurora						X
Austin Computer Systems		X				
Autodesk						X

	Col 1	Col 2	Col 3	Col 4	Col 5	Col 6
Avid	X			X		X
AVR Technology		X				
AXA Corp.						X
Aydin Controls		X				
Bag End				X		
Barco		X				
BCD Associates			X			
Best Shot						X
Beyer Dynamic				X		
Big Noise Software				X		
Black Belt Systems						X
Broadcast Television Systems						X
Broderbund						X
Brown-Wagh	X					X
Byte By Byte						X
CalComp		X				
Canon		X				
Cardinal Technologies	X	X				
Cayman Graphics					X	
CBS News Archives						X
CEI	X					
Centaur Development	X					X
Chase Technologies			X			
Chyron	X					
Cinenet						X
Classic Images						X
CMS		X				
Coda				X		
Commodore International		X				
Communications Specialties	X					
Community				X		
Compaq		X				
Compix Media	X					
Comprehensive Video Supply			X			X
CompuAdd Computer		X				
Compunic Electronics	X					
Computer Friends	X	X				
Computer Modules	X					
Computer Specialties	X					
Corel Systems, Inc.						X
CoSA						X
Costem	X					
Covox				X		
Crown International				X		
Crystal Graphics						X
Cubicomp						X
Data Translation	X					X
Dell Computer		X				
DeWolfe				X		
Diamond Computer		X				
Diaquest			X			
Digidesign				X		
Digital Arts						X

Digital Audio Labs					X		
Digital Creations		X					X
Digital F/X		X		X			X
Digital Micronics	X					X	
Digital Processing Systems				X	X		
Digital Vision		X					
Digivox					X		
Disney Software							X
Display Research Lab		X					
Display Tech		X					
DNF Industries				X			
Dr. T's Music Software					X		
Dreamlight Images							X
Dubner				X			
Dynaware					X		X
E-Machines			X				
E-Mu Systems					X		
Eastman Kodak			X				
Echolab		X					
Eclipse Technologies					X		X
Educorp							X
Electric Image							X
Electro-Voice					X		
Electronic Arts							X
EMC		X					
Emulex			X				
Energy Productions							X
Ensemble Designs		X		X			
Envisio		X					
Epson			X				
Equilibrium Technologies							X
Everex Systems		X	X				
Exabyte			X				
Fabulous Footage							X
Fast Electronic		X					
Film Bank							X
FirstCom Broadcast Service					X		
Fish Films							X
Focus Graphics				X			
Folsom Research		X					
Fractal Design							X
Fresh					X		
Fujitsu			X				
Future Video		X		X			
Gene Michael Productions					X		
Generation Systems			X				
Genoa Systems Corp.		X	X				
Gold Disk Software				X			X
Graphisoft							X
Grass Valley Group		X					X
Great Valley Products		X					X
Greatsounds					X		
Hal Leonard Publishing					X		

Company								
Halland Broadcast Services					X			
Heifner Communications	X							
Hewlett Packard		X						
High Res Technologies	X							
Hitachi		X				X		
Homrich Communications				X				
Horita				X				
Hot Shots & Cool Cuts								X
Hotronic	X							
Houston Insts./Summagraphics		X						
Howtek		X						
HSC Software					X			X
I-Den Videotronics Corp	X							
IBM	X	X			X			
Idek		X						
IEV International	X		X					
Ikegami		X						
Image Bank								X
Image Logic				X				
Image North Technologies							X	
ImageWare								X
Imageways								X
Imaging Technology, Inc.	X							
Immix	X							
Impulse								X
In-Motion	X							
InnoVision								X
Intelligent Resources	X							
Interactive Media Technologies				X				
International Video Network								X
Invisible Touch					X			
J.L.Cooper					X			
JBL					X			
Jovian Logic	X				X			
JVC						X		
KDI	X							
Kesser								X
Key Tronic Corp.		X						
Klipsch					X			
Korg					X			
Koss					X			
Kurzweil					X			
Lapis Technologies	X							
Lazerus								X
Light Source Computer Images				X				
Linker Systems				X				
Logitech		X						
Lotus								X
Lyon Lamb				X				
MacGillivray Freeman								X
Macproducts		X						
Macromedia					X			X
Magni	X							

Company						
Mark of the Unicorn				X		
Mass Microsystems	X	X				
Masterclips						X
Matrox	X	X				
Maxoptics		X				
Maxtor		X				
McQ Productions			X			X
McRoberts Software						X
Media Pedia						X
Media Vision				X		
Merkel Films						X
Micro Frontier						X
Micro Technology Unlimited				X		
MicroGrafx						X
Micropolis		X				
Microsoft		X		X		
MidiSoft				X		
Military Channel						X
Mirror Technology		X				
Mitsubishi		X			X	
Motion Works						X
Mouse Systems		X				
Mus-art				X		
Musicator				X		
Nanao		X				
NEC		X				
Network Music				X		
New Media Graphics	X					
NewTek	X					X
Nikon		X				
Nissei Sangyo America		X				
Northern Media	X					
Northgate Computer Systems		X				
Nucleus Electronics			X			
Nutmeg Systems		X				
Octree Software						X
Olduvai Corp						X
Omnicomp	X					
Omnimusic				X		
Opcode Systems				X		
Optibase	X					
Orchid Technology		X				
Oxxi						X
Paltex	X					
Panasonic		X	X		X	
Parker Adams Group				X		
Passport				X		
Peavey				X		
PEP			X			
PG Music				X		
Philips		X				
Phoenix						X
Photron	X					

	1	2	3	4	5	6	7
Pinnacle Micro		X					
Pioneer		X			X		
Pipeline Digital			X				
Pixar							X
Pixel Resources							X
Presentation Graphics Group				X			
Presentation Technologies		X					
Profusion Group			X				
Promusic				X			
Prosonus				X			
Quantum		X					
Quark							X
Questel	X						
Radius	X	X					
Rainbow Software							X
Ramsa				X			
Rapid Technology	X						
Raster Graphics		X					
RasterOps	X	X					
Ray Dream							X
Redlake Corp	X						
Reliable Communications	X						
Relisys		X					
Reply Corp.		X					
RGB Computer & Video			X				
RGB Dynamics	X						
RGB Spectrum		X					
Ricoh		X					
Roctec	X						
Roland		X		X			
Ron Sawade Cinematography							X
Ross Systems				X			
RTG Music				X			
Sampo		X					
Samsung		X					
Samtron		X					
San Francisco Canyon Co.						X	
Sanyo		X			X		
Seagate		X					
Seiko Instruments		X					
Selectra	X		X				
Sennheiser				X			
SFV International						X	
Sharp		X					
Sigma Designs		X					
Signature				X			
Silicon Graphics	X	X					X
Smith Audio Visual	X						
Software Publishing Corp.							X
Sonic Solutions				X			
Sony		X	X	X	X		
Sound Ideas				X			
Sound Source Unlimited							X

Company	Col 1	Col 2	Col 3	Col 4	Col 5
Spectral Innovations				X	
Specular International					X
Steinberg/Jones				X	
Storage Solutions		X			
Strata					X
Sundance			X		
SuperMac Technology		X			
Syndesis					X
SyQuest		X			
Tandy Corporation		X			
Tannoy				X	
Tascam				X	
Taxan		X			
TEC		X			
Technical Aesthetics Operations			X		
Tektronix		X			
Television Program Enterprises					X
Texas Instruments		X			
Texture City					X
Time Arts					X
TOA				X	
TouchVision Systems	X				
Travelview					X
Trompeter				X	
Truevision	X				X
Trycho Music				X	
Turbo Music				X	
Turtle Beach Software				X	
Twelve Tone Systems				X	
United Pixels and Lines					X
Universal City Studios					X
Valentino				X	
Vega				X	
Vestax				X	
Video Tape Library					X
VideoLinx	X				
VideoLogic	X				
Videomail	X				
Videomedia			X		
VIDI					X
ViewSonic		X			
Virtus					X
Vision Software					X
Visionetics	X				
Vividus					X
Voyager Co.					X
Voyetra				X	
Wacom Technology		X			
WangDAT		X			
Wangtek		X			
Waveframe				X	
Wavefront Technologies					X
Western Digital		X			

Will Vinton				X
Willow Peripherals	X			
Wolfetone			X	
Worldwide Television News				X
WPA Film Library				X
Wyse/Amdek		X		
Xaos				X
Yamaha			X	
Zenith Data Systems		X		
ZSoft				X

Few patterns can be discerned among the competitors in the postproduction products market segment of desktop video. Some are large, such as Sony, Panasonic, Adobe, IBM, Apple, and Compaq, with products serving multiple markets both inside and outside of desktop video environments. Some are very small, such as Gryphon, ZSoft, the Profusion Group, and Media Pedia. The majority fall into this category, or a mid-sized category.

Some are growing rapidly, as in NewTek, Videomedia, and Electric Image. Others are more established and mature, such as Electro-Voice, Zenith Data Systems, and Tandy Corporation.

Some come from backgrounds in the computer industry, others from the musical products industry, and others from the broadcast video industry. Some offer broad lines; others offer single products.

As time goes on, and the desktop video postproduction market matures, a few of the smaller organizations will succeed and become medium-sized or larger organizations. Most will fail, or be absorbed by larger organizations. Many of the larger companies will take more of an active interest in the growing desktop video market and expand their lines to cover more functional areas. New, small organizations will continue to spring up to serve market niches.

Issues

Vaporware and Hype

As in the early days of the personal computer industry, many postproduction products have been announced before they could be shipped, some years in advance of delivery. First Unit delivery dates as announced are rarely met. These conditions have led to a lot of confusion among the potential users of desktop video systems. They are confronted by a barrage of advertising and hype about products which are not yet available thereby diverting their attention from those that are.

Worse yet, many of the products do not live up to their hype when they are available. Some are full of "bugs" or other malfunctions; others are unfit for the purpose for which they are being marketed. Most, if not all, marketing campaigns for desktop video postproduction products stress the technical capabilities for creating video productions provided by their products, but carefully ignore the very real human difficulties in integrating and using these systems.

The confusion and frustration arising from these practices by desktop video manufacturers has limited the spread of positive "word-of-mouth" about these products, thereby slowing the acceptance of the new technologies. Many potential users have taken a "wait and see" attitude, preferring to wait until reality and truth are sorted out from vaporware and hype.

Training

Desktop video postproduction products manufacturers will have to somehow solve the complexities of using their products before they will become acceptable to more than the existing technically trained professionals in the video market. The most obvious way to handle this is to provide training to these users, either directly, via their sales channels, or via the educational system. Direct routes are probably not cost effective in the main, so the indirect ones are more important.

Elsewhere in this report the authors have stressed the need for sales channels to provide value added services such as integration, support, and training. In some cases, organizations such as VARs are beginning to evolve and take on this load. As in the computer industry, and for that matter the conventional video industry, desktop video can acquire trained users via the secondary, junior college, and university educational systems. This will require seeding the educational institutions with appropriate products (a la DEC or Apple), thereby encouraging them to use these products in their programs, so that they will produce graduates with desktop video product skills. Most schools are currently underfunded, and those with video programs already have suites of conventional equipment, so any growth in this area will be the result of proactive programs from the desktop video manufacturers.

Integrated Systems and Components

Total Integrated Systems and Components Market

Market Definitions and Overview

Integrated Systems and Components are those items taken collectively which replace the functions of traditional postproduction editing equipment by making possible desktop video nonlinear editing. Specifically, such functions as NTSC/RGB encoders and decoders, full-motion and still image frame grabbers, 24-bit color graphics adapters and accelerators, Film/Video converters, video compression boards and software, video switchers, editing software, print to tape software, SEG/DVE devices and software, are included along with the miscellaneous items allowing viewing and capture of television signals on a personal computer platform. This category is the heart of the desktop video revolution; the products in this category, more than any others, are the ones making it technologically possible to produce video presentations with a desktop system.

Integrated Systems and Components represented only 1.4 percent of the total desktop video production products revenues in 1989. This percentage grew to 12.3 percent in 1992 with the introduction of desktop video offline, linear systems, and is forecasted to decline slowly to 10.7 percent of the overall $12 billion desktop video postproduction market by 1999, as digital video components gradually assume the roles covered by Integrated Systems and Components in the early 90's.

Integrated Systems

At the present time, many of the functions listed above are provided via discrete devices from different manufacturers. Some manufacturers have begun combining functionality and offering packaged systems to be added to personal computer platforms as a turnkey package.

Such systems typically include the graphics i/o adapters, a compression adapter, a video switcher, editing software, and print to tape software, although other combinations are also available.

Frame Grabbers

There are a number of varieties of frame grabber products differing mostly in the bit-depth of the colors they can acquire and in the speed at which they can acquire images. The only ones acceptable for desktop video are those which can acquire 24-bit color images in real-time, meaning 30 frame grabs per second.

NTSC/RGB Encoders and Decoders

Computers typically operate in RGB video mode. That is, they input and output video signals as an unmixed set of signals describing the relative strengths of the red, green, and blue primary color components of the image. As described elsewhere in this document, video equipment operates in NTSC composite video mode or in a number of variations off of the component-video structure. In a mixed computer-video system, as is required by desktop video, some translation between these differing signal formats must occur. The translation involves matching the resolutions, scan rates, and other technical factors between the different formats. The output, in order to be acceptable for professional quality work, must be clean and flicker-free. Devices which perform these functions are available for less than $100 up to more than $5000, depending on the quality level and features provided.

Revenues and Revenue Growth Rates

Revenues from the sale of integrated systems and components in 1989 totaled only $0.6 million, due to a relative lack of integrated systems and limited sales of computer-based postproduction components into the emerging desktop video market. By 1992, this had changed dramatically, and revenues grew to $123.9 million. Revenue growth rates started exceptionally high (over 2200 percent in 1990) as newly developed products such as the Video Toaster met pent-up demand. By 1992, revenue growth had slowed to the more reasonable 99.1 percent.

Revenue growth is expected to slow throughout the rest of the survey period as this category endures the extreme pricing declines typical of new high technology product families. By 1995, revenue growth rates are expected to decline to 43.5 percent, although revenues themselves are forecasted to rise to $447.4 million. By 1999, revenues for integrated systems and components are expected to reach nearly $1.45 billion.

Revenue growth by the end of the decade is expected to slow to 35.3 percent per year, providing an overall survey period revenue CAGR of 42.1%.

Fig. 6-3:	Integrated Systems and Components Unit Shipment and Revenue Forecasts 1989-1999			
Year	Units (000)	Revenues ($M)	Revenue Growth(%)	Unit Growth(%)
1989	0.1	0.6	----	----
1990	3.8	15.0	2269.7	2421.0
1991	17.0	62.2	316.0	352.2
1992	35.2	123.9	99.1	107.4
1993	62.2	204.3	64.9	76.4
1994	103.1	311.7	52.5	65.8
1995	168.1	447.4	43.5	63.1
1996	268.8	608.1	35.9	59.9
1997	420.1	798.3	31.3	56.3
1998	639.4	1069.3	33.9	52.2
1999	940.5	1447.0	35.3	47.1
TOTAL			42.1%	59.9%

Unit Shipments and Pricing Trends

Unit shipment growth is expected to perform much better than revenue growth for the period surveyed. A unit of integrated systems and components is defined as a single hardware or software product, or a collection of hardware and software products collectively sold, which performs single or multiple postproduction video development functions. Only those items sold as part of, or in support of, a central desktop video postproduction system are counted in this category.

Unit shipments for 1989 were extremely low, barely registering for purposes of this report, for reasons noted above. By 1992, unit shipments had risen to 35,200, driven mostly by the explosive sales growth of the NewTek Video Toaster. Unit shipment growth for 1992 was recorded at 107.4 percent, already exceeding the corresponding period's revenue growth, due to the beginning of competitive pricing pressures. The years of 1993 through 1995 are forecasted to be key growth years for desktop video in general, and integrated postproduction systems and components in particular, culminating in shipments of over 168 thousand units in 1995, representing a growth of 63.1 percent over the previous year. The delta between unit shipment growth and revenue growth for 1995 is nearly 20 percentage points, reflecting the anticipated strong downward pressure on pricing as the technology begins to mature and significant competition develops.

By 1999, unit growth is forecasted at a still healthy 47.1 percent per year, maintaining the approximate 20 point advantage over revenue growth.   1999 unit shipments are anticipated to exceed 940 thousand units. Unit growth for the survey period is prognosticated at 59.9 percent, versus revenue growth at 42.1 percent.

Pricing is expected to decay strongly until 1997 as more and more products enter the market and existing products evolve into lower cost versions. After 1997, the desktop video postproduction market is expected to begin reaching maturity, with unit growth rates continuing to drop and with pricing beginning to level off.

Market and Technology Trends

Qualitative Trends

Postproduction is the heart of conventional video development. It is the most costly and time consuming phase of the process, therefore it is the one with the most room for improvement with the advent of new technologies. Integrated Systems and Components are the heart of the desktop video movement. This category contains the postproduction elements which are central to the editing and output of video and audio and most obviously results of the trend to digitization. This category is therefore the nexus of the growth of desktop video and the attendant revolution in the video development process.

Digitization

As explained earlier in this study, video postproduction is moving from an analog, tape-based, linear process to a digital, disk-based, non-linear one. Key to this movement is the development of digital integrated systems and components based on personal computers which allow the digitization, editing, and retrieval of video and audio, replacing the all-analog special-purpose systems common to conventional video development.

Although analog tape will remain an efficient and common distribution media for video programming well into the future, given both the current VHS VCR / Television installed base as well as the economies of this media versus alternatives, the use of videotape as an intermediate development media for this programming will decline significantly with the advent of fully digital desktop video systems. A key effect of this will be the use of lower quality acquisition devices and formats, since the generational loss problems of analog formats can be largely avoided via use of digital processing, assuming that the acceptable output quality for most programming (NTSC television and VHS formats) remains as it is today.

Increasing Integration

The recent trend has been for the increased integration of postproduction functions into single devices or turnkey systems. This trend can be anticipated to hold for the future as components are incorporated into VLSI functionality, thus reducing the size, complexity, and cost of these products while improving reliability and usability. As of 1992, many required postproduction functions are implemented in separate cards and devices, often offering separate and disparate user interfaces. Over the next several years, more and more of these systems will be collected into highly integrated bundles with common user interfaces, a la the Avid Media Suite Pro, an integrated system which began shipping in early 1993.

This increasing trend toward improved integration and functionality will put development time pressures on the manufacturers, forcing them to shorten product cycles and recoup investments in shorter periods of time if they are to remain competitive with other market entrants providing the next generation of functionality.

Interface Standardization

One of the difficulties with integrating disparate functionality developed by different vendors is in the interfacing of the functional elements. Often, this is done at a "least common denominator" level, requiring the functional elements to implement significant redundancies. This can be avoided if the element developers can agree on an interface standard allowing free exchange of information between the elements and the specialization of functionality within a given element.

The desktop video industry is so new that few of these interface standards have developed. Apple's QuickTime and Microsoft's Video For Windows are two such software-based standards. Intel's DVI, the JPEG and MPEG compression standards, and the AIFF file format are others. The bus structures of the common desktop video personal computer platforms represent yet more standards. These are useful, but do not define how a software edit controller might interact with a JPEG compression board, for example.

In 1992, a group of vendors headed by Avid Technology defined a standard called OMF for Open Media Framework. This consortium now includes over 80 companies, including Silicon Graphics, Digidesign, Grass Valley Group, JVC, Truevision, Alias Research, and C-Cube Microsystems . The standard allows for the exchange of information on the interprocess level among desktop video components, thus allowing for the tight coupling of integrated systems comprised of elements from different suppliers.

It is reasonable to expect the continued development of such standards as desktop video evolves.

Digital Video

Digital video products, although listed in this report as preproduction products because of their current applicability, will actually become more applicable to the postproduction process in the near future, thus putting considerable pressure on existing integrated systems. Digital video systems such as SuperMac's Digital Film, when combined with software products like Adobe's Premiere, will soon represent significant competition to integrated systems providers like Avid, who are currently performing essentially the same functions, but with higher quality. This will have two dominant effects: decreased average pricing and reduced complacency from established vendors. The digital video vendors are largely established competitors in the cutthroat personal computer industry, and are therefore familiar with competitive pressures; the integrated systems providers are largely veterans of the conventional video world, a much less competitive environment.

Competitive Analysis / Market Share
Competitive Environment

Competitors in the Integrated Systems and Components subsegment of the desktop video postproduction market are typically small- to medium-sized organizations who either focus entirely on desktop video applications, like Avid Technology and Digital F/X, or focus on the general area of computer-based graphics and video systems, as in Matrox and Magni. Suppliers compete primarily on terms of features/functions provided, personal computer platforms supported, and editing strategy (online/offline, linear/nonlinear) supported.

Most of the competitors in this subsegment sell via video dealers and the emerging desktop video VARs. Some of the competitors, those arising from a computer graphics orientation versus the conventional video orientation, employ computer dealers instead of, or in addition to, video-oriented dealers.

Structure

Participants in the Integrated Systems and Components segment of the desktop video postproduction market tend to fall into two categories: those who attempt to provide complete editing solutions, and those who provide only elements (outside of specific Machine Control Products as listed in a later section of this chapter) of postproduction systems based on personal computer platforms. The integrated systems vendors may obtain elements of their systems from other providers.

The integrated systems providers are denoted in Figure 6-4 with an asterisk. At times, the differentiation between an integrated system and a component is not always clear-cut. For example, NewTek is listed as an integrated system supplier, but its products are typically part of complex systems composed of components from several manufacturers. The Video Toaster, NewTek's primary product, can either be considered a component of the resultant integrated heterogeneous system, or an integrated system in itself, as it provides many different video postproduction functions. Arbitrarily, it is listed as an integrated system.

Likewise, it is at times difficult to differentiate some postproduction components from the digital video hardware listed in Chapter 4. Generally, the hardware listed in that chapter is not capable of full-speed, full-size, full-color video transfers and/or CD-quality stereo audio recording and playback. In addition, some of the products listed in this section perform machine control, like those listed under Machine Control Products later in this chapter. Generally, the ones in that section perform only machine control functions; the ones listed here perform machine control, complicated transitions, full motion video acquisition, and other functions. Products are listed in this section according to a "best fit" criterion.

Thankfully, most of the Integrated Systems and Components listed here are either full motion video boards or VGA to NTSC conversion devices. These products, and video compression hardware, are clear components in video postproduction editing systems and belong in this category.

Many of the full motion video board producers also manufacture general computer graphics adapters for personal computer platforms, having started in that product area and moved upscale into full motion products as graphics hardware evolved. Examples include Magni, Radius, RasterOps, Genoa, Cardinal, Matrox, and Truevision. Some of the competitors in this area offer products as an expansion to their already impressive graphics workstation products, including Everex, IBM, and Silicon Graphics. A third group of competitors is specifically focused on the desktop video market. These vendors include Avid, Digital F/X, Centaur, NewTek, EMC, Immix, and TouchVision.

At this time, no vendor can be said to be dominant, although Avid has acquired the largest portion of the high-end postproduction integrated systems sales, and NewTek has sold the most low-end integrated systems.

<table>
<tr><td colspan="2">Fig. 6-4:   List of Selected Vendors
                       Integrated Systems and Components</td></tr>
<tr><td>Company</td><td>Products</td></tr>
<tr><td>ADDA</td><td>VGA-AVer</td></tr>
<tr><td>Advanced Digital Imaging (ADI)</td><td>Digital Magic</td></tr>
<tr><td>Advanced Digital Systems</td><td>Videokey</td></tr>
<tr><td>Aitech International Corp.</td><td>ProVGA/TV Plus, VideoSurge, ProPC/Video</td></tr>
<tr><td>ASDG</td><td>T-Rexx Professional</td></tr>
<tr><td>Avid Technology *</td><td>Media Suite Pro, Media Composer series</td></tr>
<tr><td>Brown-Wagh</td><td>VideoLinX</td></tr>
<tr><td>Cardinal Technologies</td><td>SNAPplus</td></tr>
<tr><td>CEI</td><td>Wizard AV, Video Wizard</td></tr>
<tr><td>Centaur Development</td><td>OpalVision</td></tr>
<tr><td>Chyron</td><td>Centaur</td></tr>
<tr><td>Communications Specialties</td><td>Coconut</td></tr>
<tr><td>Compix Media</td><td>SuperBoard</td></tr>
<tr><td>Compunic Electronics</td><td>MVW-500, FTN-1000, FTP-1000</td></tr>
<tr><td>Computer Friends</td><td>ColorSnap series, SuperChroma Encoder, FastCompress</td></tr>
<tr><td>Computer Modules</td><td>VideoMux 8X4</td></tr>
</table>

Computer Specialties	ScanDo series
Costem	TeleFrame VCE
Data Translation	Data 100, ColorCapture
Digital Creations	SuperGen 2000, SuperGen, DCTV
Digital F/X *	Video F/X, Video F/X Plus, Soft F/X
Digital Micronics	Digital Editmaster, Digital Broadcaster
Digital Vision	ComputerEyes/RT
Display Research Lab	MR VP
Display Tech	Mac Display/Link
Echolab	PC-3
EMC *	PrimeTime editor, EMC2, EMC Tracks
Ensemble Designs	Envoy
Envisio	Pressto
Everex	Vision VGA with Overlay
Fast Electronic *	Video Machine
Folsom Research	Otto
Future Video	V-Station 1, 1-PC, II, II-PC
Genoa	VGA2TV
Grass Valley Group	videoDesigner
Great Valley Products	G-Force Combo,G-Lock, ADDI
Heifner Communications	Toaster Cozzy
High Res Technologies	VGA Video Gala
Hotronic	AS11
I-Den Videotronics Corp	IPX-50
IBM	ActionMedia II
IEV International	SimulScan,VIP-8800
Imaging Technology, Inc.	Visionplus
Immix *	Video Cube
In-Motion	Picture Perfect
Intelligent Resources	Video Explorer
Jovian Logic	Genie, VIN Plus,Olivia
KDI	TV Link
Lapis Technologies	L-TV
Magni	VGA Producer Pro
Mass Microsystems	QuickImage 24
Matrox *	Studio, Personal Producer, Illuminator series
New Media Graphics	Super Video Windows, Super Motion Compression
NewTek *	Video Toaster, Toaster Workstation, Toaster Link
Northern Media	The Video Navigator
Omnicomp	Sweet 16, ViVA, ViVA Basic
Optibase	MPG series, Optitools, Model 100 and 500, Series 2000
Paltex	EDDiSX
Photron	IND/24
Questel	CGV-10
Radius	Radius TV

Rapid Technology	Visionary, Visionary Video 601
RasterOps	24S w/Accelerator, Framegrabber 324NC, ColorBoard 364, ProVideo 32, VideoExpander
Redlake Corp	Tape Caster, Spectrum NTSC, Spectrum NTSC+
Reliable Communications	FrameBuffer
RGB Dynamics	TR-1500, CDR-950, TC-100, CDR-150, CDR-250
Roctec	RocGen Plus, RocKey VGA
Selectra	Its A Wrap
Silicon Graphics	Sirius Video, Cosmo Compress
Smith Audio Visual	Y/C Plus
TouchVision Systems	D/Vision
Truevision	VideoVGA 16, VIDI/O, Targa series, nuVista+
VideoLinx	PTV
VideoLogic	Mediator
Videomail	VMC-1 , VMC-3
Visionetics	VIGA+
Willow Peripherals	Laptop TV, VGA-TV GE/O

Issues

Editing

One of the key differentiators in terms of products in the Integrated Systems and Components market subsegment is whether the product is an online system, an offline system, or a combination, and whether the system employs linear or nonlinear editing techniques. Although the trend in desktop video is toward online, nonlinear systems, other combinations are still prevalent because of the current limitations of digitized video, as explained elsewhere in this report.

It is far more common to find offline, nonlinear systems and online, linear systems among current desktop video offerings. Competition within these categories are often based on platform support and price, whereas competition across categories is based on functionality.

Platform Structures

Early desktop video postproduction systems were focused on the Commodore Amiga platform and the Apple Macintosh. As the market has evolved, the various "PC-compatible" units have begun to obtain market share as postproduction platforms. Recent introductions by Silicon Graphics indicate that the Indigo workstation will also become a key desktop video postproduction platform.

Integrated Systems and Components vendors typically tailor their products to support only one of the available platform structures, although some, e.g. FAST Electronics, have products that support several different personal computer structures. Vendors who are locked into a particular bus structure or personal computer operating system have limited themselves to a small portion of the overall market, as some users would rather not switch their underlying personal computer platforms, with which they have significant investments in hardware, software, training, and experience, in order to obtain technology from a given vendor, no matter how wonderful it might be.

Vendors who wish to dominate this segment of the market, which tends to drive the rest of the desktop video market, will offer products which support several different platforms and allow the customers to choose the ones which fit their overall needs best.

Misinformation

As mentioned earlier in this chapter, the desktop video postproduction market, and the Integrated Systems and Components segment which drives it, is a hotbed of misinformation and hype. Products are introduced and marketed well before availability, advertised shipping dates slip by months or years, and products are often hurried to market well before the bugs have been ironed out. In addition, the competitors evolving out of the personal computer market are prone to making exaggerated claims about the video capabilities of their products which turn out to be inaccurate.

The result is a lot of confusion in the potential buying public. Some potential buyers have decided to sit by and watch the dust settle before they choose a direction.

Competitors have contributed to the confusion with their "FUD" sales and marketing strategies (FUD = Fear, Uncertainty, and Doubt - attributed to the IBM Corporation) in which buyers are urged to "wait for my product...That one will be obsolete!" . This has led to even more cycles of early announcements and nonshipping products as competitors are pressured to respond. Integrated Systems and Components competitors who succumb to this strategy are ripe for the "Osborne Effect", named after the personal computer company who announced a superior product many months before it was available, thus killing sales of its existing products and driving the company out of business.

Bells and Whistles

Integrated Systems and Components not only bring equivalent functionality vis a vis conventional video systems to desktop environments, but also add the power of the computer to the mix, thereby adding hundreds of new features and functions unavailable with conventional technology. This has several effects. First, it will provide more features and functions, e.g. strange DVE transitions or animated effects, for those who have been limited by conventional technology. Second, it will further confuse neophyte video producers who will clutter their programs with unnecessary and distracting transitions and effects. Third, it will provide more ammunition for the hype artists who will happily contrast products based on specsmanship.

The latter effect almost forces competitors to add unnecessary "bells and whistles" to remain competitive on the data sheet. Reality is that most of these additional functions and features will only occasionally, if ever, be used

Customer Acceptance

Postproduction, and in particular editing, is the most important element of creating a video program. Integrated Systems and Components include those devices which control video editing and video switching. Although the technology is now available which allows a neophyte to own his or her own video postproduction system, the knowledge necessary to integrate and utilize this technology is not as easily obtainable.

Leading vendors will sign and nurture VARs who are capable of solving these product integration and customer support problems. Those vendors who do not address these problems directly or via their sales channels will have difficulty obtaining product acceptance by customers.

In addition to focused, product-directed training, there is also a need for general training in video and audio techniques. The availability of low cost video development equipment, including Integrated Systems and Components postproduction products, has opened the available market for video programming development to a wide audience, most of which is unskilled in any facet of video development. Schools, universities, and private training organizations will see an increased demand for video artistry training, and as this training becomes available, it will improve the customer acceptance of desktop video technologies, thereby feeding demand.

Mergers and Acquisitions

Another issue in this segment is the consolidation of suppliers via mergers and acquisitions. Grass Valley Group, a longtime conventional video supplier of editing systems and a minor participant in the desktop video market, is a subsidiary of Tektronix. Adobe Systems has a stake in Digital F/X, who in turn owns Waveframe. Immix is owned by Carlton Communications. RasterOps bought Truevision. Avid Technology bought DiVA and Flamingo Graphics, one a digital video software company and the other a computer graphics software organization.

Continued consolidation should be noted as the desktop video market gains momentum and standards begin to develop. This will strengthen some vendors, those producing the de facto standard products, and weaken some of their competitors. Often, these weaker competitors will have technologies or supplementary products of use to the stronger competitors, and will therefore be absorbed in mergers and acquisitions.

Market Shares

As of the end of 1992, NewTek, who largely founded the desktop video movement by itself, has the largest market share at 70.9%, in terms of units shipped. Although this seems a dominant position, it is being eroded quickly by other product lines as new technologies hit the market and as products are developed for personal computer platforms other than the largely ignored Amiga.

Truevision, now a subsidiary of RasterOps, has the next largest market share at 16.2 percent, based on their success with full motion video boards such as the NuVista+ product. This share can also be expected to decline with the growth of new competitors in the desktop video market.

Avid Technology and Digital F/X, two pioneers in integrated desktop video systems based on Apple Macintosh platforms weigh in with 2.0 and 1.0 percent of the market, respectively. Avid is poised for explosive growth with the advent of its new Media Suite Pro product line, bringing industrial-quality, nonlinear, online, digital editing capability under the $30,000 mark. Avid's high end products, the Media Composer line, continue to gain market share in production environments, predominantly as offline systems for professional studios.

Digital F/X brought out the combination online/offline, linear/nonlinear Video F/X suite in 1991. It became immediately popular among the Mac enthusiasts who were looking for a low-cost editing suite. Technical difficulties, marketing difficulties, and lack of organizational direction has hampered Digital F/X's growth. As of press time, Digital F/X has just undergone a massive reorganization in which some of their key personnel were dismissed. Their outlook is uncertain at this time.

There are a number of other competitors who had not yet gained over 1 percent of the market as of the end of 1992, yet deserve attention. EMC, a pioneer along with Avid of nonlinear editing, has introduced a new product line based on ISA-bus personal computers. Matrox came on strong in 1992 with their Studio product line, a linear editing system based on EISA-bus platforms. IBM introduced the ActionMedia II board and TouchVision mated it with its D/Vision editing and compression software. This product began shipping in 1993. Data

Translation began shipping their long-awaited Data 100 board. Immix introduced the innovative, powerful VideoCube in early 93 as a strong competitor to Avid, EMC, and the other existing desktop video integrated systems vendors. FAST Electronic introduced the Video Machine for both Mac and ISA-bus platforms. Overall, these new competitors, as well as the new products from the market leaders, will reshape this segment for 1993 and later years.

Of course, as the digital video vendors such as Radius, RasterOps, SuperMac, and Adobe continue to improve their product lines, these products will become viable postproduction systems and will also compete in this category. It will be interesting to watch Integrated Systems and Components to see how it shakes out in the coming years.

<table>
<tr><td colspan="2">Fig. 6-5:   1992 Market Shares
               Integrated Systems and Components</td></tr>
<tr><td>NewTek</td><td>70.9%</td></tr>
<tr><td>Truevision</td><td>16.2%</td></tr>
<tr><td>Avid Technology</td><td>2.0%</td></tr>
<tr><td>Digital F/X</td><td>1.0%</td></tr>
<tr><td>Others</td><td>9.9%</td></tr>
<tr><td></td><td>--------</td></tr>
<tr><td>TOTAL</td><td>100.0%</td></tr>
</table>

Highlights of Selected Vendors

NewTek

NewTek, of Topeka, Kansas, is the granddaddy of the desktop video revolution. The Video Toaster ($2495) was among the first full-motion, broadcast-quality, personal-computer dependent products to hit the market. The Toaster, as it is commonly called, is a software package and a board which plugs into a Commodore Amiga platform and provides production and postproduction video switching capability with effects, similar to standalone units costing tens of thousands of dollars. The Toaster accepts video input from four different sources and directs them to two output channels, Program and Preview. It includes a linear keyer, over 100 different transitions under either automatic or manual control, a 24-bit frame grabber, external

GPI triggers, luminance keying, a character generator, a real-time color processor, a paint program (Toaster Paint), and a 3D animation program (LightWave 3D).

The Toaster comes in several forms. The board/software set is available and is the most common variation. A complete Toaster Workstation ($4595 up), including an Amiga platform is also sold. Toaster Link ($595) is a SCSI interface between the Toaster workstation and a Mac platform, allowing exchange of control and data between the two. A version of the Toaster Link for PC-compatibles has been announced, but not yet delivered.

The Toaster lacks edit control capability, audio features, machine control, and other functions. These functions are provided by third-party products, such as RGB Computer and Video's AmiLink line, or Smith Audio Video's Y/C Plus product. Indeed, a whole industry, composed of dozens of companies, has grown up around NewTek and the Video Toaster.

Truevision

Truevision, of Indianapolis, Indiana, began life as a division of AT&T. It was purchased from AT&T by the employees and the renamed Truevision quickly became a force in the graphics adapter market, with products like the TARGA+ high-resolution graphics adapters/frame grabber combination. Truevision was recently acquired by RasterOps, a Silicon Valley firm also specializing in graphics adapters, and is now operated as an independent subsidiary.

Truevision's ATVista and NuVista+ boards bring full-motion video capabilities to high resolution graphics adapters/frame grabbers. The NuVista+ board is the heart of Avid's Media Suite Pro system and offers full-motion, full-size, 24-bit color video digitization and playback. Truevision also offers the VideoVGA 16 graphics adapter, VIDI/O test equipment, VideoMaker+ transitions software, Bravado series multimedia boards, VideoScript presentation software, and TIPS imaging software.

Avid Technology

Avid, of Tewksbury, Massachusetts has developed quite a reputation among the film and television community with its Media Composer lines of desktop video systems Media Composer systems are typically used to generate workprints via digital nonlinear editing processes. When the workprint is approved, the Media Composer can generate an industry-standard EDL for use by an expensive online system in order to produce the final edited program.

The Media Composer Series 200 line provides 24-track CD-quality audio editing and mixing, titling, graphics import and transition, timeline-based editing, digital transition effects, freeze frame, slow/fast/reverse motion, fit to fill, EDL export, optional print to tape capability, and optional switcher control. It is based on an Apple Macintosh IIci platform and utilizes two multisync monitors. The Series 2000 is based on an Apple Macintosh Quadra 900, uses larger monitors, has the same general features and options as the Series 200, and adds four channel audio monitoring, optional VLAN machine control, an optional MIDI fader control device, and optional advanced audio mixing features.

The Media Composer line ranges in price from about $20,000 to over $100,000. In early 1993, Avid began shipping the innovative Media Suite Pro, priced at $9995 for the hardware and software necessary for use with an Apple Macintosh Quadra 950 platform. Configured systems range in price from about $25,000 to over $50,000. The Media Suite Pro offers industrial-quality, online, nonlinear editing, allowing a video developer to input source video and audio footage, edit the footage in the desired order utilizing timeline tools, add transitions, add and mix audio and graphics, and print the results to tape as a finished master. The Media Suite Pro is composed of 4 boards for the Quadra, including Truevision's NuVista+ and Digidesign's AudioMedia II, listed elsewhere in this Chapter, as well as the software necessary for integrating the product. The Media Suite Pro software is derived from the Media Composer software and presents a similar user interface.

The Media Suite Pro includes an integrated titler, PICS/PICT/QuickTime file import and export capability, 16 transitions and 16 DVE moves, print to tape capability, digital waveform monitor and vectorscope, audio pan and volume controls for 4 virtual tracks, audio and graphics mixdown capability, stereo audio input and output at CD-Quality resolution, and 640x240 (30 field) video resolution, utilizing motion JPEG compression. The Media Suite Pro requires at least 2GB of fast disk storage, and either one multisync monitor a combination of a multisync monitor and a Mac color monitor. Composite and S-Video inputs and outputs are available.

Avid sells the Media Composer line direct to end users and via professional video dealers. It sells the Media Suite Pro line via authorized resellers, including VARs and professional video dealers. Other Avid products include Audio Vision, a digital audio editing suite based on the Composer structure, and products from its DiVA and Flamingo Graphics subsidiaries, including VideoShop and Bola32.

Digital F/X

Digital F/X is located Mountain View, California and was founded in 1986. One of its first products was the Composium, a high-end, conventional video, graphics compositing system. In 1991, Digital F/X began shipping the Video F/X desktop video system. The Video F/X is a combination of software and hardware attached to an Apple Macintosh II personal computer form. Most of the hardware is located in a separate chassis outside the Mac itself.

The Video F/X combines video switching, edit control, audio mixing, graphics and CG, and non-linear editing functions in a single unit. The Video F/X can either be used as an offline system, producing EDLs for online work, or as an online system. It can be used in linear editing mode, controlling source VTRs and record VTRs, or in conjunction with Soft F/X, as a nonlinear system. In nonlinear mode, the output of the Video F/X system is an EDL only, as it can only digitize, store, and retrieve 8-bit representations of video data.

A later enhancement, the Video F/X Plus, includes a jog/shuttle knob, additional graphics capabilities, a MIDI interface, an A/B roll option, and PICS animation control.

Other Competitors

Fast Electronic U.S., Inc., out of Natick, Massachusetts, and a subsidiary of the German firm Fast Electronic GMBH of Munchen (Munich) introduced the Video Machine in 1992 and began shipping its first version in early 1993. The VideoMachine is hardware and software which provides A/B roll editing, CG, hardware transitions and effects, online edit control, EDL export, a 2-channel video switcher/mixer, eight audio input channels, digital audio mixing, two audio output channels, and, machine control. The first version is configured for ISA-bus personal computers; a Mac NuBus version is scheduled for mid-93 shipment.

The Video Products Group of Matrox Electronic Systems, Ltd., of Dorval, Quebec, Canada, offers two key products for linear editing on EISA-bus platforms. The first is Personal Producer, a software package introduced in 1991 and offering Windows-based editing functions roughly analogous to that provided by Adobe Premiere or DiVA VideoShop. Personal Producer provides A/B/C roll control, wipes, other basic transitions, two-dimensional DVE effects, video compositing, switcher control, keying, audio mixing, and machine control functionality.

In 1992 Matrox introduced the hardware to support Personal Producer as its Studio product. Studio consists of 5 EISA-bus cards which provide 3 DVE channels, 3 time base controllers, 6 stereo audio channels, a VTR controller, a 32-bit graphics frame buffer, allowing support of 8 composite or 4 S-Video inputs and control of up to 3 input plus one output VTR deck. As of early 93, Matrox has announced, but not yet made available, nonlinear editing capabilities for the Studio system.

A Studio A/B roll system, less audio components, VTRs, and TBCs lists for $9995. It requires an EISA- bus PC, 8MB RAM, 80+ MB disk, VGA and NTSC monitors, stereo speakers, DOS & Windows, plus two to four time code capable VTRs. A complete A/B/C roll system is $15,990, less the video decks, PC platform, and audio components.

Matrox is also known for its line of video adapters, including the Illuminator 16 product used in the Studio.

Intelligent Resources Integrated Systems, Inc., of Arlington Heights, Illinois is the manufacturer of the Video Explorer, a $7995 competitor to the Truevision NuVista+ product.

Like the Truevision product, the Video Explorer is a NuBus card for use in a Macintosh system, offers 4:4:4:4 digital processing, dockable input and output modules of various configurations, and a modular interconnection bus called the VideoBahn. D1 and RGB input and output modules are currently available, with composite video and YUV modules in the works. The modules can conceivably be mixed and matched, allowing video acquisition from Betacam SP and output to D1 recorders. The Video Explorer is definitely a component; it must be mated with a number of products to become a complete postproduction system. Third parties offer compatible edit control, digital disk interfacing, special effects, character generation, animation, paint, character generation, and other solutions compatible with the Video Explorer.

Optibase, Inc., of Canoga Park, California, is a leader in board-level products which accomplish MPEG and JPEG video compression. Optibase offers Model 100 and 500 JPEG turbo accelerator boards, a JPEG developer's toolkit, an MPEG developer's toolkit, Series 2000 MPEG cards for ISA-bus PCs, the MPG-1000 MPEG compression card for multimedia applications, and a bundle of JPEG multimedia software. Their MPEG products are based on a proprietary hardware codec, called the MPG-1000. Their software codec is called Optitools. Both are available separately.

RGB Dynamics, Inc., of Erlanger, Kentucky, not to be confused with RGB Computer and Video or RGB Spectrum, two other competitors in the desktop video market, focuses on the problems of converting video signals between different formats. They offer the $2395 TR-1500 Translator, a scan converter to adapt computer video board output to composite, component, or S-Video (Y/C) video signals. The Translator is a standalone product, as is the CDR-150 and CDR-250 rackmount units, which convert RGB or Component video signals to composite, S-Video, and other output signals. The CDR-950 ($1250) is an ISA-bus card compatible with Amiga or PC-compatible platforms, and converts RGB signals into composite and S-Video outputs. Their TC-100 unit transcodes component video to RGB, or vice versa.

Smith Audio Visual provides the Y/C Plus unit ($949), with works in conjunction with the Video Toaster to add S-Video capability to that product. The Y/C Plus features up to four S-

Video (Y/C) inputs, four composite inputs, two S-Video program outputs, four composite monitor outputs, and one Toaster preview composite output.

Personal Computer Platforms

Total Personal Computer Platforms Market

Market Definitions and Overview

Personal Computer Platforms include personal computers whose intended or actual primary use is as the central processor of a desktop video postproduction system, or of any other function within the scope of desktop video, as well as peripherals such as disk drives, computer monitors, keyboards, mice, trackballs, jog/shuttle controllers, scanners, digitizing tablets, projection monitors, and CD ROM players. Only those incremental units used for desktop video purposes are counted in this category.

In 1989 , Personal Computer Platforms represented 33.3 percent of the total desktop video postproduction products revenues. This percentage dropped to 25.7 percent in 1992 as the other subsegments in the postproduction market grew and the focus shifted away from the Commodore Amiga and toward the Apple Macintosh. By 1995, the segment is forecasted to reclaim 38.4 percent of the postproduction market as the focus shifted away from linear recording and control systems to digital, nonlinear systems based on PC platforms. The share is forecasted to drop slightly in 1999 to 32.6 percent of the nearly $12 billion desktop video postproduction market, in terms of units shipped.

CPU Units

The heart of a personal computer platform is the CPU unit, typically including a chassis and power supply, the CPU circuit board, some peripheral controllers, floppy and hard disks, and room for more circuit boards and storage devices. The CPU units include an interconnection structure known as a "bus" which allows the various components to intercommunicate. Various manufacturers make products which conform to the major bus orientations.

Apple Computer's Macintosh personal computer products, in the main, conform to the NuBus specification, as do the peripheral products which are Apple-compatible. IBM personal computers, as well as those of the many various "clone" manufacturers, conform to one of three different standards: the ISA bus (Industry Standard Architecture, or AT-bus), the EISA bus (Extended Industry Standard Architecture), or the MCA bus (Micro Channel Architecture). For purposes of this study, these product families comprise the bulk of the personal computer CPU units used for desktop video purposes. Also for purposes of this study, all Apple Macintoshes and all IBM clones have been lumped together in order to generate gross platform revenues and unit shipments.

Apple Macintosh products are based on the Motorola 68000 family of microprocessors and run an Apple-provided operating system. Third party software for the Mac family must comprehend these constructs. IBM clone personal computers are based on the Intel 80x86 family of microprocessors and run a plethora of operating systems, including MS-DOS, UNIX, OS/2, and Windows. The vast majority of units applicable to desktop video run the Microsoft Windows operating environment.

Recently, Silicon Graphics introduced the Indigo family of workstations, bringing graphics workstation processing power into the personal computer platform price range. The Indigo is based on a MIPS R3000A and R4000A RISC microprocessors and runs SGI's UNIX implementation. This system is anticipated to gain market share as desktop video matures and more processing power is needed for the applications.

Disk Drives

Most CPU units also include a magnetic "hard" disk drive with a capacity between 20 megabytes and 200 megabytes. Some systems employ larger drives, but few employ drives with capacities suitable for video capture and playback and nonlinear editing.

Those systems will require additional disk storage, either magnetic or optical in nature, allowing fast random access to over 1 gigabyte (1 billion bytes) of information. These drives can either be mounted internally or externally via fast interfaces such as SCSI-II. The optical drives include both magneto-optical and phase-change mechanisms.

A special case of optical storage is the CD ROM drive. Each drive is capable of accessing at least one CD ROM holding up to 660 megabytes of digital information representing graphic images, audio, text, databases, animations, etc. CD ROM drives are typically outboard systems and are read-only devices suitable only for information retrieval, rather than storage.

Output Devices

Computers require visual output devices in the form of RGB video monitors. These differ somewhat from the monitors used for video production in terms of vertical and horizontal frequencies supported, resolutions provided, and packaging options. They are also usually less expensive. Most personal computers employ monitors sized from 14 diagonal inches to 20 diagonal inches.

An alternative to a computer monitor, or an addition in some cases, particularly suitable to presentation and demonstration applications is a projection device. A projection device allows the viewing of the computer's visual output by a large number of people, typically by projecting an image of the output on a wall or other white surface. Some projection devices provide their own light sources; others require the use of overhead projectors.

Input Devices

Personal computers utilize a variety of input devices, dominated by typewriter-like keyboards. Most keyboards for desktop personal computers employ over 100 keys, including alphanumeric keys, function keys, special command keys, and a numeric keypad section. Computers which utilize Graphic User Interfaces (GUIs), such as the Apple Macintosh family or IBM-compatibles using the Microsoft Windows program, also utilize a mouse or trackball to maneuver an arrow-shaped cursor around the screen. These "point and click" interfaces allow less sophisticated users access to the power of the computer.

Desktop video users will also employ several other input devices. Scanners allow the input of still graphic images into the computer; the PC accumulates the information provided by the scanner and loads it into a graphic file for later use by applications software. Digitizing tablets allow direct input of rectilinear position information, e.g. map coordinates or graph plots, into the computer. Jog/Shuttle controllers allow the desktop video user access to user controls similar to those prevalent in the conventional video industry. Conventional video professionals are enamored neither of the personal computer keyboard, nor of the mouse or trackball, as a means of controlling the edit process. Jog/Shuttle controllers provide a bridge between the older and newer technologies in regard to user controls.

Revenues and Revenue Growth Rates

1989 revenues for personal computer platforms were $14.1 million as conventional video postproduction suites began using personal computers and graphics software to replace dedicated titling, paintbox, and animation systems. Revenue growth exceeded 100 percent for the years between 1990 and 1992 as the introduction of new graphics software, integrated systems and components such as the NewTek Video Toaster and the Digital F/X Video F/X system drove new personal computer sales. 1992 ended with $270.9 million in personal computer platform revenues, representing a growth rate of 143.0 percent over the previous year.

Revenue growth in personal computer platforms is expected to moderate, but remain very strong for the remainder of the survey period. In 1995, revenues are anticipated to reach exceed $1.74 billion, an increase of 70.3 percent over the prior year. By 1999, revenues are forecasted to reach $6.64 billion, an improvement of 29.2 percent over 1998.

Revenue growth for the period surveyed is forecasted at a very healthy 57.9 percent, reflecting the underpinning of personal computer platforms to the entire desktop video movement.

Fig. 6-6:	Personal Computer Platforms

Unit Shipment and Revenue Forecasts 1989-1999				
Year	Units (000)	Revenues ($M)	Revenue Growth(%)	Unit Growth(%)
1989	3.7	14.1	----	----
1990	8.1	30.5	117.0	120.3
1991	30.0	111.5	265.0	270.6
1992	74.0	270.9	143.0	146.7
1993	149.7	539.9	99.3	102.3
1994	289.5	1023.2	89.5	93.4
1995	513.6	1742.6	70.3	77.4
1996	827.5	2638.8	51.4	61.1
1997	1286.7	3775.1	43.1	55.5
1998	1946.8	5140.6	36.2	51.3
1999	2857.9	6640.8	29.2	46.8
TOTAL			*57.9%*	*65.7%*

Unit Shipments and Pricing Trends

Unit shipments are anticipated to grow slightly faster than revenues, as the personal computer platforms continue to drop in price for given functionality, with the gap widening as the years pass. Units of personal computer platforms include base CPU systems plus bundles of necessary peripherals purchased for primary use in desktop video systems.

In 1989, shipments of personal computer platforms totaled 3700 units. By 1992, this figure had risen to 74 thousand units, reflecting a growth of 146.7 percent over the prior year. 1995 shipments are forecasted at 513,600 units, a rise of 77.4 percent over 1994. The end of the survey period, 1999, is expected to see shipments of nearly 2.86 million units, an increase of 46.8 percent over the prior year. The unit shipment CAGR for the period surveyed is forecasted at 68.5 percent, a small delta over the revenue growth CAGR of 57.9 percent.

Although strong pricing pressures are anticipated in the personal computer platforms subsegment, desktop video will require increasing functionality and storage capability, helping stabilize the average purchase price of desktop video personal computer platforms and mitigating the overall downward trend in pricing for this segment. This stabilizing effect will override the natural downward pricing trend in pricing up until about 1995 when the desktop video market begins to mature and normal pricing effects resume for the latter part of the decade.

Market and Technology Trends

Qualitative Trends

Video on Board

One of the current limitations of personal computer platforms is the separation of general purpose processing and video processing via a relatively slow input/output bus. There is a trend toward putting the video processor closer logically to the central processor, thus enhancing the computer's ability to process the vast amounts of video data prevalent in applications such as desktop video. Apple has indicated that it will soon release a line of personal computers with integrated video capabilities, thereby improving the applicability of these systems to desktop video.

Faster, Faster

At the same time, the continuing trend in personal computers is for speed, in terms of computing power, bus transaction speed, and storage transfer rates. Current microprocessor technologies are barely able to handle compressed video thruputs at the present time; it is reasonable to expect continued performance improvements in this area. Likewise, a limitation in a personal computer's ability to process full-motion, full-size, artifact-free video is the bus structure central to the information flow. Common bus structures are nominally fast enough for compressed video data, but not uncompressed data. Improvements in high-capacity disk drive transfer rates will also be required for the next generation of desktop video systems.

The performance curve for these three different functional areas has been pretty steep over recent history and there is every indication that it will remain so.

Workstation Infiltration

It is interesting to note that the workstation class of computers incorporate many features which are beneficial to the processing demands of desktop video processing, including multitasking operating systems, virtual memory and storage systems, integrated graphics, and integrated networking. At the same time, it is interesting to note that only Silicon Graphics (and to a lesser extent the now repositioned NeXT) have pursued the desktop video market. It would be reasonable to expect competition in this area from other workstation vendors, such as Sun and Hewlett Packard.

Disk Drive Capacity

Current compression technologies require 1GB of storage space for each 15 minutes or so of stored video. As of early 1993, it is difficult to obtain single storage devices with over 2GB of total storage. The combination of such sizes with thruput rates sufficient to transfer full-motion video to and from the disk is extremely difficult to locate; even so, this only allows approximately 30 minutes of online video storage in a single device.

Again, extrapolating historical data, it is reasonable to anticipate the development of 5-10GB devices in the near future with transfer speeds sufficient for video i/o.

CD-ROMs

The growth of the multimedia market has led to the development of the MPC or multimedia personal computer, which includes an integral CD-ROM storage device. Whereas these devices are read-only and very slow (compared to video i/o requirements), the trend toward integrating these devices in standard personal computer platforms provides a high capacity read-only storage device for video applications, such as MIDI and audio file playback, background art, fonts, etc.

Newly announced technology which allows read/write capability for CD-type devices is at present too slow and too expensive to be considered desktop video technology. There is the possibility that this technology can evolve over the next few years into an affordable means for storing video data.

DSP on Board

Another trend in personal computer platforms is the coming integration of audio digital signal processing (DSP) circuitry on the motherboards of systems, rather than via outboard or plug-in devices. This will give common personal computers the ability to process 16-bit, CD-quality audio with integral circuitry such as that common in products by vendors like Digidesign.

Competitive Analysis / Market Share

Competitive Environment

The personal computer industry has stagnated in recent years after nearly a decade of explosive growth. One reason is the relative lack of new applications to which personal computers can be applied. Multimedia represents a new application, as does desktop video.

As the personal computer industry grew and coalesced around standard platforms and other interface structures, price became the dominant competitive issue. The emergence of new application areas with few fixed standards, such as multimedia and desktop video, offers new competitive vistas for the developers of personal computer products. Although much of the demand in the multimedia and desktop video markets will be for standardized, mass market elements, some of it will be for products which manufacturers can differentiate on a basis of performance, thereby reducing some of the margin pressures they have felt in recent years.

Structure

Thanks to the personal computer explosion in the 1980's, this category is one of the most diverse and competitive ones associated in any way with desktop video. Originally dominated by a few key vendors, such as Apple and IBM, the personal computer market has attracted thousands of small, entrepreneurial organizations and larger, established firms, each of whom may choose to compete across a broad range of products or a specific product niche area. Products tend to congregate around established standards, typically defined by operating systems vendors or CPU unit suppliers, with other vendors supplying supplementary products. In some cases, the CPU unit and operating systems structures are closely controlled by the developer organizations and there are few essentially identical product offerings for buyers to choose among.   In other cases, the CPU unit and/or operating systems structures are considered "open" and there are numerous competitors who provide similar products, competing on a basis of price/performance.

In all cases, third parties have developed compatible products for given CPU unit ("bus") and operating system structures and fierce competition has developed among them. Competition is typically based on pricing among the more standardized product lines and a combination of price and performance among others.

Where severe pricing competition exists, particularly in the PC-compatibles segment of the market, the dominant vendors have evolved into either offshore, Asian-based corporations, or U.S. companies with offshore manufacturing. In more exclusive product niches, U.S. organizations can compete equally, or on better terms, than offshore companies.

Desktop video products are such a product niche. Until standards develop, U.S. companies (and some Canadians) are likely to hold the largest market share in such products as Integrated Systems and Components, Machine Control Products, and Concept Development Tools.

Personal Computer Platforms are essentially personal computers and a bundle of standard peripherals. They are not unique to desktop video markets, and are therefore subject to the same competitive pressures as the general personal computer market. Vendors compete in the same ways. Offshore-manufactured products are serious contenders in most standardized product areas, such as monitors and disk drives, and domestic products dominate restricted-market product areas such as operating systems, scanners, and storage arrays.

| Fig. 6-7: | List of Selected Vendors |
| | Personal Computer Platforms |

Company	Product Lines
Abaton	scanners
Adaptec	adapters (storage)
ALR	ISA/EISA/MC-bus CPUs, notebooks
Apple Computer	NuBus CPUs, monitors, notebooks, printers, mice, disk drives, software, keyboards, scanners, CD-ROM drives
Archive	tape drives, adapters
AST	ISA/EISA-bus CPUs, notebooks
ATI Technologies	adapters
Austin Computer Systems	ISA//EISA-bus CPUs, notebooks
AVR Technology	scanners
Aydin Controls	monitors
Barco	monitors
CalComp	plotters
Canon	scanners, printers
Cardinal Technologies	adapters
CMS	tape drives
Commodore International	Amiga family CPUs, monitors
Compaq	ISA/EISA-bus CPUs,notebooks, printers
CompuAdd Computer	ISA/EISA-bus CPUs, notebooks
Computer Friends	scanners, printers
Dell Computer	ISA/EISA-bus CPUs, monitors, notebooks
Diamond Computer	adapters
E-Machines	monitors, adapters
Eastman Kodak	printers
Emulex	adapters (storage)
Epson	ISA-bus CPUs, printers, scanners, notebooks, optical drives
Everex Systems	ISA/EISA-bus CPUs, notebooks, adapters
Exabyte	tape drives
Fujitsu	ISA-bus CPUs, printers, scanners
Generation Systems	monitors
Genoa Systems Corp.	adapters
Hewlett Packard	ISA/EISA-bus CPUs, printers, plotters, scanners, disk drives
Hitachi	monitors, CD-ROM drives, disk drives, optical drives, video walls
Houston Instruments/Summagraphics	digitizing tablets, plotters
Howtek	scanners
IBM	ISA/MC-bus CPUs, monitors, notebooks, printers,

	keyboards, adapters
Idek	monitors
Ikegami	monitors
Key Tronic Corp.	keyboards, input devices, mice
Logitech	mice, scanners, input devices
Macproducts	monitors
Mass Microsystems	monitors
Matrox	adapters
Maxoptics	optical drives
Maxtor	disk drives
Micropolis	disk drives
Microsoft	systems software, mice
Mirror Technology	monitors, scanners
Mitsubishi	monitors, printers
Mouse Systems	mice, scanners
Nanao	monitors
NEC	ISA-bus CPUs, monitors, printers
Nikon	scanners
Nissei Sangyo America	monitors
Northgate Computer Systems	ISA/EISA-bus CPUs, notebooks
Nutmeg Systems	monitors
Orchid Technology	adapters
Panasonic	ISA-bus CPUs, notebooks, disk drives, optical drives, printers, monitors
Philips	CD-ROM drives, monitors
Pinnacle Micro	optical drives
Pioneer	CD ROM drives, optical drives
Presentation Technologies	monitors
Quantum	disk drives
Radius, Inc.	monitors, adapters
Raster Graphics	plotters
RasterOps Corp.	monitors, adapters
Relisys	monitors
Reply Corp.	MC-bus CPUs
RGB Spectrum	media wall display
Ricoh	scanners
Roland	plotters
Sampo	notebooks, monitors
Samsung	monitors, notebooks, printers
Samtron	monitors
Sanyo	notebooks, printers
Seagate	disk drives
Seiko Instruments	printers, monitors
Sharp	notebooks, scanners
Sigma Designs	adapters, monitors

Silicon Graphics Inc	Indigo workstations, graphics adapters
Sony	monitors, CD-ROM drives, optical drives
Storage Solutions	disk drives
SuperMac Technology	monitors, adapters, printers
SyQuest	disk drives
Tandy Corporation	ISA-bus CPUs, monitors, printers, notebooks
Taxan	monitors
TEC	printers, scanners
Tektronix	printers
Texas Instruments	ISA/EISA-bus CPUs, notebooks, printers, adapters
ViewSonic	monitors
Wacom Technology	digitizing tablets
WangDAT	DAT drives
Wangtek	tape drives
Western Digital	disk drives, adapters
Wyse/Amdek	ISA/EISA-bus CPUs, notebooks, monitors, adapters
Zenith Data Systems	ISA/EISA-bus CPUs, monitors, notebooks

Issues

Dominant Platforms

In the early years of desktop video, 1989-1991, the Personal Computer Platform of choice was the Commodore Amiga family because of the emergence of the NewTek Video Toaster. In fact, in recent years the Toaster has almost single-handedly driven sales of Amiga family.

Following closely on the heels of the Amiga was the Macintosh family from Apple, mostly because of its strong presence in the computer graphics market. PC-compatibles have been slower to penetrate the desktop video market, but recent developments in this area have made this family of products stronger contenders. In 1992 Silicon Graphics introduced the Indigo platform, combining the low cost of a personal computer with the power of a graphics workstation.

The popularity of the Mac family and PC-compatibles in the general market, and the SGI workstations in the high-end graphics and animations markets indicate that these will eventually become the dominant platforms for desktop video applications. Already, powerful desktop video systems from such vendors as Avid and Digital F/X are based on Mac platforms and systems from Matrox, EMC, and FAST are based on the PC structure. Avid has announced an intention to port its Media Suite Pro and Media Composer families over to the Indigo platform.

It is unclear whether the Toaster, and the products which support it, can continue to sustain the Amiga family as viable desktop video platforms.

Outboard Processing

Some vendors, notably Digital F/X and Immix, have chosen to utilize outboard proprietary bus structures in addition to a personal computer (Apple Mac in these cases) platform. Although this sort of structure improves performance of the video system, it introduces a number of complications into a desktop video platform. One is sheer size of the combined system. Another is the power consumed. A third is the additional cost of the extra chassis.

Perhaps more important is the divergence from a general purpose bus structure product, the underlying benefit and driving technology of desktop video in the first place, to a special purpose device, albeit one with a connection to a standardized platform.

Market Shares

Market shares in this area are not broken out by vendors, explicitly, but by general classes of platforms, as units are counted as bundles of products which form the base for desktop video systems. Each bundle contains a CPU unit, at least one video monitor, a keyboard, disk storage, an operating system, and an average set of peripherals, including mice, optical disks, scanners, printers, digitizing tablets, etc. As different vendors provide these various components, it is impossible within the scope of this research to break the individual vendors out in terms of market share. Such breakouts are available in studies of the personal computer market. The general composition of the platforms are important for purposes of a desktop video study, not the individual vendors who supply them.

There are four current forms of Personal Computer Platforms for desktop video use. The largest share is held by Commodore and the other devotees to the Amiga family of platforms.

This group of vendors, in which Commodore itself is the major supplier, accounts for 81.1 percent of Personal Computer Platform sales, in terms of 1992 units. The reason for this dominant position is the same as the reason NewTek holds the lead in Integrated Systems and Components: the phenomenal success of NewTek's Video Toaster. This share is eroding as products configured for other platforms, particularly the Apple Macintosh and PC-compatibles families, enter the market.

The second largest market share in Personal Computer Platforms, at 10.8 percent, is held by Apple Computer and complementary manufacturers.   Apple is the dominant vendor within this group, thanks to a broad array of products, including its Macintosh family of CPU units, monitors, keyboards, mice, scanners, printers, CD-ROM drives, disk drives, operating systems software, motion video software, adapters, and a host of other products. The Apple family is charging hard against the Commodore family lead, thanks to the introduction of a broad array of Integrated Systems and Components based on the Apple Macintosh platforms and the broad base of graphics products already available for Apple products.

Also making a charge at the leader, albeit a later one, are the PC-compatibles. PC-compatible Personal Computer Platforms are those ISA-bus, EISA-Bus, and Microchannel-bus units based on Intel family microprocessors and Microsoft MS-DOS and Windows operating systems. Microsoft is a key vendor in this area, although they are known primarily for software only. IBM, the founder of this classification with their initial PC, PC-XT, and PC-AT product lines, is also a key contributor with its PS/1 and PS/2 product lines, including a broad array of products. In this product area, like almost no other, there are thousands of vendors providing various platform components and competing in either single or multiple product areas. Other vendors include: Dell Computer, Compaq, Intel, Everex, AST, Wyse, Reply Systems, Western Digital, Seagate, Panasonic, ViewSonic, Hewlett Packard, Texas Instruments, and lots more. PC-compatibles acquired 7.6 percent of the desktop video Personal Computer Platforms subsegment in 1992 and can be expected to continue to gain share as more and more ISA/EISA/MC-bus products become available in the near future.

Bringing up the rear, in terms of market share but certainly not in terms of capabilities, is the Silicon Graphics Indigo platform and compatible products. SGI is making a strong play for desktop video and general medium-range graphics applications markets with this product, seeking support and compatible product development from a number of third party vendors. At present, SGI is the dominant vendor in this area, but new products are being introduced almost daily. The sheer power and reasonable pricing of this workstation platform family will make it a serious contendor in the desktop video market, although 1992 market share is only about 0.5 percent

No other platform family captured Personal Computer Platform market share in 1992, although it is possible that families centered around Sun workstations, NeXT systems, Hewlett Packard workstations, and other systems may gain limited market share in the future.

Fig. 6-8:   1992 Market Shares
                 Personal Computer Platforms

Platform Family	Share
Amiga-centered	81.1%
Mac-centered	10.8%
PC-Compatibles	7.6%
Indigo-centered	0.5%
Others	0.0%
TOTAL	100.0%

Highlights of Selected Vendors

Commodore International, LTD

Commodore is based in West Chester, Pennsylvania, but is registered as a Bahamian corporation. Its Amiga personal computers, including the Amiga 2000 and 4000 product lines, have extensive video and audio capabilities, which made them attractive to the desktop video pioneer NewTek, who in turn utilized these capabilities to develop the Video Toaster product family.

Despite features such as NTSC video and built-in PC-compatible ISA bus structures, the Amiga family has struggled for market share throughout its life. The Toaster gave it a strong boost, and in the opinion of many, saved the Amiga platform from extinction. With the strong pressure from the more popular Apple and PC-compatible product families in the desktop video market, it is doubtful that Commodore will retain much of the market share it has acquired there.

Commodore sells most of its products via distributors and authorized dealers. They have followed NewTek's lead in seeking out desktop video dealers and VARs to move their products along with the Video Toaster. They have also arranged an OEM deal with NewTek in which NewTek bundles an Amiga platform into its Toaster Workstation product line.

Apple Computer

Apple, the legendary and prototypical Silicon Valley computer company founded by visionary nonconformists in the 70's has evolved a respected corporate giant in the 90's. Headquartered in Cupertino, California, Apple today is one of the dominant vendors of the personal computer market, offering a broad range of products based around their internally-developed bus structures, innovative graphical user interfaces, operating systems, and other systems software. Apple products include the Macintosh IIci, IIsi, Quadra 700, Quadra 900, Quadra 950, and new Centris 610 and 650 CPU units. They also provide Powerbook and Duo notebook PCs, accessories, printers, disk drives, mice, keyboards, scanners, CD-ROM drives, powered speakers, and a host of other peripherals to their CPU units.

Apple is most famous for their graphical user interface (GUI) to their operating system for the Macintosh family, which replaced text-based commands with point-and-select icon-based control. This innovative concept was immediately popular with artists and other creative types who had little desire to learn complicated commands. The popularity of the Apple Macintosh with the artistic community led in turn to the development of Mac-based paint, font-generation,

3D animation, and other graphical programs, some of which are listed later in this chapter under Graphics Software Products. It has also led to the growth of the Mac in the desktop video environment, which is populated primarily by the same artistic, computer-phobic personnel.

Apple's early advantage in this GUI area has been offset somewhat recently by the development of Windows for PC-compatibles and for the Gem operating environment popular on the Amiga. Even powerful UNIX-based workstations such as the SGI Indigo have their own GUI front-ends based on the X-Windows specification. Apple products are still perceived by many computer illiterates as being more user friendly and easier to learn how to use than competive structures, so Apple and compatible vendors are likely to continue to gain market share in the desktop video environment.

Apple has never chosen to rest on its laurels. It has always been an innovative organization, and this trend continues today. Apple's development of the QuickTime standard for digital motion video is a critical factor in the growth of digital video technologies, leading to low-cost, prevalent, online, nonlinear video editing systems, the cornerstone of the desktop video movement.

Apple markets their products through authorized dealers and VARs, selling to the latter via computer distributors.

Microsoft

This Redmond, Washington giant practically owns the operating system market for PC-compatibles, thanks to IBM's selection of MS-DOS as the basis for the PC, PC/XT, and PC/AT product lines. Microsoft followed this coup with the development of the Windows operating system in order to compete with the GUI operating system of the Apple Macintosh family. Microsoft also developed the OS/2 operating system in conjunction with IBM, although it has disassociated itself from that product in recent years. Although a number of vendors provide the base CPU units and peripheral hardware in the PC-compatible market segment, Microsoft provides or had a hand in providing the operating systems for over 95 percent of these units.

Microsoft is also a key vendor in software applications for Windows, MS-DOS,and Macintosh operating environments. They produce Word, a leading word processing program, and Excel, a leading spreadsheet, and a broad range of other applications, including presentation software, project management software, artistic tools, etc. Microsoft has also produced Video for Windows, an operating system extension similar to Apple's QuickTime structure, which provides a framework for digital video applications in Windows-based personal computers.

Microsoft markets their products via distributors, dealers, and mail order.

IBM

IBM, once the proverbial 400-pound gorilla of the personal computer market, is no longer quite as dominant, but is still a force to be reckoned with. The Armonk, New York firm is known primarily for its mainframes and minicomputers and for its legitimization of the personal computer industry via the introduction of the PC and PC/XT in the early 80's. Prior to IBM's entry in the market, personal computers were considered toys; IBM brought legitimacy, an open bus structure, and marketing clout, almost single handedly creating the personal computer market as it is known today.

IBM, despite its annoying tendency to go its own way and create, rather than adhere to, industry standards, is a still-formidable producer of computers, monitors, and notebook pcs, as well as a broad range of peripherals, communication devices, and larger computer systems. IBM's recent collaborations with Intel have led to the introduction of its Ultimedia line of personal computer products and a focus on multimedia and desktop video applications. Although most of these products are inadequate for desktop video purposes, the focus on digital video applications indicates that IBM will be a contender in desktop video in the coming years.

IBM markets their products via direct sales (in conjunction with larger systems sales) and via a network of authorized dealers.

Silicon Graphics

Silicon Graphics, Inc., of Mountain View, California, is known primarily for its high-powered computer graphics workstations, often costing in excess of $100,000. Such products have been adopted for use by the Hollywood film and video community, but are far too expensive for use by desktop video producers.

SGI solved this problem a couple of years ago with the introduction of the Indigo product line. These lower-cost (under $20,000) products are based on RISC microprocessors from SGI's MIPS subsidiary, run a variant of the UNIX operating system, and have powerful graphics and audio processing capabilities. SGI has taken an aggressive third-party development posture with this product line, intending to become serious competitors in the professional graphics and video markets. They have developed cooperative projects with key video suppliers as Chyron and Avid Technology.

SGI is expected to gain market share at the high end of the desktop video market in the coming years. They have classically marketed their products via direct sales, but the Indigo line is being sold via a number of channels, including authorized dealers and mail order.

The Texans

Compaq Computer Corporation, of Houston, Texas, was the first serious competitor in the PC-compatible market pioneered by IBM. Today, it is the leader of the of the PC-compatible vendors, with over $4 billion in sales of ISA- and EISA-bus PC platforms, notebooks and other portables, printers, and a range of other products. Compaq followed IBM's lead also in utilizing authorized retailers to sell their products.

Fellow Texans at Dell Computer Corporation in Austin exploited the growing strategy of utilizing mail order firms to move standardized personal computers and peripherals. Dell grew into one of the largest suppliers of PC-compatibles, including EISA- and ISA-bus CPUs, in the late 80's.

The Japanese

A number of Japanese organizations have also entered the personal computer market, focusing primarily on peripherals such as disk drives, monitors, and printers. A key supplier of PC-compatible monitors is NEC, the Nippon Electric Corporation, who also makes a line of desktop ISA-bus computers, a line printers, and numerous other peripherals.

Panasonic, a series of divisions of the Matsushita Corporation, is a key vendor in several segments of the desktop video market, including Personal Computer Platforms. Panasonic produces and markets hard drives, optical drives, printers, monitors, PCs, and notebooks, among other products.

Most of the Japanese suppliers, including NEC and Panasonic, utilize distributors to remarket to dealers and VARs.

Machine Control Products

Total Machine Control Products Market

Market Definitions and Overview

Machine control products are those software and hardware items which control external recording and playback systems from personal computer platforms. They include both internal boards and software products as well as external devices which provide this functionality.

In 1989, machine control products represented 15.5 percent of the total video production products shipments. This percentage began to drop almost immediately as the desktop video postproduction products market emerged and is expected to continue this decline throughout the survey period.   This is because machine control products are either becoming more integrated with other desktop video systems, including Recording and Playback Devices and Integrated Systems and Components, or are being obsoleted by the trend to digital video. By 1999, machine control products are forecasted to comprise only 1.9 percent of the nearly $12 billion desktop video postproduction products market.

Revenues and Revenue Growth Rates

1989 revenues from the sales of machine control products totaled $6.7 million. Revenue growth rates, as in almost all other segments of the desktop video market, were exceptionally high in the initial years of desktop video emergence, 1990 and 1991, and dropped precipitously to 35.0 percent for 1992, when revenues totaled $52.3 million.

In 1994, revenues are expected to peak at $65.7 million, and drop the following year to $60.3 million, representing a negative revenue growth of -8.3 percent. The extreme dropoff in revenue growth is anticipated because of continuing integration of machine control products into integrated systems, an intermediate move into lower priced software-based products, and the eventual practical obsolescence of the entire category of products as postproduction systems become all-digital in the latter 90's.

Following the downturn to negative growth rates in 1995, revenue growth is anticipated to remain slightly negative for the rest of the survey period. 1999 revenues are forecasted at $52.7 million, a decrease of 3.7 percent from the previous year. Overall revenue CAGR is forecasted at 0.1 percent for the period surveyed.

Fig. 6-9:	Machine Control Products Unit Shipment and Revenue Forecasts 1989-1999			
Year	Units (000)	Revenues ($M)	Revenue Growth(%)	Unit Growth(%)
1989	1.7	6.7	----	----
1990	4.6	14.6	119.0	170.4
1991	15.1	38.7	165.0	227.2
1992	25.4	52.3	35.0	68.7
1993	38.6	62.7	19.9	51.8
1994	56.2	65.7	4.8	45.5
1995	79.3	60.3	(8.3)	41.1
1996	107.4	55.5	(7.9)	35.4
1997	136.1	54.8	(1.2)	26.7
1998	156.2	54.8	(0.1)	14.8
1999	170.9	52.7	(3.7)	9.4
TOTAL			*0.1%*	*31.3%*

Unit Shipments and Pricing Trends

Unit shipments are forecasted to fare somewhat better than revenues, at least in terms of sustained growth. Units of machine control products are defined as single hardware or software entities or single hardware/software combinations which provide recording device control for desktop video postproduction systems.

In 1989, shipments of machine control products totaled 1700 units. Unit growth was very strong in 1990 and 1991 and declined somewhat in 1992 to 68.7 percent, following shipments of 25,400 units. Unit shipment growth dropped off significantly during the remainder of the survey period but remained far stronger than the revenue growth rates for the corresponding periods. The reason for this is the early movement from all-hardware products to hardware/software bundles, to software only solutions, prior to the virtual obsolescence of the entire category by all-digital, non-linear postproduction systems as the survey period draws to a close.

1995 shipments are anticipated to reach over 79,300 units, a growth of 41.1 percent over the prior year. 1999 shipments are pegged at over 170,9000 units, an increase over 1998 of 9.4 percent. Total period shipment CAGR is 31.3 percent, a significant delta over revenue CAGR, indicating the strong pricing pressure in this subsegment as the software technologies evolve, followed by those of non-linear editing.

Prices of Machine Control Products are expected to drop precipitously in the 1993-1995 timeframe as software-only solutions become more popular and digital video editing catches on. By the end of the decade, desktop video should be dominated by digital video postproduction systems which will not require frame-accurate control of linear media, thereby rendering the product category almost obsolete.

Market and Technology Trends

Qualitative Trends

Field Logging Products

Conventional video production involves hours in postproduction "logging" or defining the starting and ending points of each recorded segment of a video production on the source tapes. In recent years, several desktop video tools have been developed which allow logging of source tapes during the postproduction process, thus speeding the already time-consuming and expensive postproduction phase. These tools, and notebook computers, will be used extensively in desktop video productions, thus maximizing the time spent on the more expensive (even in desktop video suites!) postproduction equipment.

Field logging tools are evolving as software-only or software-dominant products, thereby reducing the manufacturing costs of these items, which is in turn generally reflected in the price to the eventual consumer.

Digitization

As postproduction systems become increasingly all-digital affairs, the requirements for analog recording and playback devices will decrease substantially. Accordingly, the demand for devices which control these decks will also decrease substantially.

Those analog recording and playback devices which will be required will not be required to have frame accurate control, since the nonlinear editing systems will maintain frame accuracy during editing and can output edited "master" tapes at full frame rates. At the same time, frame-accurate decks are becoming available for desktop video applications at lower and lower prices. These decks often incorporate machine control features within the framework of the recording device, or in conjunction with a RS-232-C connection to the host desktop video system.

Competitive Analysis / Market Share

Competitive Environment

Machine Control Systems are closely tied to the Recording and Playback Systems they control. With a few exceptions, each Recording and Playback System, even within a given manufacturer's line, has irregularities in its interfaces to Machine Control Systems which require a great deal of customization to adapt to. Accordingly, most machine control systems have historically competed on the basis of which individual VTRs they control. One vendor would select VTRs A, B, and C, and another would make products for VTRs X, Y, and Z. Some standards are beginning to develop which will lessen this problem. Sony's VISCA protocol, among others, are typical of this industry development.

In the desktop video market a dichotomy exists between preferred acquisition media (hence equipment) and editing media. The Hi-8 format is preferred for video acquisition, and has machine control interface capability, but it is currently unsuitable for editing (see Chapter 2). The S-VHS format, while suitable for editing, is available in only a very few camcorders which are machine controllable. The control formats for Matsushita S-VHS products is significantly different from the Sony Hi-8 products, so it is difficult to develop single machine control solutions to handle both.

Since there is no single machine control interface standard to coalesce around, Machine Control Products are very dissimilar and do not compete against each other on a basis of price alone. Rather, more important are the VTRs supported, the breadth of functionality provided, the speed at which they operate, and how available they are to the buyers (quality of distribution).

Desktop video Machine Control Products are those which are based on personal computers. There are also consumer-level and professional-level edit and animation controllers which are standalone devices, operating independently from any computer control. These are not included in this section as Machine Control Products, but they do compete against the products listed here, both in consumer and in conventional video markets.

Structure

The vast majority of suppliers of Machine Control Products specialize in this area. Exceptions include Panasonic, Sony, Digital F/X, Gold Disk, the now-defunct AT&T Graphics Software Labs, and the ubiquitous Comprehensive Video Supply (via its subsidiary CV Technologies). As this is a small market niche, the specialty firms tend to be small, with the more successful ones slightly larger.

Those firms who compete in other product areas fall into two general categories: the video supemarket suppliers (Sony, Panasonic, Comprehensive Video Supply), and the desktop video suppliers focusing on editing and graphical software (Digital F/X, Gold Disk, AT&T GSL). The larger firms rely on professional video dealers for sales; Machine Control Products are adjuncts and supplementary sales to those of VTRs, cameras, and editing systems. The smaller firms focus on edit and animation control, selling directly to end users, via professional video dealers, and through VARs as part of integrated, heterogeneous video editing systems.

<table>
<tr><td colspan="2">Fig. 6-10:   List of Selected Vendors
Machine Control Products</td></tr>
<tr><td>Company</td><td>Products</td></tr>
<tr><td>Abbate Video</td><td>VideoToolkit</td></tr>
<tr><td>Advanced Digital Imaging</td><td>MacVAC, MacAnim8</td></tr>
<tr><td>ARTI</td><td>Clark Media Controller, Pro:mc, Pro:mc-v, VideoPublisher</td></tr>
<tr><td>AT&T GSL</td><td>StudioMaster</td></tr>
<tr><td>BCD Associates</td><td>BCD 450, BCD-2000A</td></tr>
<tr><td>Chase Technologies</td><td>Soft VTR</td></tr>
<tr><td>Comprehensive Video Supply Log</td><td>Edit Master, Edit Master Mac, Log Master, Visual Master, Edit Lister, EDL Translator, Edit Tracker, Cutter, MacAnimator, MacAnimator Plus, VideoMac, MacRemote</td></tr>
<tr><td>Diaquest</td><td>DQ-Animaq, Series II, DQ-MAC232, DIGI-COMP, DQ-422+, DQ-50P, DQ-TACO</td></tr>
<tr><td>Digital F/X</td><td>Video F/X TapeMaker</td></tr>
<tr><td>DNF Industries</td><td>ST60, ST100</td></tr>
<tr><td>Dubner</td><td>Scene Stealer</td></tr>
<tr><td>Ensemble Designs</td><td>InMotion</td></tr>
<tr><td>Editing Technolgies Corp</td><td>Ensemble Pro</td></tr>
<tr><td>Focus Graphics</td><td>ImageCorder</td></tr>
<tr><td>Future Video</td><td>Editlink 2200, 2200/TC, 2200/TCG, 3300, and 3300/TC, EC-1000 Pro MkII, EC 1000 Pro/TC MkII, EDL-2000, EDL-1000A, EDL-2000/FX, EditLink 2000-DT, DT/TC.</td></tr>
<tr><td>Gold Disk</td><td>Video Director</td></tr>
<tr><td>Homrich Communications</td><td>EZV2</td></tr>
<tr><td>Horita</td><td>Time Code Toolkit</td></tr>
<tr><td>IEV</td><td>Revolution</td></tr>
<tr><td>Image Logic</td><td>Log Producer</td></tr>
<tr><td>Interactive Media Technologies</td><td>IMTX 8000 system</td></tr>
<tr><td>Linker Systems</td><td>The Animation Stand</td></tr>
<tr><td>Light Source Computer Images</td><td>The Sequencer</td></tr>
<tr><td>Lyon Lamb</td><td>MiniVAS, MicroVAS, ENC-7, ProVAS</td></tr>
<tr><td>McQ Productions</td><td>MacAnimator</td></tr>
<tr><td>Nucleus Electronics</td><td>Personal SFC</td></tr>
<tr><td>Panasonic</td><td>AG-A570, AG-A96</td></tr>
<tr><td>PEP</td><td>Shotlister</td></tr>
<tr><td>Pipeline Digital</td><td>AutoLog</td></tr>
</table>

Profusion Group	Soft-Edit-Pro 750, Pro-1000, Pro-2000, Pro-3000, Pro-500
RGB Computer & Video POD,	AmiLink/PRO, AmiLink/VT, AmiLink/CIP, AmiLink AmiLink Logger, AmiLink/CI
Selectra	VuPort
Sony	CI-1000 Vbox
Sundance	Sundance System Q-Cut A/B Roll, Sundance Controller
Technical Aesthetics Operations	Editizer
Videomedia	V-LAN hardware, OZ, Animax, VLX-RP, VLX-2R, PACE, Micron, SuperMicron, AutoPICT, VLAN/CX

Issues

Linear Thinking

As vendors begin to standardize around a few de facto or de jure interface standards, Machine Control Products will reduce to software and interface cables. This software is already becoming available and will continue to grow in importance throughout the rest of the survey period. One use of this software will be in logging and pre-editing source material, which is almost always done on a linear recording media like videotape, regardless of the editing techniques to be employed later.

Most software vendors will try to adopt linear editing paradigms for their Machine Control Products regardless of the eventual destination of the source material. If some of the limitations of linear editing are carried over into the products, they will be less than optimum for use in conjunction with nonlinear editing systems. Other vendors will develop products based on nonlinear editing paradigms.

Graphical EDLs

Early Machine Control Products employed text-oriented command structures suitable to video professionals, but less so to novices. Use of graphical user interfaces with Machine

Control Products will become more common, allowing video novices to edit without learning command line structures like those for EDLs.

Market Shares

Three companies have the largest market shares in the Machine Control Products subsegment of the desktop video postproduction market, followed by a number of other suppliers with sub-ten percent shares.

The largest share, as of 1992, has been captured by Videomedia with its V-LAN product family. The V-LAN line includes the software and hardware necessary to implement a local area network among compatible video devices. Videomedia is the creator of this technology and the largest supplier of compatible products, although many other vendors provide compatible hardware and software products, including vendors of Integrated Systems and Components and Recording and Playback Devices. Videomedia captured 31.2 percent of the Machine Control Products market in 1992.

Close on the heels of Videomedia is RGB Computer and Video, the creators and marketers of the AmiLink family of edit control products. The Amilink product line was developed to provide edit control capability for the Video Toaster product from NewTek. It has since been expanded to provide edit control functions for a number of other families of products. RGB Computer and Video, not to be confused with RGB Spectrum or RGB Dynamics, two other competitors in the desktop video market, garnered 25.1% of the Machine Control Products subsegment in 1992.

Diaquest provides a line of animation control hardware for various platforms and has captured 11.0 percent of the Machine Control Products market subsegment as of 1992 Products include Mac, PC-compatible, and Amiga-compatible adapters controlling RS-232-C, RS-422, and other formats of VTR interfaces, as well as standalone products.

Comprehensive Video Supply, the supermarket of the desktop video industry, supplies a broad line of hardware and software products for edit control, tape logging, EDL translation, and other machine control functions. It has acquired 5.5% of the Machine Control Products subsegment with these offerings.

Gold Disk is the world's largest publisher of Amiga software products and has diversified into products for the Apple Macintosh and PC-compatibles. Gold Disk offers the Video Director, a low-cost, cuts-only video editing, clip logging, and titling package for both the Amiga and Windows-based platforms. Gold Disk has 3.4% of the 1992 market for Machine Control Products, thanks to its sales of the Video Director.

Future Video acquired 2.1 percent of the market via sales of several lines of edit control products, including both hardware and software. Products include the EditLink series of hardware controllers and the EditList Manager editing software.

The only other vendor to acquire more than 1 percent of the Machine Control Products market in 1992 was Sundance, who just barely made it at 1.0 percent. Sundance makes the Sundance System Q-Cut software and the Sundance Controller for edit control of serially connected VTRs.

Fig. 6-11:   1992 Market Shares
                    Machine Control Products

Company	Shares
Videomedia	31.2%
RGB Computer & Video	25.1%
Diaquest	11.0%
Comprehensive Video Supply	5.5%
Gold Disk	3.4%
Future Video	2.1%
Sundance	1.0%
Others	20.9%

TOTAL	100.0%

Highlights of Selected Vendors

Videomedia

Videomedia, of San Jose, California is the developer of theV-LAN universal control network for video devices. V-LAN is a software/hardware system for controlling multiple video devices, such as VTRs, via a personal computer. It supports frame accuracy and SMPTE time code and up to 31 simultaneously connected and controlled devices. The V-LAN transmitter is connected to the host personal computer via an RS232C serial connection or via a bus interface card, and to multiple receivers via coax cable. The receivers are each connected to the various video devices via their control connections, including RS232C ports, LANC ports, RS422 ports, or even GPI triggers.

Products such as the V-LAN-T transmitters, and V-LAN-R, V-LAN-S, and V-LAN-G, receivers provide the hardware necessary to implement a V-LAN control structure. Videomedia also offers the VLX-2R dual receiver and V-LAN/CX - industrial/commercial receiver. The VLX-2R module fits in the VLX rackmount chassis; the V-LAN/CX utilizes LANC, Control-M (Panasonic), and Sony VISCA protocols to control inexpensive prosumer quality VTRs. Animax is a hardware controller card for Amigas and PCs which can be configured to control single VTRs or as a V-LAN-T transmitter.

Videomedia also offers OZ, a V-LAN compatible, PC-based desktop video editing software package for the Mac and Windows-based platforms. Various versions of OZ provide cuts-only editing, A/B roll editing, and switcher control. Videomedia provides the PACE professional, V-LAN compatible animation control module, Micron and SuperMicron edit controllers, and AutoPICT animation control software.

RGB Computer & Video

RGB, out of Riviera Beach, Florida, is the creator of the AmiLink family of edit control products. RGB has been in business since 1986 and has been producing AmiLink products since 1987. AmiLink is most often used in conjunction with the Video Toaster from NewTek in order to provide the Toaster with edit control. AmiLink operates over the V-LAN structure developed by Videomedia.

The AmiLink/PRO Production Editor runs on on Amigas, OS/2-based, or Windows-based PCs. It can control up to 16 source VTRs and 4 record VTRs at one time, reads VITC and LTC time code, and provides GPI triggers, serial switching control, single frame animation control, audio mixer control, EDL management, and extensive edit control. AmiLink/VT is a board-based hardware product. AmiLink/CIP is a stripped down version of the PRO system, allowing users to interface with "prosumer" quality VTRs. AmiLink POD is jog shuttle input device with a control keyboard. AmiLink Logger is tape logging software for for Windows, Amiga, and OS/2 environments. AmiLink/CI is a version of AmiLink/PRO optimized for industrial decks

Diaquest

Diaquest, of Berkeley, California, provides a series of bus-connected and standalone animation controller hardware and the software to support them. The DQ-Animaq ($2595 or $3395, depending on version) is a Macintosh-based animation controller designed for desktop video and broadcast applications. It features frame accurate video recording, and when used with a video graphics board, it allows users to digitize moving images and then composite them with 2d or 3d graphics to create rotoscoping or texture-mapping special effects. DQ-MAC232 is a software-only animation controller for RS232C compatible VTRs; the DIGI-COMP option adds frame accurate digitizing and alpha channel compositing features.

The DQ-422+ ($2380) and DQ-50P ($2780) are board-level controllers for PC-compatibles. Action Animator software ($695 if purchased w/hardware, $995 without hardware) is also available for use with these products. The DQ-TACO ($2195) is abailable for Amiga platforms.

For standalone situations, Diaquest offers the Series II animation controllers providing serial ($2995) control or serial/parallel control ($3995).

Comprehensive Video Supply

CVS, of Northvale, New Jersey, markets an array of Machine Control Products developed by its CV Technologies subsidiary, along with a broad spectrum of other desktop and conventional video products. CVS acts as a combination OEM, distributor, manufacturer, and dealer for products in almost every category covered by this report.

Edit Master and Edit Master Mac ($750 each) are cuts-only editing packages for PC-compatibles or Mac platforms. They control multiple RS232C-connected VTRs for simple editing. Log Master ($595) is a videotape logging software package for PC-compatibles. Visual Log Master is an upgrade, as is the multiuser Log Master Plus. Edit Lister ($750) is software package for PC-compatibles which provides Edit Descision List cleaning. EDL Translator ($695) is an software package for PC-compatibles used to convert EDLs among multiple formats. Edit Tracker ($695) is an EDL tracing program for PC-compatibles. Cutter is a cuts only editing system with an upgrade path to Edit Master, again for PC-compatibles. MacAnimator and MacAnimator Plus are a Mac based animation controllers.

Gold Disk

Gold Disk, Inc., was founded in 1984 as an Amiga software company rapidly became one of the world's leading Amiga software providers. Now based in Torrance, California, Gold Disk offers a range of software products for the Amiga, Windows-based, and Macintosh personal computer platforms.

In addition to a range of multimedia authoring, graphics, and presentation software products, Gold Disk also makes and markets the Video Director, a low-cost ($200) personal videotape editing package. Video Director offers VCR-like controls and produces cuts-only video prints by controlling LANC-compatible VTRs. Each package includes a serial LANC cable for interfacing the serial port of a personal computer with compatible VTRs and camcorders.

Future Video

Future Video, of Aliso Viejo, California, builds and markets a line of hardware and software used for edit control.   Some of their low-end products are standalone models used for consumer video editing.

Their desktop video line includes the Editlink 2200 ($695), 2200/TC ($1195), 2200/TCG ($1395), 3300 ($1295), and 3300/TC ($1795). Each Editlink 2200 product is a ISA-bus card that plugs into a PC-compatible platform and controls two VTRs using either Sony's LANC interface, or the 5-pin serial interface from Panasonic. Each can read Sony's 8mm time code, has an RS232C interface for controlling VTRs, and works in conjunction with Future Video's EditList Manager 2000 software. The TC and TCG versions add SMPTE time code functions. The 3300 series is similar, except that it allows true A/B roll editing. Again, the TC version adds a SMPTE time code reader.

The EC-1000 Pro MkII ($695) and EC 1000 Pro/TC MkII ($1195) are combination standalone/PC-based edit controllers.   The EDL-2000 ($395) and EDL-1000A ($295) are Amiga products. Future video also offers EDL-2000/FX ($595) Edit List Manager software, EditLink 2000-DT ($695) and 2000-DT/TC ($1195) VTR controllers.

Sundance

Sundance Technology Group of Irving, TX offers three Machine Control Products: the Sundance System Q-Cut Mac based editing system for serial-connected VTRs, the Sundance Controller, and the Q-Base tape logging system.

Others

Panasonic offers the AG-A570 edit controller for connecting two AG-5700 S-VHS VTRs to a personal computer via a RS232C port. The AG-A570 allows assemble editing, video inserts, and audio dubbing, as well as audio/video inserts. It offers a jog/shuttle knob and control keys for deck control.   The AG-A96 provides the same function for two AG-1970 decks.

The AG-1970 and its older sibling, the AG-1960 are Panasonic's industrial/prosumer quality S-VHS VTRs. These systems can be adapted for use in desktop video systems via such products as the AG-A96, or Selectra's VuPort. Selectra Corporation, of Walnut Creek, CA, offers the VuPort for $799. This hardware device provides a specialized interface between the RS-232-C port of a personal computer and the Panasonic AG-1960 VTR. It provides the inexpensive AG-1960 with the frame accurate control normally available on much more expensive decks.

The Sony CI-1000 Vbox is a computer/video interface which employs the VISCA protocol developed by Sony for control of its VTRs via their LANC interfaces. It requires appropriate VISCA-compatible editing software, such as that provided by Homrich Communications Homrich provides VISCA control software for PC-compatible platforms via its EZV2 ($299) software package. EZV2 provides edit control, level controls for audio, assemble editing, time code searching, and video insert editing.

Audio Systems

Total Audio Systems Market

Market Definitions and Overview

Audio systems comprise all postproduction audio processing hardware and software, including digital signal processing hardware and software, MIDI equipment, software, and libraries, audio libraries, audio amplifiers and speakers, headsets, and audio patch panels. Audio Systems represented 0.6 percent of the total video postproduction products revenues in 1989. This percentage stayed relatively constant through 1992 and is forecasted to grow to 2.0 percent by 1995. By 1999, audio systems are forecasted to obtain 4.1 percent of the overall $12.8 billion postproduction products market.

DSP Hardware and Software

Audio production, like video production, has historically utilized all-analog technology. In recent years it has become possible to convert analog audio signals to digital information, store it on a computer disk, process it in digital mode, and convert it back to audio for playback. The analog to digital conversion, digital to analog conversion, and digital processing require a combination of hardware and software known collectively as digital signal processing (DSP) systems.

DSP software includes packages which synchronize digitized audio to MIDI tracks and to SMPTE time code, perform frequency equalization, perform noise gating and compression, shift audio frequency pitches, allow cut and paste editing, and/or perform digital effects such as reverberation, echo, flanging, etc.

MIDI

The electronic musical instrument manufacturers defined MIDI, or Musical Instrument Digital Interface, as a way of interconnecting musical instruments and computers. MIDI allows the creation and playback of command information to musical instruments, thereby allowing computer-based products called sequencers to "play" musical instruments such as synthesizers, samplers, and drum machines.

MIDI has application to desktop video in the area of soundtrack development. It is possible to synchronize the MIDI commands to SMPTE time code, and thus to recorded audio and video. MIDI products include sequencers, typically software-only products which run on personal computers, interfaces between computers and MIDI equipment, interfaces between MIDI equipment and SMPTE-compatible equipment, synthesizers (instruments which create or "synthesize" an instrument sound on command), samplers (instruments which play a recorded audio "sample" on command), and libraries of MIDI musical compositions on CD's or floppy disks.

The combination of a MIDI library with a suitable MIDI sequencer, interface, and synthesizer gives the desktop video user a means of adding background music to video productions without the need of paying licensing fees or becoming a musician. With a little training and developed skill, the user can alter the instrumentation or structure of a musical piece, thereby fitting the piece to the video material without undue repetition.

Audio Libraries

Some desktop video users will opt for prerecorded background music available on compact disc or other media. These "buyout" libraries offer single-payment unlimited licenses for use of the recorded material, unlike the licensing fees charged for use of popular recorded music. The disadvantage of these libraries versus MIDI libraries is the inability to change the structure or instrumentation of a piece. A given piece might last for 5 minutes; if the video production lasts for 6, the producer must either repeat part of the piece (and synchronize the added piece to the original during editing), or must tack on part of another piece. A MIDI composition would allow duplication of a verse or chorus or movement in order to stretch the piece to fit the allotted time frame, or even a change in tempo for the same effect.

Amplifiers, Speakers, and Headphones

All professional quality audio equipment operates at analog "line levels". This electrical amplitude is incapable of driving speakers directly, so an amplifier is required to boost these signal levels in order to drive either speakers (for group listening) or headphones (for private listening). Existing consumer stereo equipment has sufficient audio quality for this purpose, although it is typically overfeatured, overpowered, oversized, and overpriced for the application.

A desktop video audio system should employ an audio amplifier of between 3 and 50 watts of power (10 is reasonable), small 2- or 3-way speakers of sufficient power, and a good set of headphones. The speakers should be shielded against electromagnetic interference if they are to be located near the video monitor or monitors. Some manufacturers are offering amplified speaker sets for the multimedia market; these are typically sufficient for desktop video, although ones allowing independent volume controls for each speaker should be avoided. Better speaker/amplifier combinations will, of course, provide more accurate reproduction of the recorded audio. Those applications in which professional-quality audio is desired will be better served by use of a higher-power, higher quality, and correspondingly higher cost amplifier and speaker sets.

Headphones are typically used in office environments or other situations where audible playback is not possible or desirable. As in the case of speakers, the better the quality of headphones utilized, the more accurate the representation of the recorded audio signals. In most cases, the lightweight piezoelectric headphones common with portable radios and CD players are sufficient for this purpose, although the more professional producers will opt for headphones in the $100 to $300 range.

Audio Patch Panels

In many applications, the configuration of audio inputs and outputs must be changed in order to meet different needs. This can be done in several ways; the least costly, but most time consuming and likely technique to cause wasted time from misconfigurations and cable breakage is reconfiguration by hand. This involves disconnecting cables and reconnecting them in the appropriate manner. As many of the cable connections are located on the rear of audio equipment, this is a trying process at best.

Another way of doing this is via the use of an appropriately sized audio mixer. All of the audio inputs from microphones, playback decks, CD players, synthesizers, and the like can be routed to the inputs of the mixer. The outputs of the mixer can then be routed to the amplifier and speakers, the headphones, the record decks, and other output devices. An audio mixer offers a level of control and flexibility beyond the needs and capabilities of many, but within the requirements of some professional-quality desktop video producers.

A third way of performing the same function, offering many of the best features of the previous two techniques, is the use of an audio patch panel. This can be either a passive device, collecting all of the interconnections in an accessible and standardized panel in which the signal routings are accomplished via use of patch cables or switches, or an active device under the control of a personal computer.

Revenues and Revenue Growth Rates

1989 revenues from sales of audio systems in the desktop video environment were practically zero. Although revenues from sales of these products are not ever anticipated to generate a large proportion of total desktop video revenues, this subsegment is anticipated to be one of the fastest growing in terms of both revenues and unit shipments.

Following strong growth years in 1990 and 1991, revenue growth moderated somewhat to 161.1 percent for 1992. Revenues for that year totaled approximately $600,000. By 1995, revenues are anticipated to reach $6.5 million, a growth of 111.4 percent over the prior year. The high growth rates for audio systems in the early years of the surveyed period are caused by the general growth of the desktop video market, the youth of digital audio systems in general, the relative lack of desktop video audio systems as the desktop video boom began, the evolving requirement for higher and higher audio quality in recorded presentations (CDs vs. LPs, DAT vs. Audio Tape), and the need for audio solutions regardless of the chosen video technology (linear, nonlinear, digital, analog, online, offline, etc.).

1999 revenues are forecasted to reach $73.5 million, an increase of 76.0 percent over 1998. Revenue CAGR for the survey period is forecasted at 98.8%, indicating exceptionally strong and steady growth of this segment over the decade. The growth rate will slow somewhat in the latter years of the decade as the desktop video market matures, more systems integrate higher-quality audio systems with other products, and the audio products market is better penetrated.

Fig. 6-12: Audio Systems
Unit Shipment and Revenue Forecasts 1989-1999

Year	Units (000)	Revenues ($M)	Revenue Growth(%)	Revenue Growth(%)
1989	0.1	0.0	----	----
1990	0.2	0.1	127.0	152.2
1991	0.8	0.3	293.0	336.7
1992	2.0	0.6	135.0	161.1
1993	5.0	1.4	128.7	147.2
1994	12.0	3.1	124.5	141.9
1995	27.4	6.5	111.4	127.3
1996	56.8	12.7	95.1	107.5
1997	107.7	23.3	83.4	89.7
1998	199.4	41.8	79.4	85.1
1999	361.7	73.5	76.0	81.4
TOTAL			*98.8%*	*109.9%*

Unit Shipments and Pricing Trends

Unit shipments are also anticipated to remain very strong over the survey period. A unit of audio systems is a single hardware or software item, or the combination of items (as in a pair of speakers) used for a single purpose, intended for audio postproduction in a desktop video suite. Only those products meeting this criteria are counted in this category, although many identical products will be sold into other markets, including professional audio and musical instruments markets.

1989 shipments totaled only about 100 units, mostly sales of audio libraries and some initial sales of DSP boards and software. By 1992, shipments had risen to 2000 units, a growth rate of 161.1 percent over 1991. Unit shipment growth is anticipated to remain high throughout the remainder of the survey period as digital audio and MIDI music revolutionize audio for video in the 90's.

By 1995, unit shipments are forecasted to reach 27,400 units, a growth of 127.3 percent over the prior year. By 1999, this figure is expected to reach 361,700 units, with growth of 81.4 percent over 1998. Unit shipment CAGR for the survey period is forecasted at 109.9 percent, a slight delta over the strong 98.8 percent anticipated for revenue growth. The small difference between the two indicates the minimal pricing pressure anticipated for this subsegment, as prices are already extremely low for most products in this category.

Market and Technology Trends

Qualitative Trends

Price and Performance

In recent years, there have been a number of advances in audio systems (beyond the recording of audio information; this is covered in Chapter 5) allowing vastly improved performance and capabilities at very reasonable prices. This is a result of several factors.

First, the development of DSP (digital signal processing) technology has allowed complex analog functions to be implemented in low-cost digital circuitry instead of the more expensive analog means previously used. The DSP technologies have become more and more powerful in recent years at relatively stable pricing, thereby allowing more and more functionality to "go digital" at reduced prices to the market, as well as allowing never before available functionality because of the power of the technology. DSP technology has made practical the digitization and playback of audio information, more realistic sounding electronic instruments such as synthesizers and samplers, and complex audio processing such as reverberation and echo in low-cost, reliable systems. DSP hardware also underpins the growth of digital audio software.

Second, the emerging multimedia market has driven the demand for small, powerful speaker systems. These systems, often with integral amplification and some tone control, allow low-cost, high-quality audio reproduction.

Synthetic Sound

Improving synthesizer and sampler capabilities, including synthesis algorithms, memory capacity, sampling rates, and bit resolution, have allowed these artificial sound sources to more realistically emulate natural sounds. Early synthesizers were monophonic (one note at a time). Current models can play 16 or more notes at the same time. Early synths required extensive setup time before they could make any single sound; current models can be setup automatically can make multiple different sounds simultaneously. For example, a modern synthesizer can sound like a piano, a saxophone, and a snare drum at the same time. Early synths sounded very "synthy", or artificial; modern synths can be practically indistinguishable from acoustic musical instruments, or can be made to sound just like an early synthesizer.

Samplers once produced very imperfect reproductions of recorded sounds due to limitations of available memory, sampling rates, and bit resolutions. Current sampler technology produces quality in excess of CD recordings for longer times, thanks to improved technology and memory capacity.

The upshot of all of this is that artificially produced music and sound effects can sound as realistic as "the real thing". Most modern music employs some amount (almost all in some cases) of synthesized or sampled audio information. The same is true for conventional video and film productions, although the budgets of many of these allow for orchestras, recorded sound effects, and the like.

Desktop video environments will typically eliminate these high cost services by utilizing the capabilities of synthetic sound, in the form of samplers, synthesizers, and other digital audio products.

MIDI Acceptance

Pro musicians are hooked on MIDI. Danny Elfman, who produced the scores for such feature films as "Batman", and Jan Hammer of "Miami Vice" fame are prominent MIDI musicians. MIDI allows a single creative individual to control vast arrays of complex sound creation, modification, and recording equipment.

Use of MIDI instruments is just catching on in the conventional video environment, particularly among the non-musicians who are attempting to integrate sound tracks with finished video presentations. Desktop video is anticipated to help hasten the acceptance of MIDI in the video environment.

Combinations of MIDI/Digital Audio products are becoming more prevalent, thanks in part to the success of Creative Labs' Sound Blaster in the multimedia and games segments of the personal computer market. These products, although useful for introducing audiences to the potentials of MIDI instrumentation and digitized audio, are typically of insufficient quality for professional presentations. Desktop video requires CD-quality stereo digitized audio and realistic-sounding sound effects and instrumentation for scores. These features are not usually available in low-cost sound boards.

A major problem with MIDI acceptance among non-musician consumers, such as video producers, has been the difficulty of understanding and utilizing the tools for sequencing and editing MIDI sequences. Most of the MIDI sequencer, editor, and librarian programs have been written for the musically literate instead of those desiring only to slightly modify and play back

MIDI sequences for video purposes. This situation is improving; some vendors are offering stripped-down sequencing programs for playback-only purposes.

Music for Non-Musicians

Of course, before non-musicians can utilize MIDI to create video scores, someone else has to create a MIDI composition or convert an existing composition to a MIDI format. MIDI musicians, like conventional musicians, are available for hire to either compose music or play compositions for video presentations. This method of obtaining music for video is the most expensive of the available alternatives, although it does produce the most unique result.

Most video producers, particularly desktop video producers, shun the first alternative and turn instead to purchasing rights to music, either popular or custom-composed, in its final audio form distributed via cassette tape, DAT tape, or CDs. There are several forms of this music. Most requires payment of "needle drop" and other fees for the amount of music used in each copy of a video presentation. Another alternative is the use of "buyout" music, in which the purchaser obtains unlimited use rights for the recorded audio for a fixed fee. This is popular among desktop video producers who merely need background music of an appropriate "feel" for a program.

The problem with recorded music is that it is impossible to change the tempo or instrumentation as desired, and it is very difficult to change the structure or length of the composition. MIDI sequences are easy to modify in this manner and libraries of MIDI sequences have recently become available. Using an appropriate MIDI editor or sequencer, it is possible for even a non-musician to change the tempo of a piece, change a trumpet solo to a xylophone solo, duplicate a verse or a chorus, or shorten or lengthen the piece to fit the video program.

Competitive Analysis / Market Share

Competitive Environment

Providers of Audio Systems typically are not comprehensive in nature; rather, with a few exceptions, they tend to specialize on one or two areas of sound reproduction and generation. Areas of concentration are: sound reproduction (speakers, amps, headphones), sound synthesis (samplers, and synths), digital audio, MIDI (software and control devices), and sound libraries.

Audio Systems are somewhat split between distribution paths, with sound reproduction and sound synthesis devices typically being marketed through professional audio and musical equipment dealers, and digital audio and MIDI products split between this channel and computer-oriented dealers, with some MIDI products available through mail order organizations. Sound libraries, typically the output of smaller organizations, have been marketed primarily through mail order, as this is the most affordable method for small suppliers to reach large markets. With the advent of multimedia, some of the sound reproduction products are beginning to move into the computer channels, as have some of the consumer-quality sound synthesis products.

Providers of sound reproduction devices tend to be older, stable organizations who may also compete in the Audio Acquisition Products subsegment covered in Chapter 4 of this report. Although there have been some new entrants into this market, most of the participants have been there for some time as sound reproduction technologies are neither new nor fast-changing, leading to few market opportunities for new participants to gain market share.

Digital audio, on the other hand is very new, and the participants in this subsegment are changing almost daily. There are a few dominant suppliers, but none so entrenched that a superior competitor could not displace. There are perhaps two dozen total manufacturers making digital audio solutions applicable to desktop video.

MIDI products suppliers, including software vendors and sound synthesis manufacturers, are composed of about a dozen key manufacturers and hundreds of smaller, entrepreneurial firms.

Structure

As in each of the other sections of this report, Figure 6-13 is intended to show a representative, but not exhaustive, sample of the competitors in the Audio Systems market. As discussed above, each of these suppliers tends to provide a limited set of the possible functionality combined under the umbrella of "Audio Systems".

It is important to note that the primary market for Audio Systems products is not the desktop video market. These products are intended for professional and semi-professional musicians; they just happen to be applicable to desktop video use, since desktop video developers tend to need some of the same functionality as musicians.

The only vendors who provide products in more than a couple related product areas are Korg, Peavey, Roland, and Yamaha, companies known best for their electronic musical instruments. These companies have diversified their basic musical instrument lines (synthesizer and sampler keyboards, etc.) with ancillary products (MIDI and digital audio software and hardware, etc.). Most of the vendors providing Audio Systems specialize in a single product area, such as MIDI software or music libraries. These vendors tend to be small- to medium-sized organizations with limited development and marketing staffs.

| Fig. 6-13: | List of Selected Vendors |
| | Audio Systems |

Company	Product Lines
Acoustic Research	speakers
ADA	amps, speakers
AirCraft	music libraries
AKG	headphones
Altec Lansing	speakers, amps, powered speakers
Antex	digital audio hardware
Apple	speakers
Aris Entertainment	special effects and music libraries
Associated Production Music	music libraries
Audio Technica	headphones
Avid Technology	digital editing systems
Bag End	speakers
Beyer Dynamic	headphones

Big Noise Software	MIDI software
Coda	MIDI software
Community	speakers
Covox	MIDI hardware and software
Crown International	test equipment, amps
DeWolfe	music libraries
Digidesign	digital audio hardware and software
Digital Audio Labs	digital audio hardware and software
Digital Processing Systems	digital audio hardware and software
Digivox	MIDI software
Dr. T's Music Software	MIDI software
Dynaware	MIDI software
E-Mu Systems	synths
Electro Voice	speakers
FirstCom Broadcast Service	music libraries
Fresh	music libraries
Gene Michael Productions	music libraries
Greatsounds	sound effects libraries
Hal Leonard Publishing	MIDI sequence libraries
Halland Broadcast Services	music libraries
HSC Software	music libraries
IBM Corp	digital audio hardware
Invisible Touch	MIDI sequence libraries
J.L.Cooper	MIDI hardware
JBL	speakers, powered speakers
Jovian Logic	digital audio hardware
Klipsch	speakers
Korg	synths, accessories, digital audio systems, samplers, sequencers
Koss	headphones
Kurzweil	synths
Macromedia	digital audio hardware and software
Mark of the Unicorn	MIDI software
Media Vision	digital audio hardware
Micro Technology Unlimited	digital audio hardware and software, MIDI hardware
Microsoft	digital audio software
MidiSoft	music libraries, MIDI software
Mus-art	MIDI sequence libraries
Musicator	MIDI software
Network Music	music and sound effects libraries
Omnimusic	music libraries
Opcode Systems	MIDI hardware, software; digital audio software
Parker Adams Group	MIDI sequence libraries
Passport	MIDI software, digital audio software
Peavey	samplers, synths, MIDI hardware, speakers, amps
PG Music	MIDI software

Presentation Graphics Group	MIDI sequence libraries
Promusic	music and sound effects libraries
Prosonus	MIDI sequence libraries, sound effects libraries
Ramsa	speakers
Roland	speakers, synths, powered speakers, samplers, digital audio
Ross Systems	speakers
RTG Music	MIDI sequence libraries
Sennheiser	headphones
Signature	music libraries
Sonic Solutions	digital audio systems
Sony	headphones
Sound Ideas	sound effects libraries
Spectral Innovations	digital audio hardware
Steinberg/Jones	MIDI software, digital audio software
Tannoy	speakers
Tascam	patch bays
TOA	speakers
Trompeter	patch bays
Trycho Music	MIDI sequence libraries
Turbo Music	MIDI sequence libraries
Turtle Beach Software	synths (board level), digital audio hardware and software
Twelve Tone Systems	MIDI software
Valentino	music and sound effects libraries
Vega	speakers
Vestax	speakers
Voyetra	MIDI software, MIDI sequence libraries, digital audio software
Waveframe	digital audio systems
Wolfetone	music libraries
Yamaha	speakers, amps, synths, samplers, digital audio and MIDI hardware

Issues

Distribution Channels

As noted above, the distribution channels for Audio Systems is different from that of
most video systems, and different still from the evolving desktop video channels. Video dealers
are notoriously unschooled in audio products, and even less so in musical instruments or
computer-based digital audio products. Computer dealers are also unfamiliar with audio
systems, in the main. Musical products dealers tend to be both video- and computer-illiterate.

Combining these product families into a single, viable channel with the knowledge necessary to support each technology will be a significant benefit. Over the next five or so years, as the desktop video market matures, and desktop video VARs emerge, this trend should become more prevalent. The implication is that dealers who wish to market desktop video products will have to acquire the expertise in their organizations for each of the component technologies in order to be effective.

Non-Musicians

Not only will the distribution channels have to change in order to reach the desktop video user, but the products themselves will have to adapt to the limited audio and musical expertise of these new customers. Current MIDI and audio tools are designed for the musician and reflect this bias in their operation. Most desktop video users will not be musicians, and certainly not skilled ones. Manufacturers will need to develop easier to use products in order to tap the potential of desktop video applications for their products.

Mergers and Acquisitions

As desktop video matures, expect the merging of computer, video, and audio firms into single entities. Some of this has already begun. For example, Creative Labs, a key multimedia digital audio and video hardware provider, recently purchased E-Mu, maker of the Proteus line of synthesizes. Harman International owns JBL, Urei, Soundcraft, DOD, and Digitech. Mark IV owns Electro-Voice and Altec-Lansing. Fujitsu and Roland, another Japanese organization, have been working jointly on some digital audio products.

Market Shares

The market shares shown in Figure 6-14 are for Audio Systems, the application of audio and musical products to the desktop video postproduction market, not for any other application of these products to any other market. Most of the manufacturers listed here participate in a number of other markets, possibly even including Audio Acquisition Products for desktop video production.

The Audio Systems market is currently very fragmented, with no vendor controlling more than a 10 percent market share. There has also been limited penetration of sound synthesis products and the associated MIDI software and hardware products into the desktop video environments as of 1992, so the dominant product categories are speakers, sound libraries, and digital audio.

```
Fig. 6-14:        1992 Market Shares
                  Audio Systems


Company                   Share


Roland                     8.6%
Digidesign                 6.8%
Acoustic Research          3.5%
JBL                        2.3%
Network Music              1.9%
Steinberg/Jones            1.7%
Opcode Systems             1.6%
Passport                   1.2%
Yamaha                     1.1%
Others                    71.3%

                          --------
TOTAL                    100.0%
```

Highlights of Selected Vendors

Roland

Roland Corporation U.S., of Los Angeles, California, manufactures samplers and synths, powered speakers, MIDI hardware, and digital audio products. Powered speakers include the MA-12C Micro Monitor ($160) set, a 10W stereo amplifier and two magnetically shielded speakers, the MA-7 speaker set, and the MA-20 (15W/channel) set. Synthesizers and samplers include the U-220 RS-PCM rackmount synth, the JV-880 MultiTimbral Synth (also rackmount), the SC-55 Sound Canvas ($795), the SC-7 Sound Module, the SP-700 rackmount sampler unit, and the S-770 and S-750 rackmount sampler units. Keyboard-equipped synthesizers are also available. MIDI products include the industry standard MPU-401 ISA-bus to MIDI interface and the CF-10 MIDI fader unit ($240).

Digidesign

Digidesign, of Menlo Park, California was founded in 1984 and is the world's leader in digital audio workstations. Digidesign is focused only on digital audio hardware and software.

Digidesign's flagship product is Pro Tools, a $5995 4-channel digital audio hardware/software system which can be expanded in 4 channel increments up to 16 channels ($5000 each set of 4). Sound Tools, a 2 channel system upgradeable to 4 channels or to Pro Tools ($3495), is a junior version of Pro Tools. Digidesign has also provided the AudioMedia card since 1990, upgrading it to the AudioMedia II in 1992.   The AudioMedia card is a 2-channel non-expandable system. All of Digidesign's products provide CD-quality sound for each channel as well as DSP processing functions such as equalization and noise gating.

Recently, Digidesign added the ProMaster 20 for stereo mastering, the Session 8 and Session 8 XL PC -based 8-channel digital audio systems, and AudioMedia LC, a low-cost version of the AudioMedia II card.

Acoustic Research

Acoustic Research, a long respected name in high-fidelity speaker systems, also offers a line of powered speaker systems. The Powered Partner 22 ($109) is a 3W system, the Powered Partner 42 ($229) is an 8W system, and the Powered Partner 570 ($399) and 622 ($349) systems add subwoofer units.

JBL

JBL, of Northridge, California, and a division of the Harman International Corporation, is a well-known speaker cabinet manufacturer, offering a range of products from consumer stereo products, to professional audio studio monitors, to multimedia speakers. JBL also offers all-weather products, subwoofers, speaker components, amplifiers. Their 4206,4208, 4408A, 4410A, and 4412A Studio Monitors are particularly appropriate for desktop video soundtrack mixing and for general audio studio applications.

Network Music

Network Music, of San Diego, California produces a range of music and sound effects libraries, available under a number of licensing arrangements. The libraries consist of sounds and original music compositions recorded onto CD-ROM for use in television, radio, and video presentations such as commercials, promotional pieces, and industrial programs.

Steinberg/Jones

Steinberg/Jones, of Northridge, California, makes the CuBase family of MIDI software products for the Amiga, Macintosh, and Windows-based families of personal computers. CuBase is essentially a MIDI sequence editor and player. Versions of CuBase add digital audio recording and playback capabilities.

Time Bandit, another Steinberg/Jones product, utilizes the capabilities of digital signal processing functions to adds harmonic processing capabilities to digital audio information.

Opcode Systems

Opcode is based in Palo Alto, California and is the leading Macintosh MIDI software provider in the market today. Products include the Vision sequencer program, the EZ Vision basic MIDI sequencing package, and the Studio Vision sequencer with digital audio recording and playback capability. AudioShop is Opcode's digitized sample editor. Other products include the Studio 3 and Studio 5 MIDI interface and time code translation hardware units.

Passport

Passport Designs, of Half Moon Bay, California, is another key manufacturer and marketer of MIDI software. Products include MasterTracks Pro ($395), a professional MIDI sequencer program for Windows or Mac platforms. It includes digital audio support. Trax is a less capable MIDI sequencer for Mac or Windows platfomrs, TurboTrax is another sequencer for Mac platforms, Alchemy ($695) is a digitized sample editor w/DSP effects for the Mac, AudioTrax ($299) is a 64 track, 8-bit digital audio and MIDI recorder for the Mac, MusicTime ($249) is a sheet music editor for Windows and Mac platforms, Encore ($595) is a professional sheet music editor for both Mac and Windows platforms, and Score is a music scoring program for Windows units.

They also make a multimedia product called Producer for creating multimedia presentations.

Yamaha

Yamaha, a division of the Japanese conglomerate, is a diversified musical and audio products manufacturer. Their DX7 synthesizer broke new ground in the area of music synthesis and the underlying technology has been used in scores of products from sound cards to performing keyboards. Yamaha is also known for high-quality musical instruments such as grand and electric pianos, saxaphones, trumpets and other horns, and other synthesizers and samplers. Yamaha also manufactures mixer units, speakers, power amps. digital audio systems, and miscellaneous MIDI hardware.

Recording and Playback Systems

Total Recording and Playback Systems Market

Market Definitions and Overview

Recording and Playback Systems are comprised of that equipment needed to store video images for later retrieval and playback. These systems include video tape recorders (VTRs), including the subset of video cassette recorders (VCRs), rewritable laserdisc systems, and video patch panels.

Recording and Playback Systems represented 42.0 percent of the total desktop video postproduction products revenues in 1989. This percentage dropped to 27.2 percent in 1992 as desktop video allowed the use of less costly recording devices as well as fewer of them per postproduction suite. The percentage share of recording and playback systems is forecasted to drop steadily throughout the survey period as desktop video systems move more into the pure digital domain, thus reducing the need for outboard recording decks. In 1999, recording and playback systems is forecasted to drop to only 4.2 percent of the overall $12 billion desktop video postproduction products market.

VTRs and VCRs

A video tape recorder, or VTR, is the basic recording and playback device for the video industry. There are a number of different tape formats supported by VTRs, including most which involve tape incorporated into plastic cassettes. VTRs which support these plastic cassettes are referred to specifically as video cassette recorders, or VCRs. For the purposes of this report, the more general VTR will be used to describe the recording devices.

Some camera systems, known as camcorders and described in the Chapter 5, incorporate VTRs. Some VTRs are playback-only, thus becoming somewhat oxymoronic. For the majority of desktop video uses, the VTRs involved will be considered standalone, playback and record units.

VTRs are also differentiated by their ability to utilize SMPTE time code. Time code allows precise referencing of each individual frame of a recorded program, a requirement for conventional editing systems. Desktop video systems may or may not require this capability, depending on the degree to which they support nonlinear editing. This is important, as time code-compatible VTRs are considerably more expensive than those of comparable quality without time code.

TBCs and Time Code Generators

Those systems which require time code for precise editing also require devices to generate time code signals and other devices to synchronize to these signals. The device which generates time code signals is called, logically enough, a Time Code Generator. The device allowing the synchronization of two or more time code signals is called a Time Base Corrector, or TBC. These devices have been historically available in the conventional video market as standalone, often rack-mounted electronic devices, and will continue to do so.

Many modern VTRs include these functions within the VTR electronics, thus obviating the need for external devices. Again, the need for any form of time code equipment is largely dependent on the editing system; nonlinear systems typically do not require such capability.

Time code equipment is listed in Chapter 5 as part of video acquisition products, since time code is first applicable when initially recording video, as well as later in the postproduction editing process.

Laserdiscs

Laserdiscs store large amounts of analog data on a media similar to a Compact Disk, but larger. Laserdisc units provide nonlinear access to this analog data, some offering both read and write capability. Laserdiscs which provide this read/write capability typically cost in the $50,000 price range and are not expected to be commonly used with desktop video systems.

More commonly, laserdiscs will represent a source of captured video and audio information to be edited and combined with other video and audio information, including graphics, to create a final presentation. Systems for this purpose can be obtained for under $1500 from vendors such as Pioneer and Panasonic. Midrange systems allowing Write Once Read Many (WORM) cartridges, and either composite or component video output can be had for $10,000 to $20,000. Media is typically available for around $300; each piece stores 20 to 40 minutes of video and audio.

Laserdisc systems are typically computer controllable. As such, they are appropriate as controllable video sources. Those capable of recording are useful for recording animations in a frame by frame mode and then playing the completed sequence back at full speed for recording to tape.

Patch Panels

In complicated video systems employing multiple cameras, monitors, VTRs, and other components, it is usually very inconvenient to make and break the connections between the various elements. Often the connection points are located on the rear of rack-mounted items and are less than fully accessible. A Patch Panel is a passive device which mounts in plain view and allows the quick reconfiguration of connections via standard, short cables. More complex devices, employing computer control and electronic switching of connections, are available for some applications.

Tape Formats

Prior to 1991, the dominant tape format used in desktop video postproduction was Sony's U-Matic SP. This 3/4" cassette format offers professional quality, but the devices which utilize it are quite bulky and costly. In 1991 and 1992 the Hi-8 format and the S-VHS format began to replace U-Matic SP as the dominant desktop video format. Hi-8 is a very small format appropriate for hand-held camcorders which offers approximately the same quality as U-Matic SP. S-VHS is very similar to the popular VHS 1/2" format, except it offers significantly higher image quality, comparing well with Hi-8 and U-Matic SP. S-VHS decks often offer the capability of dual-mode operation, allowing the playing from or recording to VHS cassettes, which is important for small-scale distribution.

Sony, the dominant supplier of Hi-8 equipment, is positioning the tape format as ideal for video acquisition because of its compact size and moderate recording duration. Because of the small width and thickness of the Hi-8 tape itself, the metal oxide particles which actually store the recorded data begin flaking off after a relatively few passes through VTRs. This results in "dropouts", minute but visible imperfections in the video images reproduced from the tapes. Accordingly, the Hi-8 format is currently not preferred for editing purposes in postproduction, as traditional non-linear editing requires a great deal of tape shuttling, rewinding, and other passes through the VTR deck. Other popular "prosumer", "industrial", or even "broadcast" quality formats such as S-VHS and Betacam SP do not suffer this problem, at least in the magnitude experienced by Hi-8 users. On the other hand, S-VHS and Betacam SP tape cassettes are significantly larger and bulkier than Hi-8 products, and are therefore less applicable to camcorder applications. It has become common to see professional organizations utilize Hi-8 equipment for video acquisition, but copy their footage to Betacam SP tape for non-linear editing.

Revenues and Revenue Growth Rates

Revenues from sales of recording and playback systems totaled $50.9 million in 1989. Revenue growth followed the same pattern as most other subsegments of the desktop video market in 1990 through 1992 as the desktop video market emerged, driving sales of recording and playback systems used in conjunction with the base postproduction systems. 1992 revenues reached $439.5 million, a growth of 101.8 percent over 1991's revenues.

By 1995, revenues from sales of recording and playback systems is expected to exceed $805 million, although revenue growth rates are expected to drop precipitously in the years between 1992 and 1995 and turn negative for the rest of the survey period. This downturn in revenue growth is a function of three separate processes: first, the utility in lower-cost, prosumer-grade VTRs made possible by desktop video systems; second, the anticipated pricing curve of these systems; and, third, the decrease in VTRs per desktop video system from a high of 2.5 in 1989 to a low in 1999 of less than 0.5, as camcorders and all-digital systems decrease the need for dedicated recording and playback systems. As the desktop video market emerged, the dominant recording technolgies were the expensive U-Matic SP and Betacam systems and the inadequate VHS and 8mm systems. Professional users, the earliest adopters of desktop video, focused on the more expensive Betacam and U-Matic SP systems, making the average pricing for Recording and Playback systems very high. As the S-VHS and Hi-8 technologies emerged in the early 90's, desktop video users switched en masse to these newer, less expensive recording technologies, driving the average cost of Recording and Playback Systems down. This trend is expected to continue throughout the remainder of the decade.

1999 revenues are anticipated to decline to $351.8 million, a decrease of 29.0 percent from the prior year. Revenue growth for the survey period is forecasted at a CAGR of -3.1 percent.

Fig. 6-15:	Recording and Playback Systems Unit Shipment and Revenue Forecasts 1989-1999			
Year	Units (000)	Revenues ($M)	Revenue Growth(%)	Unit Growth(%)
1989	4.6	50.9	----	----
1990	10.2	81.0	59.1	121.0
1991	34.5	217.8	169.0	236.3
1992	78.1	439.5	101.8	126.7
1993	127.7	632.4	43.9	63.5
1994	183.9	792.3	25.3	44.0
1995	236.7	805.5	1.7	28.7

1996	286.6	751.1	(6.8)	21.1
1997	327.3	651.9	(13.2)	14.2
1998	355.5	495.6	(24.0)	8.6
1999	371.1	351.8	(29.0)	4.4
TOTAL			(3.1)%	24.9%

Unit Shipments and Pricing Trends

Unit shipments are anticipated to remain stronger than revenue growth for the survey period, for the reasons defined above. A unit of recording and playback systems is a single hardware product used to record and playback videotape or laserdiscs in conjunction with desktop video postproduction systems.

1989 shipments of recording and playback systems totaled 4600 units. High growth rates followed for 1990 through 1992, culminating in 126.7 percent growth and shipments of over 78 thousand units for 1992. By 1995, unit shipments are expected to grow to 236,700 units, an increase of 28.7 percent over the prior year. 1999 shipments are forecasted at 371,100 units, a growth of 4.4 percent over 1998. Unit shipment CAGR for the survey period is forecasted at 24.9 percent. This is much stronger than the anticipated revenue growth of -3.1 percent, due mostly to the extreme pricing pressures in this subsegment from the trend to lower-quality VTR decks as desktop video matures.

As explained above, the pricing pressures are due to a trend away from expensive U-Matic SP and Betacam equipment to Hi-8 and S-VHS products, from time code compatible equipment with integral TBCs to industrial-quality systems without these capabilities, and to general technological learning curve pricing pressures.

Market and Technology Trends

Qualitative Trends

Effects of Technology

As with most complex electromechanical products, Recording and Playback Systems are subject to a great deal of technological improvements as new recording technologies, VLSI integration, mechanical systems, amd packaging techniques emerge. These systems have acquired increasing sophistication and performance at decreasing retail pricing throughout their history, so it is reasonable to expect a continuance of this trend.

Systems appropriate for use with desktop video suites will therefore become more capable and easier to use at lower and lower prices. Industrial, prosumer, and even consumer systems will provide performance levels currently available only in expensive, complex, hard-to-use professional systems. Digital recording systems will become affordable in the mid- to late-90's. The trend toward including TBCs in VTRs will continue. Even patch panels, currently manual devices, will acquire improved technology, with electronic patch panels becoming more prevalent and affordable.

Effects of Nonlinear Editing

At the same time technology is improving the available Recording and Playback Systems, other desktop video technologies are reducing the numbers of these units required. The trend toward digital editing and predominantly digital signal paths has two effects on the use of Recording and Playback Systems.

First, the decreased signal degradation available in digital processes allows less of a differential between acquired video and audio signal quality and that which is eventually displayed via presentation devices, e.g. VCRs and televisions. Unless there is a dramatic increase in the required signal quality and resolution required at the delivery end of the process, there can be an effective reduction in the signal quality and resolution required at the acquisition end, therefore throughout the entire video development process. These lower-quality recording systems are less expensive, complex, and cantankerous than the finely-tuned professional systems they replace.

Second, the use of digital, non-linear processes for editing video presentations lessens requirements for time code compatibility, as time code is essentially a placekeeping mechanism for linear recording systems. Digital systems have their own processes which allow frame accurate cuts, transitions, and other functions, and do not need time code to perform this function. As time code capability is an expensive function in Recording and Playback Systems, desktop video will therefore allow use of lower cost Recording and Playback Systems lacking this expensive functionality.

Another possible effect in some smaller desktop video environments, a result of the two primary effects, is that some desktop video environments will be able to utilize the same device, e.g. a camcorder, as both a video acquisition device and a Recording and Playback System for saving a recorded master tape on an analog videotape format.

Competitive Analysis / Market Share

Competitive Environment

The consumer segment of the video recorder/player market is stagnant. The EIA (Electronic Industries Association) has reported fairly flat sales for the last several years in this end of the market. The broadcast-quality segment is still growing, but prices in this segment are falling rapidly as new technologies evolve. The midrange between the two extreme market segments, in terms of product quality and cost, is growing rapidly, thanks to the technological advances of Hi-8 and S-VHS.

Recording and Playback Systems for desktop video purposes focus on this midrange product area. The midrange was once defined as two different markets, the "prosumer" market for advanced consumers and semiprofessionals, and the "industrial" market for professional, non-broadcast users. Today, the prosumer and consumer market boundary is considerably blurred and the edge between industrial and broadcast is no longer so clearly defined. In fact, many devices previously considered of "prosumer" quality are now available in common consumer retail outlets and are used in professional, broadcast video programming.

The rough segmentation in this area is now as follows: if the product produces insufficient resolution (e.g. 8mm and VHS systems) for broadcast applications, it is a consumer product. If the product includes time code capability or digital recording, and/or costs over $10,000, it is a broadcast product. Everything else is effectively an industrial product.

The same competitors offer products in the industrial and broadcast ranges, and dominate the consumer end as well. Competition in the consumer end is based on price and performance, and in the other two markets on performance and functionality.

Structure

The Recording and Playback Systems subsegment of the desktop video market is dominated by a few, very large, Japanese industrial giants. Many products sold under other brand names in the consumer market are actually built by these giants.

Thanks to the blurring of capabilities between consumer-oriented products and the "prosumer" quality VCRs, some of the consumer products will be applicable to desktop video. There is a more diverse group of vendors for this class of products than for the industrial/broadcast range of products. The upper range is the almost exclusive domain of three vendors, who are also the largest suppliers in the lower range.

<table>
<tr><td colspan="2">Fig. 6-16:   List of Selected Vendors
                  Recording and Playback Systems</td></tr>
<tr><td>Companies</td><td>Product Lines</td></tr>
<tr><td>Hitachi</td><td>consumer VCRs</td></tr>
<tr><td>JVC</td><td>VTRs, consumer VCRs</td></tr>
<tr><td>Mitsubishi</td><td>VTRs</td></tr>
<tr><td>Panasonic</td><td>VTRs, consumer VCRs, digital VTRs</td></tr>
<tr><td>Sony</td><td>VTRs, consumer VCRs, digital VTRs, WORM laserdiscs</td></tr>
<tr><td>Pioneer</td><td>consumer VCRs, videodiscs, rewritable videodiscs,</td></tr>
<tr><td>Sanyo</td><td>consumer VCRs</td></tr>
</table>

Issues

Formats

The key issue for desktop video, and other professional video, developers is output quality in terms of image resolution. Although the American public is apparently satisfied with VHS quality as a distribution format resolution, a higher quality format is needed for the production process of video acquisition and the postproduction processes of editing and mastering.

S-VHS and Hi-8 formats are sufficient for these needs, at least in industrial-quality applications, and perhaps even for broadcast-quality work. Betacam resolution is certainly sufficient.

Many desktop video enthusiasts will begin their work in 8mm or VHS and soon discover the inadequacies of these formats. Still others, those evolving from the professional videographer ranks, will begin their work in Betacam, only to find that the quality is overkill for many requirements. Most will reach a happy medium with an industrial quality format.

Usability

Another key issue in Recording and Playback Systems is the usability of the equipment. Most industrial-quality equipment has dozens of switches and connectors on front and back as well as supplementary menu-selected functions, accessible by flipping switches and turning knobs. As more and more video-illiterates enter the desktop video market, this complexity will be very confusing to the average Joe who cannot program the clock on his home VCR.

Clearly, some effort must be applied toward reducing the complexity of industrial-quality video equipment so that good ole Joe Average can figure it out.

Market Shares

As in the Video Acquisition Products market segment discussed in Chapter 5, three key vendors dominate the market for Recording and Playback Devices. Sony, with 39.4 percent, has the leading market share as of 1992 because of the continued use of U-Matic and Betacam equipment in desktop video production, as well as the availability of S-VHS VTRs. Sony's

LANC and VISCA protocols for machine control have also contributed to the popularity of their products.

Panasonic and JVC, the two subsidiaries of Matsushita Electric, collectively account for a larger market share than Sony, but individually own smaller shares. Panasonic, due mostly to the popularity of the AG-1960 S-VHS VTR, accounted for 33.5 percent of the Recording and Playback Systems market segment in 1992. JVC contributed an additional 21.2 percent.

Other vendors, including Mitsubishi, Pioneer, and Hitachi, contributed an additional 5.9 percent market share. No other vendor was responsible for more than 1 percent of the market.

Fig. 6-17:   1992 Market Shares
              Recording and Playback Systems

Companies	Shares
Sony	39.4%
Panasonic	33.5%
JVC	21.2%
Others	5.9%

TOTAL	100.0%

Highlights of Selected Vendors

Sony

Sony Corporation provides one of the most comprehensive audio/video product lines among all of the vendors supplying desktop video products. They supply VTRs in a number of different quality ranges and formats, editing equipment, monitors, projection systems, digital VTRs, color printers, audio mixers, microphones, cameras, camcorders, accessories, machine controllers, and more.

Sony was the developer of the Betamax, 8mm, Hi-8, Betacam, Betacam SP, U-Matic, and U-Matic SP tape formats. They continue to make VTRs supporting most of these formats, plus those pioneered by its rival, Matsushita. Sony's product line includes the CVD-1000 Vdeck Hi-8 VTR, which delivers over 400 lines of resolution, records RC time code, and reads both RC time code and Sony Professional 8mm time code. It also includes AFM Hi-Fi stereo audio plus a PCM digital audio track, 3 video inputs (S-Video, 2 composite), a mic/audio mixer, a mic jack, a builtin fader for video or audio fades, wireless remote control, VISCA compatibility, and software for Macintosh computers.

The SVP-9000 S-VHS Hi-Fi Player and SVO-9600 S-VHS Hi-FI Player/Recorder are positioned directly against the Panasonic AG-7650 and AG7750 professional quality units. The EVO-9650 is a single-frame recording VTR especially for transferring animations to videotape. The EVO-9700 is Sony's Hi-8 desktop editing deck, incorporating both a player and recorder, S-Video and composite inputs and outputs, over 400 lines of resolution, PCM stereo audio, a jog/shuttle knob, and a builtin 8mm time code generator/reader. Sony also provides the PVW-2800, PVW-2650, PVW-2600, BVW-60, BVW-65, BVW-70, and BVW75 Betacam SP units, portable Betacam SP units, U-Matic SP VTRs, 8mm consumer VCRs, S-VHS and VHS VCRs, D-1 and D-2 VTRs, and WORM laserdiscs.

Sony markets its professional quality items through authorized video dealers and direct to major consumer organizations. It moves its consumer quality items through mass distribution outlets like major retailers, superstores, and audio/video retailers.

Panasonic

Panasonic, a group of subsidiaries of the Japanese giant Matsushita Electric, is also a very diverse supplier of professional and consumer quality video development equipment. Matsushita developed the VHS, S-VHS, VHS-C, S-VHS-C, and MII tape formats, and its companies, including Panasonic and JVC, focus mainly on product lines incorporating these standards. Like Sony, Panasonic supplies a broad range of products for video and audio acquisition, editing, and recording.

The AG-5700 S-VHS Hi-Fi Editing VCR includes an RS232C interface for control of playback, recording, and editing functions. It is a lightweight unit, allowing easy portability, and offers high speed fast forward/rewind functions. The AG-1970 S-VHS Hi-Fi Editing VCR includes an integral TBC and a jog/shuttle knob. The AG-1960, one of the most popular units for desktop video applications, is similar to the newer AG-1970. The AG-7650 and AG-7750 are professional quality S-VHS playback and record/playback VTRs and include jog/shuttle knobs, time code compatibility, builtin TBCs, RS-422 control interfaces, Dolby noise reduction, and dub inputs and outputs.

Panasonic sells its products in a manner similar to Sony, with direct and professional dealer channels for professional quality equipment, and mass market retailers for consumer items.

JVC

JVC is a subsidiary of The Victor Corporation, which is in turn owned primarily by Matsushita. This tends to put Panasonic and JVC in the same positions of using Matsushita technology and competing against its arch-rival, Sony. JVC offers an extensive product line, but not as broad as that offered by either Panasonic or Sony.

The BR-S822U is a full featured, professional editing recorder for S-VHS or VHS applications, offering RS422 and RS232C control functions and optional plug-in TBCs. It retails for $6100 in its base configuration, but can go for as much as $8300 with options. The BR-S622U, its recorder/player twin, subtracts some of the editing capabilities of the 822, but retails for $4500 (less TBCs, VITC capability, etc.). The slightly less capable and less expensive BR-S611U and BR-S811U pair is also available. JVC also offers VHS equipment, editing consoles, tape duplicating systems.

Graphics Software Products

Total Graphics Software Products Market

Market Definitions and Overview

Graphics Software Products include animation programs, morphing programs, titling and character generation programs, and paint programs, as well as software which provides special graphics and file translation functions. These various packages are used to develop still or moving graphic images used in video postproduction; only those packages used with desktop video systems for this purpose are counted in this category. In 1989, Graphics Software Products represented 7.5 percent of the total desktop video postproduction products revenues, partly because graphics applications such as character generation were among the first computer-based solutions to move into the conventional video market. This percentage increased rapidly to 27.3 percent in 1992, and is forecasted to grow to 48.1 percent of the $12.8 billion postproduction products market by 1999.

CG and Titling Programs

One of the simplest, and most universal, forms of graphics software is the titling program, or "CG" in video parlance. These programs, in general, create graphics files composed of lettering over backgrounds. The lettering is selectable by the user, both in terms of characters used, as well as font styles, sizes, kerning, shadowing, and other features. The backgrounds can typically be selected as opaque solid, opaque textured, transparent (overlay over video), or even with graduated coloring.

CG functions are often combined with "paint" functionality in more versatile graphics programs, but are also available in dedicated titling packages.

A major factor in titling software is the concept of "aliasing", or the development of rough edges on characters as they are scaled from their stored sizes to display sizes. One way to solve this problem is via "antialiasing" algorithms; another is to use vector-based graphics, which do not exhibit this problem. A popular vector-based graphics format is EPS (Encapsulated PostScript).

Paint Programs

A paint program gives the user basic to advanced drawing tools, allowing the creation of complex images. Typical paint program tools include the emulation of various-sized drawing instruments, color "fill" functions, palette selection and configuration functions, cut and paste functions, erase functions, geometrical shape insertion functions, and limited file import and export capabilities.

Paint capability is often the most basic functionality provided by any complex graphics software package, including animation, 3-D design, and titling packages.

Animation Programs

Animation is the process of giving artificial images movement. Animated sequences are typically combined with audio and still graphics to simulate live action or provide extra emphasis in video and multimedia presentations. Animation software is required to create animated sequences.

Animation software products essentially expand on basic drawing tools, such as paint programs, by creating movement and variation in a given image over time. They often work by defining elements within a given image as "objects" and then defining the movements of the objects relative to each other.

Animation software is available for two dimensional and three dimensional graphics development and in basic and advanced versions. Animation programs often include titling and/or paint functionality.

Morphing Programs

A new computer-generated video image effect has become popular in recent years. Although it works on captured video images, it is effectively a computer-based graphical function, so it requires a Graphics Software Product in order to implement it.

Morphing is the gradual transition of the features of a given image or image element to the features of a second image, typically done in real time on a moving video image. An example is the sequence at the end of Michael Jackson's "Black and White" video.

Morphing is typically a function of standalone software packages, although it is reasonable to expect the inclusion of this effect in future comprehensive graphics packages.

Special Graphics Programs

The last major category of Graphics Software Products is a catchall category and includes image touchup software, image librarians, and file format translators. Image touchup software allows image sizing, orientation, coloring, and even composition changes, on either artificial (graphics) or captured (video) images. Image librarians allow the cataloguing of groups of still and moving images so that they can be easily accessed and utilized in video, multimedia, and other visual programming. File translators import a number of different graphics file formats, manipulate the graphics information as necessary, and then export the graphics information in one of a number of different formats for use in other applications.

Revenues and Revenue Growth Rates

Graphics software products are anticipated to be one of the major growth areas in the whole desktop video market, as personal computer software is anticipated to replace an array of special purpose, expensive systems in use in conventional video. 1989 revenues for this subsegment totaled only $0.8 million as the fledgling desktop video market began to emerge.

1990 through 1992 were periods of extremely high growth, both in terms of revenues and unit shipments, for the graphics software products subsegment of the desktop video market. From a peak rate of 849.4 percent in 1990, revenue growth declined to a more reasonable 110.0

percent in 1992, reflecting $51.5 million in actual revenues. By 1995, revenue growth is anticipated to decline further to 93.5 percent, following $393.4 million in revenues for that year. By 1999, revenues are forecasted to near $3.5 billion, an increase of 47.0 percent over the prior year. Revenue CAGR for the survey period is forecasted at a very healthy 97.5 percent.

Fig. 6-18:	Graphics Software Products Unit Shipment and Revenue Forecasts 1989-1999			
Year	Units (000)	Revenues ($M)	Revenue Growth(%)	Unit Growth(%)
1989	0.9	0.8	----	----
1990	9.7	7.5	849.4	1017.0
1991	34.1	24.5	225.0	253.3
1992	74.6	51.5	110.0	118.8
1993	109.3	103.5	101.0	46.5
1994	183.1	203.3	96.5	67.5
1995	339.3	393.4	93.5	85.3
1996	718.6	783.1	99.1	111.8
1997	1434.4	1427.1	82.2	99.6
1998	2643.6	2354.1	64.9	84.3
1999	4425.4	3459.9	47.0	67.4
TOTAL			*97.5%*	*76.2%*

Unit Shipments and Pricing Trends

Units of graphics software products are defined as single graphics software packages intended for use in desktop video postproduction. Only those packages intended for this purpose are counted in this category, although identical packages are used for other purposes in the personal computer industry.

Shipments for 1989 totaled only 800 units as desktop video systems had not yet fully emerged as target systems for graphics software. By 1992, this figure had risen to 74,600 units, a growth of 118.8 percent over the prior year. 1995 shipments are anticipated to exceed 339 thousand units and 1999 shipments to total over 4.4 million.

Unit growth rates are anticipated to drop in 1993 as in the preceeding years from the extraordinary explosion at the beginning of the decade. Starting in 1994 unit growth is anticipated to rise as desktop video devotees purchase new software, existing users add packages to their systems, and more expensive software associated with workstation-class personal computer platforms begins to become a larger percentage of software sold. This upward trend is anticipated to last until 1996, when unit growth rates are forecasted at 111.8 percent, and then decline gradually for the rest of the decade as the market becomes more saturated. A strong unit shipment CAGR of 74.2 percent is forecasted for the survey period.

Although individual item pricing is anticipated to decline continuously throughout the survey period, the number of packages purchased per desktop video system is anticipated to rise as new applications are developed, and higher-priced packages associated with workstation-class desktop video platforms are assumed to gain market share in the next several years.

Market and Technology Trends

Qualitative Trends

Functionality and Usability

When Graphics Software Products were first developed for personal computers, they were limited to monochrome drafting programs and basic color "paint" programs. Today's programs provide complex color drawing tools, photo touchup tools, image animation and morphing, and file import and export capability, at times in single packages. As the overall graphics software market, as well as that segment associated with desktop video, matures, more of these functions will be integrated into single packages.

With integration of functionality comes complexity, which often means hard-to-use products. At the same time graphics software programs are acquiring additional functionality, they are also becoming easier to use, thanks to Graphic User Interfaces (GUIs) and better attention to how users use the products.

Competitive Analysis / Market Share

Competitive Environment

Graphics Software Products is one of the most hotly contested subsegments of the desktop video market, for several reasons. First, most of the products listed here are applicable to the general personal computer graphics market in addition to the desktop video market. The personal computer graphics market is much more established and much larger than the desktop video graphics software market, and this size has encouraged a number of vendors to develop innovative products for it. Second, software development is not a capital-intensive industry. Many competitors in the graphics software industry began as moonlighting, garage shop-type operations. The low (in terms of capital required) barriers to entry in this type of industry allow many more competitors to enter than in industries which require significant capital investment, say hard drive manufacturing or camcorder design.

Structure

As a fast-growing industry segment with low barriers to entry, Graphics Software Products has attracted a broad range of competitors, from small fly-by-night organizations to major manufacturers like Aldus, Macromedia, and Software Publishing Corporation. As few of the products in this category are focused exclusively on desktop video applications, few of the companies which produce them are focused exclusively on this emerging market. Most compete in the general computer graphics arena, focusing on still art creation, animations, or other general purpose markets. The growing multimedia and desktop video markets have opened new sales opportunities for these vendors and some have chosen to tailor products specifically for these markets.

The list in Figure 6-18 is a far-from-exhaustive list of Graphics Software Products which can be, and are, used for desktop video postproduction applications including still art and background creation, photographic and motion video touchup, titling or character generation, animation, and morphing. It is however a representative list of the sorts of products in this category and includes the market leaders.

The diversity of vendors in this subsegment leads to a diverse set of distribution channels for their products. Smaller organizations have focused on direct sales and sales through authorized dealers. Larger organizations utilize mail order firms and distributors to reach end users, small computer dealers, and VARs. They typically sign larger dealers to direct contracts.

Fig. 6-19:   List of Selected Vendors
                 Graphics Software Products

Companies	Products
A+ Development	AutoPaint
Abvent	Zoom
Activa International	Real3D
Adobe	Photoshop, Illustrator, Dimensions 3-D,Streamline, Collector's Edition clip art libraries, fonts
Aegis	VideoScape
AIM Graphics	AIM-3D
Al Giddings Images Unlimited	stock footage
Aldus	PhotoStyler, FreeHand, Gallery Effects, SuperPaint
Aldus/Silicon Beach	Super 3D
Alias	PowerAnimator, Animator, Full Color Retouch, Sketch, Upfront
Archive Films	stock footage
Aris Entertainment	clip art libraries, QuickTime libraries
ASDG	MorphPlus, Art Department Professional
AT&T GSL	Sculpt 3D, Comet CG, RIO, Sable
Aurora	Liberty
Autodesk	Animator, 3D Studio, Animator Pro, Studio 2
Avid	Bola32
AXA Corp.	Camera F/X, Ink & Paint, Producer, Watercolor
Best Shot	stock footage
Black Belt Systems	Imagemaster
Broadcast Television Systems	The Fixer
Broderbund TypeStyler	GP
Brown-Wagh	3D Workshop, PC Animate Plus
Byte By Byte	Sculpt 3D, Sculpt 4D
Cayman Graphics	TyPerCard
CBS News Archives	stock footage

Centaur Development	OpalPaint
Cinenet	stock footage
Classic Images	stock footage
Comprehensive Video Supply	PICS Tools, Mac Video Titler, MacCaption
Corel Systems, Inc.	Corel Draw!
CoSA	After Effects, Additional Effects
Crystal Graphics	TOPAS, MacTOPAS, Flying Fonts!, 3D Designer, Desktop Animator
Cubicomp	Workspace
Data Translation	VideoQuill
Digital Arts	RenderManager, DGS
Digital Creations	DCTV Paint
Digital F/X	Titleman
Digital Micronics	Vivid24
Disney Software	Animation Studio
Dreamlight Images	stock footage
Dynaware	Dynaperspective
Eclipse Technologies	Madison Avenue
Educorp	stock footage
Electric Image	Electric Image Animation System
Electronic Arts	Deluxe Paint 4, Studio/32
Energy Productions	stock footage
Equilibrium Technologies	deBabelizer
Fabulous Footage	stock footage
Film Bank	stock footage
Fish Films	stock footage
Fractal Design	Painter, Sketcher
Gold Disk Software	Animation Works Interactive, Professional Draw
Graphisoft	Mac3D
Grass Valley Group	videoDesigner
Great Valley Products	CineMorph, Image F/X
Hot Shots & Cool Cuts	stock footage
HSC Software	Kai's Power Tools; ImagePrep
Image Bank	stock footage
Image North Technologies	Inscriber Fontmaker
ImageWare	ImageWizard
Imageways	stock footage
Impulse	Imagine
InnoVision	PrimeTime, Montage
International Video Network	stock footage
Kesser	stock footage
Lazerus	Radiant/PC
Lotus	Freelance Graphics
MacGillivray Freeman	stock footage
Macromedia	MacRenderMan, FilmMaker, Life Forms,

	TitleMaker, ClipMedia clip art libraries, SwivelMan, Swivel 3D Pro, Three-D, SwivelArt, QuickPICS
Masterclips	clip art libraries
McQ Productions	Video Titler
McRoberts Software	LUNA
Media Pedia	stock footage
Merkel Films	stock footage
Micro Frontier	Colorit!
MicroGrafx	Picture Publisher, Draw
Military Channel	stock footage
Motion Works	PROMotion, ADDMotion
NewTek	Toaster Paint, Lightwave
Octree Software	Caligari 3D
Olduvai Corp	VideoPaint
Oxxi	SpectraColor
Phoenix	Phoenix 3D
Pixar	NetRenderMan, RenderMan, ShowPlace, MacRenderMan, Typestry
Pixel Resources	PixelPaint Professional
Quark	QuarkXPress
Rainbow Software	F16
Ray Dream	Ray Dream Designer, JAG, addDepth
Ron Sawade Cinematography	stock footage
San Francisco Canyon Co.	stock footage
SFV International	stock footage
Silicon Graphics	Iris Inventor
Software Publishing Corp.	Harvard Draw, Harvard Graphics
Sound Source Unlimited	stock footage
Specular International	Infiniti-D
Strata	StrataVision 3D, StrataType 3D
Syndesis	InterChange Plus
Television Program Enterprises	stock footage
Texture City	stock, background libraries
Time Arts	Oasis, Lumena
Travelview	stock footage
Truevision	TIPS
United Pixels and Lines	Ultimate Backgrounds
Universal City Studios	stock footage
Video Tape Library	stock footage
VIDI	Presenter Professional; Modeler Pro
Virtus	Virtus Walk Through
Vision Software	CameraMan, Renderize
Vividus	Cinemation
Voyager Co.	stock footage
Wavefront Technologies	Advanced Visualizer, Visualizer Paint, Composer,

	Visualizer Translators
Will Vinton	Playmation
Worldwide Television News	stock footage
WPA Film Library	stock footage
Xaos	Pandemonium, nTitle
ZSoft	Photo Finish

Issues

Incompatibilites

Although all of the tools listed in Figure 6-19 are applicable for desktop video postproduction purposes, this does not mean that they can be used in conjunction. Each software package is configured for a particular personal computer platform and operating system structure. In addition, each package produces or uses different file formats which may not be transferrable even among applications based on the same personal computer platform.

There are variations in resolutions and bit depths, fonts, and font types supported. Some products support keying, others do not. Some produce bitmapped images; some produce vector files.

These various incompatibility problems are typically addressed in a small way by each separate package, as well as on a more global scope by file translation utilities. The problem is likely to get worse before it gets better as the desktop video market presents an opportunity for the creation of new incompatibilities between products.

The emergence of standards from dominant vendors and industry committees tend to reduce the confusion by allowing the industry to standardize on common formats, thus allowing free interchange of information from one program to another.

Processing Power

As graphics software programs become more and more capable, they tend to require more performance from the "engines" powering them, the personal computer platforms. The increasing percentage of desktop video postproduction work being done in the digital domain via graphics programs will continue to load these personal computer platforms and drive the development of new generations of CPUs and dedicated graphics processors.

Artistry

As in the other areas of desktop video, the ability to afford and own Graphics Software Products does not necessarily imply the technological and artistic capabilities to use them. All software packages, in general, require the development of certain computer skills in potential users. Generally, the providers of these packages adequately convey the information necessary for the users to develop these skills.

On the other hand, Graphics Software Products are tools to automate and record an artistic process. Artistry cannot be obtained from a manual; it is typically the result of years of study and practice. Although these tools will provide the users with the technology to accomplish graphical arts tasks such as creating animations, titles, and other graphics, the artistry necessary to create professional-quality output must be obtained elsewhere.

Market Shares

With the diversity in Graphics Software Products, and the sheer numbers of vendors and packages, it is difficult for any vendor to obtain a significant market share unless its products are bundled with other popular products. Such is the case with the market leader in Graphics Software Products, NewTek, developer and marketer of the innovative Video Toaster product line.

NewTek bundles two graphics packages with every Toaster sold. The first is Toaster Paint, a general purpose paint package. The other is Lightwave 3D, a 3D modeling, animation, and special effects package. Sales of these two packages accounted for 33.5 percent of the Graphics Software Products subsegment in 1992.

The remaining market share was divided among the hundreds of software products vendors, with only six garnering more than a 1 percent share. The leader of the middle six was Autodesk, developers of AutoCAD, who obtained a 7.3 percent share based on sales of their Animator and 3D Studio packages. Following Autodesk was Centaur Development at 6.7%, based mostly on bundled sales of its OpalPaint paint package with its high resolution OpalVision graphics adapter.

Adobe led the charge among the Macintosh software providers with its Photoshop and Illustrator programs, acquiring 3.5 percent of the subsegment in 1992. Macromedia, with its broad range of animation and graphics tools, gathered another 3.2 percent. Corel, based mostly on sales of Corel Draw, its graphical illustration program, took 2.7 percent of the 1992 sales in terms of units shipped.   Crystal Graphics, developers and marketers of the TOPAS products marketed by AT&T until early 1993, as well as several other Graphics Software Products, took a 1.7 percent share, counting the contribution of the TOPAS products (which they reobtained in 1993) with their branded products.

<table>
<tr><td colspan="2">Fig. 6-20:   1992 Market Shares
                Graphics Software Products</td></tr>
<tr><td>Companies</td><td>Shares</td></tr>
<tr><td>NewTek</td><td>33.5%</td></tr>
<tr><td>Autodesk</td><td>7.3%</td></tr>
<tr><td>Centaur</td><td>6.7%</td></tr>
<tr><td>Adobe</td><td>3.5%</td></tr>
<tr><td>Macromedia</td><td>3.2%</td></tr>
<tr><td>Corel</td><td>2.7%</td></tr>
<tr><td>Crystal Graphics *</td><td>1.7%</td></tr>
<tr><td>Others</td><td>41.4%</td></tr>
<tr><td></td><td>--------</td></tr>
<tr><td>TOTAL</td><td>100.0%</td></tr>
<tr><td colspan="2">* Includes TOPAS products.</td></tr>
</table>

Highlights of Selected Vendors

NewTek

NewTek, of Topeka, Kansas, manufactures and markets the Video Toaster family of products described elsewhere in this chapter as well as other places in this report. Each Toaster is bundled with two software products, Toaster Paint and Lightwave 3D, to enable users to create the graphics and titles necessary to develop professional quality video presentations.

Toaster Paint is an icon-driven paint program and includes a titling function with builtin fonts. It can import text and generate text shadows, but does not antialias. Lightwave 3D is a high-level graphics and animation program. It includes real-time perspective windowing, fast rendering, and excellent special effectss and texture mapping.

Autodesk

Autodesk, of Sausalito, California, is best known for their market-leading computer aided drafting package, AutoCAD. They also provide several powerful animation and modeling packages which can work independently or in conjunction with AutoCAD.

Animator is a very feature-rich animation package, loaded with options, which runs on PC-compatible platforms. It offered poor resolution for desktop video purposes, so Autodesk introduced Animator Pro as a major enhancement to the basic Animator package. Animator Pro added high resolution, two-dimensional, 24-bit capabilities. The $795, MS-DOS package includes both animation and paint functions in a single program.

3D Studio ($2995) is another MS-DOS package which works with AutoCAD to creating high-resolution 3D models. It includes modeling, materials editing, rendering, animation, and special effects power. It also includes a CD-ROM of 3D textures, objects, an animations. Studio 2 is another high end modeling package, offering fast rendering and links to AutoCAD.

Centaur

Centaur Development, of Redondo Beach, California, makes and markets the OpalVision 24-bit graphics subsystem for Amiga platforms. Included in the bundle is a highly regarded 24-bit paint program, OpalPaint. The success of OpalPaint and OpalVision in the desktop video market is due primarily to the dominance of the Amiga platform and the Video Toaster in the early years of the market's development.

OpalPaint is a real-time, 24-bit capable paint package that overcomes many of the disadvantages of Toaster Paint, bundled with the Video Toaster from NewTek. OpalPaint provides a full range of drawing tools and an expandable library of image processing modes with adjustable parameters. It also includes full texture-mapping capabilities, transparancy and color gradients, multiple work modes, nozzle brushes, predefined palettes, and many other tools.

Adobe

Adobe Systems, of Mountain View, California is a well-known and formidible graphical software developer and marketer. Their PostScript image description language essentially redefined the way personal computers generate printed images.

Their PhotoShop program, available in both Windows and Mac versions as of early 1993, is an $895 image processing program, offering excellent file import and export ability, paint tools, color adjustment tools, and image transformation tools to rotate, stretch, skew or distort images. It also offers filters for image correction and special effects, color separations, PostScript support, and cross-platform compatibility. PhotoShop is the world's leading photo design and production tool whose versatility has direct application to desktop video development. Its full palette of tools for editing and enhancing images allows users to create images from scratch or manipulate existing artwork.

Illustrator, also available in both Windows and Mac versions, is a $695 PostScript drawing program. A UNIX-based version is also available. Illustrator provides text tools for titling, graphing tools, 24-bit color support, and color separations. Other Adobe products include Dimensions 3-D, a 3D modeling program announced in late 92, Streamline, a file conversion utility, theCollector's Edition, a library of predrawn PostScript artwork, and a broad range of fonts for titling.

Macromedia

Macromedia, of San Francisco, California, is a leading provider of multimedia and graphics software solutions, predominantly for Macintosh platforms. They offer one of the broadest ranges of Graphics Software Products lines among all of the competitors in this category. The growing importance of the Mac platform in desktop video applications is sure to make their relative market share grow.

Swivel 3D Pro ($695) is a 3D modeling package which produces PICS files that can be imported into Director, Macromedia's powerful multimedia authoring program. Swivel 3D Pro was the first Mac program to feature linking: it lets users design models with constrained motion between parts of the model. It offers 24-bit color, interfaces with animation controllers, and provides file import and export capabilities.

MacRenderMan is a 3D graphics rendering package. The 3D product creates photorealistic 3D animations from previously created images and offers compositing functions. FilmMaker ($695) is a two-dimensional animation package which interfaces with animation controllers to print animated sequences to videotape. Life Forms is a human figure animation program which lets the modeler realistically duplicate human motion. Its primary applications are in choreography or as a human motion visualization tool. TitleMaker is a $149 titling package. SwivelMan ($895) combines features of Swivel 3D Pro with support for RenderMan RIB files.

Macromedia also supplies the SwivelArt graphics model libraries, ClipMedia CD-ROM animation libraries, and the QuickPICS file utility.

Corel

Corel Systems, Inc. provides Corel Draw!, a high quality graphics tool for MS-DOS platforms. This drawing and text manipulation tool is both powerful and easy to use and can be configured to run under Windows operating environments. Draw! includes more than 100 typefaces and is compatible with Ventura Publisher, Aldus Pagemaker, and other DTP pkgs. It can import files from Lotus 123, scanners, clip art libraries, and other sources.

Crystal Graphics

Crystal Graphics, of Santa Clara, California, is the developer of TOPAS, MacTOPAS, and TOPAS Desktop, three 3D animation and illustration packages remarketed by AT&T Graphics Software Labs until their demise in early 1993. Crystal Graphics is now marketing these products themselves under the names TOPAS, TOPAS for the Mac, and Crystal Desktop Animator. TOPAS, for PC-compatibles, now sells for $3995. TOPAS for the Mac now retails for $2995, and Crystal Desktop Animator is available for $1995.

Crystal 3D Designer, a 3D modeling package for PC-compatibles, sells for $995, and offers much the same capabilities as Desktop Animator, minus the animation. Flying Fonts! is an animated titler package for PCs.

Crystal sells primarily through VARs and other authorized resellers.

Others

CoSA, of Providence, Rhode Island offers After Effects ($1295), a Graphics Software Product which allows compositing and layering of QuickTime Movies, PICS sequences, and PICT images. Each layer can be positioned, scaled, rotated, masked, filtered, and made transparent over time. All effects can be time based. After Effects uses Adobe Premiere and Photoshop plug-in filters and offers high quality rendering, full antialiasing, and PAL/NTSC output. It supports full motion video, multiple track editing, alpha channel, and multiple undo and redo. After Effects began shipping in late 92.

The Additional Effects package was released in early 93 as an enhancement to After Effects. Starting in 1993, After Effects is also bundled with SuperMac's DigitalFilm digital video product.

Electric Image, of Pasadena, California, manufactures the Electric Image Animation System ($7500), a high-end animation program. EIAS includes 3D graphics, animations, VTR control, file conversion, and digital compositing. It also allows shadow casting, transparancy mapping, and environmental (mirror) mapping. It provides file import functions and different shading techniques and runs on Macintosh personal computer platforms.

InnoVision, of San Leandro, California, develops and markets the PrimeTime professional titling and effects software. PrimeTime runs on PC-compatible platforms and is also bundled with the Magni VGA Producer Pro graphics adapter. It offers 9 standard font styles (more available via options), anti-aliasing, drop shadows, texture mapping, highlighting and glow functions, kerning, edit functions, and text roll and crawl functions. PrimeTime is available in four configurations: SVGA, no animation ($400), TARGA-compatible, no animation ($900), and either with animation ($600,$1200 respectively)

Innovation also offers Montage ($500), a 24-bit titling and graphics compositing package for the Amiga platform and Video Toaster applications.

Chapter 7
Strategies For Success

Overview

There will be a number of strategies employed by desktop video manufacturers in order to be successful in this emerging market. Some of the strategies are being employed now; others will develop over time. Some strategies being used presently will prove ineffective over time and will be discontinued, e.g. the current practice of announcing products months or years before they are available in hopes of influencing current purchase decisions.

At this point in time, the following strategies have emerged as critical to the majority of players competing in the market. They are likely to remain important over time.

Strategies Based on Price/Performance

Desktop video is based on the premise that creating video presentations with certain tools offers a cost and development time advantage over substitute techniques, i.e., conventional video methods. Accordingly, the advantages that desktop video products offer over substitute products are in the area of price/performance. Not only must desktop video products offer price/performance advantages over substitute products, but they must also offer either price or performance, or both, advantages over competitive products in order to obtain and maintain market shares and profitability.

At the present time, most competitors are differentiating their products on the basis of price vis a vis the conventional video substitute products and performance versus competition within the desktop video market. Over time, many will choose to differentiate their products by price versus all competition, offering a "standard" functionality set and low prices in order to satisfy the majority of consumers who require undifferentiated products. Other vendors will choose to compete through functionality, performance, or perhaps even specialized applications within the broader desktop video market areas and will price their products above the baseline set by the "standard" products.

Either strategy is likely to be successful. Until "standard" products emerge in each category, it will be difficult for both consumers and manufacturers to determine which products fall into which marketing strategy. As the market matures, the manufacturers of the "standard" products will grow rapidly. So will the manufacturers of the "clones" to follow, both in terms of quantity of competitors and revenues. Margins, on the other hand, will decrease continually as increased competition forces prices lower and lower, forcing many competitors out of the market and leaving it to the best capitalized manufacturing organizations.

The competitors who focus on providing exceptional performance, functionality, or application focus at reasonable prices have less margin pressure with which to contend. On the other hand, they are also less likely to achieve high revenue numbers because of the limited markets they will pursue vis a vis the "standard" product competitors. The "niche" competitors will be better able to hold their product prices steady, assuming that they are able to add technological advancements to them at a pace that keeps the products significantly differentiated from those in the "standard" categories.

Those manufacturers who attempt to offer largely undifferentiated products at premium prices will not be successful very long. The U.S. market, and the world market as a whole, has been educated during the personal computer revolution about the differences between marketing hype and reality and will readily choose the low-cost vendor who offers a "standard" product over a "brand name" product.

Strategies Based on Distribution

Pricing and functionality is irrelevant if manufacturers cannot deliver products to the eventual end users or consumers. Therefore, acquisition of distribution channels and appropriate exercise of those channels will be critical to the development of the desktop video market and the manufacturers of products for that market.

Those manufacturers who choose to compete in the pricing arena will require distribution channels capable of moving large volumes of products so that the manufacturers will be able to capitalize on their manufacturing economies of scale, thus reducing their costs and keeping product margins at reasonable levels. This implies a requirement for mass marketing channels such as mail order, mass merchandisers, and even a network of dealers via stocking distributors. There is no doubt that as "standard" products become available, these channels will evolve and become critical to the success of the manufacturers employing them.

A limiting factor to the development of these channels for desktop video products, as well as to the emergence of "standard" products, is the current technological complexity of desktop video systems. As desktop video combines computer, audio, and video technologies, it requires technical skills in each area in order to integrate a desktop video system as well as to properly utilize it. Current mass distribution channels are either organized along a single technological boundary, e.g. computer dealers or professional audio mail order houses, or are unable to offer technical assistance in any area, e.g. Wal-Mart, Sears, etc.

In addition, the vast majority of product categories within the boundaries of desktop video have not yet produced "standard", mass-market products. Current products are differentiated mostly on the basis of performance or functionality and few clear market "winners" have emerged. Until this happens, demand for these products will not reach a point where mass merchandisers will be interested in them.

In the meanwhile, the combination of integration complexity and varied product functionality offers two opportunities to desktop video manufacturers. First, they can implement product improvements to reduce the complexities of use and integration of their products and to standardize on a set of functionality for given product categories, thus making the products more palatable to mass markets. Second, they can develop alternate channels of distribution which can overcome the technological issues of desktop video and move products to the emerging user base.

It is this second path that leads to the anticipated growth of Value Added Resellers or VARs in the desktop video market. The vast majority of desktop video products manufacturers in the short term, and the niche manufacturers in the long term, will be best served by cultivating these emerging desktop video specialists. They offer the advantages of superior computer skills and low technology entrenchment relative to the majority of existing professional video and professional audio dealers, as well as an improved focus on corporate and other markets which will be the largest growth areas for desktop video. They offer the advantages of video and audio expertise over computer dealers. They offer training and integration support, clear advantages over mail-order firms for dealing with desktop video integration and usage problems.

Strategies Based on Training and Support

The manufacturers of desktop video products can also differentiate themselves by the level of support and training they offer directly to end users and their chosen distribution channels. Because of the complexities of integrating the computer, video, and audio technologies of desktop video, the market has been slow to accept the emerging products, particularly given the general lack of integration support, education, and training provided by the manufacturers and unavailable from the current distribution channels.

It is a known fact that word of mouth is the most effective form of advertising and that it is a reflection of customer satisfaction, which in turn is determined by factors such as ease of use, ease of integration, product quality, and quality of related services from the manufacturers or their representatives. Most important to development of a positive word of mouth reputation is the perception that the manufacturers, their representatives, and their products meet the expectations of the buyers, the end users of those products.

The extravagant marketing claims of some desktop video manufacturers have induced the perception that desktop video development is a simple, inexpensive process. It is, in a relative sense, compared to the enormously expensive and incredibly complex process of creating video presentations using conventional video equipment. It is also far more difficult than programming a VCR clock, installing a personal computer hard drive, or setting the timing on an automobile engine, feats well beyond the technical capabilities of a large segment of the populace.

For positive customer satisfaction leading to increased positive word of mouth advertising, it will be necessary for the manufacturers of desktop video products to reduce the complexities of their products either via technological innovations or via training and support. Since the distribution channels for desktop video are just now slowly developing, it is somewhat unreasonable for the manufacturers to depend on the channels to deliver this training and support without assistance.

Successful manufacturers in the desktop video arena will follow the lead of organizations such as Autodesk and Aldus in the CAD and Desktop Publishing markets. These companies invested heavily in training and support as their markets were developing, reaped the positive benefits including word of mouth advertising, and are currently market leaders. Other companies who relied on users to self-educate or on their sales channels to provide the support necessary to integrate these evolving technologies for end users suffered slower acceptance and correspondingly lower market shares.

Strategies Based on Product Positioning

Some desktop video vendors, including major manufacturers such as Panasonic and Sony as well as smaller firms like Comprehensive Video, will offer a broad range of products, each positioned to attack an element of the desktop video market. These companies will rely less on the strengths of individual products and more on the overall breadth of their product lines, thus positioning themselves as one-stop suppliers to the market.

Other manufacturers, such as Avid Technology or Sachtler, will offer narrower product lines focused on particular functions in the video development process, e.g. postproduction editing or lighting in the cases of the example organizations, and will distinguish themselves by offering products for a range of applications within these functions. Avid, for instance, offers editing products from its DiVA subsidiary for multimedia editing, the Media Suite Pro line for industrial-quality videotape editing, and its Media Composer line for broadcast-quality applications. Sachtler offers a range of lighting products from low cost, portable, easy to use lighting kits to complex, expensive stage lighting systems.

Some companies will adopt a twist on the above strategy, offering a single product for multiple computing platforms. An example is Gold Disk Software, who manufactures similar products for the Macintosh, PC-Compatible, and Amiga platforms.

Still other manufacturers are emerging and will continue to emerge as single-product suppliers. This strategy is very precarious and few companies will survive long with a single product. Most will be overcome by the competition. Many will evolve similar to Avid, Sachtler, or Gold Disk by offering variations on their now-successful first product into related application areas or for other platforms. A very few will be successful as single-product suppliers.

Strategies Based on Industry Alliances

A key element of any emerging market is the development of standards and standard products around which the market focuses. Desktop video has to date evolved few of these standards, although it has adopted a few from the overlapping markets of multimedia, personal computers, professional video, and professional audio.

First among these, because of the importance of the personal computer platform as the center of a desktop video system, is the standardization of these platforms in terms of hardware interfaces, user interfaces, and operating systems. The current leaders in the desktop video market are the Commodore Amiga platform and the Apple Macintosh series, with PC-compatibles of the ISA, EISA, and MCA sub-varieties gaining ground quickly. The Silicon Graphics Indigo family will also compete strongly in the desktop video market and entries are expected from Sun Microsystems, Hewlett Packard, DEC, and other classic workstation vendors.

More important than the maker of the platform itself is the concept of the platform as the basis of an integrated group of products from multiple vendors. Since no vendor can supply every item or function needed by the desktop video market (or any other market for that matter), the ability to integrate interoperable hardware and software with a basic platform is critical to the success of this market. Some vendors will choose a particular platform family with which to make their products compatible. Others will make their products compatible with multiple platforms.

Critical to the emergence of any personal computer family as a standard desktop video base is the availability of a software structure allowing appropriate intercommunication of desktop video hardware and software. Standards such as Apple's QuickTime and QuickTime for Windows offer such frameworks for the Macintosh and PC-compatible platforms. The Microsoft Video for Windows competes in the PC-compatible market, and Avid's OMF standard incorporates several platforms and operating systems, and is even compatible with QuickTime. Manufacturers who desire to create personal computer-based hardware or software for the desktop video market are best served by ensuring that their products are cognizant of these emerging standards.

Some manufacturers have already begun to congregate around individual standards. For instance, there is the PC-compatible crowd, who are developing products for the ISA, EISA, and MCA platforms, based on the MSDOS, Windows, or OS2 operating systems working in conjunction with Intel's DVI compression technology and products such as Microsoft's Video for Windows. This group includes IBM, Intel, Microsoft, Matrox, Asymetrix, Editing Machines Corporation, Truevision, and others.

The Apple-centric group has focused on the Macintosh II platform (e.g. the Quadra family), System 7, and QuickTime, and includes such vendors as Apple, Adobe, SuperMac, Radius, RasterOps, Avid, Digital F/X, Gryphon, CoSA, and others. Similar groups are focusing on the Amiga platform and on the new SGI Indigo platform.

Two other strategic alliances are of particular note and are outside of the boundaries of open standards. The first is the collaboration between Avid Technology and Silicon Graphics. These two firms, in addition to their joint involvement in the OMF standard development, have cooperated on multiple fronts, giving Avid access to SGI's graphics technologies and markets and

SGI access to Avid's video technologies. SuperMac Technology and Adobe Systems also have a cooperative arrangement to mutual benefit. SuperMac developed what is now Premiere and sold it to Adobe, who then licensed it back to SuperMac for bundling with SuperMac's hardware products. Adobe also sells the product to other hardware vendors.

Finally, some desktop video manufacturers are merging with or acquiring companies or product lines which provide them with broader ranges of solutions for desktop video markets. Macromedia acquired MacRecorder from Farallon, giving it an audio tool to complement its multimedia authoring and graphics software products. Macromedia itself is the merger of Macromind, Authorware, and Paracomp, each bringing specific strengths to the whole. Avid acquired DiVA, giving it a low-end editing product to supplement its line. RasterOps acquired Truevision, giving it a line of PC-compatible products to supplement its existing Mac product line.

It is reasonable to expect continued action in all three areas of industry alliance detailed above. More standards will evolve and product lines from multiple manufacturers will coalesce around them. A few will dominate the desktop video market. Firms will select other organizations with complementary products, technologies, and/or distribution channels, and will enter into strategic relationships with them. Some of these relationships will be more than arm's-length strategic partnerships; some will develop into mergers or acquisitions providing the major party with new resources in terms of product lines, technologies, or distribution channels.

Chapter 8
Profiles of Selected Companies

<table>
<tr><td>Abbate Video, Inc.
14 Ross Avenue
Floor 3
Millis, MA 02054</td><td align="right">(508)376-3712</td></tr>
</table>

Company Background

Abbate Video is a small, entrepreneurial organization founded by two brothers, Mark and Jeff Abbate, and a confederate, Phil Palombo, which has been marketing an evolving product, now known as the VideoToolkit for the past two years. Typical of many emerging desktop video operations, Abbate Video is funded primarily by the founders and bootstrap financing. VideoToolkit was developed by the founders as a moonlighting project and sales have recently expanded to allow them to pursue the business as a full-time occupation. Like other small, poorly funded operations, Abbate has been limited in its use of advertising and merchandising programs, relying instead on relatively inexpensive public relations techniques in order to increase product awareness in the desktop video market.

Company Strategies

Abbate's general strategy has been to develop, manufacture, and market software-based solutions to improve the productivity of existing video production techniques by using the power of computers to automate some of the processes. The products are low cost and utilize the power and memory of a computer to organize and simplify a tedious set of tasks, that of logging source video footage and of creating cuts-only workprints. The products are also applicable to the emerging multimedia market as they can optimize the acquisition of footage for QuickTime movies.

Abbate has tried several approaches to marketing their products, including direct sales, use of national or regional sales representation firms, and dealers. They are currently focusing on using direct advertising to generate direct end user sales and dealer leads. When possible, they are establishing dealers among those resellers with a desktop video focus. They have also established cooperative marketing arrangements with Adobe, including product information with every package of Premiere 2.0 shipped. Abbate has also employed a very successful public relations campaign, resulting in a number of positive reviews in leading industry publications.

Products

VideoToolkit, Abbate's only current product line, is a series of software & cabling packages for videotape logging, assembly, and cuts-only video movie making. VideoToolkit is available in various configurations matching to the target machines being controlled. Each configuration runs on a Macintosh system and controls one or two analog VTR machines, allowing the user to log source footage and assemble it into work prints or simple cuts-only video programs. The packages, priced at $279 or $299 depending on the configuration, also support QuickTime, VISCA, LANC, and RS422 control. The VideoToolkit software is an upgrade of a previous product called On Track.

<table>
<tr><td>Adobe Systems, Inc.
1585 Charleston Road
P.O. Box 7900
Mountain View, CA 94039</td><td>(415)961-4400</td></tr>
</table>

Company Background

Adobe was founded in 1982 by current chairman John Warnock and John Geschke. With funding from Apple in 1984, Adobe was able to develop Postscript and introduce it to the market as 1985. Postscript rapidly became an industry standard for the transfer of graphics information between personal computers and printers, including those of Apple, and Adobe's success was assured. Adobe is now publicly traded on the NASDAQ market with annual revenues in excess of $250 million.

Company Strategies

Adobe has chosen to specialize in acquiring, developing, marketing, and selling graphics software tools for personal computer platforms. Adobe has been able to consistently grow its business via strategic acquisitions of products and organizations which are compatible with this focus. In 1981, Adobe acquired a stake in Digital F/X, a leading desktop video system supplier, and purchased Reeltime from SuperMac Technology, renaming it Premiere and launching it to the multimedia and desktop video markets. In 1992, Adobe acquired two other firms and a stake in a third, and announced a graphics paint program, Illustrator, and the upgrade of Premiere, version 2.0.

Adobe also improves its technology positions and access to markets via strategic relationships with other vendors. Besides Digital F/X and Verity, Adobe enjoys continuing relationships with Apple, SuperMac, RasterOps, and Microsoft, among others.

Products

Premiere, announced in 1991 and significantly upgraded in 1992, is a key desktop video product. Technical limitations in the current product, as well as the hardware products with which it is sold, limit its current utility to the multimedia market, but it is evident that the editing package will soon be suitable for video postproduction. Premiere allows the combination of live video, animation, audio, still images, and graphics into a single presentation. Version 2.0 adds antialiased animated titling, rotoscoping, chroma keying, EDLs, time code compatibility, machine control, and other features to an already impressive package. SuperMac, who developed the core package under the name Reeltime and sold it to Adobe, continues to bundle the product with its VideoSpigot and Digital Film product lines.

Illustrator is a multiplatform (Mac, DEC Ultrix, SGI, NeXT, Windows) graphic design tool including the ability to import text, perform color separations, create charts, and overlay clip art. The $695 product is suitable to perform titling and other still graphics functions on desktop video systems. A leading graphics tool, PhotoShop, provides the ability to import, manipulate, and export graphics files on the Macintosh platform. The $895 package allows the design of electronic artwork via the integral paint and illustration tools, or the touchup of color or black and white images via the integral image processing tools and filters. Dimensions 3-D, a three-dimension modeling tool was announced in late 1992.

<table>
<tr><td>Apple Computer, Inc.
20525 Mariani Avenue
Cupertino, CA 95014</td><td>(408)996-1010</td></tr>
</table>

Company Background

Apple Computer develops, manufactures, and markets personal computer systems for business, education, government, and home users around the world. Apple is one of the key elements in the technology, business, and culture associated with the Santa Clara Valley, better known as Silicon Valley, in Northern California. It was founded in a garage by two icons of Silicon Valley, Steve Jobs and Steve Wozniak, was incorporated in 1977, and currently has annual sales in excess of $5 billion per year.

To some extent, Apple has helped create both the desktop video movement as well as the associated multimedia market. Apple's products have long been the preferred personal computer platforms for artistic professionals, due to their intuitive graphical user interfaces. Third party providers have capitalized on Apple's inroads into graphics and other artistic environments by providing innovative paint, animation, and titling programs, which have been slowly but steadily adopted by the conventional video industry, hastening its computerization and the oncoming of desktop video. Apple's development of the QuickTime standard in 1991, while more immediately applicable to the multimedia market, has helped establish a framework for the growing digital video movement which will soon allow all-digital video editing, thereby revolutionizing video programming development.

Company Specialties

Apple, partially because of its highly visible, but precarious, strategy of bucking the prevailing trend of personal computer development, has a history of technological and market exploration and innovation. This focus on innovation has allowed Apple to develop key elements such as the graphical user interface and to focus on educational and artistic markets with great success. Apple has also been strong in developing strategic relationships with key developers in emerging technology areas, including such suppliers as Xing Technology, SuperMac Technology, Sony, and Radius, leading to key developments in the digital video underpinnings to the desktop video market.

Apple is also known for continuous product line upgrades, typically adding higher performance products to its line at least on an annual basis. This allows Apple to replace older, less capable technologies and revamp its line to keep pace with competing platform manufacturers.

Products

Apple offers a variety of personal computer platforms based on the 68030 and 68040 microprocessors as well as 24-bit color peripherals. The 68040 devices include the Quadra family and the newer Centris family of workstations; the 24-bit color peripherals include monitors and graphics adapters. The performance provided by these high end products are required for true digital processing of video.

Apple has also incorporated a number of developments into its System 7 operating system enhancements which are useful in desktop video applications. These include system-level support for MIDI devices and for analog video, two key elements of desktop video program development. This, of course, is in addition to QuickTime itself, a system-level manager of dynamic data types, hardware peripherals, and compression algorithms, providing integration of voice, text, audio, MIDI control, graphics, video, and animation into coherent, controllable file structures.

Although QuickTime is intended for Apple-based platforms, Apple has recently released QuickTime for Windows, allowing the playing of QuickTime "movie" files on Windows-based personal computer platforms.

<table>
<tr><td>Autodesk, Inc.
2320 Marinship Way
Sausalito, CA 94965</td><td>(415)525-2763</td></tr>
</table>

Company Background

Autodesk was founded in 1982 as a graphics software tools provider to the engineering and technical markets. They went public in 1985. They are best known as the developers, manufacturers, and marketers of AutoCAD, the leading personal computer CAD drafting package. They have also developed multimedia, general purpose graphics, and even virtual reality products.

Company Strategies

Autodesk's primary strategy has been to offer high functionality tools in a low cost package. Using this strategy, they became the leading provider of personal computer CAD tools. Most of the company's revenues have come from their CAD products, specifically the industry leading AutoCAD package, although Autodesk is working hard to move into other markets. Autodesk's core customers are engineers and architects who also have need for other graphical and calculation-intensive tools, such as 3D design packages. Autodesk has responded by offering products such as their 3D Studio to address these needs.

Autodesk is not specifically focused on the desktop video market. Rather, they offer several packages applicable to multimedia and general 3D graphics development which have been adopted by elements of the desktop video market in lieu of other available tools. Autodesk's tools are focused on the PC-compatible segment of the personal computer market.

Products

Autodesk is best known for AutoCAD, the leading CAD product for the personal computer market.   It introduced Animator, a low-end multimedia animation package, in 1989 and upgraded it to Animator Pro in 1991. Animator Pro is a $795, medium-level animation program for real-time playback. It includes paint tools, utilities for converting animations from other formats, up to 1024x768 support, graphics tablet support, and improved font support.

3D Studio is Autodesk's $2995 high-level 3D graphics and animation program. 3D Studio offers some VTR control capability as well as image processing functions, object deformation tools, and CD ROM samples.

<table>
<tr><td>Avid Technology, Inc.
Metropolitan Technology Park
One Park West
Tewksbury, MA 01876</td><td>(508)640-6789</td></tr>
</table>

Company Background

Avid Technology's self-professed charter is to provide "software solutions and systems integration for digital media to production, postproduction facilities, broadcast organizations, ad agencies, government and corporate media departments worldwide." Founded in 1987, Avid has rapidly become a major player in professional video editing systems, and a leader of the desktop video movement. Their products are all based on Apple Macintosh platforms at this time, although there are plans to port their products to PC-compatibles and Silicon Graphics' Iris Indigo workstations in the near future.

As of early 1993, Avid Technology is the only organization who is delivering a digital desktop video product suitable for near-broadcast quality, on-line, video postproduction. Their

Media Suite Pro product, announced in 1992 and shipping in early 1993, provides an eloquent statement as to the potential of desktop video.

Avid products have been used to edit television series, including LA Law, Civil Wars, American Detective, and The Wild West, feature films, movies of the week, documentaries, and commercials for such products as Diet Coke, McDonald's, Nike, and Budweiser. They have also been used to create music videos for artists such as Mariah Carey, Huey Lewis and the News, John Mellencamp, U2, and C+C Music Factory.

Avid is privately held and has made an IPO as of early 1993.

Company Strategies

Avid's initial products are focused on broadcast-quality production markets such as video production and postproduction houses and broadcast organizations. Avid attacked these markets via direct sales and the classic video dealer channel. With the advent of the Media Suite Pro in early 1993, Avid now has a product suitable for corporate or governmental video development, and has expanded its distribution channels to include desktop video VARs. Avid markets its products worldwide in 24 different countries via direct sales offices and a network of international distributors. In 1991, roughly 10% of Avid's sales were in Japan alone.

Avid has entered into a significant strategic partnership with Silicon Graphics, Inc. SGI and Avid working on several joint projects, including the porting of the Avid-led OMF standard to SGI's Iris Indigo platforms, Avid building SGI's JPEG compression board for the Indigo, and Avid porting the Media Suite Pro software to the Indigo. SGI is now bundling OMF with its Iris workstations.

Avid has recently purchased two complementary organizations to add products to its basic suite. Avid acquired Flamingo Graphics in 1992 in order to acquire the Bola 32 product, a graphics generation program. Avid acquired DiVA in 1993 in order to protect its flanks from low end digital video editing solutions, led by such products as Adobe's Premiere.

In 1992, Avid announced the Open Media Framework (OMF) strategy, a data interchange structure analogous to Apple's QuickTime, but for high-end professional-quality digital media products and platforms. Avid has enlisted a number of organizations as participants in OMF development, including such industry leaders as JVC, Grass Valley Group, Truevision, Digidesign, Polaroid, Eastman Kodak, Alias Research, Fluent Software, Lyon Lamb, Intelligent Resources, Radius, Montage, Matrox, and C-Cube Microsystems. The OMF group agreed with Apple to incorporate QuickTime into the standard, allowing interchange between OMF-compatible systems and QuickTime-compatible systems.

Products

Avid's first product line, the Avid/1 Media Composer, was introduced and shipped in 1989. It rapidly took the professional video industry by storm, allowing the production of video programming in fractions of the time required for preexisting systems. In 1991, Avid followed with the Media Composer 200 and 2000 series, further lowering the price and expanding the capabilities in non-linear desktop video systems.

The Media Composer 200 line starts with the entry level model 230 system, which uses a graphical bin analogy and advance time line for video editing, provides audio waveform editing, dissolves, fades, and comes with a waveform monitor and vectorscope (in software). The model 240 adds 24 tracks of CD-quality audio, 16 digital wipe patterns, freeze frames, and slow motion capability. The model 250 adds multicamera editing and auto assembly. The Media Composer 200 series is priced between $25,000 and $50,000 and comes with two color multisync monitors and a 1GB optical drive.

The Media Composer 2000 is a high-end desktop video product starting at around $60,000 and going upwards, depending on capability. Avid also offers a series of software products for the Media Composer systems, including MediaMatch, MediaMix, MediaLog, and AudioVision, adding expanded audio, tape logging, and media integration capabilities to the base systems.

Avid's Media Suite Pro was announced in 1992 and began shipping in early 1993. It is a complete desktop video on-line editing system producing near-broadcast quality output via digital editing. It incorporates the only full-motion, full-frame video compression product shipping as of early 1993. The Media Suite Pro lists for $13,500 including a 2GB optimized optical hard drive, software, and four boards for the Mac Quadra. It employs the Truevision NuVista+ card, mated with a proprietary Avid Motion JPEG card, plus Digidesign's AudioMedia II card, plus Atto Technology's SCSI-II adapter. The Media Suite Pro includes an integrated title generator and imports PICT, PICS, AIFF, and QuickTime file types. Unlike its Media Composer siblings, the Media Suite Pro is not intended for off-line applications, so it does not support EDLs, but it does support SMPTE time codes. Media Suite Pro compositions can be imported into Media Composers for generation of EDLs if desired.

The product offers 4 channels of digital audio, with full editing and mixdown capabilities, and can input or output two channels at a time. It offers 16 digital transitions including wipes and fades, plus 16 DVE effects. Output resolution is better than Hi-8 or S-VHS quality, and near U-Matic SP. The Media Suite Pro can capture video and record output to tape in real-time, storing up to 30 minutes of footage on a 2GB drive. The current product is only available for the Macintosh Quadra platform, but Avid is developing SGI Indigo and PC-compatible versions for near-term release.

<table>
<tr><td>Digidesign, Inc.
1360 Willow Road, Suite 101
Menlo Park, CA 94025</td><td>(415)688-0600</td></tr>
</table>

Company Background

Digidesign was founded in 1984 and has built a solid reputation for design and manufacture of high quality, digital audio products. Products such as Pro Tools and AudioMedia II are largely responsible for the digital audio revolution, replacing multitrack analog tape recorders in many professional and semiprofessional video and audio production and postproduction facilities.

Company Strategies

Digidesign is focused on designing, manufacturing, and marketing digital audio production tools for the Mac platform. They have also recently announced two products for the PC-compatible market. All of their products are high-quality hardware, software, or integrated bundles which provide multichannel digital audio processing capabilities.

Digidesign's target consumers are professional and semiprofessional musicians, video and audio postproduction facilities. Digidesign sells through professional audio dealers, high-end musical equipment dealers, mail order, and to a limited extent, direct sales to end users. Field sales offices are located in Paris, New York, Chicago, Los Angeles, Nashville, near major centers of audio and video production and postproduction.

Digidesign focuses on state-of-the-art product engineering and innovation. They believe in high quality engineering and strong technical support over marketing and sales hype. For this reason, they are highly respected in the isolated and insulated worlds of video and audio postproduction, but are largely unknown outside of those markets. Approximately 25% of Digidesign's employees are engineers.

Products

Pro Tools, Digidesign's flagship product, has set the standard for digital audio recording and postproduction. The hardware/software system provides 16-bit, CD-quality sound for 4-16 inputs and outputs (base system provides 4 inputs and 4 outputs, can be expanded by adding additional boards), waveform editing, mixing, MIDI file editing and playback, track bouncing, parametric equalization, and a host of other features. The $5995 to $24,995 system is very popular with professional musicians, audio recording studios, and video postproduction houses.

The slightly less capable, and less expensive at $3495, offering is Sound Tools II. It offers 4 inputs and outputs, CD-quality 16-bit sound, waveform editing, parametric and graphic equalization, compression, and other features. It can be upgraded to Pro Tools for $3495.

The most applicable product to desktop video applications is the AudioMedia II card, which is bundled with Sound Designer II software for a total of $1295. The NuBus card offers stereo input and output, CD-quality 16-bit sound, and SMPTE synchronization. The software provides waveform editing, compression, graphic and parametric equalization, and noise gating. The AudioMedia II board is used in products such as the Avid Media Suite Pro to provide exceptional audio processing power.

Recent product introductions from Digidesign include ProMaster 20, Session 8, Session 8 XL, and AudioMedia LC. ProMaster 20 is a system suitable for stereo digital audio mastering, offering 20 bits of resolution and 104dB of signal to noise ratio for its two input and output channels. Session 8 and Session 8 XL are multitrack recording systems with the general capabilities of Pro Tools in a fixed 8 input / 8 output configuration. Versions for PC-compatibles are available now; versions for the Macintosh platform are planned for the near future. The AudioMedia LC is a less capable version of the AudioMedia II system.

Other products include Pro Store, a high speed rack mounted SCSI hard disk drive; Turbosynth, a modular sound synthesis program; SampleCell, a 16-voice, 16-bit sample playback software package; Q-Sheet A/V, MIDI/SMPTE automation software; and, Video Slave Driver, a peripheral product which synchronizes Digidesign products to "house sync" in professional video applications.

<table>
<tr><td>Gold Disk, Inc.
385 Van Ness Avenue, Suite 110
Torrance, CA 90501</td><td>(310)320-5080</td></tr>
</table>

Company Background

Gold Disk was founded in 1984 in Ontario, Canada, and started by developing Amiga software products. By May 1991, it was the largest worldwide publisher of Amiga software, recognized as a leader in desktop presentations and business productivity tools in the Amiga market. In 1989, Gold Disk opened an office in the Los Angeles area which became the main office for the company. In 1991, it introduced Animation Works for the Mac and Animation Works Interactive for the Windows environment, becoming a multiplatform software developer.

Company Strategies

Gold Disk's published mission is to provide leading edge products that work together in the creation, integration, and delivery of next generation presentation technologies. Its principal business is the development and publishing of desktop presentation and application development products for Windows-based PCs, Macs, and Amigas. It markets to business, education, and government organizations, with particular emphasis on cross industry multimedia presentation developers.

Gold Disk sells directly to end users and indirectly via dealers and personal computer distributors such as Merisel, Ingram Micro, and Soft-Kat.

Gold Disk was an early supporter of the MPC standards and develops products compatible with those multimedia standards.

Gold Disk is privately held.

Products

Gold Disk started out in the Amiga market with products such as PageSetter, Professional Page, ComicSetter, Professional Draw, MovieSetter, and ShowMaker. In late 91, they introduced VideoDirector for the Amiga platform; they ported it to the Windows environment in 1992.

VideoDirector, is a low-cost ($200) personal videotape editing package, similar to Abbate Video's VideoToolkit. It offers VCR-type controls and produces cuts-only video prints by controlling LANC-compatible VTRs. It provides a serial LANC control cable for interfacing with compatible decks and camcorders.

Other Windows-based products include ScreenCrazeII, a screen saver; Professional Draw, a graphics development package; AddImpact!, a multimedia presentation package for OLE compatible spreadsheets, word processors, and other presentation programs; and, Animation Works and Animation Works Interactive. Animation Works ($100) and Animation Works Interactive ($495) are multimedia authoring tools which provide powerful animation and graphics development features as well as sequence editing and playback functions. Animation Works Interactive allows the creation of interactive multimedia programs for applications such as kiosks or training programs.

Macintosh-based programs include Animation Works ($200) and Astound ($399). Astound is a desktop presentation software package, allowing the combination of music, narration, QuickTime videos or animations, moving text transitions, and cel animations into a multimedia presentation.

<table>
<tr><td>Gryphon Software Corporation
3298 Governor Drive
P.O. Box 221075
San Diego, CA 92122</td><td>(619)454-6836</td></tr>
</table>

Company Background

Gryphon was founded in three individuals in 1991 and began marketing their Morph program in 1992. Morphing is the process of gradually converting one image object into another. It was made popular via feature films such as "The Abyss" and "Terminator II" and the "Black and White" music video from Michael Jackson. Although the morphing for those projects was accomplished on much higher power workstations, Morph brings this capability to the Macintosh platform.

Company Strategies

Gryphon is currently a single-product company. They market directly to end users and indirectly via dealers and mail order. In addition, they have recently been able to sign major distributors such as Ingram Micro to move their products to small dealers and VARs.

Products

Morph ($149) is Gryphon's sole product at this point. It runs on a Macintosh II or Quadra platform, imports PICT files and exports either PICS files, QuickTime files, or collections of PICT files. Morph requires the user to define "key points" in each input image which provide the axes around which the program gradually modifies one image to another.

<table>
<tr><td>Macromedia, Inc.
600 Townsend Street
San Francisco, CA 94103</td><td>(415)252-2000</td></tr>
</table>

Company Background

Macromedia is the result of several mergers and acquisitions beginning with the formation of Macromind in 1984 by Mark Canter and several of his artist and musician friends, the acquisition of Paracomp in 1991, and the merger with Authorware in 1992. Macromedia develops, acquires, markets, and sells a broad range of software-based products focused on the graphics, animation, and multimedia authoring markets. These products are equally applicable to the emerging desktop video market.

Company Strategies

Macromedia's merger of product lines and distribution strategies from its component organizations gives it a powerful set of tools to develop and market high and low range authoring solutions across multiple platforms. Macromind's focus on the Macintosh multimedia market, Authorware's focus on high end multimedia in the PC-compatible market, and Paracomp's general concentration of animation have combined to present a formidable competitor in the multimedia tools market.   Macromedia's professed goal is to become the dominant supplier in this market.

Macromedia sells directly to some end users, but primarily markets its products through the indirect channels of computer distributors, dealers, and VARs.

Products

Authorware, a high-end multimedia authoring product, was developed by the Authorware corporation element of Macromedia. This product, an icon-based presentation and multimedia building environment in UNIX, Macintosh, and Windows versions, has been popular in the corporate world for developing training applications. Many of these training applications are now being converted to videotape for distribution, thus making Authorware a desktop video tool, as well.

The key Macromedia product for desktop video applications has been Director, a low-end concept development tool allowing creation of storyboards. Director includes a paint program and a multimedia database which holds information on imported PICT images, scrapbook sequences, graphics files, text, animations, and sound. Director is Mac-based. A lower range product, Magic, produces animated presentations, but lacks some of the high end features of Director. It is also a Mac-based package.

<table>
<tr><td>Matrox Electronic Systems, Ltd.
Video Products Group
1055 St. Regis Boulevard
Dorval, Quebec, Canada H9P 2T4</td><td>(514)685-2630</td></tr>
</table>

Company Background

Matrox, an established high-end video card manufacturer for PC-compatible platforms, formed the Video Products Group in late 1991 in order to develop, manufacture, and market desktop video systems.

Company Strategies

With the formation of the Video Products Group in 1991, Matrox set goals to market innovative desktop video production products, including hardware that incorporates the latest digital processing technology, software that provides easy-to-use, intuitive user environments, and integrated systems that combine the two.

Matrox designs, develops, manufactures, and markets its own products. It has a headquarters location in Quebec, Canada, plus offices in New Jersey, England, and Hong Kong, allowing it access to most of the major markets in the world.

Products

Matrox introduced Personal Producer in late 1991, a Windows-based software product roughly analogous to Adobe's Premiere, DiVA's VideoShop, or Avid's Media Suite Pro software. It is an editing and control package which works in concert with suitable hardware modules to provide typical desktop video postproduction editing functionality. The software provides A/B/C roll capability, wipes and other basic transitions, 2D DVE processing, video compositing, video switching, keying, audio mixing and control, and machine control features.

In 1992, Matrox followed with the hardware necessary to capitalize on the power of Personal Producer. Its Studio board set consists of 5 EISA-bus cards which provide 3 DVE channels, 3 time base controllers, 6 stereo audio channels, a VTR controller, a 32-bit graphics frame buffer, allowing support of 8 composite or 4 S-Video inputs and control of up to 3 input plus one output VTR deck. Although the system shipping as of late 1992 was a linear-editing system only, meaning that it requires the use of external source VTRs, Matrox has announced an intention to add a Motion JPEG card to the system, allowing it to become a non-linear system, similar to the Avid Media Suite Pro.

<table>
<tr><td>NewTek, Inc.
215 SE Eighth Street
Topeka, KS 66603</td><td>(913)354-1146</td></tr>
</table>

Company Background

It's hard to believe that the desktop video revolution started in Topeka, Kansas. But it did, in 1990, with the introduction of the Video Toaster from NewTek. NewTek actually started earlier, introducing its first product in 1985, following on with a succession of other multimedia products, all of which financed development of the Video Toaster. All of NewTek's products were based on the Commodore Amiga 2000 platform because of its excellent video processing capabilities. The Toaster, as it is often abbreviated in industry use, was no exception.

The introduction of the Toaster came at an opportune time. The underlying technology had been recently developed, the market had a lot of pent-up demand, and there were no competitive products under the $100,000 price range. Out comes the Toaster at about $1600, and desktop video is born. Over 40,000 of these units have been sold since then, giving the struggling Amiga a reason to be, and providing video production and postproduction capabilities for thousands of prior video illiterates, as well as improving the capabilities of a significant block of video professionals. A measure of the impact of the Toaster is that some 25 percent of its owners have expressed an interest in upgrading their VTRs and cameras to BetaCam equipment, or professional quality, although many were rank video amateurs when they first got their Toasters.

Company Strategies

Although the Toaster was developed for the Amiga platform, NewTek has announced variations which connect to both Macintosh and PC-compatible platforms. As of late 1992 these were not yet successfully shipping, but the promise of their availability will dramatically expand their market beyond that provided by the slow-selling Amiga. NewTek's development strategy has been to continually add features to the product line, dramatically expanding its already impressive set. Cross-platform functionality is a good example of this feature expansion.

Despite its functionality, Toaster products do not include such features as edit control or audio editing. NewTek has relied on 3rd party organizations, albeit without a great deal of encouragement, to provide these functions. Indeed, a whole industry, composed of dozens of companies, has grown up around NewTek and the Video Toaster.

NewTek itself is mostly a development organization. They rely on a third-party organization out of Minneapolis to provide their sales and channel marketing. NewTek sells through some distributors, but mostly through a limited set of authorized dealers and VARs. NewTek also relies on strong public relations, participating in many trade shows and other industry events. They have distributed over 100,000 copies of their "Revolution" promotional videotape, which was produced using Video Toasters, to industry observers and participants at trade shows.

NewTek had the desktop video market to themselves for quite a while, but now competitive products are beginning to multiply. NewTek will have to continue to innovate on their product in order to maintain their lead over the newly emerging digital video products arriving in 1992 and 1993.

NewTek is privately held.

Products

NewTek's only significant product is the Video Toaster, which contains everything but the kitchen sink in terms of functionality, other than audio and edit control. It is essentially a single card, plus over 30MB of software, which reside in a Commodore Amiga system. The

Amiga can be a standalone platform or can be controlled via ToasterLink, a SCSI connection to an Apple Macintosh or a PC-compatible platform. Because of technical difficulties, the standalone version is the only one which is commonly available.

The Toaster is predominantly a video switcher, controlling the video signals from four different inputs and directing them to two video outputs, program and preview. It includes a linear keyer, over 100 different transition types with either automatic or manual control, a 24-bit frame grabber, external GPI triggers, luminance keying, a character generator, a real-time color processor, a paint program, and a 3D animation program. A typical Toaster workstation is $4595 and includes the Toaster board and software, a Commodore Amiga with 52MB of disk and 7MB of RAM. The system also requires three monitors, at least two VTRs with time base correctors, an accelerator card, and a Vectorscope / Waveform monitor.

Toaster Paint, the paint and character generation program provided with the Video Toaster, provides a good selection of fonts and paint tools, can handle shadowing, and can import text from other programs, although it cannot antialias the fonts. Lightwave 3-D is the high level 3D graphics and animation package bundled with the Toaster.

<table>
<tr><td>Opcode Systems, Inc.
3950 Fabian Way, Suite 100
Palo Alto, CA 94303</td><td>(415)856-3333</td></tr>
</table>

Company Background

Opcode is one of the leading MIDI vendors, focusing mainly on software such as sequencers and librarians, but also offering hardware necessary to interconnect MIDI-compatible musical instruments, electronic effects devices, and personal computers.

Company Strategies

The company has focused on the computer end of the MIDI business, unlike companies like Roland, Korg, and Yamaha, who focus on the musical instrument end. The company develops, manufactures, and sells hardware and software products based on the Apple Macintosh platform. These products are sold predominantly to high-end musical equipment dealers, who in turn market to professional and semi-professional musicians.

Opcode has also developed a general software structure known as OMS (Opcode MIDI System) which allows Opcode's various products to interchange data. This allows their products to interact easier than those of competitive organizations.

Products

Opcode's flagship product is Vision, a MIDI composition and sequencing program allowing the user to create or import MIDI files, assign instrumentation, and play the stored sequences via an attached synthesizer. Opcode offers a high end version of Vision, called Studio Vision, which adds the capability of recording, editing, synchronizing with MIDI instrumentation, and playing back of digitized audio. They also offer a low-end product, EZ Vision, for hobbyists, educators, and MIDI newcomers who do not require the power of Vision or Studio Vision.

Other software products include the Galaxy librarian, allowing the creation, storage, editing, retrieval, and interchange of sound "patches", or individual sound creation programs for synthesizers, drum machines, samplers, etc. Cue is a film scoring system allowing the synchronization of MIDI sequences to SMPTE time code and visual cues. A new product, SoundTrack provides a set of over 100 prerecorded general MIDI song sequences and a Hypercard-based indexing and playback system. It allows non-musicians the ability to select and playback MIDI music.

Opcode also offers a line of hardware products which enable the connection of a Macintosh to multiple MIDI devices. Timecode Machine is a MIDI-to-SMPTE(LTC) converter in a standalone unit. MIDI Translator is a simple 1-in, 3-out, Mac-to-MIDI adapter. Studio +2 is a more powerful Mac-to-MIDI interface, allowing 2-in, 3-out capability and serial port (printer and modem) pass through switching. Studio 3 is similar, offering 2-in, 6-out capability, serial port pass through, plus MIDI-to-SMPTE(LTC) synchronization. Studio 4 is similar to Studio 3, but with 8-in, 10-out capability. Studio 5 is Opcode's high end hardware product, offering the functions of a Mac-to-MIDI interface, a MIDI patchbay, a MIDI processor, and a SMPTE synchronizer in a single rackmount unit. It offers 15 independent ins and outs, allowing a wide range in patching capability. All Opcode hardware devices are compatible with their software products.

<table>
<tr><td>Panasonic, Inc.
One Panasonic Way
Secaucus, NJ 07094</td><td>multiple, see Chapter 9</td></tr>
</table>

Company Background

Panasonic is not an individual organization, rather it is a series of subsidiaries of the giant conglomerate Matsushita Electric Industries Company, Ltd. of Japan. Panasonic is divided into a series of trading companies focused on individual markets in the United States and worldwide. Products marketed by Panasonic are manufactured by other divisions of Matsushita.

Even though they are actually separate organizations under the Matsushita umbrella, the public perceives Panasonic to be a distinct, integral organization. For purposes of this report, it is helpful to consider this to be so, although the products mentioned below actually come from several different organizations.

Company Strategies

Panasonic's general strategy, and that of many of its Japanese conglomerate competitors is to provide high quality, innovative, electronic devices at affordable prices. They constantly innovate, providing rapid turnover in product lines, in order to include the latest functionality or technological cost advantages in the various products.

Panasonic Communications and Systems Company markets an extensive line of office automation equipment in the U.S., including notebook computers, printers, color monitors, CD-

ROM drives, other optical disk drives, scanners, copiers, fax machines, typewriters, telephones, pagers, and POS equipment. Panasonic Broadcast and Television Systems Company markets a series of professional video cameras, camcorders, and VTRs, audio tape recorders, editing equipment, video components, audio mixers, audio amplifiers, DAT tape decks, video monitors, and LCD projectors. Other divisions handle consumer quality VTRs and camcorders, microphones, stereo audio equipment, and a host of other electronic products.

Panasonic sells its computer products through dealers and distributors, its consumer products through mass merchandisers and technology super stores, and its video and audio products directly to end users or through professional video and audio dealers.

Panasonic is a key proponent, along with another Matsushita subsidiary, JVC, in promoting VHS, VHS-C, S-VHS, and S-VHS-C formats for videotape acquisition, editing, and playback. Its prime competitor is Sony, who promotes the 8mm, Hi-8, U-Matic SP, and BetaCam SP formats. Sony has the edge in video quality, Panasonic and JVC the edge in market acceptance, thanks to the dominance of VHS over the now obsolete Beta format pushed by Sony. S-VHS is being positioned as an upgrade to VHS, since VHS tapes can be viewed on S-VHS equipment. VHS-C has been largely ignored, since S-VHS-C offers the same size advantages (in terms of cassette size and play lengths) and offers higher quality. Both compete with Hi-8, which has the lead in compact camcorders over the bulkier S-VHS units from Panasonic and others.

Products

Key Panasonic products include the AG-1960 and AG-1970 S-VHS VTRs.   The 1960 is a an editing recorder/player that provides S-VHS resolution, hi-fidelity stereo sound, Jog/Shuttle capability, color control, and serial edit control. It does not offer SMPTE time code capability. The AG-1970 is a recent upgrade to the 1960 product, adding an integral TBC and improved audio quality at a lower price, $1199. The AG-7650 and AG-7750 professional quality VTRs add time code capability and extra options for $3495 and $4895, respectively.

Panasonic markets a line of professional quality S-VHS cameras and camcorders, starting with the AG-455 camcorder at $1599, the AG-460 2-CCD camcorder at $2900, and the WV-F250B 3-CCD color video camera at prices ranging from $3195 up, depending on features. Panasonic also offers a range of VHS, S-VHS, VHS-C, and S-VHS-C consumer and prosumer quality camcorders for the mass market.

Panasonic color video monitors include the 13" BT-H1350Y, the BT-H1360Y, and the BT-S1370Y at $969, $729, and $599, respectively. They offer decreasing levels of functionality, but all include a builtin speaker, S-Video and composite inputs, a headphone jack with volume control, and a metal cabinet. Panasonic also offers 7", dual 7" rackmount, 9", 10", 19", 20" and 25" video monitors in various configurations They also offer LCD projection systems for wide screen viewing.

The Panasonic LF-7010 is a 1GB optical disk drive offering removable cartridges, phase-change technology, a SCSI-II interface, and compatibility with both WORM and read/write media. A Panasonic OEM, Optical Access International of Woburn, MA, has written a driver for this unit allowing it to store real-time video and audio with such products as the Digital F/X Video F/X or Digidesign's Pro Tools.

Panasonic offers a variety of CD-ROM drives, videodisc players and recorders, and computer equipment, all applicable to desktop video.

<table>
<tr><td>RasterOps, Inc.
2500 Walsh Avenue
Santa Clara, CA 95051</td><td>(408)944-4398</td></tr>
</table>

Company Background

RasterOps was founded in 1987 and went public in 1990. They produce approximately $100 million in annual sales through the design, manufacture, and marketing of Macintosh based graphics adapters.

Company Strategies

RasterOps' professed mission is to design, manufacture, and market photorealistic color-imaging products. The company regards digital video as falling within these boundaries and has been one of the early entrants into the digital video / desktop video market.

RasterOps is based in Santa Clara, California, but also operates sales offices in Europe and the Far East. Until recently, they sold their products primarily through dealers; they have recently added several key distributors to handle smaller dealers and VARs.

In 1992, RasterOps acquired two organizations in order to expand their market presence. The key deal was the acquisition of Truevision, another digital video leader. Until this acquisition, RasterOps was focused on the Macintosh market; Truevision's range of products for the Macintosh and PC-compatibles broadens their product line substantially. In addition, Truevision's focus on using distributors to reach VARs will help RasterOps broaden their distribution channels.

RasterOps has also signed OEM deals with Sony and DEC to develop digital video technology for those companies' products.

Products

RasterOps has been known for some time as a leading manufacturer of Macintosh video adapters and currently offers a wide range of these products. More importantly, as far as desktop video is concerned, they have developed a line of video capture and playback boards, compression products, and a video encoder, which work in conjunction with a suitable QuickTime editor, e.g., Adobe's Premiere, to provide an integrated digital video solution.

The key components are the 24STV, 24MxTV, and 24XLTV video boards, the MediaTime video/audio board, the MoviePak compression daughterboard, and the Video Expander II outboard encoder. Any of the four video boards can be mated with MoviePak and the VideoExpander, providing various functionality levels for desktop video production.

The 24STV offers 30 frame per second output and near real-time capture, composite and S-Video input, and 640x480 resolution. The 24MxTV ($2199) is similar and offers 832x624 resolution for larger monitors. The 24XLTV ($3499) is similar, but offers additional RGB inputs and supports displays up to 21" in size. MediaTime accepts input from composite or S-Video sources, provides CD-quality stereo audio recording and playback, and supports 640x480 monitors with video in a window. MoviePak, shipping in early 1993 for $1999, is a daughterboard to each of these graphics adapters which adds Motion JPEG compression at up to 30:1 ratios, allowing 30 frame per second 640x480 video. The Video Expander II is an outboard standalone device which encodes an interlaced RGB (Mac video) signal into NTSC composite, S-Video and RS-170 RGB outputs for recording to tape or viewing on other types of monitors.

The Editing Aces bundle of MoviePak, MediaTime, and Video Expander II is available from RasterOps for $4697 as of early 1993.

<table>
<tr><td>Silicon Graphics, Inc.
2011 North Shoreline Boulevard
Mountain View, CA 94039</td><td align="right">(415)960-1980</td></tr>
</table>

Company Background

Silicon Graphics is an established workstation vendor, competing with the likes of DEC, Hewlett-Packard, and Sun Microsystems in the computer graphics, CAD, CAM, and simulation markets. Their products are based on a derivative of the UNIX operating system and proprietary hardware and bus structures. They have recently become very well known in the film and television industry because people like George Lucas and his Industrial Light and Magic organization use SGI products to create dazzling special effects for movies like "Terminator II", "Lawnmower Man", and "The Abyss".

In 1991, SGI introduced the low-end Iris Indigo product line, their first under-$10,000 products. These products brought high-quality graphics capability and CD-quality audio to the power of a workstation at affordable pricing. Accordingly, they were immediately met with a great deal of acclaim. More importantly, SGI began a strong campaign of encouraging the porting of 3rd party applications over to the Indigo platform in order to make it more palatable to the personal computer user base. Offerings from Adobe, Alias Research, Time Arts, Autodesk, Frame Technology, Wavefront, SoftImage, Interleaf, Informix, Valid Logic, and others are being ported to the Indigo. SGI has signed a licensing agreement with Insignia Solutions, Inc. for their SoftPC emulation program, allowing Windows applications to run on the Indigo and other SGI workstations in 1993. SGI is working to port Apple's QuickTime to the platform. Avid Technology has announced plans to port its Media Suite Pro desktop video system to the Indigo in 1993. In short, the Indigo has become and will continue to be a comer in the high-quality graphics and video workstation market.

Silicon Graphics was founded by former Stanford University professor Jim Clark in 1982 after his work on a DARPA (Defense Advanced Research Projects Agency) project which also provided the seeds for Sun Microsystems and MIPS. Clark gathered up some of his doctoral students and founded SGI as a purveyor of "visual computing".

Company Strategies

Silicon Graphics is positioned as a supplier of workstations for visual computer applications. Their primary market has been the engineering and scientific community with applications such as CAD, CAM, and graphic simulations. Recently, they have penetrated the film community and have enjoyed success providing the graphics horsepower for special effects in feature films.

Strategic relationships are critical to SGI's success. In 1992, they acquired longtime supplier MIPS and purchased minority stakes in Control Data Corporation and Alias Research. They aborted a deal with Compaq Computer in which Compaq was to purchase almost $200 million of SGI stock and the two companies were to exchange technologies. Eight other companies, including NEC, Toshiba, and Tandem bought into SGI in 1992, hoping to acquire some of SGI's industry leading graphics technology as well as some of their profits.

SGI has licensed some graphics technology to Microsoft and has entered into a strategic relationship with desktop video pioneer Avid Technology. SGI will work in Avid's OMF consortium to develop interoperable digital video applications and platforms and Avid is developing SGI's full-motion video compression board. Avid also has announced plans to port the Media Suite Pro and the Media Composer software over to the Iris Indigo platform. Silicon Graphics has also announced strategic partnerships with Soft Image and Alias Research.

SGI has traditionally manufactured high-quality, high-performance, high-priced workstations. They break this mold with the Iris Indigo, a workstation in personal computer clothing. It remains to be seen if SGI can be successful with a low-range product in a market where there is much more competition than is familiar or comfortable. Still, SGI is working hard to establish a reputation with the personal computer market. They are working with third party software developers in order to port popular packages to the Indigo platform. They are also selling direct, via mail order, for the first time.

Products

SGI is most known for its computer graphics workstations sold to companies like Walt Disney Studios, Industrial Light & Magic, NASA, and Boeing for up to $500,000. Because of the cost of these products, they are inapplicable for desktop video applications, although they are used extensively in feature films and episodic television production.

The Iris Indigo, announced in 1991, is positioned as a PC rather than a workstation. In its simplest configuration, the Indigo is priced at $7995 and offers 30MIPS of performance. Configurations are available with higher power, more disk drive storage, and other features, raising the configured price to around $30,000, more than for a high-powered personal computer, but far less than for a typical graphics workstation.

Indigo uses MIPS RISC microprocessors. The low end employs the R3000 device and the high end products use the R4000. Monitors are offered, ranging from 16" to 19" in size. Video boards, compression boards, and CD-ROM drives are options. The base system provides high-performance 3D graphics, CD-quality audio inputs and outputs, builtin Ethernet and SCSI II ports, two serial ports, and one parallel port.   The Indigo runs SGI's implementation of UNIX, called IRIX, as well as the OSF/Motif window manager.

<table>
<tr><td>SuperMac Technology, Inc.
485 Potrero Avenue
Sunnyvale, CA 94086</td><td>(408)245-2202</td></tr>
</table>

Company Background

SuperMac is a manufacturer and marketer who focuses on high-resolution graphics hardware for the Macintosh personal computer market. They have made forays into software development and into products for other personal computer platforms, but have consistently concentrated on their mainline business.

In 1991 Apple Computer announced QuickTime, a standard for information interchange for multimedia hardware and software. Within two weeks of its announcement, SuperMac introduced the VideoSpigot as the first digital hardware product compatible with QuickTime, along with the Reeltime software it developed to control the hardware. SuperMac soon thereafter sold the Reeltime package to Adobe, who released it as Premiere. The rest, as they say, is history. SuperMac sold a substantial quantity of Video Spigots, in their various configurations, despite their limitations in terms of audio and video acquisition and playback quality.

In 1992 SuperMac announced the DigitalFilm product, a true desktop video competitor. It began shipping the product in early 1993 and encountered some problems which forced SuperMac to issue a product-wide bug fix and to retool the product with the fixes. Despite these difficulties, SuperMac is expected to become a major force in the digital desktop video market in the very near future.

Company Strategies

SuperMac focuses on the publishing, prepress, business productivity, and digital video markets. All of their products represent productivity improvements for these markets. SuperMac takes a business posture of being customer responsive, quick to advance technology via VLSI, and levering their technology and market knowledge to bring innovations to the market.

SuperMac sells indirectly through a worldwide network of over 1600 authorized resellers, distributors, VARs, OEMs, and mail-order firms. They support 38 authorized distributors in over forty different countries.

SuperMac has established strategic relationships with a number of organizations, including Quark, Electronics for Imaging, Adobe, Apple, Microsoft, Asymetrix, Storm Technology, and Macromedia. Some of these are developmental and others are co-marketing relationships only. For instance, SuperMac bundles Adobe's Premiere with its Video Spigot and DigitalFilm product lines, Macromedia's MacRecorder with their Spigot and Sound product, and Microsoft and Asymetrix products with its VideoSpigot for Windows product, which was recently sold to Creative Labs. SuperMac worked with Storm Technology to develop their Thunderstorm line of graphics adapters.

SuperMac's relationship with Adobe is somewhat unique. Recognizing its limitations in software marketing, SuperMac sold Reeltime to Adobe, and then licensed it back (as Premiere) for bundling with its hardware. When Adobe obtained Reeltime, it also obtained the chief engineer responsible for it. Agreements in 1991 and 1992 have continued the relationship wherein SuperMac bundles Premiere with its hardware and continues to work with Adobe to improve it.

SuperMac is publicly held since mid-92, trading on the NASDAQ exchange.

Products

SuperMac's key desktop video product is the DigitalFilm system, which began shipping in 1993. It is a Macintosh NuBus card which provides a high level digital video capture and playback system. DigitalFilm allows users to capture full screen video and stereo sound to hard disk at 30 frames per second, and to output the video back to a VTR at full speed. It, like several other digital video products, simulates 640x480 video resolution by a technique called scan line doubling.

DigitalFilm ($5999) supports 24-bit color on large screen monitors, Motion JPEG image compression and decompression with adjustable compression ratios up to 70:1, QuickTime, SMPTE time code with frame accuracy, VDIG, 8- or 10-bit audio at sample rates up to 44.1kHz, key frame motion control animation, EDLs, keying, and output to composite, S-Video, and RGB. DigitalFilm is bundled with Adobe's Premiere. As of early 1993, SuperMac made DigitalFilm's components available individually. These include DigitalFilm Player, DigitalFilm Recorder, and DigitalFilm Encoder & Breakout Box.

SuperMac's Video Spigot family is one of the largest selling digital video product lines. It includes the Video Spigot, Spigot & Sound, and the Video Spigot Pro. Each comes in a number of versions for the various Macintosh platforms and range in price from $499 to $1899, depending on capability. All are based on a single card which supplies composite video capture and playback capability. Capture and playback rates are largely a function of the horsepower of the personal computer platform, but range from a low of about 5 frames per second to a high of about 20. The frame size is also limited, typically supporting only video-in-window sizes of 80x60 to 320x240. The Spigot and Sound configurations add MacRecorder and Sound Edit Pro from Macromedia, allowing stereo audio capture and playback.

SuperMac also offered a version of the Video Spigot for Windows-based platforms, but recently sold this product lines to Creative Labs, creators of the Sound Blaster and Video Blaster.

SuperMac is best known for a line of 8- and 24-bit graphics adapters and monitors. They also offer color dye-sublimation thermal transfer printers, display calibrators, and supplies for their printers.

Chapter 9
List of Selected Companies

3M Visual Systems Division
P.O. Box 2963
Austin, TX 78769
(800)328-1371

Acer America Corporation
2641 Orchard Parkway
San Jose, CA 95134
(408)432-6000

Acoustic Systems
415 East St. Elmo Road
Austin, TX 78745
(800)749-1460
FAX: (512)444-2282

Ad Lib, Inc.
220 Grande-Allee East, Suite 850
Quebec, Quebec, Canada G1R 2J1
(418)529-9676

Adobe Systems, Inc.
1585 Charleston Drive
P.O. Box 7900
Mountain View, CA 94039
(415)961-4400

Adrienne Electronics
11994 Marjon Drive
Nevada City, CA 95959
(916)265-8288
(916)265-3805

Advanced Digital Imaging
22 Rocky Knoll
Irvine, CA 92715
(714)725-0154

Advanced Logic Research (ALR), Inc.
9401 Jeronimo
Irvine, CA 92718
(714)581-6770

Advanced Remote Technology, Inc. (ARTI)
307 Orchard City Drive, Suite 204
Campbell, CA 95008
(408)374-9044

Advent Computer Products
449 Santa Fe Drive, Suite 213
Encinitas, CA 92024
(619)942-8456

Agfa Matrix Division
Agfa Corporation
One Ramland Road
Orangeburg, NY 10962
(914)365-0190

AimTech Corporation
20 Trafalgar Square
Nashua, NH 03063
(800)289-2884

Aircraft Production Libraries
162 Columbus Avenue
Boston, MA 02116
(800)343-2514
FAX: (617)542-7222

AITech International Corporation
1564 Centre Pointe Drive
Milpitas, CA 95035
(408)946-3291

AKAI Professional
P.O. Box 2344
Fort Worth, TX 76113-2344
(817)336-5114
FAX: (817)870-1271

AKG Acoustics
1525 Alvarado Street
San Leandro, CA 94577
(510)351-3500
FAX: (510)351-0500

Aldus Corporation
411 First Avenue South
Seattle, WA 98104
(206)628-2320

Alesis Corporation
3630 Holdrege Avenue
Los Angeles, CA 90016
(310)558-4530
FAX: (310)836-9192

Alias, Inc.
110 Richmond Street East, 4th Floor
Toronto, Ontario, Canada M5C 1P1
(416)362-9181
FAX: (416)362-0630

Alpha Technologies
6921 Cable Drive, Suite 100
Marriotsville, MD 21104
(410)781-4200

Altec Lansing
10500 West Reno Avenue
Oklahoma City, OK 73126
(405)324-5311
FAX: (405)324-8981

American Studio Equipment
8922 Norris Avenue
Sun Valley, CA 91352
(818)768-8922

Ampex Corporation
401 Broadway
Redwood City, CA 94063
(415)367-4161
FAX: (415)367-2841

AmPro Corporation
35 Cabot Road
Woburn, MA 01801
(617)932-4800
FAX: (617)932-8756

AMTEL Systems
310 Judson Street, Unit 6
Toronto, Ontario, Canada M8Z 5T6
(416)251-3355
FAX: (416)251-3977

AMX Corporation
Video Products Division
12056 Forestgate Drive
Dallas, TX 75243
(214)222-0193

Antex Electronics Corporation
16100 South Figueroa Street
Gardena, CA 90248
(310)532-3092

Anton Bauer, Inc.
One Controls Drive
Shelton, CT 06484
(203)929-1100
FAX: (203)929-9936

Apple Multimedia Lab
3220 Sacramento Street
San Francisco, CA 94115
(415)346-0535

Applied Research and Technology (ART)
215 Tremont Street
Rochester, NY 14608
(716)436-2720
FAX: (716)436-3942

Associated Production Music
6255 Sunset Boulevard, Suite 820
Hollywood, CA 90028
(213)461-3211
FAX: (213)461-9102

AST Research, Inc.
2121 Alton Avenue
Irvine, CA 92714
(714)863-1333

Asymetrix Corporation
110 110th Avenue NE, Suite 711
Bellevue, WA 98004
(206)462-0501

Atlas/Soundolier
1859 Intertech Drive
Fenton, MO 63026
(314)349-3110
FAX: (314)349-1251

AT&T Graphics Software Labs
3520 Commerce Crossing #300
Indianapolis, IN 46240
(317)844-4364
FAX: (317)575-0649

ATI Technologies, Inc.
3761 Victoria Park Avenue
Scarborough, Ontario, Canada M1W 3S2
(416)756-0718
FAX: (416)756-0720

ATronics International, Inc.
1830 McCandless Drive
Milpitas, CA 95035
(408)942-3344
FAX: (408)942-1674

Audio Accessories, Inc.
Mill Street
Marlow, NH 03456
(603)446-3335
FAX: (603)446-7543

Audio-Technica US, Inc.
1221 Commerce Drive
Stow, OH 44224
(216)686-2600
FAX: (216)686-0719

Audiotronics
7428 Bellaire Avenue
North Hollywood, CA 91605
(818)765-2645

Autodesk, Inc.
2320 MarinshipWay
Sausalito, CA 94965
(800)525-2763
FAX: (415)331-8093

Avid Technology, Inc.
Metropolitan Technology Park
One Park West
Tewksbury, MA 01876
(508)640-6789
FAX: (508)640-1366

Aydin Corporation
700 Dresher Road
Horsham, PA 19044
(215)657-8600

Aztek
17 Thomas
Irvine, CA 92718
(714)770-8406
FAX: (714)770-4986

Barco, Inc.
1000 Cobb Place Boulevard
Kennesaw, GA 30144
(404)590-7900
FAX: (404)590-8042

BCD Associates
7510 North Broadway #205
Oklahoma City, OK 73116
(405)843-4574

Bencher, Inc.
333 West Lake Street
Chicago, IL 60608
(312)263-1808

Beyer Dynamic
56 Central Avenue
Farmingdale, NY 11735
(516)293-3200
FAX: (516)293-3228

Bogen Photo
565 East Crescent Avenue
Ramsey, NJ 07446
(201)818-9500

Brightstar Technology, Inc.
1450 114th Avenue, Suite 200
Bellevue, WA 98004
(206)451-3697

Brooktree Corporation
9950 Barnes Canyon Road
San Diego, CA 92121
(619)452-7580

Brown-Wagh Publishing
130-D Knowles Drive
Los Gatos, CA 95030
(408)451-0900

Byte By Byte Corporation
9442A Capital of Texas Highway North
Suite 650
Austin, TX 78759
(512)343-4357

C. Itoh Electronics, Inc.
2505 McCabe Way
Irvine, CA 92714
(714)660-1421
FAX: (714)757-4488

Calaway Editing
a division of Dynatech Corporation
535 Race Street
San Jose, CA 95126
(408)295-8814
FAX: (408)295-6409

Canon U.S.A., Inc.
1 Canon Plaza
Lake Success, NY 11042
(516)488-6700

Carvin
1155 Industrial Avenue
Escondido, CA 92029
(800)854-2235
FAX: (619)747-0743

Chinon America, Inc.
Information Equipment Division
660 Maple Avenue
Torrance, CA 90503
(800)441-0222

Cine 60, Inc.
630 Ninth Avenue
New York, NY 10036
(212)586-8782
FAX: (212)459-9556

Claris Corporation
5201 Patrick Henry Drive
P.O. Box 58168
Santa Clara, CA 95052
(408)727-8227

Colortran, Inc.
1015 Chestnut Street
Burbank, CA 91506
(818)843-1200
FAX: (818)954-8520

Columbine Systems, Inc.
1707 Cole Boulevard
Golden, CO 80401
(303)237-4000
FAX: (303)237-0085

Commodore International Ltd.
1200 Wilson Drive
West Chester, PA 19380
(215)431-9100
FAX: (215)431-9156

Communication Specialties
89A Cabot Street
Hauppage, NY 11788
(516)273-0404

Compaq Computer Corporation
20555 FM149
Houston, TX 77070
(713)370-0670

Comprehensive Video Supply
148 Veterans Drive
Northvale, NJ 07647
(201)767-7990
FAX: (201)767-7377

Compression Laboratories, Inc.
2860 Junction Avenue
San Jose, CA 95134
(800)225-5254

CompuAdd Corporation
12303 Technology Boulevard
Austin, TX 78727
(512)250-2530

Computer Associates, Inc.
711 Stewart Avenue
Garden City, NY 11530
(800)645-3003

Computer Associates International, Inc.
10505 Sorrento Valley Road
San Diego, CA 92121
(619)452-0170
FAX: (619)452-4421

Computer Friends, Inc.
14250 NW Science Park Drive
Portland, OR 97229
(503)626-2291

Computer Prompting Corporation
3408 Wisconsin Avenue N.W. #201
Washington, DC 20016
(202)966-0980
FAX: (202)966-0981

Conrac
600 North Rimsdale Avenue
Covina, CA 91722
(818)966-3511

CoSA
14 Imperial Place, Suite 203
Providence, RI 02903
(401)831-2672

Covid, Inc.
2400 West 10th Place #4
Tempe, AZ 85281
(602)966-2221
FAX: (602) 966-6728

Creative Labs, Inc.
1901 McCarthy Boulevard
Milpitas, CA 95035
(408)428-6600

Current Music Technology
146 Paoli Pike
Malvern, PA 19355
(215)647-9246

Cybernetics Products, Inc.
Oxberry Division
180 Broad Street
Carlsstadt, NJ 07072
(201)935-3000
FAX: (201)935-0104

Data Translation, Inc.
100 Locke Drive
Marlboro, MA 01752
(508)481-3700
FAX: (508)481-8620

Datacube, Inc.
4 Dearborn Road
Peabody, MA 01960
(508)535-6644
FAX: (508)535-5643

Diaquest, Inc.
1440 San Pablo Avenue
Berkeley, CA 94702
(510)526-7167

Digidesign, Inc.
1360 Willow Road, Suite 101
Menlo Park, CA 94025
(415)688-0600
FAX: (415)327-0777

Digital Arts
7050 Convoy Court
San Diego, CA 92111
(619)541-2055
FAX: (619)541-2655

Digital Electronics Corporation
31047 Genstar Road
Hayward, CA 94544
(415)489-4700
FAX: (415)489-3500

Digital F/X, Inc.
755 Ravendale Drive
Mountain View, CA 94043
(415)961-2800
FAX: (415)961-6990

Digital Processing Systems
55 Nugget Avenue #10
Scarborough, Ontario, Canada M1S 3L1
(416)754-8090

Digital Video Applications Corp. (DiVA)
a divsion of Avid Technology, Inc.
222 Third Street, Suite 3332
Cambridge, MA 02142
(617)491-4147

Digital Vision, Inc.
270 Bridge Street
Dedham, MA 02026
(617)329-5400
FAX: (617)329-6286

Display Technologies
1355 Holmes Road
Elgin, IL 60123
(708)931-2100
FAX: (708)931-2120

DOD Electronics Corporation
5639 South Riley Lane
Salt Lake City, UT 84107
(801)268-8400

Dotronics, Inc.
160 First Street SE
New Brighton, MN 55112
(612)633-1742

Dr. T's Music Software, INc.
100 Crescent Road
Needham, MA 02194
(617)455-1454

E-Machines, Inc.
9305 SW Gemini Drive
Beaverton, OR 97005
(503)646-6699
FAX: (503)641-0946

E-Mu Systems
1600 Green Hills Road
Scotts Valley, CA 95066
(408)438-1921

Editing Machines Corporation
1825 Q Street NW
Washington, DC 20009
(202)232-4597
FAX: (202)234-1847

Electric Image
117 East Colorado Boulevard, Suite 300
Pasadena, CA 91105
(818)577-1627

Electro-Voice
600 Cecil Street
Buchanan, MI 49107
(616)685-6831
FAX: (800)955-6831

Electrohome, Ltd.
809 Wellington Street North
Kitchener, Ontario, Canada N2E 1V8
(519)744-7111
FAX: (519)749-3131

Electronic Arts, Inc.
1820 Gateway Drive
San Mateo, CA 94404
(415)571-7171

Electronic Script Prompting
6129 Western
Clarendon Hills, IL 60514
(800)543-0346
FAX: (708)887-0389

Elmo Manufacturing Company
70 New Hyde Park Road
New Hyde Park, NY 11040
(516)775-3200

Ensemble Designs
PO Box 993
Grass Valley, CA 95945
(916)478-1830
FAX: (916)478-1832

Ensoniq
155 Great Valley Parkway
Malvern, PA 19355
(215)647-3930

Farpoint Technologies
1127 Wood Hollow Drive
Marietta, GA 30067
(404)612-8652

Fast Electronics U.S.
5 Commonwealth Road
Natick, MA 01760
(508)655-FAST

Fast Forward Video
18200C West McDurmott
Irvine, CA 92714
(714)852-8404
FAX: (714)852-1226

FirstCom Music House
13747 Montfort, Suite 220
Dallas, TX 75240
(214)934-2222
FAX: (214)392-3454

Fluent Machines, Inc.
1881 Worcester Road
Framingham, MA 01701
(508)626-2144

Focus Graphics, Inc.
1191 Chess Drive, Suite B
Foster City, CA 94404
(415)377-0596
FAX: (415)377-0598

FOR.A Corporation of America
313 Speen Street
Natick, MA 01760
(508)650-3902
FAX: (508)651-8729

Form and Function
1595 17th Avenue
San Francisco, CA 94122
(800)843-9497

Fostex Corporation of America
15431 Blackburn Avenue
Norwalk, CA 90650
(310)921-1112
FAX: (310)802-1964

Fractal Design Corporation
335 Speckels Drive
Aptos, CA 95003
(408)688-8800

Frezzolini Electronics
5 Valley Street
Hawthorne, NJ 07506
(201)427-1160
FAX: (201)427-0934

Fujitsu America, Inc.
3055 Orchard Drive
San Jose, CA 95134
(408)432-1300

Furman Sound
30 Rich Street
Greenbrae, CA 94904
(415)927-1225

Future Video Products, Inc.
28 Argonaut, Suite 150
Laguna Hills, CA 92656
(714)770-4416

General Electric Company
Projection Display
Electronics Park, Bldg. 6-205
Syracuse, NY 13221
(315)456-3277

General Electric Lighting
Nela Park
East Cleveland, OH 44112
(216)266-6969
FAX: (216)266-2662

Genoa Systems Corporation
75 East Trimble Road
San Jose, CA 95131
(408)432-9090
FAX: (408)434-0997

Gold Disk Software, Inc.
385 Van Ness Avenue, Suite 110
Torrance, CA 90501
(310)320-5080

Grass Valley Group
PO Box 1114
Grass Valley, CA 95945
(916)478-3000
FAX: (916)478-3180

Gryphon Software Corporation
3298 Governor Drive
P.O. Box 221075
San Diego, CA 92122
(619)454-6836

GTE/Sylvania Lighting Products
Sylvania Lighting Center
100 Endicott Street
Danvers, MA 01923
(508)750-2404

Headland Technology / Video Seven
46221 Landing Parkway
Fremont, CA 94538
(510)623-7857
FAX: (510)657-8013

Heurikon Corporation
8000 Excelsior Drive
Madison, WI 53717
(608)831-0900
FAX: (608)831-4249

Hewlett-Packard Corporation
P.O. Box 10301
Palo Alto, CA 94303
(415)857-1501

Hewlett-Packard Signal Analysis Division
1212 Valley House Drive
Rohnert Park, CA 94928
(707)794-1212
FAX: (707)794-4620

Hitachi Denshi America, Ltd.
150 Crossways Park Drive
Woodbury, NY 11797
(516)921-7200
FAX: (516)921-0993

Hitachi Home Electronics
Multimedia Systems Division
401 West Artesia Boulevard
Compton, CA 90220
(800)369-0422

Hitachi Sales Corporation of America
401 West Artestia Boulevard
Compton, CA 90220
(213)537-8383

Hollywood Edge
7060 Hollywood Boulevard, Suite 1120
Hollywood, CA 90028
(800)292-3755
FAX: (213)466-5861

Horita
PO Box 3993
Mission Viejo, CA 92690
(714)489-0240

Hotronic
1875 South Winchester Boulevard
Campbell, CA 95008
(408)378-3883
FAX: (408)378-3888

I-Den Videotronics Corporation
9620 Chesapeake Drive #204
San Diego, CA
(619)492-9239
FAX: (619)279-2569

IBM Corporation
Old Orchard Road
Armonk, NY 10504
(914)765-1900

IBM Desktop Software
472 Wheelers Farms Road
Milford, CT 06460
(800)426-7699

IBM Multimedia Information Center
P.O. Box 2150
Atlanta, GA 30301-2150
(800)426-9402

Ikegami Electronics (USA), Inc.
37 Brook Avenue
Maywood, NJ 07607
(201)368-9171

ILC Technology, Inc.
399 Java Drive
Sunnyvale, Ca 94089
(408)745-7900
FAX: (408)475-0829

Image Graphics, Inc.
917 Bridgeport Avenue
Shelton, CT 06484
(203)926-0100
FAX: (203)926-9705

Image North Technologies, Inc.
180 King Street, Suite 360
Waterloo, Ontario, Canada N2J 1P8
(518)570-9111

In Focus Systems, Inc.
7770 S.W. Mohawk Street
Tualatin, OR 97062
(800)327-7231

Innovision Optics
1318 Second Street #31
Santa Monica, CA
(310)394-5510
FAX: (310)395-2941

Instant Replay Corporation
4525 Wasatch Boulevard, Suite 335
Salt Lake City, UT 84142
(801)272-0671

Intel Corporation
3065 Bowers Avenue
Santa Clara, CA 95051
(408)987-8080

Intelligent Resources
3030 Salt Creek Lane, Suite 100
Arlington Heights, IL 60005
(708)670-9388

Interactive Media Technologies
7320 E. Butherus #200
Scottsdale, AZ 85260
(602)289-4689
FAX: (602)443-3086

Interactive Solutions
1720 South Amphlett Boulevard, Suite 219
San Mateo, CA 94402
(415)377-0136

JBL Professional
8500 Balboa Boulevard
Northridge, CA 91329
(818)893-8411
FAX: (818)893-3639

J.L. Cooper Electronics
125000 Beatrice Street
Los Angeles, CA 90066
(310)306-4131

John Morley & Associates
120 South Victory Boulevard, Suite 103
Burbank, CA 91502
(818)955-8990
FAX: (818)955-9667

Jovian Logic Corporation
47265 Fremont Boulevard
Fremont, CA 94538
(415)651-4823

JVC Information Products Co.
2903 Bunker Hill Lane #102
Santa Clara, CA 95054
(408)988-7506
FAX: (408)727-7533

JVC Professional Products Co.
41 Slater Drive
Elmwood Park, NJ 07407
(201)794-3900
FAX: (201)253-2077

JVC Professional Products Company
41 Slater Drive
Elmwood Park, NJ 07407
(201)794-3900
FAX: (201)523-2077

Karl Heitz, Inc.
34-11 62nd Street, PO Box 427
Woodside, NY 11377
(718)565-0004
FAX: (718)565-2582

Kawai America Corp.
Professional Products Group
2055 East University Drive
Compton, CA 90224

Korg
89 Frost Street
Westbury, NY 11590
(516)333-9100
FAX: (516)333-9108

Lake Compuframes
P.O. Box 890
Briarcliff Manor, NY 10510
(914)941-1998
FAX: (914)941-0159

Lasergraphics, Inc.
17671 Cowan Avenue
Irvine, CA 92714
(714)660-9497
FAX: (714)660-8042

Lazerus
2821 Ninth Street
Berkeley, CA 94710
(510)845-1237

Leader Instruments Corporation
380 Oser Avenue
Hauppage, NY
11788
(516)231-6900
FAX: (516)645-5104

Lexicon, Inc.
100 Beaver Street
Waltham, MA 02154
(617)891-6790
FAX: (617)891-0340

Linker Systems
13612 Onkayha Circle
Irvine, CA 92720
(714)552-1904

Listec Video
30 Oser Avenue
Hauppage, NY 11788
(516)273-3020
FAX: (516)435-4544

Logitech, Inc.
3 Budway
Nashua, NH 03063
(603)880-8479

Lotus Development Corporation
55 Cambridge Parkway
Cambridge, MA 02142
(617)577-8500

Lowel Light Manufacturing Company
140 58th Street
Brooklyn, NY 11220
(718)921-0600
FAX: (718)921-0303

Lyon Lamb Video Animation Systems, Inc.
4531 Empire Avenue
Burbank, CA 91505
(818)843-4831
FAX: (818)843-6544

Mackie Designs, Inc.
12230 Woodinville Drive
Woodinville, WA 98072
(800)258-6883
FAX: (206)487-4337

Macromedia, Inc.
600 Townsend Street, Suite 310
San Francisco, CA 94107
(415)442-0200
FAX: (415)626-0554

Magic Teleprompting, Inc.
1390 Waller Street
San Francisco, CA 94117
(415)626-5283
FAX: (415)626-2762

Magni Systems, Inc.
9500 S.W. Gemini Drive
Beaverton, OR 97005
(503)626-8400
FAX: (503)626-6225

Manhattan Production Music
311 West 43rd Street, Suite 702
New York, NY 10036
(800)227-1954
FAX: (212)262-0814

Mark of the Unicorn, Inc.
222 Third Street
Cambridge, MA 02142
(617)576-2760

Mass Microsystems
810 West Maude Avenue
Sunnyvale, CA 94086
(408)522-1200

Mathematica, Inc.
402 South Kentucky Avenue
Lakeland, FL 33801
(813)682-1128

Matrox Electronic Systems, Ltd.
Video Products Group
1055 St. Regis Boulevard
Dorval, Quebec, Canada H9P 2T4
(514)685-2630
FAX: (514)685-2853

Matthews Studio Equipment
2405 Empire Avenue
Burbank, CA 91504
(818)843-6715

Media Cybernetics
8484 Georgia Avenue
Silver Spring, MD 20910
(800)992-HALO

Media Pedia Video Clips
22 Fisher Avenue
Wellesley, MA 02181
(617)235-5617

Media Vision
47221 Fremont Boulevard
Fremont, CA 94538
(510)770-8600

Megascan Technology
42 South Street
Hopkinton, MA 01748
(508)435-2600
FAX: (508)435-9166

Micro Display Systems
755 East 31st Street
Hastings, MN 55033
(612)437-2233
FAX: (612)437-7325

Micrografx, Inc.
1820 North Greenvile Avenue
Richardson, TX 75081
(214)234-1769
FAX: (214)234-2410

Microsoft Corporation
One Microsoft Way
Redmond, WA 98052
(206)882-8080

Microtech International
158 Commerce Street
East Haven, CT 06512
(203)468-6223

Microtime, Inc.
1280 Blue Hills Avenue
Bloomfield, CT 06002
(203)242-4242
FAX: (203)242-3321

Midisoft Corporation
P.O. Box 1000
Bellevue, WA 98009
(206)881-7176

Miller Fluid Heads (USA) Inc.
410 Garibaldi Avenue
Lodi, NJ 07644
(201)473-9592
FAX: (201)473-9693

Mitsubishi Electric Sales America
800 Cottontail Lane
Somerset, NJ 08873
(201)563-9889
FAX: (201)563-0713

Moniterm Corporation
5740 Green Circle Drive
Minnetonka, MN 55343
(612)935-8151
FAX: (612)933-5701

Motion Works, Inc.
#300 - 1334 West 6th Avenue
Vancouver, BC, Canada V6H 1A6
(604)732-0289

MSC Technologies, Inc.
2600 San Tomas Expressway
Santa Clara, CA 95051
(408)988-0211

Musco Mobile Lighting, Ltd.
Highway 63 South, PO Box 73
Oskaloosa, IA 52577
(515)673-0491

Nady Systems
6701 Bay Street
Emeryville, CA 94608
(510)652-2411
FAX: (510)652-5075

Nanao USA Corporation
23510 Telo Avenue #5
Torrance, CA 90505
(213)325-5202
FAX: (213)580-1679

NEC Electronics, Inc.
401 Ellis Street, PO Box 7421
Mountain View, CA 94039
(415)960-6000

NEC Home Electronics
Professional Systems Division
1255 Michael Drive
Wood Dale, IL 60191
(800)562-5200

NEC Technologies, Inc.
Professional Systems Division
1414 Massachusetts Avenue
Boxborough, MA 01719
(508)264-8000
FAX: (508)264-8673

NEC Technologies, Inc.
1255 Michael Drive
Wood Dale, IL 60191
(708)860-9500

Network Music
11021 Via Frontera
San Diego, CA 92127
(619)451-6400
FAX: (619)451-6409

Neumann USA
6 Vista Drive
Old Lyme, CT 06371
(203)434-5220
FAX: (203)434-3148

New Media Graphics Corporation
780 Boston Avenue
Billerica, MA 01821
(508)663-0666
FAX: (508)6678

New Video Corporation
1526 Cloverfield Boulevard
Santa Monica, CA 90404
(310) 449-7000 telephone
(310) 449-0132 fax

NewTek, Inc.
215 S.E. Eighth Street
Topeka, KS 66603
(913)354-1146

Nova Systems, Inc.
50 Albany Turnpike
Canton, CT 06019
(203)693-0238
FAX: (203)693-1497

nView Corporation
11835 Canon Boulevard
Suite B-107
Newport News, VA 23606
(804)873-1354

O'Connor Engineering Labs, Inc.
100 Kalmus Drive
Costa Mesa, CA 92626
(714)979-3993
FAX: (714)957-8138

Octree Software, Inc.
311 West 43rd Street, Suite 904
New York, NY 10036
(212)262-3116

Olduvai Corporation
7520 Red Road, Suite A
South Miami, FL 33143
(305)665-4665
FAX: (305)665-0671

Omnicomp Graphics Corporation
1734 West Belt North
Houston, TX 77043
(713)464-2990
FAX: (713)827-7540

Omnimusic
52 Main Street
Port Washington, NY 11050
(800)828-6664
FAX: (516)944-6586

Opcode Systems, Inc.
3950 Fabian Way, Suite 100
Palo Alto, CA 94303
(415)856-3333
FAX: (415)856-3332

Optical Media International
180 Knowles Drive
Los Gatos, CA 95030
(800)347-2664

Orchid Technology
45365 Northport Loop West
Fremont, CA 94538
(510)683-0300
FAX: (510)490-9312

Owl International, Inc.
14218 NE 21st Street
Bellevue, WA 98007
(206)747-3203

Packard Bell
9425 Canoga Avenue
Chatsworth, CA 91311
(818)773-4400

Panasonic Broadcast Systems Co.
One Panasonic Way
Secaucus, NJ 07094
(201)348-7671

Panasonic Broadcast Systems Company
One Panasonic Way
Secaucus, NJ 07094
(201)348-7000
FAX: (201)348-7549

Panasonic Communications & Systems Co.
Professional/Industrial Video
One Panasonic Way
Secausus, NJ 07094
(800)553-7222

Panasonic Industrial Company
2 Panasonic Way
Secaucus, NJ 07094
(201)348-7000 / 742-8086

Parallax Graphics, Inc.
a subsidiary of Dynatech Corporation
2500 Condesa Street
Santa Clara, CA 95051
(408)727-2220
FAX: (408)980-5159

Passport Designs, Inc.
100 Stone Pine Road
Half Moon Bay, CA 94019
(415)726-0280

Paul Mace Software
400 Williamson Way
Ashland, OR 97520
(503)488-2322

Pinnacle Systems, Inc.
2380 Walsh Avenue
Santa Clara, CA 95051
(408)970-9787
FAX: (408)970-9798

Pioneer
600 East Crescent Avenue
Upper Saddle River, NJ 07458
(201)327-6400

Pioneer Communications of America, Inc.
Optical Memory Products Division
Sherbrooke Plaza
600 East Crescent Avenue
Upper Saddle River, NJ 07458
(201)327-6400
FAX: (201)327-9379

Pioneer Electric Corporation
2265 East 220th Street
Long Beach, CA 90810
(213)835-6177

Pipeline Digital
45-508 Loli'i Street
Kaneohe, HI 96744
(808)235-0335

Pixar
1001 West Cutting Boulevard
Point Richmond, CA 94804
(510)236-4000

Pixelworks, Inc.
7 Park Avenue
Hudson, NH 03051
(603)880-1322
FAX: (603)880-6558

Presentation Technologies, Inc.
743 N. Pastoria Avenue
Sunnyvale, CA 94086
(408)749-1959

Prime Image, Inc.
19943 Via Escuela
Saratoga, CA 95070
(408)867-6519
FAX: (408)926-7294

Profusion Group
5009 Blue Bell Avenue
Valley Village, CA 91607
(800)551-8868

Promusic
6555 NW 9th Avenue, Suite 303
Fort Lauderdale, FL 33309
(305)776-2070
FAX: (305)776-2074

Prosonus
11126 Weddington Street
North Hollywood, CA 91601
(800)999-6191

Proxima
6610 Nancy Ridge Drive
San Diego, CA 92121
(619)457-5500
FAX: (619)457-9647

Q-TV
104 East 25th Street
New York, NY 10010
(212)460-9050
FAX: (212)529-9679

QSI Systems
73 Raymond Avenue #8
Salem, NH 03079
(603)893-7707

Radius, Inc.
1710 Fortune Drive
San Jose, CA 95131
(408)434-1010
FAX: (408)434-0127

Ramtek Corporation
1525 Atteberry Lane
San Jose, CA 95131
(408)954-2700
FAX: (408)954-0118

RasterOps Corporation
2500 Walsh Avenue
Santa Clara, CA 95051
(408)944-4398
FAX: (408)562-4065

Ray Dream, Inc.
1804 North Shoreline Boulevard
Mountain View, CA 94043
(415)960-0768

Recognition Concepts, Inc.
P.O. Box 8510
Incline Village, NV 89450
(702)831-0473
FAX: 9702)831-8035

Redlake Corporation
15005 Concord Circle
Morgan Hill, CA 95037
(408)779-6464

Relisys
320 South Milpitas Boulevard
Milpitas, CA 95035
(408)945-9000
FAX: (408)945-0587

RGB Spectrum
2550 Ninth Street
Berkeley, CA 94710
(510)848-0180
FAX: (510)848-0971

Roland Corporation US
7200 Dominion Circle
Los Angeles, CA 90040
(213)685-5141
FAX: (213)722-0911

Sachtler Corporation of America
55 North Main Street
Freeport, NY 11520
(516)867-4900
FAX: (516)623-6844

Sampo America, Inc.
5550 Peachtree Industrial Boulevard
Norcross, GA 30071
(404)449-6220
FAX: (404)447-1109

Samson Technologies
262 Duffy Avenue
Hicksville, NY 11801
(516)932-3810
FAX: (516)932-3815

Samsung Information Systems America, Inc.
3655 North First Street
San Jose, CA 95134
(408)414-5400

Sanyo Fisher (USA) Corporation
1200 West Artesia Boulevard
P.O. Box 5177
Compton, CA 90224
(213)537-5830
FAX: (213)635-4643

Sennheiser Electric Corporation
6 Vista Drive
Old Lyme, CT 06371
(203)434-9190
FAX: (203)434-1759

Sharp Electronics Broadcast Group
Professional Products Division
10 Sharp Plaza
Mahwah, NJ 07430
(201)529-8731
FAX: (201)529-9636

Sharp Electronics Corporation
Professional Products Division
Sharp Plaza
Manwah, NJ 07430
(201)529-8731

Shure Brothers, Inc.
222 Hartrey Avenue
Evanston, IL 60202
(708)866-2542
FAX: (708)866-2279

Sigma Designs, Inc.
46501 Landing Parkway
Fremont, CA 94538
(510)770-0100
FAX: (510)770-0110

Sigma Electronics, Inc.
1184 Enterprise
East Petersburg, PA 17520
(717)569-2681

Silicon Beach Software, Inc.
a subsidiary of Aldus Corporation
9770 Carroll Center Road, Suite J
P.O. Box 261430
San Diego, CA 92126
(619)695-6956

Silicon Graphics, Inc.
2011 Shoreline Boulevard
Mountain View, CA 94039
(415)960-1980
FAX: (415)961-0595

Snell & Wilcox, Ltd.
2454 Embarcadero Way
Palo Alto, CA 94303
(415)856-2930
FAX: (415)857-1434

Software Publishing Corporation
1901 Landings Drive
Mountain View, CA 94039
(415)962-8910

Sony Business and Professional Group
3 Paragon Drive
Montvale, NJ 07645
(201)930-1000

Sony Corporation of America
Sony Drive
Park Ridge, NJ 07656
(201)930-1000

Sony Corporation of America
Computer Peripheral Products Division
655 River Oaks Parkway
San Jose, CA 95134
(408)944-4136

Soundcraft
8500 Balboa Boulevard
Northridge, CA 91329
(818)893-4351
FAX: (818)893-3639

Specular International
233 North Pleasant Street
Amherst, MA 01004-0888
(413)549-7600

Steinberg/Jones
17700 Raymer Street
Northridge, CA 91325
(818)993-4091

Strand Lighting
18111 South Santa Fe Avenue
Rancho Dominguez, CA 90221
(213)637-7500

Strata, Inc.
249 East Tabernacle, Suite 201
St. George, UT 84770
(801)628-5218

Sun Microsystems, Inc.
2550 Garcia Avenue
Mountain View, CA 94043
(415)960-1300
FAX: (415)969-9131

Sundance Technology Group
6341 Campus Circle Drive, Suite 100
Irving, TX 75038
(214)550-8338
FAX: (214)869-1026

SuperMac Technology, Inc.
485 Potrero Avenue
Sunnyvale, CA 94068
(408)245-2202
FAX: (408)735-7250

Tandy Corporation
1800 One Tandy Center
Fort Worth, TX 76102
(817)390-3700

TASCAM / TEAC Professional Division
7733 Telegraph Road
Montebello, CA 90640
(213)726-0303

Taxan Corporation
18005 Cortney Court
City of Industry, CA 91748
(818)810-1291

Tecmar, Inc.
6225 Cochran Road
Solon, OH 44139
(216)349-1009
FAX: (216)349-0851

Tektronix, Inc.
14150 SW Karl Braun Drive
Beaverton, OR 97077
(503)923-0333
FAX: (503)923-4434

Telescript
445 Livingston Street
Norwood, NJ 07648
(201)767-6733
FAX: (201)784-0323

Theatre Service & Supply
1792 Union Avenue
Baltimore, MD 21211
(301)467-1225

Theatre Vision International
5426 Fair Avenue
North Hollywood, CA 91601
(818)769-0928

Time Arts, Inc.
3436 Mendocino Avenue
Santa Rosa, CA 95403
(707)576-7722
FAX: (707)576-7731

TOA Electronics, Inc.
601 Gateway Boulevard
South San Francisco, CA 94080
(415)588-2538
FAX: (415)588-3349

Toshiba America Information Sys., Inc.
Disk Products Division
9740 Irvine Boulevard
Irvine, CA 92718
(800)456-DISK

TouchVision Systems, Inc.
1800 Winnemac Avenue
Chicago, IL 60640
(312)989-2160
FAX: (312)989-2144

Triplett Corporation
1 Triplett Drive
Bluffton, OH 45817
(419)358-5015

Truevision, Inc.
a division of RasterOps Corporation
7340 Shadeland Station, Suite 100
Indianapolis, IN 46256
(317)858-TRUE
FAX: (317)576-7700

Turtle Beach Systems
P.O. Box 5074
York, PA 17405
(717)843-6916

Twelve Tone Systems
P.O. Box 760
Watertown, MA 02272
(617)273-4437

Vantage Lighting
175 East Paul Drive
San Raphael, CA 94903
(415)468-6220

Vicon Industries
525 Broad Hollow Road
Melville, NY 11747
(516)293-2200
FAX: (516)293-2627

Video Associates Labs
4926 Spicewood Springs Road
Austin, TX 78759
(512)346-5781
FAX: (512)346-9407

Video International Development Corporation
65-16 Brook Avenue
Deer Park, NY 11729
(516)842-1815

Video Logic Corporation
6807 Brennon Lane
Chevy Chase, MD 20815
(202)452-6077
FAX: (301)652-6584

VideoLogic, Inc.
245 First Street
Cambridge, MA 02142
(617)494-0530

VideoMail, Inc.
568-4 Weddell Drive
Sunnyvale, CA 94089
(408)747-0223

Videotek, Inc.
243 Shoemaker Road
Pottstown, PA 19464
(215)327-2292
FAX: (215)327-9295

VIDI
16309 Doublegrove Street
La Puente, CA 91744
(818)918-8834

Vinten Broadcast, Inc.
44 Indian Lane East
Towaco, NJ 07082
(201)263-4000
FAX: (201)263-8018

Virtus Corporation
117 Edinburgh South, Suite 204
Cary, NC 27511
(919)467-9700

Visual Information Technologies, Inc.
2460 Lotus Drive
Plano, TX 75075
(214)596-5600

Visual Software
6425 Hollywood Boulevard, Suite 300
Los Angeles, CA 90028
(800)669-7318

Vividus Corporation
651 Kendall Avenue
Palo Alto, CA 94306
(415)494-2111

Voyetra Technologies
333 Fifth Avenue
Pelham, NY 10803
(914)738-4500

Wavefront Technologies
530 East Montecita Street
Santa Barbara, CA 93103
(805)962-8117

Willow Peripherals
190 Willow Avenue
Bronx, NY 10454
(212)402-0010
FAX: (212)402-9603

Workstation Technologies, Inc.
10884 Sky Park Circle
Irvine, CA 92714
(714)250-8983

WYSE Technology, Inc.
3471 North First Street
San Jose, CA 95134
(408)473-1200

Yamaha Corporation of America
Professional Products Division
6600 Orangethorpe Avenue
Buena Park, CA 90620
(714)522-9011
FAX: (714)739-2680

Zenith Data Systems Corporation
1000 Milwaukee Avenue
Glenview, IL 60025
(312)391-7000

Chapter 10
Methodology

This study is derived from three key sources: secondary research, primary research, and the personal expertise of the authors.

Secondary research included acquiring product literature, press releases, and brochures of desktop video competitors and over 3500 related articles in industry journals, trade magazines, newspapers, computer and video magazines via library research. From this secondary research, initial primary research strategies were determined and background information files were built.

Primary research included in-depth telephone and face-to-face interviews with over 80 officers and product management professionals in key competitor, reseller, and end user organizations within the desktop video market.

The authors of this report are also founders of Desktop Video Products, a key Northern California multiple services organization focusing on the desktop video market. They were able to draw upon their own expertise in interpreting some of the information obtained from primary and secondary research. The authors have over 35 years of experience in the personal computer and desktop video industries, including time managing the personal computer analysis section of a major industry research firm, as well as the technical (2 engineering bachelor's) and business (1 MBA) educational backgrounds to cope with the complexities of the desktop video technologies and market.

The desktop video market is forecasted in terms of unit shipments, revenues, and growth rate projections for the period between 1989 and 1999. These forecasts are based on raw data obtained from the primary and secondary research, as triangulated against market forecasts obtained from other Market Intelligence Research Corporation and competitive reports on the multimedia and conventional video markets as well as information from the Electronic Industries Association and the U.S. Department of Commerce.

From this cumulative research, the authors were able to develop discussions on industry trends, industry history and technology, competitive environments and analyses, and strategies for success. Lists of desktop video companies as well as profiles of a selected few are included with the report.

Chapter 11
Glossary

1" - a videotape format historically used in broadcast production, typically flat to 4.5MHz bandwidth for excellent quality. Surpassed only by D1, D2, D3, or BetaCam and BetaCam SP formats. Signal integrity concerns such as differential gain and differential phase typically less than 4%.

2D - two dimensional. A concept used in modeling and animation in which shapes are defined in terms of two axes, typically x & y, and the third dimension, z, is ignored. 2D graphics are the simplest graphics, but lack the depth dimension of 3D graphics.

2D Effects - video editing effects which act on a frame of video in two-axis manipulation only. Split screen, mirroring, slide across, and expand are examples..

3/4" SP (or 3/4" U-Matic SP) - a videotape format developed by the JVC Corporation as an upgrade to the older, 3/4" U-Matic format. 3/4" SP adds an improved y/c video signal and high-fidelity stereo audio to the U-Matic capabilities. Well suited to corporate video quality and often used in field video and low budget broadcast situations. Capable of 260 to 340 TV scan lines of resolution.

3D - three dimensional. A concept used in modeling and animation in which shapes are defined in terms of three axes, x, y, and z, used to represent length, width, and depth.

3D Effects - video editing effects which act on a frame of video in a three-axis manipulation, by providing perspective or by affecting the whole of an image without respect to the 2D nature of a frame (such as fades or dims).

8mm - a consumer-quality videotape format capable of 250 TV scan lines of resolution. This format is being supplaually described as the number of horizontal versus the number of vertical pixels (as in 640x480 or 1024x768) displayable on a given monitor. In analog video, such as NTSC, resolution is described as the number of scan lines displayable on a given monitor. Horizontal and vertical resolution are not always equal.

Retrace - return of the electron beam to the left side or top of the screen after a horizontal or vertical scan.

RGB - an acronym for red, green, and blue, the three primary additive colors. By mixing different quantities of red, green, and blue light, any color can be created. Computer monitors and televisions use this concept to create the various colors they display. The number of colors displayable is limited only by the number of graduations possible in each primary color. In analog systems, such as television, there are an infinite number of graduations available. In digital systems, this is a finite number, limited by the bit-depth of the image and the ability of the graphics adapter and monitor to differentiate the different colors. Often, a monitor will be controlled by separate red, green, and blue signals, comprising an "RGB" interface.

Rolloff - a modeling term describing the rate at which apparent light intensity decreases as a function of angle away from a spotlight's direction. A value of zero means that the light intensity is constant over the area illuminated.

Saturation - the degree to which a color is diluted by luminance, or white light. For example, the degree of saturation is what differentiates a light pink from a deep red of the same hue.

Scan Lines - the individual horizontal scans of the electron beam across a display's surface. Scan lines are also used to indicate resolution, in that a display capable of 525 scan lines is of higher resolution than one which can handle 400 scan lines.

SECAM - an acronym for Systeme Couleur Avec Memoire, the television broadcast standard for France, the former USSR, and various eastern European countries. Like PAL, SECAM is based on a 50Hz power system, but it utilizes a different encoding process and displays 819 lines interlaced at 50 fields per second. SECAM is not compatible with NTSC or PAL, though conversion between the standards is possible.

Sequencer - a program or device which outputs MIDI programs to synthesizers, samplers, and other MIDI-compatible electronic music instruments. Some advanced synths or samplers have builtin sequencers.

Shading - a modeling process that gives objects dimension by controlling the way one or more light sources illuminate objects. Most sophisticated shading techniques provide smooth transitions on curved objects and let objects cast shadows.

Shuttle - advancing or reversing a VTR deck by discrete steps at a variable speed. Usually by use of a jog/shuttle knob.

Smoothing - the electronic process of eliminating the jaggies. Also known as antialiasing.

SMPTE - an acronym for the Society of Motion Picture and Television Engineers

SMPTE Time Code - or simply time code, is a timing standard for videotape production, developed by SMPTE, which makes it possible to accurately describe any individual frame on a videotape. SMPTE time code is used in industrial and professional quality video equipment in order to ensure frame accuracy in audio and video edits. The time code signal is incorporated directly onto tapes to provide tape-position information and control information for editing. A "bi-phase mark signal" of 80-bits per frame reveals precise tape position. 32 of the 80 bits, commonly referred to as "User Bits" are available for use as control information during videotape editing. The SMPTE time code signal is recorded as either LTC or VITC. The position-information frame count corresponds with the frame number of the color synchronization (00-29). The User Bits can be sued to insert roll numbers, control commands (necessary for playing back video tapes with commercials), character information, etc.

Solid Model - a modeling term describing a model relating the surface into boundaries which define mass. Mass properties may be associated with various boundary definitions in the model.

Specular - a modeling term describing the component of reflection seen at a surface point of an object which is produced by reflection about the surface normal. It depends on the observer position, whereas the diffuse component does not. Often this appears as a highlight.

Spline - a mathematically defined curve used instead of polygons for describing 2D and 3D objects.

Split Editing - a video editing technique in which the video clips and matching audio clips are modified separately, allowing the audio portions to overlap other video clips as desired.

Storyboard - a series of panels or pictures (usually sketches) designed to show how a production will look. Comic books are essentially storyboards.

Surface Model - a model relating edge lines into polygonal or curved boundaries which define the exterior or interior "skin" of an object. Surface properties may be associated with the polygonal or curved boundaries.

Surface of Revolution - a modeling term defining an object made by rotating a polygon or other shape around an axis. Also called a sweep.

S-VHS - a video format developed by the JVC Corporation as an enhancement to the VHS format and a replacement for older, 3/4" U-Matic systems. S-VHS uses 1/2" tape in a VHS-sized cartridge, along with y/c signal encoding, and high-fidelity stereo audio. S-VHS is also known as Super VHS and provides a vertical resolution of 400 scan lines. S-VHS employs S-Video signaling.

S-Video - a video signal that separates luminance from color using y/c encoding. This method does not reduce the bandwidth or compromise the RGB components and results in images of higher resolution and better color quality than composite video.

Sync - an abbreviation for synchronization.

Sync Generator - a device or component that generates the sync signals required for overlay, editing, effects, and other purposes.

Synchronization - the process of coordinating two or more processes or events; in video, this generally applies to locking the timing of several signals together.

Sync on Green - some computer systems combine the sync signals with the green color signal. Special circuitry is required to utilize this form of sync signal.

TBC - an acronym for Time Base Corrector.

Texture Map - a modeling term describing a 2D or 3D pattern that is applied to the object surface during the shading computation. The advantage to texture is that the complexity of appearance does not have to be modeled in the object geometry.

TIFF - an acronym for Tag Image File Format, a computer graphics file format developed by Aldus, Adobe, and Apple. It is particularly suited for representing scanned images and other large bitmaps. The original TIFF saved only black-and-white images in uncompressed forms. Newer versions support color and compression. TIFF is a neutral format designed for compatibility with both Macintosh and PC-compatible applications.

Time Base Corrector - a device that allows video recorded by different sources at potentially different speeds to be synchronized and edited; minute variations in recording speed, if uncorrected, can affect editing control and image quality.

Track - a grouping of homogenous data within a movie file. Typical track types might include video, sound, transitional effects, closed captioned text, MIDI data, etc. Also, areas of information on a videotape or laser disk. These may include video, audio, and control tracks.

Transition - a visual effect which occurs between two different frames.

Translate - a modeling term meaning to move in position while keeping the same angular orientation.

Tweening - the creation of a series of animation computer graphic frames between two previously created frames. When it comes time to create motion, some programs can perform tweening (also known as in-betweening).

U-Matic - a 3/4" videotape format

Underscan - the opposite of overscan, in which the raster scan lines do not stretch all of the way from horizontal edge to edge, but leave borders.

VCR - an acronym for video cassette recorder.

Vector Graphics - computer graphics defined by primitive geometric objects of given values. The vector definition is resolution independent and therefore maintains integrity at various zoom intervals and on devices of varying resolution.

Vectorscope - a device, typically an analog instrument, which is used in the calibration of the electrical equipment acquiring, editing, storing, and reproducing color images.

Vertical Sync - a pulse used to trigger the vertical retrace of a scanning electron gun from the bottom of the frame back to the top left. Also the name of the individual signal in some interfaces which conveys this information.

VGA - an acronym for Video Graphics Array, defined by IBM, and representing a computer graphics adapter capable of 640x480 resolution.

VGA Pass-Through - the ability of some VGA adapters and some high-resolution graphics adapters to interconnect and pass VGA signals through the high-resolution adapter for display on a high-resolution monitor.

VHS - an acronym for Video Home System, a 1/2" videotape cassette format pioneered by Panasonic and JVC, which allows 240 scan lines of resolution. It is the most popular videotape format in the world today and is used for the vast majority of programmed videotapes for lease and sale.

VHS-C - an acronym for Video Home System - Compact, a miniaturized version of the popular VHS videotape cassette format.

Video - the representation of a desired image via electrical and photoelectric means. In a broad sense, video encompasses the conversion of live or artificial images into electrical signals, the processing, transfer, and storage of these electrical signals, and the conversion of the electrical signals back into a representation of the original images. An alternative definition: a program stored on videotape is also called a "video".

Video Cassette Recorder - a device designed for recording and playback of video and audio signals to and from videotape cassette cartridges. Also known as VCRs, for short, video cassette recorders are specific forms of video tape recorders, or VTRs.

Video Overlay - a method of combining a paint image (computer graphics) and a live video image.

Video Tape Recorder - a device designed for recording and playback of video and audio signals to and from magnetic tape. Also known as VTRs, for short, video tape recorders define the general form of this type of recording equipment; VCRs, or video cassette recorders, are specific implementations of VTRs. Professional quality equipment is typically denoted as VTRs, whether or not cassettes are used, whereas consumer quality equipment typically uses the VCR designation.

VITC - an acronym for Vertical Interval Time Code, SMPTE time code superimposed onto the vertical blanking interval of the video signal. Advantage is that time code can be read even when a helical scanning VCR is in the Pause or Slow mode

VTR - an acronym for video tape recorder.

Waveform Monitor - a device, typically in the form of analog instrumentation, which displays a visual representation of a NTSC-compatible video signal waveform. Waveform monitors are used to calibrate the signal levels sent between pieces of video equipment.

Window Dub - also known as a burnin dub, a copy of a raw tape with time code "burned in" to a window on each frame, allowing the user to know the exact time code associated with each frame.

Wireframe - a superimposed, three-dimensional grid that aids in the manipulation of an image.

Work Prints - rough, intermediate versions of a video program, created for use in concept approval.

Y/C - a type of component video signal found in S-VHS, Hi-8, and 3/4" SP video formats that separates a signal's brightness (luminance, "y") and color (chrominance, "c") information to maintain better picture quality. This is an intermediate step in image resolution between standard composite video and component video.

Y/C Crosstalk - also called buzz, looks like rolling black and white beads and occurs because a rapid transition of color is decoded as a transition in luminance. You can minimize this by choosing less saturated colors and avoiding drastic jumps in hue.